Writing Young Adult Fiction

FOR

DUMMIES®

Writing Young Adult Fiction
FOR DUMMIES®

by Deborah Halverson
Award-winning author and editor

Foreword by M. T. Anderson
National Book Award Winner

WILEY

Wiley Publishing, Inc.

Writing Young Adult Fiction For Dummies®

Published by
Wiley Publishing, Inc.
111 River St.
Hoboken, NJ 07030-5774
www.wiley.com

Copyright © 2011 by Wiley Publishing, Inc., Indianapolis, Indiana

Published simultaneously in Canada

For general information on our other products and services, please contact our Customer Care Department within the U.S. at 877-762-2974, outside the U.S. at 317-572-3993, or fax 317-572-4002.

For technical support, please visit www.wiley.com/techsupport.

Wiley also publishes its books in a variety of electronic formats and by print-on-demand. Some content that appears in standard print versions of this book may not be available in other formats. For more information about Wiley products, visit us at www.wiley.com.

Library of Congress Control Number: 2011930126

ISBN: 978-0-470-94954-2 (cloth); ISBN: 978-1-118-09289-7 (ebk); ISBN: 978-1-118-09290-3 (ebk); ISBN: 978-1-118-09291-0 (ebk)

Manufactured in the United States of America

10 9 8 7 6 5 4 3 2

WILEY

About the Author

Deborah Halverson edited books with Harcourt Children's Books for ten years — until she climbed over the desk and tried out the chair on the other side. Now she is the award-winning author of teen novels including *Honk If You Hate Me* and *Big Mouth*. Armed with a master's in American Literature and a fascination with pop culture, Deborah sculpts stories from extreme places and events — tattoo parlors, fast-food joints, and, most extreme of all, high schools.

Deborah is also the founder of the popular writers' advice website DearEditor. com, a frequent speaker at writers' conferences nationwide, and a writing teacher for groups and institutions including the Extension Program of the University of California, San Diego. She freelance edits fiction and nonfiction for both published authors and writers seeking their first book deals. By conducting word-by-word line editing or more general substantive editing, Deborah helps authors hone their storytelling voices, synchronize age-appropriate language and subjects, and develop stories that appeal simultaneously to young readers and to adults such as parents, teachers, and librarians.

Deborah lives in San Diego, California, with her husband and triplet sons. For more about Deborah, visit her author website at www.deborahhalverson. com and her writers' advice website at www.deareditor.com.

Dedication

For Robin Cruise, who gave me not one but three big breaks . . . and more importantly, her friendship

Author's Acknowledgments

On my first day as an editorial assistant with Harcourt Children's Books, the managing editor walked me down the hall to view an art show of newly arrived paintings for a picture book then in production. I stood among a bustling crowd of editors, designers, production people, marketing gurus, and inventory, financial, legal, and support staff — all of whom had dedicated their careers and personal passions to creating entertaining and enlightening books for children — and it hit me: I'd found my people. I discovered that day what I've come to love about the writers and producers of children's books: They are a true community that cheers, collaborates, and works its knuckles to the bones in support of literature for young readers. The enthusiastic participation of the writers, agents, and editors who have contributed their expertise to the information you hold in your hand reflects that.

I extend immense thanks to the inspiring writers and teachers who've lent their voices to this book: M. T. Anderson, Kathi Appelt, Karen Cushman, Jennifer Donnelly, Jean Ferris, Cynthia Leitich Smith, Darcy Pattison, Mary E. Pearson, Gary Soto, Deborah Wiles, and Jane Yolen. Add to their voices those of my trusted children's book agent Erin Murphy and my friend Senior Editor Kate Harrison.

Then there are those whose words are not directly quoted in this book but whose insight and expertise fill its pages: former publisher and all-around publishing visionary Rubin Pfeffer, editorial veteran Diane D'Andrade, vice president and editorial director Jeannette Larson, author Bruce Hale, author and copyright/free speech attorney Randal Morrison, publishing attorney Lisa Lucas of Lucas LLP, and publicists Barbara Fisch and Sarah Shealy of Blue Slip Media and Antoinette Kuritz of Strategies Literary Public Relations.

And just as no story would be complete without its grand finale, I extend my deepest appreciation to my agents for this book, Matt Wagner and Anna Johnson, whose idea it was to turn me into a dummy; to my editorial team: acquisitions editor Tracy Boggier, technical editor Barbara Shoup, copy editor Danielle Voirol, and especially project editor Vicki Adang, whose humor pervades this book as much as my own; to my husband, Michael, who champions me with absolute abandon, and my three sons, who inspire me to embrace every day as a new adventure; and last but far from least, to my mentor and friend Robin Cruise, the managing editor who ushered me into that art show on my very first day in publishing.

Publisher's Acknowledgments

We're proud of this book; please send us your comments at http://dummies.custhelp.com. For other comments, please contact our Customer Care Department within the U.S. at 877-762-2974, outside the U.S. at 317-572-3993, or fax 317-572-4002.

Some of the people who helped bring this book to market include the following:

Acquisitions, Editorial, and Media Development

Project Editor: Victoria M. Adang

Acquisitions Editor: Tracy Boggier

Senior Copy Editor: Danielle Voirol

Assistant Editor: David Lutton

Editorial Program Coordinator: Joe Niesen

Technical Editor: Barbara Shoup

Editorial Manager: Michelle Hacker

Editorial Assistant: Rachelle S. Amick

Cover Photos: © iStockphoto.com/DNY59

Cartoons: Rich Tennant
   (www.the5thwave.com)

Project Coordinator: Katherine Crocker

Layout and Graphics: Corrie Socolovitch

Proofreader: Nancy L. Reinhardt

Indexer: Valerie Haynes Perry

Special Help
   Jennette ElNaggar, Todd Lothery

Publishing and Editorial for Consumer Dummies

   Diane Graves Steele, Vice President and Publisher, Consumer Dummies

   Kristin Ferguson-Wagstaffe, Product Development Director, Consumer Dummies

   Ensley Eikenburg, Associate Publisher, Travel

   Kelly Regan, Editorial Director, Travel

Publishing for Technology Dummies

   Andy Cummings, Vice President and Publisher, Dummies Technology/General User

Composition Services

   Debbie Stailey, Director of Composition Services

Contents at a Glance

Table of Contents

Foreword

. . . .

Do you remember the first time you, as a child, really fell into a book? When you turned the first page, you were sitting there on the sofa or lying on the floor or trapped in the back of a car with screaming siblings . . . and then a few more pages flipped, and you were no longer aware of pages or words or hair-pulling. You found yourself someplace else: standing on a mountaintop, sneaking through an underground lair, or curled up inside a hollow tree. You were completely lost in another world. It's an amazing sensation.

Our early experiences reading books can be intense. Every day, children are spirited away from bedrooms and kitchens and classrooms and the seats of buses. Toddlers demand the same book night after night, until they can recite each page and shout out each rhyme before their dozy parents can. Very few people are as passionate about books as children are. Kids devour books — in some cases, literally.

If you write to stir the emotions of readers, to move people deeply, to change people's lives, then you should consider writing for young adults. Who else will read your book 12 times? Who else will try to steal a copy from the library? Who else will sleep on top of your book? Who else will make a diorama of your book with the main character played by a Styrofoam cup? Who else, in short, will invest themselves imaginatively in your world like a young person will?

Young readers are still constructing their understanding of life. They do not yet know the ways of their species nor the ways of the world. As they read stories, they learn about justice and injustice, happiness and sadness, glory and delight and sorrow.

They also learn the rules of *story*. They learn how some novels reflect their lives and some novels take place on other worlds. They learn a grammar of stories — how sometimes things move quickly and sometimes things move slowly, how characters are different from and similar to real people, how plot twists happen and what makes a joke funny. Books for young people, after all, train us all to appreciate literature for adults — as well as to make some sense of our own teeming, crazy world.

So as you think about writing stories for young adults, remember that your audience will greet you ecstatically — but they'll also have high expectations. They will be fervent in their reactions, positive and negative. (Few adults, on finding a book boring, will throw it under the bed, start kicking the floor, and turn purple.) It's an amazing journey to take with a young person. I hope you enjoy it — and that you someday find young readers lost in your book, sunk in your world, whisked away from their bedrooms, their kitchens, their buses, exploring a place you made. That, after all, is one of the greatest gifts you can give them — and yourself.

—M. T. Anderson
National Book Award Winner, National Book Award Finalist, L.A. Times *Book Prize Winner, and two-time Michael L. Printz Honor Book Author*

Introduction

● ●

*W*ith young adult book sales rising and bestselling authors exploding onto the scene with multibook contracts and movie deals, aspiring writers of young adult (YA) fiction are more numerous than ever. But the appeal of writing YA fiction is more than creating high-profile bestsellers. It's writing for kids. It's expanding their vocabulary and their imaginations. It's forming reading habits for life. And it's adding to the impressive body of young adult literature, with its rich narrative voices, satisfying story arcs, intriguing concepts, natural and revealing dialogue, and robust characterizations. Young adult fiction isn't just for kids anymore; it has heft for grown-ups as well.

Your path to writing YA fiction likely began with your own passion as a young reader, so you know firsthand the joy kids find in books. Now you're going to create that for others. You've chosen a fulfilling mission. The realm you're entering — the children's book world — is an amazing community of writers, editors, agents, librarians, teachers, supporters, and champions of young readers. And then there are the readers themselves. You'd be hard-pressed to find a more sensitive, loyal, and responsive audience.

Young adult literature is a moving target as it transforms with each new generation of readers, but some things don't change: Young readers always want a great read. They want books in which they can see themselves and learn about the world and their place in it, all in ways that enlighten and entertain them. Your job is to meet those expectations. That's not as simple as it sounds, because you face challenges that writers for adult fiction don't: You need to talk to teens, to talk like teens, and, sometimes, to talk as if you were a teen yourself. That takes special craft skills and an understanding of your unique audience — the way they think, their interests, their fears, and their dreams.

This book helps you understand that audience so you can work your craft accordingly. I also explain how to operate in the very particular young adult fiction marketplace, because when all is said and done, you're entering a business with risks, rewards, and rejection. I explain how to think like a kid but strategize your novel and your career like an adult. Welcome behind the scenes of young adult fiction!

About This Book

My goal in writing this book is to provide you with the tools you need to become a published author of young adult fiction. To that end, I serve up a full plate of writing techniques, along with insights and tips to apply in all phases of crafting your young adult novel. I want to help you get and stay inspired, understand the ins and out of the YA publishing world, avoid common mistakes in trying to reach young readers, submit your manuscript to editors and agents with confidence, and move boldly into the realm of self-promotion. Above all, I hope to guide you in developing a voice and style that appeals to young readers and that is wholly, comfortably yours.

Writing is an abstract endeavor, and the way to make it tangible is to offer examples. So I've filled this book with examples. Tons of them. Exercises, too, so you can apply the skills at hand directly to your project. Working through the exercises chapter by chapter can take your fiction from idea to final manuscript. Along the way, I cover the fine points of writing craft in a comprehensive and how-to manner to help you meet readers' needs . . . and your own. Where step-by-steps are appropriate, I've stepped. Where checklists provide focus, I've checked. Where do's-and-don'ts drive things home, I've done. But know that there's no such thing as a recipe for the Great American YA Novel. Too much depends on how each writer blends the ingredients together. But there *are* ingredients, and I give those to you here. The bewitching brew you concoct with them is up to you.

Don't feel you have to read this book from cover to cover. You can skip around if that suits you, picking out topics as your needs dictate at any given time. This book is modular, meaning that even if you start in Chapter 12, the information still makes sense. However, if you prefer to work your way from idea to final bound book, I've organized the information so you can start at Chapter 1 and read straight through to the end.

Conventions Used in This Book

I use the following conventions in this book:

- ✔ Technical writing and publishing terms appear in *italics* and are followed by easy-to-understand definitions.

- ✔ Web addresses appear in `monotype`.

- ✔ I vary pronoun gender throughout the book, although you may find more *she*'s than *he*'s. The ranks of children's book publishing are abundant with women, as is the readership, so if I do lean, I'm sure it's toward the feminine.

✔ I use the term *young adult fiction* as the world at large does — as a comprehensive label for two distinct publishing categories: *middle grade fiction* (or simply MG) for ages 9 through 14 and *young adult fiction* (YA, also called *teen fiction*) for ages 12 through 17. Within the children's book industry, people frequently distinguish between MGs and YAs. When making the distinction in this book is necessary, I do so. But know that all the craft, submission, and marketing information work for both MG and YA fiction because the storytelling techniques are essentially the same and the same publishing players handle both categories.

✔ I use sidebars throughout the book to share my teaching podium with award-winning and bestselling young adult novelists. The material in these gray boxes, written by the guest authors, provides insight into how successful authors wield the skills you build in this book. At the end of each sidebar, I list some of the author's books. The best way to find out how to write for young adults is to read exemplary YA novels — start with these.

What You're Not to Read

You can skip parts of this book altogether if you want to. Information that accompanies a Technical Stuff icon offers extra insight into the process and business of YA fiction, but it's not crucial reading. The same goes for the gray-shaded sidebar boxes that pepper the chapters. That extra material is meant to fill out your knowledge of the industry and offer you examples of how pros do what I'm explaining how to do, but you won't sabotage your career by skipping the sidebars.

Foolish Assumptions

Just as you make assumptions about your young readers, I'm making some assumptions about you:

✔ **You want to be published.** This is your first stab at writing fiction, and you need to know where to start. Or you're a published writer in another category, and you want to try your hand at YA. Or perhaps you've been submitting your YA manuscripts but haven't yet landed a deal, and you want to change that. Regardless of your experience level, your goal is to see your name on the cover of a printed-and-bound YA novel.

✔ **You've got a story to tell.** Ever notice how many people say they have a book in them? You're one of them — only you're ready to act, and you have an idea already in the chamber. All you need now is the know-how to develop it.

✔ **You want to be a better writer.** Whether you're a newbie needing the basics or a veteran writer aiming to brush up, you want techniques and tips that you can put to work immediately with tangible results — and you want those techniques broken down in a way that lets you apply them with your own personal flair.

✔ **You want to enlighten and entertain young people between the ages of 9 and 17.** Young adults are still figuring out who they are and how this world works, and their novels play a part in their explorations. You want to contribute to their journey into adulthood — or at least make them smile as they forge onward.

If you see yourself anywhere in this list, then you'll find the information in this book edifying and productive.

How This Book Is Organized

I've arranged this book in a logical sequence, leading off with an overview of young adult fiction's unique marketplace and readership before jumping into the happy task of ushering you from your initial story idea through the development, submission, and promotion of your published novel. I provide exercises at every step so you can build your novel as you move through the book.

Part 1: Getting Ready to Write Young Adult Fiction

Writers don't just sit down at a computer and spit out the Great American YA Novel. They must plan, brainstorm, and analyze first. During your prewriting phase, you pinpoint your exact audience in the wide young adult age range, find an angle that makes your story stand out from the masses, prep your writing space so you can work efficiently and distraction-free, and discover what makes young adult literature so different from every other literary category out there — and why it's so darn great.

Part 11: Writing Riveting Young Adult Fiction

This part of the book helps you turn your ideas into a solid first draft by taking you step-by-step through the novel-development process. You shape your plot, sculpt believable characters, develop a convincingly youthful narrative voice and natural dialogue, and manipulate the setting to enhance all those elements. Along the way, you find techniques for connecting with an audience whose sophistication and maturity is in flux.

Part III: Editing, Revising, and Formatting Your Manuscript

Revising is writer's jargon for the act of rewriting parts of your story — adding things to it, rearranging parts of it, and removing things altogether — all with the intent of transforming your solid-but-not-yet-perfected first draft into a seamless, flowing final draft. This part tells you how to effectively tackle the items on your revision list and experiment with fixes in a constructive, confident, and safe way. Find out how to assess what you've done, identify what needs fixing, make a plan for fixing it, and then successfully execute that plan. I break the process down into methods and the most common boo-boos in grammar, execution, and overall storytelling. After that, you get to polish the manuscript and make it pretty.

Part IV: Getting Published

This part is all about sharing your final manuscript with the world. I tell you how to find the right agent and/or editor for you, how to craft a professional and enticing submission package, and how to promote your novel after it's published. I also demystify self-publishing so you can decide whether it suits your needs and situation better than traditional publishing.

Part V: The Part of Tens

Everyone loves lists, and the *For Dummies* people are no exception. In keeping with their tradition, I include a Part of Tens with lists that warn you about the most common pitfalls in writing young adult fiction, answer the most common publishing contract questions, and prep you for writers' conferences so you can get as much out of the experience as possible.

Icons Used in This Book

These five icons are sprinkled throughout this book to highlight information that deserves special attention.

This icon flags great strategies for employing the technique at hand or enhancing a particular aspect of your writing or story. Tips may save you time or help you come at something from an angle you hadn't considered. Try them out.

This icon means you're getting a heads-up about something you should keep in mind as you read onward.

Red alert! Every activity has its trouble spots, and writing and publishing for young adults is no different. Spare yourself confusion, dead ends, and wasted effort by heeding these words of warning.

This is extra in-depth stuff that you don't *have* to read in order to write and publish successfully . . . but it's cool to know if you feel inclined to linger.

Look for this icon when the writing bug bites or when writer's block descends. The text next to this icon gives you some direction for putting my tips and tricks into practice.

Where to Go from Here

I've done my best to organize this book so you can give it a thorough read if you're new to YA fiction and to writing in general. Or you can dip in and skim if you're just trying to brush up. The choice is up to you now.

If you're new to YA fiction, spend some time with the prewriting chapters in Part I to get to know your special audience and the categories and genres that define YA lit. If you've been in the YA realm awhile, you can dip into the craft chapters as needed to buck up skills that need bucking and to remind yourself of what you already knew but lost sight of — a common happening for writers, who must balance so much.

I'll send you into the book proper by telling you the same thing I tell all the writers I edit — bestsellers and newbies alike — and all the writing students I've ever taught: Be open and be willing to experiment. Writing is not about applying formulas, no matter how many checklists and step-by-steps I give you. The magic happens when you let your hair down and go beyond the formulas. Try new things. Do what you never thought you'd do. Let the "rules" and formulas anchor you, yes, but then get funky from there. This is YA fiction, after all, and Rule No. 1 for teens is that rules are made to be broken.

Part I

Getting Ready to Write Young Adult Fiction

The 5th Wave

By Rich Tennant

"Read this. It's a draft of a novel I'm writing for the young adult market. I want to make sure there's absolutely nothing in it you can relate to."

In this part . . .

Young adult fiction is as different from adult fiction as teenagers are from adults. It has its own rules, its own quirks, and its own very opinionated audience: teens.

Ultimately, the elements of storytelling are the same for both categories, but YA fiction writers must come at those elements with a different mindset. This part initiates you into that way of thinking. You find out what YA fiction is and how it constantly evolves, you discover the category's core traits that defy change, you target specific age ranges and genres, you choose themes and conflicts that appeal to young readers, and you get yourself organized to write. Above all, you master the first steps in creating stories that resonate deeply with teens, a wonderfully fickle, self-centered, sometimes reluctant, and ultimately fleeting readership who reads to define teens and their roles in the world — and who just plain loves a good story.

Chapter 1

The Lowdown on YA Fiction

In This Chapter

▶ Understanding what YA fiction is and isn't

▶ Exploiting YA's unique opportunities

▶ Facing YA's unique challenges

▶ Reaping the rewards of writing for young adults

The Me Generation. Generation X. Generation Next. Each new crop of teens has its own culture and view of the world and their place in it. Their fiction — collectively called *young adult fiction* — shifts with the ebb and flow. This constant state of flux creates new opportunities for aspiring and veteran writers alike. Understanding YA fiction's changing nature gives you insight into how you can fit into its future. This chapter offers a glimpse into its transitive nature while listing core traits that distinguish YA fiction despite its flux, along with the unique challenges and opportunities you face as a YA writer.

Introducing YA and Its Readers

Young adult fiction is distinguished by its youthful focus and appeal. The main characters are usually young adults (exceptions include the animal stars of Kathi Appelt's *The Underneath*), and their stories, or *narratives,* reflect a youthful way of viewing the world that puts them at the center of everything. Characters act, judge, and react from that point of view until they mature through the events in the story.

One of the unique aspects of YA novels is that they have nearly universal appeal; YA fiction offers something for every interest and everyone who can read at a middle school level or higher. The audience includes young teens who fancy tales of first love and other relationships, older teens who can't get enough of other teens' troubles, and even grown-ups who like stories that help them remember what life was like when they thought they knew it all.

Knowing what makes a YA a YA

It's easy to think that having a teen lead is what makes this fiction "young adult" fare. That matters, yes, but it's not a defining factor on its own. Many adult books feature teenagers but have adult themes and exhibit adult sensibilities, sophistication, and awareness. Here are six traits that together help distinguish young adult fiction, all of which I talk about extensively in this book:

- **Teen-friendly casts:** Teen novels star young adults with similarly aged peers who all exhibit youthful *characterizations,* or ways of thinking and behaving. These characters usually lack the empathy of an adult, worrying about how things affect them first and foremost. They don't put themselves in others' shoes well or readily, nor do they analyze why they or other people do things — at least not at the beginning of the story, before they've matured through their adventures. Adults are generally background characters or not present at all. (Chapter 5 gives you direction on writing characters that teens love.)

- **Universal teen themes:** The themes in young adult fiction are *universal* ones that real teens struggle with every day. The stories deal with issues and developmental hurdles that affect every generation, such as peer pressure and falling in love for the first time. (Flip to Chapter 2 for pointers on your theme.)

- **Accessible narrative styles:** The stories are structured with clarity, accessibility, and teen social culture in mind — perhaps with frequent paragraphing, lots of white space, short chapters, or structures that mimic journaling or electronic correspondence, such as texting or e-mail exchanges. All these style decisions depend on the intended audience's specific age and sophistication level.

- **Youthful narrative voice:** The narrators' choice of words and the sophistication of their views reflect the dramatic, often self-centered mindset of teens. Teen characters who narrate their own stories sound like real teens thanks to relaxed grammar and syntax and immature observations, whereas the adult or all-knowing *(omniscient)* narrators demonstrate an appreciation of how the teen mind works. Although first-person narration isn't a requirement, it's common enough to be called another helpful defining characteristic of YA fiction. (Chapter 9 helps you choose your narrator and have her tell the story from a teen's unique point of view.)

- **Moral centers:** Young adult stories generally have moral centers, with their young characters growing and changing in a positive way. Even if the story does not have a happy ending, the story ends with the maturing of the main character, with that new wisdom being the positive factor. These novels avoid preaching, however, letting the story demonstrate the lesson while the readers interpret the "message" for themselves, which increases their sense of independence. You reveal this wisdom through your story's plot. (Chapter 6 walks you through building a perfect plot.)

✔ **Teen-friendly concepts:** The themes may be universal, but the plots that embody those themes are unique and particularly intriguing to young adults. The events are believable within a teen's experience as well as within the fictional world of the story, and they take place in settings that teens can relate to. The stories are often timely, reflecting current events, politics, or social norms. (Chapter 7 explains how to ratchet up the tension in your story, and Chapter 8 helps you create a believable setting.)

Above all, young adult fiction is not watered-down adult fare. The stories are rich, artistic, and compelling. They respect the audience instead of coddling or talking down to readers. The "young adult" moniker is about the age and sensibility of its audience rather than the quality of the story's content.

The book that changed everything: *The Outsiders*

"Young adult literature" has only been a formal category since the late 1950s, about the time the American Library Association formed its Young Adult Services Division (now known as the Young Adult Library Services Association, or YALSA). In fact, the term *teenager* had been widely recognized only the decade before, so it's understandable that it took a while before writers focused on the angsts and dreams of that new age group.

Prior to that, stories written about kids and childhood were mostly written with adult readers in mind, and the ones written directly for young readers were often thinly veiled morality lessons rather than novels intent on exploring the experiences of that audience. There were notable exceptions like J. D. Salinger's *The Catcher in the Rye*, which signaled an interest in the emerging teen psyche in 1951 with its brooding young man caught between the worlds of childhood and adulthood, but otherwise writers had yet to connect with this emerging audience in a collective way. Even when folks did start writing novels with young adults officially in mind, the fledgling

category got little respect as anything but fluffy entertainment.

Then came 1967. That year, Viking Press published 17-year-old S. E. Hinton's *The Outsiders*, and a gang of greasy no-gooders who smoked, drank, "rumbled," and knocked up girls totally changed the tone of books written for young people. Young readers finally saw themselves in a book — their own worries, their own interests, their own potential triumphs.

The publication of *The Outsiders*, with its "real" teens, ushered in the 1970s "issue book" or "problem novel." This literary phase had authors tackling universal teen problems with fervor. Getting your period, having your first sexual experience, smoking, rape . . . these books served up social angst galore. And teens gobbled them up. Judy Blume was perhaps the queen of the issue novel, captivating young readers with hits like *Forever* and *Are You There God? It's Me, Margaret*. The topics were big, and the young characters embodied the issues and fought the battles on their own terms. Young adult fiction had come into its own.

Understanding why YA fiction is for kids

Young readers want see themselves in their books, and young adult fiction satisfies that need. Teens get stories that reflect their situations and concerns, and they feel empowered reading about kids their own age who solve their own problems. For young readers who aren't at the top of the reading spectrum, teen fiction offers reading experiences that respect and welcome them rather than intimidate. Advanced readers who are educated or sophisticated enough for books with adult themes get challenging, inspiring stories about kids their own age. All these readers can learn about our crazy, ugly, wonderful world from the safety of their reading nooks, and kids can immerse themselves in a book to escape the troubles of real life just like adults do. Young adult fiction offers teens stories about themselves and their world.

Every young adult novel is written for a very specific age range, which determines everything from theme to sentence length. I break down those age ranges in detail in Chapter 2, but for now, understand that *young adult fiction* is actually an umbrella term for two very different publishing categories:

- ✔ Middle grade fiction, aimed at kids ages 9 through 14 (also referred to as *MG* or *tween fiction*)
- ✔ Young adult fiction, or YA, for teens ages 12 through 17 (also called *teen fiction*)

Looking at why it's not just for kids

Even though young adult fiction's primary audience is tweens and teens, adult readers get great pleasure from these novels as well. More and more adults are discovering that young adult fiction is more than stories about high school girls who get crushes on high school boys and then teen angst ensues. These novels have edgy storytelling and offbeat humor; they have strong narratives, plot, and characters; and they scrutinize the complex concerns of young people under all sorts of lenses. Above all, they entertain.

In fact, some of the most ardent fans are 21-and-overs. *The New York Times* reports that 47 percent of 18- to 24-year-old women and 24 percent of same-aged men buy primarily young adult books. The same is the case for one out of five 35- to 44-year-olds. And YA lit book clubs for adults are plentiful. These adults love the timeless themes, they enjoy the trips down memory lane, and they relish the strong storytelling that fills YA fiction. A young adult novel has lessons and entertainment for every age, and the stigma of reading "a kid's book" has long since disappeared.

Books with equally strong appeal for young and old readers alike are said to have *crossover appeal*, meaning they cross over the line that divides the adult and young adult markets.

The other book that changed everything:
Harry Potter and the Sorcerer's Stone

After deep explorations into teen issues in the 1970s, young adult fiction faltered as the old issue books started feeling stale, safe, and irrelevant to kids of the '80s. As would happen time and again, the category was about to undergo change. American teen culture was venturing into darker, edgier handling of teen topics, and the market for young adult fiction sagged under the restlessness of the next emerging teen culture.

The mass market teen romance phase of the 1980s was the first real sign that the shift was taking place. There also arose an interest in multicultural stories that reflected the full range of American demographics. But the category didn't take a solid upswing until the mid-1990s with the publication of a new kind of teen novel that featured edgy, realistic themes. These books mesmerized young readers — and unsettled adults. Complex, compelling, and often experimentally structured novels like Ellen Hopkins' *Crank* pulled no punches. They showed life at its grittiest, tackling universal problems from an entirely different aesthetic. This shock-and-awe version of issue books breathed new life into the young adult fiction category. The gloves were off now, and teens responded by opening up their own wallets, for the first time taking the reins in buying paperbacks themselves in mall-based stores.

Still, an upswing is no volcanic eruption. That had to wait for the arrival of a bespectacled young wizard named Harry Potter. No one was prepared for the book that rocked the publishing world. A dozen publishers rejected J. K. Rowling's *Harry Potter and the Philosopher's Stone* before it was finally published in modest numbers in England in 1997 and shortly thereafter in America as *Harry Potter and the Sorceror's Stone*. At that point, a publishing phenomenon erupted. Both kids and adults loved the series, taking it to such sales heights that when the seventh and final volume was published in 2007, it sold a record-breaking 8.3 million copies in the first 24 hours. The series became a media empire complete with its own merchandise, movies, and even a theme park. The books were sold in chain stores, mall-based stores, and retail and warehouse stores. Harry Potter was everywhere.

The subsequent publicity boon for all young adult literature was immense. Initially books about wizardry benefitted from the interest the series, but that eventually spilled over into all categories and genres of YA lit. New and reluctant readers had discovered the joy of reading, while kids who'd been readers their whole lives found their interest turning to passion, and older readers rediscovered the world of YA literature. Thanks to Harry Potter, young adult literature reached a new level of mass-media exposure, paving the way for the commercialization that defines today's young adult fiction marketplace.

Over the years, young adult fiction has developed into an age-defying literature, most significantly with the publication of J. K. Rowling's famous Harry Potter series. When that now legendary wizard hit the scene in 1997, kids suddenly found themselves competing with adults twice or three times their age for the front of the line at Harry Potter launch parties. And then with the explosion of paranormal hits and mainstream crossovers in the early 2000s, YA fiction attained a new level of prosperity and audience appeal. Wonderfully, the classics still hold strong, creating a rich market for young adult fiction.

And let's not forget the Nostalgia Factor. Nostalgia calls adults back to the books they remember from their own teen years, like Katherine Paterson's *Bridge to Terabithia* or maybe their favorite issue books from the 1970s. Adults reread these books and share them with the young adults in their lives.

Maneuvering through the Challenges

With such a wide readership, writers of young adult fiction have great opportunities. They also have challenges that writers of adult fiction don't toil against: reluctant readers and gatekeepers.

Reaching reluctant readers

In education and publishing circles, *reluctant readers* refers to those teens and tweens who aren't so keen on spending their free time — or their assigned time, for that matter — with a book. What makes them so reluctant? Many simply haven't yet found joy in reading. Or they see reading as a chore when they could be indulging in "fun" things (such as TV, movies, video games, hobbies, and activities with friends and family) or going to school, doing homework, and participating in extracurricular activities. And then, of course, some young people simply lack solid reading skills.

Reluctant readers make up much of your potential audience, especially in the middle grade realm. You can take this into account in your fiction by

- **Putting big words in contexts that make their meaning clear:** Some kids love consulting their dictionaries, but reluctant readers aren't in that group.

- **Writing clear, tight sentences:** Even the best readers don't want to fight their way to the meaning. Keep it accessible.

- **Keeping up a fast pace:** Young readers generally don't have the patience of adults, who may stick with a slow-starting book because they've heard great things about it or are especially intrigued by the promises in the jacket flap copy.

- **Hooking young readers instantly:** Help young readers get emotionally invested right off the bat . . . or risk losing them.

Writing stories with high teen-appeal is especially important with reluctant readers, so give careful consideration to your target audience; identifying your target audience is a vital prewriting phase I cover in Chapter 2. Give these kids a reason to read instead of succumbing to frustration or to the million other things screaming for their attention.

You may hear of a subcategory of young adult fiction called *Hi/Lo*, as in *high interest, low reading level.* These books are created specifically for reluctant readers. They're packaged to look like any other book, but the text is written with their needs in mind. The stories are short, from 400 to 1,200 words, and they have many illustrations. Hi/Lo books feature distinct characters who are quickly characterized — no going on and on about anything in a Hi/Lo, which uses quick pacing to keep interest. Sentence structure is short, simple, and clear. Storylines are straightforward and avoid jumps in point of view or time. Because boys are three times more likely to be reluctant readers than girls, Hi/Los are commonly geared to boy interests, emphasizing funny situations, sports, disasters, teen conflict, family/friend problems, and street kids and gangs, and they embrace the sci-fi, mystery/spy, and adventure genres. Hi/Lo is a small, specialty subcategory. I focus this book on *trade fiction,* or the general market, which sells through standard outlets to the general reader.

Pacifying gatekeepers

Unlike writers for adults, you don't have direct access to your audience. Instead, you and your novel must wend your way through a group of people who in one manner or another screen books before they reach the kids they're written for. I'm talking about librarians, teachers, parents, book reviewers, even booksellers. These are the *gatekeepers* of young adult fiction. Every one of them has opinions about what young people should read, with some of those gatekeepers holding the purse strings.

This means you have to please a lot of people before you ever get to your primary audience. Edgy stories that offer rougher views of the world may not squeeze through the filters. Language, sex, and violence all get careful screening. In principle, that's not necessarily a bad thing; adults *should* be aware of what the young people under their wings are reading. But it does add a many-people-deep wall that writers for adults don't have to work around . . . or under or over or right through in some paper-and-ink version of the old Red Rover child's game.

Cases of banned books and censorship arguments periodically crop up in the young adult fiction news, reminding the world of the most ardent gatekeepers. But your chief awareness should lie at the level of everyday screening for age and individual appropriateness. Keep in mind the role of gatekeepers in your readers' lives as you make decisions about your story's content and word choice. Young adult novelists must by default consider their gatekeepers . . . but whether you choose to pacify gatekeepers, work within general boundaries, or blow the boundaries apart is completely up to you.

Understanding types of children's book publishers

Most people can name some big publishers, but the children's book publishing industry also has specialty publishers who target specific customers through various outlets. You should know the differences among the players if you're to become an effective player. Here's the lineup:

✔ **Traditional trade publishers:** These are the companies most people think of when they hear "publisher." Sales reps market their books to bookstores, libraries, and schools, and the books are reviewed in dedicated book media such as *School Library Journal.* These houses operate with a *traditional publishing model,* which pays authors advances against royalties while handling the editing, marketing, sales, order fulfillment, and monies. Smaller houses may offer royalties only, no advances. In most cases, the author holds the copyright to his story. (More on advances, royalties, and copyright in Chapter 17.)

✔ **Mass-market publishers:** These companies have the same advance and royalty structure as traditional houses, but the copyright may be in the company's name, or the author and house may have a joint copyright. Mass-market publishers may also publish the paperback editions of novels originally published in hardcover by a traditional trade publisher. These books are marketed to and stocked by bookstores and discount retailers such as Wal-Mart. These books get reviewed in some dedicated book media.

✔ **Packagers or book developers:** These companies generally come up with the concepts and story ideas before hiring writers to execute those plans, usually for a one-time flat fee. The packager develops the content, takes care of all editing and packaging, and then sells the project to traditional or mass-market publishers, leaving distribution and marketing to that purchasing publisher. The copyright may be joint or in the packager's name.

✔ **Educational publishers:** These companies publish curriculum-based material intended primarily for use in schools. They may pay advances against royalties, royalty only, or a flat fee. They usually employ a sales force that markets directly to educators in their schools or at conferences. These books are reviewed in education journals.

✔ **Small presses:** These companies may publish just a handful of titles a year. Not all of them publish young adult fiction; they often specialize in one or two book categories. They may offer advances against royalties, royalty-only contracts, or flat fee contracts. Small press books sometimes get dedicated book media reviews. They often market through *direct mail catalogs* sent directly to potential customers or through *wholesalers* (also called *distributors*), which means they hire independent companies to stock and distribute their books. Because of their small-operation status, they may cease operating suddenly, so there's higher risk in publishing with a small press.

✔ **Vanity publishers:** Also called *co-op publishers* or *subsidy publishers,* these companies handle the production of the book while the author foots the bill. The author also pays for the marketing and promotion (if there is any) and handles the distribution. Vanity publishers offer a percentage (varying from 3 to 40 percent) of each book sold, although sales numbers aren't usually high, and the publisher owns the ISBN (the 13-digit International Standard Book Number that uniquely identifies your book). The publisher may send out books for review at author expense, but dedicated book media rarely review them.

The Society of Children's Books Writers and Illustrators (SCBWI) warns its members to avoid any publisher that requires authors to pay for publication of their work. The distinction between vanity publishing and self-publishing is becoming quite murky as the author-services companies that aid in self-publishing expand their services menu. See Chapter 14 for more on the murkiness.

✔ **Self-publishing:** This kind of publishing puts you in the driver's seat, with all the control as well as all the monetary risk. You design, edit, produce, market, and distribute your own books. You own the copyright and your ISBN, and you keep all the money generated. Self-published books rarely get dedicated book media reviews. They can be sold through online booksellers as well as through personal author websites and at appearances, and they may be sold as e-books or take advantage of print-on-demand technology and so don't necessarily need to be physically stocked.

Self-publishing favors those who already have a platform and can sell the books as ancillary products, such as through back-of-the-room sales at speaking engagements, or when there are small, identifiable, reachable target audiences. The means for self-publishing are changing as the publishing world evolves to include electronic technologies, and opportunities for individual authors are expanding. I've dedicated Chapter 14 to self-publishing.

Enjoying the Perks of Writing for Young Adults

You may have challenges that writers for adult fiction don't have, but you also have something special going for you: your audience. Young adults are a devoted readership that's vocal about their passions — and their defiance. Their loyalties and rebelliousness create opportunities for you.

Getting new waves of readers: Long live the renewable audience!

Because new readers age into the young adult market each year, the audience for your fiction is a constantly renewing one. This is a boon for you. For each set of newcomers, the old is new. First time love is as exciting and confusing for the new batch of readers as it was for their older siblings. I talk about picking universal themes that you know will resonate with your targeted age group in Chapter 2. Your task is to come at your theme in a way that makes it fresh and relevant to those new teens on the block.

Gaining a following: The young and the quenchless

When young people like a book, they can be passionate, vocal fans. They tell their friends about it, and then their friends read it and tell their friends about it, and then you have more fans. And with social media, telling one friend can mean telling dozens at the same time. Don't discount the role of peer pressure in teen book-selecting. No young person wants to be the last to read the latest hot pick, so word of mouth is a big deal with this audience. Just as booksellers hand-sell in bookstores by recommending their favorite titles and authors to customers, so, too, kids push their picks. Get them liking, and get them talking.

You also find that teen readers stick with an author or series with fierce loyalty. They line up outside stores to buy an author's hot books, and teens even create their own book trailers (see Chapter 15). If you can hook 'em, you own 'em. Teens want *more*. And because adults are now sticking with young adult fiction even when they grow out of the official age ranges, you may keep your readers longer than you think.

Breaking the rules

A great part of writing for teens is that they're open to new ways of telling stories. They don't yet know all the "rules" adults follow — not that they'd care about them if they did know. Young adults like to test boundaries. In content, teens like to flirt with danger while secure in the belief of their immortality and safety. And in seeing rebellion and rule-breaking in stories, teens feel empowered and thrilled and validated.

In terms of writing style, teens are quite open to *different*. They haven't become wedded to the old ways, so young readers are more likely to embrace new stuff. They let a story talk about itself, for example, jumping out of the narrative to address readers. They're also willing to walk the line between fantasy and real. And still being so close to their picture book days and thus very visual, they welcome the inclusion of visual elements when that suits the story.

An example of middle grade fiction that breaks the mold is Brian Selnick's *The Invention of Hugo Cabret*, a 526-page book that blends words and pictures in a novel that had expert librarians scratching their heads while they decided what it was. A picture book? A graphic novel? A full-fledged narrative novel? They decided picture book, awarding it the 2008 Caldecott Medal for Illustrations (of which it has nearly 300), even as the National Book Award committee called it a finalist in the Young People's Literature category.

Let this knowledge free you up to explore and experiment with your own fiction, finding the right way to tell your story.

Chapter 2

Targeting Teen Readers

- -

In This Chapter

▶ Understanding the age ranges and categories

▶ Comparing teen and tween fiction

▶ Choosing your genre and theme

- -

A story that thrills a 17-year-old can completely freak out a 9-year-old. Yet young adult fiction encompasses those ages and everything in between. Most books aren't so expansive. Your goal is to target one specific age group for your story and then sync your themes and conflicts to that group's maturity level and social concerns. That means you must identify your target readers early in the process. This chapter guides you through that step, charting the standard age groups and genres, factoring in the overlap of tweens and teens, and helping you give common teen themes a fresh twist to grip readers and make your novel stand out.

Identifying Your Teen or Tween Audience

Before you start cranking out chapters, you must be able to name your *target audience* — your readers' ages and gender — along with your intended genre, which reflects your readers' interests and expectations (more on genre in a bit). Simply saying, "I'm writing for teens," isn't enough. Several age groups fall under that umbrella, each with its own emotional maturity, intellectual level, and social interests, and you have to be sure that your story ideas, theme, plot, structure, and language all jive with the age range you pick.

All seven of the craft chapters in Part II of this book help you hone your storytelling skills to suit your chosen target audience, but in this section, you take aim at your audience. After all, scoring a bull's-eye is awfully hard when you're shooting in the dark.

Choosing your age range

Some people say "young adult fiction" to mean novels written for all young readers, distinguishing these books from novels for adults. However, if you're talking to someone within the world of young adult literature — librarians and teachers, editors and agents, writers and booksellers — it's good to distinguish between *middle grade* (MG) fiction, or tween fiction, and *young adult* (YA) fiction, or teen fiction. An author who says she's "writing a YA novel" is writing for teens. She'd specifically state "a middle grade novel" or "MG" if she were writing for tweens.

Everything in this book works for both MG and YA fiction — the craft tips, the submission strategies, the marketing guidance, the whole shebang. The storytelling craft is essentially the same for each category, and the same players in children's book publishing handle all books for young readers, from toddler board books all the way up to MG and YA novels.

You need to understand both MG and YA so you can function in the biz with the movers and shakers as well as tell your story to your readers in the most effective and affecting manner. I give you the insider's view of the MG and YA categories in this section.

Breaking down the age ranges

Officially, the two categories of young adult literature — YA and MG — are further split into age ranges. Assigning age ranges to stories helps book-buyers and readers judge the age-appropriateness of the content and the writing. Table 2-1 lays out the age ranges for you.

You may find a story's age range listed on a book jacket flap or in its online bookseller listings; you can certainly find it in the publisher's catalog, which publishers usually post on their websites each season.

Table 2-1   Age Ranges for Middle Grade and Young Adult Fiction

Age Range	Category	Description
Ages 9–12	Middle Grade	Older elementary into middle school, grades 4–7
Ages 10–14	Middle Grade	Middle school into early high school, grades 5–9; these kids may be reading older MG and younger YAs
Ages 12 and up	Young Adult	Older middle school into high school, grades 7–12
Ages 14 and up	Young Adult	High school, grades 9 and up; generally understood to cap at age 17

Age groupings aren't hard-and-fast. They can vary from publisher to publisher, imprint to imprint, and bookseller to bookseller thanks to subjective preferences and the ever-morphing readers themselves. The topic of age ranges can make even the most astute publishing exec nutso, so don't live and die by these. Use them as guidelines, albeit dang good ones.

That "and up" designation in the age-range column can get a little hinky. Booksellers often favor an upper age cap so they can help their customers sort the choices. But publishers aren't crazy about limiting the readership, fearing that a teen who might otherwise enjoy a certain book will pass on it simply because she's a few months or even a few years older than the top age listed on the jacket. With many teen novels crossing over to adult audiences, an upper age limit can be very limiting indeed.

Even with the "and up" designation, teen fiction doesn't generally target readers older than 17. Although that, too, isn't hard-and-fast. Publishers and sellers used to assume that 18-and-ups would be moving on to more adult material. No more. Now there's a market for YA fiction that delves into those late teen years. The extremely successful Gossip Girl series, for example, features 17- and 18-year-olds and appeals to readers from mid-teens to menopause. And 18-year-old Bella became the most envied girl in America for her love affair and subsequent marriage to the hunky (and inconveniently undead) Edward in the Twilight series. So much for rules.

The point of age ranges is to give readers a clue about the age-appropriateness of the content and the writing. Each new generation of kids redefines *teen*, and their literature should reflect this. Your goal as a writer is to do your best to write the most age-appropriate novel you can for the bracket you choose. That's the way to connect successfully with your readers and position your book in the marketplace.

Understanding teen and tween sophistication

Some 12-, 13-, and 14-year-olds read middle grade novels with older themes, and others are already happily immersed in YA. That's why you see some overlap in the teen and tween age ranges. (Did you notice the overlap of the 12- to 14-year-olds in Table 2-1? This isn't accidental.) With the wildly varied physical and emotional development of 12- through 14-year-olds and the fact that young readers like to "read up" into age ranges above their own, you never really know who's going to read your novel. But you can make some pretty good guesses about your audience.

The shift from tween to teen sophistication starts happening around age 12. Here's how tweens and teens generally differ:

✔ **Tweens (ages 9 to 12):** Typically, tweens are focused inward, with conflicts stemming from that. They're struggling to find out who they are, first and foremost, and their book choices reflect that.

✔ **Teens (age 13 onward):** Teens are starting to look outward as they try to find their places in the world and realize that their actions have consequences in the grander scheme of life, affecting others in immense ways. These kids want more meat in their stories.

As young people's emotions, intellect, and interests change, a writer's word choice and sentence structure may become more complex, as may the plot. Chapter 9 focuses on the language techniques that allow you to adjust your storytelling for your chosen age group. Chapter 7 is where you shape your plot for the specific audience you identify here.

Understanding what's suited to tween or teen sophistication and what would be better aimed at an older audience is important. YALSA (the Young Adult Library Services Association) offers many booklists among their public resources that can help illuminate the genres, themes, and categories of young adult fiction for you — visit www.ala.org/yalsa. But don't just read the titles on those lists; read the books themselves. Lots of them. That's the only way to get a solid feel for your genre, your target audience, and the current book market. How's that for fun homework?

Targeting gender

Publishers are unabashedly vocal about their desire to reel in boy readers, especially boy tweens. Those fellas are a consistently hard-to-reach audience, and it drives book-lovers crazy. Who doesn't want boys to read for fun? Many boys already do, certainly, but not nearly in the numbers that girls do or with the frequency.

Studies give all sorts of reasons for boys' reluctance to read, from the fact that boys are slower to develop and thus their reading skills aren't as advanced as girls' to the belief that boys are uncomfortable exploring emotions in books, instead preferring gnarly explosions. In other words, boys are drawn to the action that's so easily had in video games, TV, and movies. You have to wrest boys away from these things to free up their eyes for a book.

If you want to target boys, bait your line with a theme or topic tempting enough to set aside their game controllers for. Many writers find success by offering action fare along with irreverence, silly humor, and sports themes while slipping the emotional stuff underneath. My novel *Big Mouth*, for example, is about a 14-year-old boy training to be a competitive eater — with the goal of eating 54 hot dogs (and buns!) in the time it takes the rest of us to tuck our napkins into our shirts. But under that gastric "sports story" lurks the issue of eating disorders in teen boys. Walter Dean Myers's *Hoops* is an example of not shying away from the hard stuff, coming at boys full-force even as he ensconces his drama in the boy-friendly world of basketball.

Chapter books: Sooo not YA fiction

Writers new to the children's book world often get confused about chapter books and novels, wrongly seeing chapter books as young middle grade novels. They're not. They fall squarely in the children's book category, alongside picture books.

Aimed at ages 6–9 or 7–10 (first through fourth grade), *chapter books* are a transition from beginning readers to MG novels, offering young readers experience with longer narratives and with following plot and character development across multiple chapters. These books have fully developed chapters and are roughly 100 or more pages, although those pages usually include some illustrations and decorative elements — hence their children's-book categorization. The short chapters work well for short attention spans, and the slightly larger print keeps the books from intimidating budding independent readers. Some chapter books, like the Geronimo Stilton series, graphically enhance the text itself with funky fonts and colors to keep the text blocks welcoming.

The story sophistication level is well below that of MG and YA.

The chapter book market is dominated by series, often with a main-character-and-his-sidekick formula. Familiar characters, familiar author style, and familiar themes make readers loyal to their series and stretch the series' appeal to reluctant readers — which means they get a lot of boy readers (hurrah!). Popular examples include Bruce Hale's Chet Gecko series, Barbara Park's Junie B. Jones series, Jon Scieszka's Time Warp Trio series, and Donald J. Sobol's classic Encyclopedia Brown series.

Just below chapter books are the "intermediate reader" or "transitional reader" chapter books, such as Mary Pope Osborne's Magic Tree House books. These books have chapters, yes, but they're even shorter than chapter books, making them great reads for children who are just venturing into independent reading.

For more about boys and reading, visit the website of Guys Read (`www.guys read.com`), a nonprofit literacy program for boys and men that was founded by Jon Scieszka, the Library of Congress's first National Ambassador for Young People's Literature.

Of course, boys aren't the only gender-specific audience you can write for. See the later section "Exploring common genres" for info on chick lit and other gender-related genres.

Exercise: Name your category

To ensure that you develop a story that syncs with the needs, intellect, and emotional sophistication of a single audience, get a clear bead on your category and age range early on. You don't want to discover at the end of draft one that the topic or theme of the story you so meticulously crafted for older readers is actually more suited to middle graders. Answer the following questions to help you define your category and age range before you start crafting the narrative:

✔ **Will the characters be worried about how the outcome affects them or how it affects others?** Middle graders are focused inward, and older teens start to look outward. The more mature and empathetic your character, the older he's likely to be — and thus the older your readership is likely to be.

✔ **Will your plot involve age- or grade-related events such as getting a drivers' license or passing the SAT?** Know the developmental milestones that will be at play in your novel and sync them with your audience.

✔ **Will there be violence?** Generally, the more violence there is, the higher the target age range.

✔ **Will your theme be an edgy one?** Older readers prefer riskier, rawer themes such as addiction or sexual experimentation; younger audiences are still getting their sea legs with the basic issues of puberty. You can find a list of potential themes later in "Looking at universal teen themes."

✔ **To whom is the theme of most interest and value?** Older teens like topics that make them think bigger than they currently do or that make them question themselves more deeply. Young readers tend to keep their focus a little closer to home.

Knowing Your Genre

Just because your novel is young adult fiction doesn't mean every young adult will like it. As with grown-up readers, young people develop preferences for certain types of stories. They may love sweet romantic stories, or they may like funny ones, or they may like ogres and wizards and the heroic lads who thwart them. The types of stories in the young adult fiction category — its *genres* — are gloriously plentiful.

Knowing your target genre is just as important as knowing your target age range. Readers, who can be incredibly loyal, often stick to one or two genres. Knowing their interests and expectations can help you better shape your fiction for them. This isn't to say you need to stick with one genre for your entire publishing career in a kind of reverse loyalty. Many successful authors write across genres. For example, M. T. Anderson has written serious historical YA, dark futuristic YA, action-packed humorous MG, and experimental fiction that crosses over to adult audiences, too, earning major book awards and legions of fans along the way.

Knowing the genre of your current manuscript (also called your *work-in-progress*, or WIP) is crucial. Each genre has its own way of doing things, distinct qualities that set up expectations for its readers. Whether your goal is to nurture those expectations or nuke them to oblivion, you should understand the expectations of your chosen realm. Then be able to explain what makes your story fit into your genre as well as what distinguishes it as something fresh and intriguing.

Author Cynthia Leitich Smith on paranormal fiction: More than monsters

From first kisses to first tackles, the teen years can feel like one unstoppable mass of magic and mayhem. Bodies shift, voices change, everything from a blemish to a C in English feels like the end of the world. No wonder paranormal books are popular.

YA paranormal is a bigger genre than most people think. It's not just lusty vampire drama or regency zombie gorefests, as much fun as those are. You can find the fanged, furred, and fabulous in paranormal mysteries, chick lit, historicals, and every other genre of books for young readers. Check out as many YA paranormal novels as you can. To rise above the competition, you need fresh, tasty blood, and the only way to know what's already out there is to read deep, wide, and spooky.

But be warned, intrepid writers: There's no such thing as cranking out "a vampire novel" or "a demon novel" or "a zombie novel" or "a faerie novel." Werearmadillos? Ditto. These stories are greater than their creatures. Stacey Jay's cute, perky zombie heroine in the chick lit-ish *My So-Called Death* is a far scream from Christopher Golden's fearsome fiends in his horror novel *Soulless*. What matters is not the monster but what you do with it.

Most popular are the YA paranormal romance and YA horror (or gothic fantasy) markets. The appeal of those is that kids can see their own experience in the stories — but with delicious danger and taboo teasing. A paranormal romance novel is, first and foremost, a romance novel, just one that incorporates traditional horror elements. There's nothing like a kiss in the shadows . . . with a hunky immortal. The central question typically remains: How will the couple end up together? However, magical elements and creatures heighten the literal stakes.

It's not only that Mom and Dad disapprove of the supernatural bad boy; it's that God and all of humanity view him as a threat. It's not only pregnancy she risks but her very soul.

A horror novel may have romantic elements, but at its heart lies the genuinely horrific. These monsters have teeth. They relish feeding. They need victims. Gothic fantasy considers a myriad of timeless themes such as invasion, plague, gender-power dynamics, and the beast within.

In all paranormal books, the fantasy is only compelling so far as it illuminates the real world. In my novel *Tantalize*, Quincie becomes involved with an older guy who encourages her to drink with him. What is she drinking? What will that cost her? Whose fault is it? Those questions could be answered in either a realistic or fantastical context. Magic heightens, but the way the metaphor speaks to reality is what makes the story resonate.

I'm a hybrid — a Gothic writer who weaves in some humor and romance. My stakes are high and my magic, costly. Bad things happen to good characters, and I don't promise a happy ending. But then, unpredictable endings are half the fun of reading, aren't they? And creatures of the night are anything but predictable.

Cynthia Leitich Smith is the best-selling author of the YA gothics Eternal, Tantalize, *and* Blessed, *as well as numerous award-winning books for young children. She is a member of the faculty at the Vermont College MFA program in Writing for Children and Young Adults, and her Cynsations blog is one of the top sites read by the children's/YA publishing community. Find out more about Cynthia at* www.cynthialeitichsmith.com.

In this section, I introduce you to various genres in YA fiction and talk about crossing genre boundaries in your story.

Exploring genres of YA fiction

Here's a list of genres of YA fiction, along with descriptions and novels that exemplify them. For the sake of keeping the list manageable, I've grouped the genres into three sets: general market, defined markets (categories with a narrower focus and more-limited audiences), and niche markets (small, specialized markets).

The hands-down best way to get to know your genre is to read like crazy. But don't be a passive reader. Get a notebook going, jotting down the things you like about the genre and the things you don't. Also note the common page counts, the sophistication level of the writing and the readers, and the issues and interests of that readership. If certain authors jump out at you, compelling you to race to the store for more of their books, ask yourself why. What are they doing that makes their stories stand out? Are they bucking expectations, or are they working the genre's formulas to their best effect, twisting them in satisfying or unpredictable ways? If you read in this active manner, you'll see patterns developing within a few books — patterns of the genre as well as of your own preferences. You'll probably discover as much about your desires as a storyteller as you will about the genres during this stage.

General market

Here are some general-market genres in young adult fiction:

- **Contemporary (or contemporary realism):** Featuring realistic, current settings, contemporary novels address social issues and teen problems such as eating disorders, abuse, and crime. They're also referred to as *problem novels* or *issue books.* Sample titles include *Speak* by Laurie Halse Anderson, *Fallout* by Ellen Hopkins, *Shooter* by Walter Dean Myers, and *By the Time You Read This, I'll Be Dead* by Julie Anne Peters.

- **Chick lit:** Chick lit, a popular subcategory of the contemporary genre, features teen girls who struggle (usually with social awkwardness) but eventually triumph. Sample titles include The Princess Diaries series by Meg Cabot, *Love Is a Many Trousered Thing* by Georgia Nicolson, the Gossip Girls series by Cecily von Ziegesar, and *Just Listen* by Sarah Dessen.

- **Romance:** Similar to chick lit, romance addresses family and personal development and relationships, but most importantly, romance explores romantic relationships. Sample titles include *What My Mother Doesn't Know* by Sonja Sones and *Flipped* by Wendelin Van Draanen.

✔ **Humor:** Employing situational, fantastical, satirical, or slapstick humor, humor stories commonly feature character growth through tribulations, along with humorous exploitation of teen angst. Although sometimes silly for the sake of pure entertainment, humor books often deal with real issues in a lighter, more humorous manner. Sample titles include *Love among the Walnuts* by Jean Ferris, *Burger Wuss* by M. T. Anderson, *Al Capone Does My Shirts* by Gennifer Choldenko, and books by David Lubar and Gordon Korman.

✔ **Adventure:** Fast-paced and full of action, adventure books are especially popular with boys. Popular subgenres are survival, war stories, and spies and espionage. Sample titles include *Hatchet* by Gary Paulsen, *I'd Tell You I Love You, But Then I'd Have to Kill You* by Ally Carter, and *Stormbreaker* (from the Alex Rider series) by Anthony Horowitz.

✔ **Sports:** This genre is sports as pastime and passion, featuring down and dirty game action. These books usually involve finding oneself through a sport, with characters gaining an understanding of the greater world and their individual experiences through the lessons learned participating in the sport. Sample titles include *The Boy Who Saved Baseball* by John H. Ritter, *Hoops* by Walter Dean Myers, *Pinned* by Alfred C. Martino, and *Summerland* by Michael Chabon.

Defined markets

The following genres have a narrower focus than the general-market genres in the preceding section:

✔ **Historical:** Historical novels can portray fictional accounts or dramatizations of historical figures or events, or they can explore the lives of ordinary people in different times. Regardless of the teen protagonists' role in the actual history-making events at hand, the characters struggle with universal teen issues along with the issues of their time and place. Subgenres include early American history, slavery and the Civil War, 20th-century America, and world history. Sample titles include *A Northern Light* by Jennifer Donnelly, *Bud, Not Buddy* by Christopher Paul Curtis, *Fever, 1793* by Laurie Halse Anderson, *A Year Down Yonder* by Richard Peck, and books by Ann Rinaldi and Carolyn Meyer.

✔ **Fantasy:** Fantasy is a very general term for stories that are magical or in other ways supernatural. Its knee-jerk identity as a fiction genre is usually *high fantasy,* which features elves, dwarves, and the like who often band up for epic quests involving myths and legends. There's also humorous or dark fantasy, alternate and parallel worlds, historical fantasy, gothic novels (which incorporate elements of horror), and stories about fantastical happenings in fantastical landscapes that have nothing whatsoever to do with elves or wizards. Sample titles include *The Lord of the Rings* by J. R. R. Tolkien, the Harry Potter books by J. K. Rowling, the Gemma Doyle trilogy by Libba Bray, *The Golden Compass* by Philip Pullman, *Ella Enchanted* by Gail Carson Levine, *The Lightning Thief* by

Rick Riordan, *11 Birthdays* by Wendy Mass, and books by Patricia Wrede, Jane Yolen, and Tamora Pierce.

- **Paranormal and horror:** Think vampires, werewolves, zombies, ghosts, and the undead. Paranormal and horror feature real-life (often modern-day) characters and settings with supernatural elements, magic, and/or magical creatures. Paranormal tends to be rooted in horror, as opposed to just being fantastical. Sample titles include *Coraline* by Neil Gaiman, *Tantalize* by Cynthia Leitich Smith, *Dead in the Family* by Charlaine Harris, and *Twilight* by Stephenie Meyer.

- **Science fiction/futuristic:** Subgenres include hard science, humor, alternate worlds and time travel, utopia/dystopia, speculative, post-Apocalypse, and genetic engineering. These stories often warn against the dangers of societal or technological trends. Unlike adult sci-fi/futuristic novels, YA versions usually end with hope or the sense that the world/humanity can be saved or rebuilt for the better. Sample titles include *Feed* by M. T. Anderson, *A Wrinkle in Time* by Madeline L'Engle, *The Giver* by Lois Lowry, *The Hunger Games* by Suzanne Collins, *The Eleventh Plague* by Jeff Hirsch, *Uglies* by Scott Westerfeld, and books by Orson Scott Card.

- **Mystery/crime/thriller:** Contemporary or historical, these books involve classic mystery and thriller elements such as conspiracy, crime, physical peril and suspense, and of course, good ol' teen detectivery. Sample titles include *What I Saw and How I Lied* by Judy Blundell, *The Body of Christopher Creed* by Carol Plum Ucci, *The Ruby in the Smoke* by Philip Pullman, *Only the Good Spy Young* by Ally Carter, the Pretty Little Liars series by Sara Shepard, the Nancy Drew series, and books by Joan Lowery Nixon.

Niche markets

These genres have small, specialized markets:

- **Gay/lesbian issues:** Featuring gay/lesbian themes such as gender identity issues and same-sex attractions or concerns, books in this genre often include teens who have (or are contemplating) same-sex love relationships. Sample titles include *Will Grayson, Will Grayson* by John Green and David Levithan, *Eight Seconds* by Jean Ferris, *Boy Meets Boy* by David Levithan, *Someday This Pain Will Be Useful to You* by Peter Cameron, and *My Tiki Girl* by Jennifer McMahon.

- **Multicultural:** Multicultural books are usually defined as books about people of color, such as African Americans, Native Americans, Asian Pacific Americans, and Latinos. These books feature issues of ethnicity and race. Sample titles include *The Absolutely True Diary of a Part-Time Indian* by Alexie Sherman, *Monster* by Walter Dean Myers, *Kira-Kira* by Cynthia Kadohata, and *Walk Two Moons* by Sharon Creech.

✔ **Religious/inspirational:** The religious/inspirational genre revolves around characters and plots dealing with religion, faith, and spiritual concerns. There is also a specialized Christian book market that offers young readers stories underscoring Christian values. Sample titles include *Send Me Down a Miracle* by Han Nolan and *Matilda Bone* by Karen Cushman. Titles specific to the Christian market include the best-selling Diary of a Teenage Girl series by Melody Carlson and Robin Jones Gunn's two series about Christy Miller and Sierra Jensen.

✔ **Urban, especially African American urban fiction:** Also called *street fiction/lit, hip-hop fiction,* and *gangsta fiction,* this genre exposes readers to the gritty realities of street life in urban America. It usually features African American characters living in the inner city with drug dealing, gang violence, and scenarios of street survival or escaping the ghetto. This is not a mainstream genre and is not stocked widely in school libraries due to the controversial topics, themes, and graphic nature; the books are often self-published or from small publishers. Teen street lit that does enter the mainstream usually tones down the graphic nature and incorporates warnings about the consequences of destructive or criminal behavior. Sample titles include *The Coldest Winter Ever* by Sister Souljah, the Bluford series, and *Homeboyz* by Alan Lawrence Sitomer.

Writing cross-genre novels

Most young adult novels stick to a single genre, but you can blend elements from two or more genres within a single story to create what's called a *cross-genre novel*. Want to write a western but not interested in the traditional horse-riding, six-shooter fare? Drop some unicorns and centaurs among the tumbleweeds and give it a paranormal twist. How about a high school gossip clique on Mars, blending the best of chick lit with sci-fi? Cassandra Clare peoples Victorian London with demon hunters in *Clockwork Angel,* and Scott Westerfield blends fantasy, history, and machinery in his adventurous *Leviathan* (this cross-genre blend has earned its own subgenre name: *steampunk*). Although merging genres can cause confusion for folks who wonder where to shelve the book or who to market it to, a cross-genre novel done right offers something fresh to readers of both genres.

If you want to craft your YA fiction as a cross-genre novel, here are some tips to increase your chances with agents, editors, and readers:

✔ **Stick to two genres.** Sure, you can write a horror western with a dose of high fantasy, but should you? Your audience is young people, remember. It's one thing to respect their intelligence; it's another thing to throw everything but the kitchen sink at them. Blending more than two genres may overcomplicate your novel.

✔ **Make your story more of one genre than the other.** You can lessen the shelving/marketing confusion by skewing the story to be mostly one genre so the book can be solidly categorized. Readers must know what the novel is before they can know whether it's for them.

✔ **Put story ahead of gimmick.** Gimmick may sell a few copies of your novel, but if the writing isn't great, word gets around in the form of bad customer and critic reviews — if you can land a publisher in the first place. Strive to create harmony between your chosen genres, working the elements together naturally for a full, satisfying story.

Embracing special story formats

A marvelous quality of the young adult fiction realm is its openness to alternative ways of storytelling, digressing from straight, linear narrative storytelling in order to engage curious young readers. Here are some of the special story formats you may see in YA:

✔ **Novels in verse:** These books feature novel-length narratives told through poetry, with novelistic plots and full character arcs. Sample titles include *Stop Pretending: What Happened When My Sister Went Crazy* by Sonja Sones, *The Geography of Girlhood* by Kristen Smith, *Shakespeare Bats Cleanup* by Ron Koertge, and *God Went to Beauty School* by Cynthia Rylant.

✔ **Diary/journaling:** Typically told through a succession of diary entries, these novel-length narratives are most popular in chick lit, such as *Angus, Thongs, and Full Frontal Snogging* by Louise Rennison, and contemporary fiction, such as Walter Dean Myers's *Monster*, which alternates a 16-year-old boy's journal entries with pages of a movie script he's writing. The diary format isn't limited to those genres, however. Kids of any era journal, so the format works for historical fiction, as in *Catherine, Called Birdy* by Karen Cushman, and for futuristic stories, such as *The Diary of Pelly D* by L. J. Adlington, which uses an unearthed diary

to contrast a dystopian world with a more idyllic prewar existence. Diary fiction even scores high with boy readers, as proven by the Diary of a Wimpy Kid series by Jeff Kinney.

✔ **Epistolary:** These novels tell stories primarily through letters, though they may incorporate news articles, journal entries, and other documents. Although not a new format, the modern epistolary novel for young adults is often influenced by current social media, including blogs (Gossip Girls), e-mail (*ChaseR* by Michael J. Rosen), texts and instant messaging (*ttyl* by Lauren Myracle), and the like.

✔ **Experimental:** As the name implies, *experimental fiction* for young people defies definition — although it's safe to say it embraces creative storytelling. Take Markus Zusak's *The Book Thief*, which is narrated by Death himself. As you may expect, Death doesn't feel bound by the conventions of traditional storytelling. Deborah Wiley's *Countdown* uses scrapbooked elements to supplement the narrative story, and M. T. Anderson's *The Astonishing Life of Octavian Nothing, Traitor to the Nation*, reimagines the past by mixing a historical fiction narrative with epistolary elements and traces of fantasy. And then there's Brian Selznick's graphic narrative *The Invention of Hugo Cabret*, a novel that so mixes narrative and illustrative storytelling that many in the children's book world have puzzled over whether to call it a novel, a graphic novel, or a very long picture book. What most do agree on, though, is its powerful storytelling. The book earned many awards, including the coveted Caldecott Medal, awarded for illustrative excellence in books for children.

Thinking through the Theme

A *theme* is a concept you want to teach or a message you want to convey that your protagonist (and by extension your readers) can experience. Themes give stories focus, unity, and a point. A theme is different from your story *premise*, or *idea*, where you take the concept and add a specific situation and chain of events (the *plot*). And theme is different from your genre, with all the rules and reader expectations that go with the style of story you've chosen to tell.

Consider this: When a reader goes into a bookstore, she doesn't say to the clerk, "I'm looking for a book about a grasshopper." Instead, she says, "I'm looking for a book about how wishes can come true." *Wishes coming true* is the theme. When the clerk responds, "I do have a book about wishing. It's the story of a grasshopper who wishes upon a star and his dream comes true," he's restating the theme and then offering a plot that delivers the theme.

I get all detailed about ideas and premises and plots in Chapters 4, 6, and 7. For now, theme is the thing, with my pointing out the usefulness of universal themes in YA fiction and then suggesting some ways you can make those same old concerns fresh for the current generation.

Looking at universal teen themes

YA fiction reflects the issues and concerns that kids experience as they transition from childhood to adulthood: bodies that suddenly act like flesh-and-blood Transformers, new responsibilities with startling consequences, conflict seeming to lurk around every corner, the pressures of S-E-X. . . . Regardless of time, place, and culture, everyone undergoes this metamorphosis, hopefully with minimal chaos and pain. *Timeless* or *universal* teen themes are those issues and concerns that puberty serves up to any- and everybody. Here's a sampling of universal themes:

- Self-esteem, popularity, cliques, being cool, accepting differences, fitting in
- Relationships (friendship, family, romance), first love
- Body image, sexuality (sexual identity, sexual desire), pregnancy

- ✔ Peer pressure, addictions, drugs/alcohol/sexual experimentation
- ✔ Surviving adversity, broken families, abuse (sexual, physical, emotional), poverty, dealing with death
- ✔ True meaning of happiness, real success, personal empowerment, activism, attitude, power of imagination
- ✔ School life, sportsmanship, jobs, fashion, religion/spirituality
- ✔ Accepting change, general coming of age

Universal themes open up your story to a wide audience. The more readers who can relate to your story, the more readers you'll get. Your fiction comes into its own when you mix-and-match your personal pick of universal themes with your setting (time, place, and culture, which I discuss at length in Chapter 8) and your unique plot ideas (Chapter 6).

Making timeless themes relevant today

Whether your genre is chick lit or fantasy, humor or historical, teens want books in which they can see a bit of themselves. That means throwing them universal themes with current social, cultural, and political spins.

Take the theme of popularity as an example. Many young people would give their right arm for a shot at being popular. But if they make their move and fail, the consequences can be devastating: social banishment, vandalized lockers, vicious graffiti in school bathrooms — at least, that's how past generations felt the sting. But in these days of social media, the popularity theme has a whole new feel. The public sting of being called out online, the helplessness in the face of viral rumor mills, the casual cruelty of one-click forwarding. Yikes! Fear of having your phone number written on a bathroom stall door is nothing compared to the horror of being called a slut online and seeing it repeated 500 times in cyberspace. The theme of popularity gets a fresh, new feel when you factor in the layer of fear and fragility that social media brings to the old issue.

When you start writing, go easy on your theme. Sure, I know you spent a lot of time mulling it over, figuring out the best way to get fresh with it, and of course tying it to the plot. But if you get heavy-handed with it, your readers will balk. Teens don't like being preached at. They get enough of that at school and at home, they don't need it in their books, too. Use a light touch instead, letting your readers figure out the themes by thinking about what happens to the major characters. You want to guide readers to your point, not beat them with it.

Exercise: Choose your theme

Knowing the theme for your story helps you shape your plot, develop your characters, and stay on track as you write your first draft. The following items help you pinpoint your theme, mining it from all the great ideas and plans you have for your story:

1. State the practical lesson, value, or attitude you want your readers walk away with:

   _____

   Examples: "Always believe in yourself." "Never judge a book by its cover." "Never act in anger."

2. Fill in the blank:

   I want my character to learn _____

   _____

   Examples: "to accept himself, flaws and all." "that she can overcome a wrong done to her." "that the consequences of keeping a secret are worse than those of admitting the truth."

3. Fill in the blank:

   My character must deal with _____

   Examples: a bully, an unexpected pregnancy, a betraying best friend

4. Does a famous quotation or saying best sum up what you want your readers to realize? Write it here:

   _____

   _____

   Examples: "Believe you can, and you're halfway there." "Beauty is skin deep." "Forgiveness is a gift you give yourself."

Consider your responses to Questions 1–4. Using one or two words, state the common denominator that runs through them all. Self-esteem? Body image? Peer pressure? Pick words from the sample themes in the earlier section "Looking at universal teen themes" or come up with your own word or phrase. This exercise helps you articulate your theme, the ultimate point of your story.

Making or Chasing Trends

Wait. Hold on a minute. Let me dig out my yellow flag . . . there! Do you see it waving? I need to tell you something very, very, very, very, very important: Do not chase trends. Ever. You won't catch them.

Writing takes time, submitting to agents and publishers takes more time, and publication takes freakin' forever. Generally, a full year passes between the time a book is signed and the day it hits store shelves. That doesn't factor in how long it took you to whip up that amazing manuscript.

I know following trends is tempting. A book takes the reading public by storm, and everyone reads it and then wants more books just like it. It happened with Harry Potter, and it happened with the Twilight series. Suddenly readers of all ages were clamoring for books about wizards and vampire hotties. Yes, publishers note that kind of demand and quickly buy up a bunch of manuscripts about wizards or vampires or whatever and rush them into production to meet that demand. That's capitalism at work in the book biz. But unless you already have that wizard manuscript done and ready to submit, the pipeline will be full before you can type "The End." Worse, not only will that wave have passed, but you'll just have wasted precious months on something you can't sell thanks to a glutted marketplace. It doesn't much matter whether what you wrote is good; you'll be hard-pressed to get an agent or editor to even look at it.

Your best work comes out when you're writing on something you're passionate about, not when you're slap-dashing something together because, hey, you want a piece o' that action, baby. Write the book *you* want to write.

I absolutely believe in strategizing your project for the marketplace early on, making sure it has a fresh hook (which I cover in Chapter 4) so that your earnest efforts aren't wasted on a book that has no market. Those efforts don't begin with noting the top title on the bestseller list and then slamming your fingers against your keyboard at high speed. They begin with making sure your story has a distinct place in the market, which you'll know if you've done your genre homework and identified your target audience. Armed with that information, you can give your story a twist that makes it stand out in that market, perhaps even starting your own trend. In this spirit, then, let this be your mantra: Don't chase trends; make them.

Chapter 3

Managing Your Muse

. . . .

In This Chapter

▶ Finding your best writing times and places

▶ Getting (and keeping) the words flowing

▶ Outlining and researching

▶ Keeping up with the YA writing community and industry

. . . .

*W*riting a novel is hard work and lots of it. As a YA fiction writer, you must combine creativity with productivity as you render abstract ideas into tangible collections of words on a page — hundreds of pages, in fact, all resonating with the energy and enthusiasm that prompted you to write in the first place. That's a big job.

In this chapter, you discover how to go about the job of writing YA fiction. You pinpoint your most productive writing spaces and times and get tips about protecting both. You see why you should tap into the YA community and how to get the most out of conferences and critique groups, and you find some resources that can keep you in tune with the children's book industry. You consider the ins and outs of researching and outlining, and, above all, you find ways to kick-start your writing each day, foil would-be distractions, and give dreaded writer's block the bum's rush.

Setting Yourself Up to Write

Creativity churns out ideas; productivity churns out books. This section helps you figure out when you're most productive — what time? where? under what conditions? — and how to protect your writing space and time from distractions or flat-out derailments. What's right for one writer may be wrong for another, though. Use the tips in this section to determine what's right for your personality and creative style.

Carving out your writing space

A great way to prepare to write is to set up a dedicated writing space. Where should that space be, and what should it look like? The answers are different for every writer. If you're new to writing novels, you may not have the slightest clue. In that case, think back to high school and college. Were your best writing, studying, and number-crunching done in crowded locales or in isolation? Were your legs propped up and stretched out, or did you hunch maniacally over the keyboard with metaphorical steam billowing out your ears? When you tackle tasks that require complete focus now, do you prefer to be surrounded with the familiar, or do you need to leave your home because the call of the dirty dishes is just too loud to ignore? The key to setting up to write is to know yourself.

Some folks think they need a studio built over their garage to be a writer, but you don't need a whole lot to get down and dirty with your manuscript. Here are the bare bones of it, which you can fit that into a closet if that's what's available to you:

- ✔ A small table and chair
- ✔ Your computer
- ✔ A pen and your notebook full of ideas
- ✔ Key reference books

And with today's laptops, even the table and chair aren't necessary. You can kick it on a sofa with the computer in your lap.

You need neither a mansion nor a fortune to create a writing space. Productivity isn't about the space; it's about what you need to get in the writing mood and then stay there long enough to put some words on the page. If you don't need a formal writing nook, don't set one up. There's no crime in that.

As you design a space that accomplishes that for you, here are some things to keep in mind.

Choosing the right lighting and seating

Your stories may originate in your brain and funnel out through your fingertips, but your eyes and posterior are part of the writing team, too. Keep them happy by giving them the tools they need. Proper lighting eliminates eye strain, reduces headaches, and makes your time at the computer pleasant. Choose lights with no glare, and use desk or floor lamps with bendable necks or clip-on lights to let you direct the lighting where you need it. Don't shine your light on your computer screen, and keep the shades on your window adjusted to prevent sunlight from glaring off of it.

If you're writing for an extended stretch, periodically focus your eyes on things around the room or outside your window, or just lean back and close them. No drifting off, though!

You need a quality chair for your desk and another for kicking back if you have the space, so invest in good seats. That kick-back model can be a bean-bag or an old couch — whatever's comfortable and good to your body.

Apply the rules of good ergonomics to your computer posture and desk and chair height. You want a relaxed, neutral posture to keep your muscles from straining. You can even get a foot rest designed for better typing comfort. If you're writing for long periods, get up and stretch frequently. Don't reward productive writing sessions with a sore tush.

Livening up less-than-posh places

Maybe all you can carve out for a writing space is a corner of a family room or an unused closet. If your space is small, liven it up with color. Paint the walls if you can. Tack up some sports pennants. Set a woven placement beneath your computer. If you're tucked in a corner of the living room, sepa-rate your desk from the rest of the world with a partition screen, making a space instead of simply the desk you sit at. If you're converting a walk-in closet or pantry into a mini office, add wall mirrors to give it depth and plants and posters of dreamy places to stay in touch with the outside world. Even small spaces can be happy places.

If the only space available to you is the unused basement or the old lawn-mower shed, don't feel like you've just been banished to the dungeon. Fixing up non-living spaces doesn't require money so much as imagination — of which writers have plenty! A coat of paint, cool posters or paintings from the five-and-dime, a wall collage of photos, a deliberately cheesy shower curtain dangled from cute ceiling hooks . . . you can decorate on the cheap. You don't even need new furniture. A fresh coat of paint can do wonders for a tattered desk or rusted filing cabinet. I sprayed my rusty brown filing cabinet sparkly gold and absolutely adore it.

No matter what space you choose to write in, include some items that inspire you. Surround yourself with quotations or photos of peaceful places. Frame the jackets of your favorite books or photos of writers you idolize. Keep a few favorite books nearby so you can flip them open on a moment's notice to remind yourself why you love to write.

You may also try adding music to your workspace. Many studies suggest that music helps people concentrate. It blocks out surrounding noise and gives your subconscious something to do while the rest of you focuses on your story. Wear headphones to filter out the background noise if you work in public places or in your house when others are home. Of course, some people crave silence when they write. Give music and silence a few trials each to pinpoint which scenario keeps you more focused.

Create a businesslike atmosphere

Your goal is to write an appealing novel, get it published, and make enough money to do it all again. You need to approach this task as a professional would, which includes setting up your workspace so it reflects the serious side of writing. In your work space, allow only things that are essential to your writing (sure, that stack of mail can be called "essential," but it's not essential *to your writing*), and keep the most necessary items within reach.

For a cleaner work space, get things up and out of your way with magnetic office supply baskets that stick to the file cabinet next to you. Mount small shelves just for your necessaries or buy hanging organizers. If you crave tchotchkes, keep them few and organized. Sure, desk toys are fun, but you're not there to have fun with toys; you're there to have fun with your fiction. Here's what to keep within reach:

- ✔ **Handy items for your desk:** Your notebook; a bookstand for your notebook, dictionary, or thesaurus; a cup and coaster; pens, pencils, and highlighters; tape; notecards and sticky notes

- ✔ **Handy items to have within reach:** Reference books such as a baby name book, books on the craft of writing (including this one!), inspiring novels, and a good dictionary and thesaurus

- ✔ **Handy items for nearby:** An electrical outlet; a trash can; a printer and refill paper; a bulletin board; a file system for contracts, submissions, and research

Invest in a separate backup device for your computer hard drive and keep it close by. You must save your writing frequently — preferably after every writing session. Choose a device that's small so you can keep it nearby and easy enough to operate yourself.

Nothing says "professional" like a to-do list. Use a bulletin board to post a to-do list and your writing schedule. This list is for nothing but your writing-related tasks. Those tasks can be writing business, such as "call bookstore rep to confirm signing time," or your writing goal for that session, such as "rewrite school fight scene." Get yourself a nice, thick pen for crossing things out when they're done. That step is important. It's easy to finish a day of writing and feel like you've accomplished nothing because there isn't a big stack of papers in the printer when you're done. Checking things off gives you satisfaction. Be able to look at your list quickly and make changes easily.

Now here's the hardest part of setting up and maintaining your writing space: Be organized. Don't let papers stack up on your desk. Few things are deadlier for a flowing chapter than having to stop and search through a stack to find that reference article you need to complete the scene. The chances of getting sidetracked by those other interesting articles in the stack are huge, and your train of thought is likely to race on without you. Use binders, get a hanging folder rack for the side of your desk, or set up an accordion folder. An easily accessible filing system is a must. Keep your story ideas together and store your research for each book in a designated folder or binder.

Protecting your writing time

Writing time doesn't just present itself; you must schedule it. And then, well, you gotta show up. I know, I'm stating the obvious, but in truth the first threat to your writing time is you. It's easy to choose a nagging chore over a manuscript that's hit a murky spot or to put off your writing tonight because you had a rough day at the office or to book your dentist appointment during your writing time because, hey, teeth are important. They are. But so is your writing. You must commit to its sanctity before you can ask anyone else to — and if you have family, friends, a job, and social obligations, you'll be asking that of a lot of people.

Here's the thing: You don't need huge chunks of time to write a novel. A few minutes each day can be as productive as any four-hour stint on the weekend. What matters is the quality of that time. If you show up for your writing reservation on time and ready to go, those few minutes will do you just fine.

Commit to writing a minimum of five minutes every day. I heard this tip early in my career from National Book Award Finalist Kathi Appelt. Her reasoning: If you sit down for five minutes, you're likely to stay there for ten, twenty, or far more. Or as the stunningly prolific Jane Yolen famously put it, "BIC." Butt in chair. *That*'s how you crank out books.

A lot goes into being a writer. And a lot can get in the way of it. Here are some tips to get your derrière in that chair and keep the rest of the world at bay:

- ✔ **Block out your writing schedule on the family calendar.** Marking the calendar serves as a visual reminder to everyone that your writing time has as much weight as work, extracurricular activities, or appointments. Schedule around your blocked-out times as you would a doctor's appointment or soccer practice.

- ✔ **Schedule business time.** It's easy to fill up your writing time with writing business such as researching the industry, submitting, promoting, blogging, and arranging speaking engagements. To keep that from happening, schedule a formal business time at the beginning or end of each writing session. Or set aside certain days of the week for business tasks. Put yourself on a timer if you must, but stick to it. Don't let the business of writing replace the act of writing.

- ✔ **Shut down.** Turn off your e-mail, unplug your Internet hub, erase the games from your computer, enable the voice mail–only feature on your phone. Shut down anything that can distract you from your writing. Even writing-related e-mails and phone calls can wait until your scheduled business time. People will learn not to call during your writing time because when you call back, you tell them, "Sorry I missed your call. I send all my calls to voice mail during my writing time. What can I do for you now?" Pleasant but pointed. Most people appreciate knowing the best times to reach you.

✔ **Let others know.** Tell your family that you can't be interrupted during writing time except for dire emergencies, and then remind them of that by shutting your door and posting a sign to keep needy children at bay. You don't have to be rude about it. You can write something like "Do Not Enter: Mommy loves you, but it's writing time. Please leave a note and I'll get back to you shortly." (Adjust that for the office, of course, if you're a lunch-break writer.) Leave a pad of sticky notes and a pen. Make the visitor decide whether his or her need is important enough to write a note.

✔ **Be okay with saying no.** You don't have to volunteer for *every*thing to be a good friend, parent, and employee. Learn to say no to things that violate your writing time, as in, "No, I can't take that on right now," "It's great talking to you, but I'm in my writing time," and "I would love to help you do that. I'll find you as soon as my writing time is up." Telling your lovely darlings to wait an hour is okay — you're not refusing your kids; you're training them to handle what they can during your writing time and wait a bit for the rest. That doesn't make you a terrible parent; it makes you a better one because you won't be cranky, and you'll give the child your full attention after your writing time. Trust me — I'm a triplet mom and a published author, so I know.

✔ **Trade personal time with someone else.** Want writing time? Sometimes you have to give to get. Negotiate with your significant other so that you both get time to pursue your personal interests. Set up a couple of nights a week as your nights to write, and give your partner nights to do his or her thing. *Quid pro quo* gets everyone vested in protecting that time. Or offer to take the neighbor's kids for an hour after school a couple days a week, and then let that neighbor reciprocate. You both get some *me* time, and the kids get play dates. Everyone wins.

✔ **Filter and prioritize.** Writers commonly steal their writing time from their sleep allotment. That works for some folks, but it's not ideal for your body — or fair to your family, the primary recipients of your crankiness. Can you give up something else? Probably. Most people, if they look carefully enough, can find plenty of tasks that can get the old heave-ho. Try it. List all the things you do in a week and figure out which ones you must do, which ones you can hand off to someone else, which ones don't actually need to be done at all, and which ones you can do more quickly or efficiently than you currently do them. The spare time can easily become a writing session.

Don't settle for just passing the time when you could be giving time to your passion. The average American watches five hours of television a day, according to the lovely folks responsible for the famous Nielsen ratings. Imagine all the writing you could do with 151 extra hours each month! Just giving up one show a night can gain you seven extra hours each week. Consider your other outlets, too. Are they more important than your writing?

Smaller blocks of time are easier to work into a busy schedule, so if you can only give yourself half an hour to write every day, great! By the end of the week, you'll have written for 3.5 hours. That's plenty of time to write your novel.

Setting Your Muse Loose

Writers devise all sorts of nifty tricks for getting — and keeping — the words flowing. You're sure to develop favorites yourself. This section offers some tried and true ways to capture ideas, to launch each writing session, and to take aim at writer's block should its shadowy figure dare to loom.

Capturing ideas

Ideas tend to pop into writers' heads at inopportune times — as you fall asleep, for example, or when you're cruising up the I-5. In Chapter 4, I talk about fostering ideas that have high teen appeal, but before you can foster them, you must capture them. This section gives you two ways to do that.

Exploit your downtime to capture ideas. You probably have a lot of waiting times in your life, such as waiting for the bus or commuter train, waiting for your daughter to finish lacrosse practice, or waiting in the doctor's office. Don't just tap your toe and fuss with the paper gown. Pick up a pen and jot in your notebook. These can be wonderful breakthrough moments.

Carry a notebook

Carrying a notebook is the timeworn idea-capturing method of choice for most writers. Palm-sized or full-sized, spiral or bound, the notebook's style is up to you. The point is to have a master place to write down those random thoughts that isn't the back of receipts and stray papers. Those are too easy to lose — and what do you do with them if you do get them home safely? Stack them in a box and spend precious time sorting through them? When's *that* going to happen?

If carrying even a palm-sized notebook with you when you leave home is impractical, slip a few index cards in your purse or back pocket; you can just tape the cards in your notebook when you get home. Taping is great because having to transcribe notes into your notebook is an extra step that you're likely to put it off until later — and sometimes "later" turns into "never." Keep the notebook and tape where you put your keys so that the taping becomes as much of a habit as tossing your keys into the drawer.

Your story starts with you

Wondering where all those good ideas you're capturing in your notebook are going to come from? Generating ideas may not be a matter of looking around for inspiration. Instead, try looking within:

✔ **Write what you know.** Are you a survivor of something? A minority in a social situation? A basketball buff? How does your circumstance or passion challenge, inspire, or inform you? Your YA fiction can have great depth thanks to the details you bring to bear when you write about what you know.

✔ **Write what you don't know.** Pushing yourself to learn about something new helps you learn about yourself and stay excited about your story. Novelty sparks great enthusiasm, and your research may turn up things to inspire your plot events.

✔ **Write what you like to read.** Love reading about kids who outsmart villains? Are you a sucker for sports Cinderella stories? You probably know your favorite genres and subjects well, which means you understand how those stories work and what readers want from them. Plus, knowing a section of the market well helps you craft a story that stands out from the others.

✔ **Write what you want to read.** Wish there was a book about someone dealing with a certain situation? That's an opportunity for you. Write that book.

Above all, write about what moves you. Writing young adult fiction is hard enough without trying to write what you think will sell but don't actually care about.

While at home, your master notebook should be easily accessible. Move it to your bedside table at night with a flashlight for ideas that fly by in the dark, or store it in your writing space overnight but keep index cards next to your bed. In the morning, you can tape the cards into the notebook.

Go digital

You probably have some kind of digital device, from a mobile phone to a handheld computer device, on your person at any given moment. This makes digital devices a superb way to capture fleeting ideas. Notes applications are a standard feature on digitals, with many devices having voice recorders or even apps that turn your words into type as you speak, allowing you to access them with your computer at a later time.

Or simply whip out your cell phone, call yourself, and leave a message on your voice mail. How's that for handy? I wrote much of my second novel that way, calling myself while pushing my infant triplets on their morning and afternoon walks and then retrieving those voice mails after I returned home and put those babies down to nap. If you don't already have a digital device that allows you to record notes or your voice, look into getting one.

Getting the words to flow

You work very hard to make sure you have the space and time to write, but you're no closer to your novel if those words don't flow when you sit down. Here are some tricks to help that happen.

Start each session with a writing exercise

To avoid the horror of staring at a blank screen with a blank mind, start every writing session with a writing exercise. Here are some to try:

✔ **Freewriting:** Give yourself five minutes to write whatever pops into your head, wherever it leads you, with no corrections or self-censoring. This is called *freewriting* or *stream-of-consciousness writing*. Just as jumping up and down gets your blood pumping, unfettered writing gets the words flowing.

✔ **Prompts:** Writing prompts are statements, questions, or suggestions intended to trigger your creative juices. For example, a prompt may tell you to pick a headline from the newspaper and write a fake article to go with it or to choose a cliché phrase and write about it without ever directly stating the phrase. Some prompts have you writing scenes or dialogue based on a specified scenario. Entire websites and workbooks are dedicated to writing prompts, so you'll have no shortage of ideas. You can use characters from your story, or you can write something that has nothing to do with your work-in-progress.

Choose some prompts that push you outside your normal milieu. Instead of writing sample scenes, write a postcard or a letter based on a character or plot prompt; or write a poem using a poetry prompt; or rewrite a popular song's lyrics, choosing a country song if you usually listen to pop or a rap song if you like classical. If you experiment in your writing warm-ups, you'll be more inclined to let your hair down with your novel.

Set goals

Set tangible writing goals that you can post on your calendar and check off when accomplished. Include both long- and short-term goals:

✔ **Have a goal for each and every writing session.** Aim for a set number of words, pages, or minutes. Keep the goal realistic so you can walk away feeling satisfied. A low target keeps your momentum going, your morale high, and the stress minimal. A good starting place is 500 words, two pages, or 20 minutes a day. Adjust up or down from there.

Falling short of your goals can be devastating to the creative psyche. If it's more realistic to write one page each day than two or three, then make it okay to write one. That way, you'll reach your goal and feel satisfied and productive instead of beating yourself over the head as a failure every day. A positive, productive mindset is better than a high page count any day.

✔ **Set short-term goals for your novel.** You may set monthly goals or year-end goals for word or page count. Or you may set story-related goals, such as finishing your rewrite of Chapter Three by the end of the week or completing your first draft by the end of summer. You may set skill-related goals, such as reviewing dialogue techniques and then finishing a revision pass for dialogue by a certain day.

✔ **Set an attainable end goal.** You need a grand goal for this whole writing endeavor, something that's solid, that you can see and then feel when you get there — and feel if you don't. "I want to sell a YA historical novel to a major YA publisher by [date]" is easier to work toward than "I want to be published." Attainable goals are quantified and can be broken down into steps, with time frames for accomplishing them. As they say, if you can see it, you can achieve it.

Devise incentives

Reward yourself when you reach your goals. If I've reached my weekly goal by Thursday night, I get to go surfing on Friday morning. Find your carrot and then dangle it.

On the other hand, turn up the heat if you work best when there are negative consequences for slacking off. Do your kids have negative consequences when they miss curfew? Do you have negative consequences if you miss a deadline at work? Assign consequences for not meeting your writing goals, and make them sting. If you miss your goal, deprive yourself of something you really like to do. If you can't stand disappointing others, invite Aunt Edna to visit for the summer and promise to hand her a finished first draft when she walks in the door. Don't worry — she needn't *read* said first draft (which will likely be as ugly as it is solid); just have both of you anticipating the hand-off so you'll both know if it doesn't happen. Picturing that look of disappointment on her face (or of pride, if you can't shake the happy joy stuff) may be the motivation you need to move your fingers on the keyboard instead of flipping on the vacuum for a stroll around the living room.

Avoid good stopping points

Some writers deliberately stop midflow to make sure they'll have a place to pick up the story tomorrow. They write perhaps two pages a day, good or bad, and stop there, even if they desperately want to keep going. That way, they're craving to run to that computer the next day and already have their next two pages cued up in their heads.

Bulldozing your way through writer's block

Few things strike writers with more fear than these two words: *writer's block.* The feeling of not knowing what to write is devastating to a writer, and the condition can feel like it'll go on forever. Sadly, you'd be the rare writer if you managed to avoid writer's block altogether, but you can help cut down the incidences by being aware of how to mitigate the primary factors:

- **Mind your writing time.** Neglected writing is a prime factor in writer's block. Set that writing schedule and stick to it, even if you're cranking out only a few words a day. Be a frequent and regular writer.

- **Banish perfectionism.** Be okay with writing yucky stuff. Refuse to let yourself reread on the first draft, or only let yourself reread on Fridays, with all the other days being about moving forward. Look at it like this: Yucky stuff can actually be good stuff because it gives you something to *re*write, helping you work your way to new material that's decent or even good. That's part of the process of crafting great fiction. (I discuss revision in Chapter 11.)

- **Move to the edge of your seat.** Avoid being bored with what you're writing by shaking things up. Move characters to unexpected locations so they say and do unexpected things. Let them mess up and do things you *don't* want them to do and see where that takes you. Allow yourself room to experiment. If you try to write the right thing the first time around, you'll be too cautious. Stop playing it safe.

- **Rebuild your confidence.** Self-doubt is an evil affliction of writers. If you feel your confidence faltering, pull out those writing prompts and get your sea legs back. Remind yourself that you're a great writer even if you have hit a bump in your story.

- **Remember why you're writing.** Reread those books that inspired you to write in the first place, or read the bio of a role model who energizes and empowers you.

- **Connect your story to the real world.** Research some part of your story to spark new ideas. Or consider how real-life people you actually know might handle the situation in your story, and then put your characters through those steps.

- **Unwind.** Stress is the nemesis of creativity. Physical exertion helps relieve stress, as does music. Try to view your writing as a mental escape from the challenges of life instead of as a victim of them.

- **Schedule your distractions.** Distractions are allowed . . . just limit them. If you can't stand abstaining from Facebook until the end of the day, for example, allot 10 minutes of your hour-long writing time to getting your Facebook fix and then keep the remaining 50 minutes pure and productive. Where's the guilt in that?

   Some distractions defy scheduling, such as the fallout from an emotional event. For those times, unleash your emotions on a piece of paper in a five-minute *stream-of-consciousness* exercise (unfiltered, ungrammatical, uncorrected, unchecked) and then be done with it. This release may not be a cure-all for the emotions, but it can keep them from distracting you from your writing.

Joining the challenge: A novel in a month

Need external motivation? Give National Novel Writing Month (NaNoWriMo) a whirl. With the end goal of writing 50,000 words in 30 days, NaNoWriMo is the writer's equivalent of the New York City Marathon. The 1,667-words-a-day pace may require a several-hour sprint each day (with no time for editing or revising), but the reward can be amazing: a complete first draft on Day 30. Check out founder Chris Baty's buoyant website `www.nanowrimo.org` for rules, free registration, inspiring forums with thousands of other NaNoWriMo writers, and tips for accomplishing this massive but empowering feat. The starter's gun fires on November 1, but start preparing by at least early October to give yourself time to study the helpful site and choose your subject and theme, develop your characters, and outline your plot.

You won't overcome writer's block by waiting for it to go away. Be proactive. It's a lot to expect your muse to kick in every time you sit down to write, at the precise moment your fingers reach for the keyboard. Sometimes you have to hunt that muse down. Apply a writing prompt to something in your work-in-progress, do a stream-of-consciousness exercise about a random item in your story, or write yourself a letter from your character explaining why she's gone AWOL today. Do not skip your writing session. Force your muse to engage with you.

Outlining the Right Way (for You)

Some writers swear by outlining; others swear it off. These polar stances stem from the conflicting need to know where your story is going and the desire to give creativity room to work its magic. You don't have to be so either/or. The security you can get from outlining may be just what you need to let your creativity flow. Anyway, who says you have to go whole-hog and strategize every tiny detail of your story ahead of time? You can be more general with your outline, or you can work in portions, outlining just the next few steps of your writing. I cover all those options in this section.

But first, here are some benefits of outlining:

- ✔ It helps your story stay on track. If you know where you're going, you're less likely to toddle off on tangents.

- ✔ It helps you spot inconsistencies before you build a story around them.

- ✔ It lets you screen ideas. You don't waste time writing useless scenes or storylines if you've determined in advance that they won't work out.

- ✔ It reduces your risk of writing yourself into corners.

✔ It aids in foreshadowing, which makes the sequence of events more believable. If you don't hint at things to come, a story's resolution may feel sudden, random, and too convenient.

Author Mary E. Pearson's ten tips to beat writer's block

Contrary to what I thought when I first started writing, being published does not render you immune to writer's block. Every story presents unique challenges that can undermine your confidence. I still frequently ask myself, "What kind of mess have you gotten yourself into now? This story is hopeless! It'll never make sense. I don't even know what it's about!" When I get to a spot where I feel like I can't move forward, I do all kinds of things to help me keep going:

1. I print what I've got and then highlight key points or emerging themes to help me refocus.

2. I write a one-liner (or several) that seems to describe the book.

3. I write a short jacket flap–type synopsis to try to understand what the book is about.

4. I look at emotional questions (inner plot) I have raised. Did I answer too soon and let the steam out of the story? Sometimes it's simply the last chapter or two where I took a wrong turn and I only need to rewrite those in order to move forward.

5. I remind myself that the first draft doesn't have to be perfect. Go ahead, Mary, write crap. That's what revision is for.

6. I share a partial with friends — every writer needs encouragement. (But be careful about sharing too much too soon. This can derail a lot of writers, especially if the vision for the story is fragile.)

7. I picture myself a year from now with a finished book. I know the only way I'll get there is by writing a few words each day.

8. I trick myself. I sit down and tell myself I only have to write ten words and then I can get up and do whatever I want guilt-free. Ten. That's all. But I have to do it every day. It's amazing how quickly ten words can grow into a whole page, and then the mind spins during downtime so your story is always being written. That daily jolt of writing keeps those ideas spinning.

9. I reread one of my books about craft. These are like mini-conferences and are a good shot in the arm.

10. I banish all the devils sitting on my shoulder whispering all the *shoulds* and *shouldn'ts* of writing. I literally tell myself, "You will never please everyone, so when all is said and done, you damn well better please yourself. Write the book that *you* want to write!" And I mean it.

I could go on about the many ways I've invented to help me beat doubt. The point is to keep going. Writing is hard, uncertain work, and stories have no clear pathways. Don't beat yourself up when you hit a wall. Take a moment to catch your breath and find a way around it. You can borrow one of my ways or invent your own. Ten words . . . it's like digging a little hole right under that wall, and before you know it, the wall is far behind you.

Mary E. Pearson is the author of five award-winning teen novels, including The Adoration of Jenna Fox *and* The Miles Between. *Find out more about Mary at* www.MaryPearson.com.

Outlining the whole story

If you're a planner in life, you're probably an outliner in writing. Outlining lets you plan your story, accounting for all the pieces and seeing whether they all fit together neatly. You can do this in extreme detail, or you can just list the main plot points.

Here are two standard formats for a novel outline:

- Using a string of short scene and chapter summaries, essentially writing a very long *synopsis* (formal story summary)
- Constructing a bulleted list of the events, players, conflicts, and consequences for each scene and chapter

In either case, you decide the amount of detail you want. Less detail can give you more of an organic feel as you write, satisfying your need for both a road map and creative wiggle room. Both formats should keep the *character arc* (the main character's emotional or psychological journey through the story) in mind and be able to trace it through the outline. You should also be able to trace your main plot and subplots through the finished outline. (See Chapter 5 for an in-depth discussion of character arc and Chapter 6 for info on the relationship between main plots and subplots.)

Here are four simple steps for building an outline:

1. **Divide the story into three parts: the beginning, middle, and end.**

   In the *beginning,* the main character reveals her great desire, and a catalyst sets her on her journey. In the *middle,* a succession of obstacles puts that desire in jeopardy. And in the *end,* the main character finally has an epiphany that overcomes the obstacles, allowing her to attain her goal.

2. **Subdivide each of those three parts into the events that will accomplish each part's goal.**

   This gives you your chapters. You need to account for the catalyst, the obstacles, the epiphany, and the resolution, all of which you examine extensively in Chapter 6.

3. **Break down the chapters into scenes.**

   Figure out which small events need to happen to make the overall goal of each chapter attainable and believable. Some chapters may have several scenes, and some may have only one.

4. **Go back up to Step 2 and feed in your subplot in the same manner.**

   Make sure the subplot complements or runs parallel to the main plot, converging with it in the end. (Again, more on that in Chapter 6.)

When you're done with these steps, you should be able to track the plot development and the character's emotional escalation from the opening scene to the closing one. You can go back in and fill in as much detail as you like. As you do so, look for holes, inconsistencies, improbabilities, and any other red flag that may be waving at you. Now's a great time to work out the kinks.

Resist becoming a slave to your outline. Be open to surprises, both during the outlining process and after you've begun writing. When surprises do strike, be willing to rework your outline to accommodate them. Sometimes the best ideas come after you've spent time with characters during the actual writing of the story.

Planning portions

Some writers want to know where they're going but don't necessarily want to know how they're going to get there. These folks plan their stories in portions, knowing the benchmarks they want to hit but leaving the rest to the writing process. For them, an outline acts as a general guide — a way to get a broader overview of the story — rather than a technical map. Planning the story in portions allows more flexibility than the whole-story outline while still providing the security of knowing what lies ahead.

Sometimes writers who plan in portions find outlining difficult because they don't yet know their characters. These folks first write a few chapters and only then sit down to outline. At that time, they may choose to plan all their benchmarks or just plan a few steps ahead.

Tossing out the outline

Some writers want nothing to do with an outline, deeming it far too stifling. That's completely okay. But even if you won't touch an outline with a 10-foot pole, you should do some pre-story planning. That doesn't squelch creativity. Instead, it gives you something to aim for as you work your way through your YA manuscript, page by creatively surprising page.

Here are four things non-outliners should identify before writing:

 ✔ **The main character's goal:** You can't write without an end goal, even if you aren't yet sure how you'll achieve that goal. You need to know what your character wants more than anything, because that desire pushes her past ever-increasing obstacles when giving up may seem far easier to her. She must want what she wants badly enough to forge onward.

✔ **The flaw that will handicap your main character through every crisis in the story:** In YA fiction, the main character must be on an internal journey, overcoming her flaws to become a better, more enlightened and mature person. She overcomes her big flaw during the climax, when she has an epiphany and finally exploits her strength to successfully conclude her internal journey. This is the *character arc,* which I talk about in Chapters 5 and 6.

✔ **The strength that will be your character's salvation at the climax:** You can't suddenly throw a character's strength onstage when it's needed. You must know it and give your young readers glimpses of it throughout the story.

✔ **The catalyst:** What event will push your character out of her comfort zone and launch her on her journey? This is the first big event in your book; if you know nothing else about your story, know this.

These four preplanning items keep you grounded in your work so you can't accidentally flit around from this tangent to that.

If you don't want to be restricted by an outline but are having trouble getting started on your novel, try making an outline and then never looking at it again. Use it as a writing exercise. Or consider it the first rough draft of your story, getting you to think about and interact with the characters and elements, even if you don't intend to commit to everything in it after you start the actual writing.

Outlining *after* your first draft is a sneaky way to help you assess whether you've truly nailed the story structure. Making each chapter its own item on your outline, trace your storyline from Chapter One to Chapter Last to see whether you lost track of any threads or strayed from your path.

Doing Research, YA-Style

Research? For fiction? Yes! Research isn't just about verifying facts; it's about making a story believable. Research clarifies things for you, makes you able to create richer and more believable characters, and helps you work through problematic parts of the story.

You need enough factual detail to make your story seem real, or else those teen readers of yours won't buy into it. Want to write a road romp with teens driving a car cross-country? Have them climb into "their Chevy Impala" instead of into "their car." That tells readers about the era and the personality of the driver, and it can have you researching how many miles the Impala gets to the gallon so that you pause the road trip for gas often enough to be believable. Your fiction can be high on detail or not, but generally there's stuff you can research to one degree or another. This section tackles the act of researching fiction with a young audience in mind.

All genres of YA fiction can benefit from research that fleshes out the story. Sci-fi and fantasy writers, for example, need research to make sure their world-building details are plausible. Even contemporary novels need research. Writing about a kid with a body image issue? How about lack of confidence, alcohol addiction, or peer pressure? Writing convincingly is easier if you know the causes, risk factors, symptoms, and behaviors that go along with those problems. If you want realistic settings, characters, plot, voice, and dialogue, you need to know who and what you're writing about.

Taking notes and keeping records

For each novel you write, keep a notebook, electronic document, or folder with a section for research. Include articles, your notes, and your sources, writing down full bibliography info for historical or factual research.

No matter what the detail is, note your source for it. Record whatever will help you find that source again if the info is challenged or if you want to check something. Include the following information:

- ✔ **Titles:** All book titles, article names, website names, blog names
- ✔ **Creators:** Authors, publishers, website creators, people you interviewed
- ✔ **Location info:** Page numbers, web addresses
- ✔ **Dates:** Publishing dates, creation and retrieval dates

If you're pulling a technical fact from a book, photocopy the page as *backup,* or proof for your records. If the facts are from a website or blog, print the article and tuck it into your research file, because a website can shut down or be changed at any time.

Following general research guidelines

Researching is an exercise in self-control. You have to stay focused despite interesting side topics that catch your eye, you must stick with something until you can verify or corroborate it with multiple sources, and you must say no to iffy sources. Here are some strategies for accomplishing that:

- ✔ **Turn to the experts.** Look to libraries, archives, museums, clubs, organizations, societies, and websites. Interview experts when you can. Read books on your topics, looking in the bibliographies at the end for further expert sources.
- ✔ **Use a mix of primary and secondary sources.** *Primary sources* are first-hand documents, such as articles or books written during a particular era, diaries and letters, or newsreels and photographs. You can read

diary entries from a particular time or about the issue at hand (especially those written by young people) to get insight into what it was like to live it. *Secondary sources,* such as books, articles written after the era or events, or movies made about the subject, lose out on immediacy but benefit from a broader perspective. You want both perspective and immediacy.

✔ **Trust your gut.** When you get a feeling that something is improbable, confirm the info with a second or even a third source. Printed resources (books and magazines) remain excellent sources because the publications must endure fact-checking by various editors along the way. Of course, even printed books can be wrong or out-of-date. Do what you can to establish the credibility of a source and judge its information.

Nonfiction picture books are great places to start researching. They break down facts into easily digestible chunks. You don't always need scientific explanations or thousand-page biographies. Picture books about inventions and historical events and personalities are particularly plentiful, thanks to the demand created by elementary school projects.

Finding reliable online resources

The Internet has made researching both easier and harder. You can perform complicated searches in an instant, accessing a staggering array of expert sources without leaving your desk, but you must also wade through a morass of unverified, questionable, and creatively tweaked facts and histories. Websites, public question-and-answer sites, Wiki sites (featuring user-generated content), and blogs can entice you with stuff that looks and sounds credible but is in fact biased, opinionated, misrepresented, or flat-out wrong. This section helps you find reliable info and evaluate what you read online.

Starting with credible sites

How do you know a reliable resource? Look for sites or online articles that list the author's full name, title, organization affiliation, relevant credentials, peer recognition (such as awards or publication in established journals), creation date, contact information, and reader reaction in the comments sections or in reviews of the articles. The most credible websites are

✔ University sites or other academic sources

✔ Government sites

✔ Industry publications

✔ Local historical sites

✔ Big-name media (such as *TIME* magazine)

In the case of studies, find the original source of the study instead of relying on a blog reporting about it. Many printed resources have been digitally scanned and posted, allowing you to double-check them yourself without checking them out of the library.

Sorting through questionable information

Here are some signs that you should think twice about a source:

- ✔ **Poor writing:** Your red flag should wave if the writing quality is poor and the articles are riddled with typos or poor grammar.

- ✔ **Biased language and generalizations:** As you research a topic and get a feel for its breadth, you should get an idea of whether a site seems to be leaving out important stuff or spinning facts with bias. Also watch out for generalizations, conflicts of interest, sweeping exaltations of the value of the information on the site, or intemperate language like "that jerk wouldn't know an ascot from his [*bleep*]!" (Of course, you may want subjective opinions instead of objectivity. There's a place for that in your research, too. Just know at the outset of your research whether that's what you want.)

- ✔ **Old information:** If the website hasn't been updated or if the article is old, you may have out-of-date information.

- ✔ **No contact info:** Be skeptical if a source is anonymous, offering no contact information and thus preventing anyone from following up.

- ✔ **No claims to expertise:** Personal sites and sites with user-generated content often contain material from nonexperts, people who are simply interested in a topic.

Watch out with info from Wikipedia, the online "free encyclopedia" built on user-generated content. Anyone can write or update a Wikipedia entry at any time, rendering its credibility factor low. Sometimes, people enter wrong information on purpose, virtually vandalizing the site for any number of reasons. Still, Wikipedia gives you a starting point: You can get an overview of a topic and develop research questions from its entries. After you read a Wikipedia entry, visit at least three other sources to confirm your facts. You can start that confirmation with the sources cited at the bottom of the article — just be sure they meet the criteria for reliable sources.

Blogs can be very useful. You can get the feel of a region or a social group's interests and vernacular. But be skeptical as you read. Lots of bloggers cut and paste facts that they've read elsewhere to bolster their claims and opinions, and in the process those facts get misunderstood, misrepresented, or misstated. Wording can tip you off when this happens; you get a feel for credibility as you get into researching.

If you're looking for facts, follow the trail from a blog to an expert site, either by using the links provided in the blog or by performing Internet searches for those specific facts. Most of the time, verifying or debunking a blogger's claims takes just a few minutes. The same goes for personal websites run by people or groups who claim to be "experts" on something.

Don't be a cut-and-paster of fact yourself. That's just asking for errors in your novel, which is just asking for reader corrections and criticism on blogs, in book reviews, and so on. You'll see pretty quickly how easily the errors slip in and get compounded when others cut and paste. Be skeptical, double-check, and look for reliable sources.

Doing field research to make the teen realm yours

Researching teen fiction includes studying your audience's culture and inter-actions. If you know what they're watching, listening to, talking about, and stressing about, you have a better chance of writing stories that connect with them. Subscribe to some teen magazines. Find out which radio stations are popular with the kids in your area and listen to music of your target era, place, or social group. Watch teen shows and peruse teen-centric stores.

And talk to teens. Interview them for your story. If you're writing a book about a girl equestrian, spend time at equestrian events and interview young riders at length. Prepare questions ahead of time, take good notes, and even tape the interviews if possible.

Don't just research it; live it. If you're going to write about an activity, get in there and try the activity yourself. For example, if you're writing that equestrian tale, sign up for some riding lessons so you can climb into a saddle and experience saddle soreness for yourself — and in the process find out why people fall in love with riding despite the initial pain.

Putting the brakes on research

Research is fun, it's interesting, and, let's be honest, it's a procrastination tool. But you're not a researcher; you're a writer, and a writer has to know when to say when. Here's how to help you get back to the writing:

- ✔ **Don't research your entire book upfront.** Start your project by researching your timeline/events, and then write your story. Research the details as you need them. For example, you don't need to know the history of needlepoint stitches to write your first draft about some girls in the 17th century who spend their evenings in sewing circles. Look into that stuff later, after the hard part of writing the first draft is done.

Before you start researching, make a list of things you want to know — and stick to that list. If intriguing tangents present themselves, add them to your list but don't follow them yet. Stay on target, find what you need, and then move on.

- ✔ **Leave yourself notes as you write.** Note in the manuscript margins any places where you'd like to flesh out the details. Don't stop to add the details, though, even if the facts are in your research notes. Story first, details second.

- ✔ **Focus on your story rather than on your research results.** Keep your ultimate goal in mind: a story rich in detail and steeped in believability. You needn't be an expert on every topic in your book. In most cases, "informed layperson" is just right. Find out just enough, and then rush back to your manuscript.

- ✔ **Keep your audience in mind.** Your teen readers don't need to be experts on every topic, either. Ask yourself, "Does a teen really need to know this?" If your answer is anything but a strong *yes,* stop that line of research and get back to your story.

Revealing what you know

You don't have to tell readers everything you know about a topic. Teens and tweens are reading fiction first and foremost for the story. That means all the research you're doing is meant to support and enrich the story, not supplant it. Dish out details to young readers slowly and judiciously. Establish your story first, without dumping the whole fictional world on them. You have plenty of time to fill out your world, but you have only the first few sentences to hook young readers with a character and tease the main conflict.

Leave the intricate detailing to nonfiction writers. For example, if you're writing about a character who uses herbs, mention the herbs as something she uses for a particular effect and then move on with the story. Your young readers don't need a full rundown of the benefits of those herbs, no matter how fascinating that information is to you. That's not the point of your novel.

See how other writers incorporate fact and fiction by reading novels that are set in your time and place or that feature your particular topic.

Finding Your People: The YA Community

Joining writers' organizations and attending conferences are great ways to educate yourself about YA craft and business, to network, and to find submission opportunities. And there's just something immensely bolstering about surrounding yourself with people who share your passion and particular challenges. (See Chapter 18 for more about attending conferences.)

This section covers the Society of Children's Books Writers and Illustrators (SCBWI) along with the wide world of writers' conferences. It also mentions smaller-scale critique groups, some professional publications for writers, and the benefits of joining online writing communities.

Young adult fiction is a subcategory of children's book publishing, which also includes picture books, chapter books, and so on. Although some writers' groups, publications, and conferences dedicate themselves solely to YA fiction and say so in their descriptions and names, anything with the tag "children's books" includes young adult fiction writers. Read Chapter 2 for more on the breakdown of children's book categories.

Joining a professional organization: What SCBWI should mean to you

Anyone who's serious about writing young adult fiction should belong to the Society of Children's Books Writers and Illustrators. SCBWI's website proclaims it the "largest children's writing organization in the world," and that's no exaggeration. Founded in 1971, SCBWI's worldwide membership reached 22,000 in 2010. It's the only professional organization specifically for children's book writers and illustrators.

Each year, SCBWI sponsors two annual international conferences about writing and illustrating for children, along with dozens of regional conferences and events. The nonprofit organization acts as a voice for writers and illustrators regarding children's literature, copyright legislation, and fair contract terms. It sponsors awards and grants, creates professional publications about the craft and business of children's books, and offers support to its members in the form of online forums and critique exchanges.

Agents and editors actively engage with SCBWI, respecting it as a place where new talents arise and are nurtured. These crucial pros join experienced authors and illustrators on the faculty of SCBWI-sponsored writer events. Some editors even give priority consideration to SCBWI member submissions and announce open manuscript calls through the *SCBWI Bulletin*.

SCBWI exists online with forums, e-newsletters, and pages of resources about industry and craft. But you can take part in a deeper way in its more than 70 regional chapters, which meet regularly. Check out www.scbwi.org for current membership benefits and fees.

Attending writers' conferences

Attending any writers' conference can give you valuable craft skills and insight into the publishing industry. Some conferences are designed specifically with children's book writers in mind, with a few conferences focusing solely on writing for young adults. Conferences offer the following:

- ✔ Craft tips to help you develop writing that engages young readers
- ✔ Opportunities to network with experienced writers who share your YA audience and marketplace
- ✔ Up-to-the-moment insight into the state of the children's book industry from editors, agents, librarians, teachers, booksellers, and publicity pros who toil daily in the kid lit trenches
- ✔ One-on-one interaction with children's book editors and agents

Plus, attending a conference is a great way to feel part of a like-minded community. Sometimes the lift from a conference is what you need to finish your work-in-progress.

The primary children's book writers' conference is SCBWI's Annual Summer Conference in Los Angeles (www.scbwi.org). The group also holds a winter conference every December in New York, the hub of U.S. children's book publishing. Other children's book conferences include the annual Oregon Coast Children's Book Writers Workshop (www.occbww.com) and the Big Sur Writing Workshops (www.henrymiller.org/workshops.html). Table 3-1 gives a breakdown of the kinds of conferences out there.

Table 3-1	Types of Writing Conferences	
Conference Type	*Size/Duration*	*Offerings*
National conferences	Large annual gatherings like SCBWI's Summer Conference, which well over 1,000 writers and dozens of speakers attend over the course of four days	National conference offerings are many and wide in scope, often with separate fiction and picture book tracks. Paid critique opportunities are among the offerings.
Regional conferences	Smaller, usually two- or three-day events; attendance may be in the dozens or hundreds	Editors and agents join authors in offering craft- and industry-related sessions. Paid critiques are standard.

(continued)

Table 3-1 *(continued)*

Conference Type	Size/Duration	Offerings
Local writers' group or SCBWI chapter retreats	Smaller events such as one- or two-day weekend writing retreats or writing intensives; the attendance is significantly smaller, somewhere between 20 and 30 attendees	The general approach has at least one published author and an agent and/or editor facilitating the retreat's various classes and revision blocks. Paid critiques may or may not be available.
Local writer's group or SCBWI chapter meetings	Several-hour meetings; local chapter memberships vary in size from a few writers to several dozen or even a hundred-plus; specific meeting attendance depends on scheduled speakers and topics	One or several speakers (published authors, agents, or editors) present craft- or industry-related material. Paid critiques aren't usually part of this kind of event.

Children's book writers also gather at industry trade shows, teacher/librarian conferences, and book festivals. You won't learn craft there, though. These are your places if you're a speaker, panelist, or scheduled book signer promoting your latest work as a sponsored guest of your publisher or the host organization. Primary events include Book Expo America (BEA), where publishers engage in selling rights and doing general book business; the American Library Association (ALA) Midwinter Meeting and its Annual Conference in early summer; the Texas Library Association (TLA) Annual Conference, the largest statewide librarians' conference in the country, where librarians gather to talk books and library business; and the Los Angeles Times Festival of Books and the San Francisco Book Festival, which are designed for the general public.

Budget and proximity are factors in your conference selection. If a general conference for writers in all categories is the most feasible choice for you, study its course offerings for YA sessions and YA-knowledgeable faculty before you make your final decision. Some general conferences make a point of representing the children's book world. Fill out your conference schedule with classes that tackle craft skills for all fiction regardless of audience, such as exploiting setting and plotting with tension.

When you go to a conference, be prepared and professional no matter what your role. Editors and agents go to conferences not because they have nothing better to do but because they're looking for at least one good project at each conference. Sometimes they get more, and sometimes they don't get any. Represent yourself and your work well while you're there. See Chapter 18 for tips on getting the most from conferences of any size.

Keeping up with the biz: YA-specific journals

You don't have to go to a conference to keep up with the state of children's book publishing. You should be studying the industry from home, regularly and as early in your writing career as possible. Here are the three biggest resources you should be reading:

- ✔ *Publishers Weekly:* This is the primary trade journal for the publishing industry. *PW* provides news and articles on publishing trends and reviews of new books for adults and children. Twice a year (February and July), it publishes a special edition highlighting the spring and fall seasons for children's books. (Some publishers have a third selling season, offering a new list of books every spring, fall, and winter.) Alas, a *PW* subscription isn't cheap. If budget is an issue, sign up for *PW*'s free e-newsletters: *PW Daily* and the children's book–focused *Children's Bookshelf*. Website: www.publishersweekly.com

- ✔ *School Library Journal:* This is a primary reviewer of books, multi-media, and technology for children and teens, with articles about timely topics of interest for school library media specialists. *SLJ* reviews thousands of new books for children and teens each year. Sign up for their free e-newsletters, *SLJ Teen* (for librarians, teachers, and consumers with teen-interest books and other media) and *Curriculum Connections,* which ties children's and teen books into curriculum for classroom and library use. Website: www.schoollibraryjournal.com

- ✔ *SCBWI Bulletin:* This is the bimonthly publication of the Society of Children's Books Writers and Illustrators. Available to members only, it includes a calendar of events, regional information, articles about craft and the industry, updates about publishers and agencies, and news about awards and contests. Website: www.scbwi.org

Checking out the online community

You can follow the industry and talk craft with your colleagues in online writers' forums. In addition to helping you stay abreast of the hottest industry happenings, these forums are great places to meet potential critique group members. (Jump to the next section for the benefits of critique groups.)

Verla Kay's Message Board for Children's Writers & Illustrators (www.verla kay.com/boards) is one of the most popular forums for children's book writers, as is SCBWI's members-only online community. You may expand your reading list by adding forums specific to your genre, such as SFFWorld's science-fiction and fantasy Discussion Forum (www.sffworld.com/forums). Choose the right forum for you by first sitting back and reading others' posts to get a feel for the community, its rules and etiquette, its information and know-how, and the genres most discussed there.

Joining a critique group

After your muse has started pumping out those pages, you need some feedback to know when you're on track and when you need to revise. You're just too close to the writing to judge it objectively. A productive critique group tells you what you need to hear, not what you want to hear, and the members do so constructively.

These people also form your immediate support group, something every writer needs. Writing a manuscript is a solitary act, and sharing the ups, downs, challenges, and excitement with others who share your passion can be a big boost. I remember pushing and shoving one new YA writer into a conference, only to have him call me a few hours into it to declare, "I have found my people."

Gather a core group of those people and work with them to make your YA fiction (and theirs) as great as it can be. Chapter 11 goes into the nitty-gritty of joining or forming a critique group and giving and getting critiques.

Don't ask your sweetie to be your critiquer. That's fraught with perils. Sweetie may be afraid of hurting your feelings and so won't give honest feedback. Or Sweetie may in fact be quite fine with risking your feelings for the sake of honesty — but you won't much care for getting criticism from Sweetie. That's just too close to the bone. Most importantly, Sweetie probably isn't as in tune with teen fiction as you are. You need to hear from people who can be objective, whose criticism isn't loaded with other baggage, and who know how to write teen fiction.

Part II
Writing Riveting Young Adult Fiction

In this part . . .

Ladies and gentleman, it's time to get funky. Here, you get to plot, twist things around, rile up your characters, talk funny, and force your readers to turn the pages. This is the fun part. This is the part where you get to write!

Using the hook as your foundation, find out how to build a story from concept to final book, making all the pieces teen-friendly along the way. Discover how to tell the story, who should tell it, who should be in it, where it'll take place, and how the events will play out. In this part, I discuss five elements of storytelling, offering techniques, tricks, potential snags, and solutions to help you hone these elements in a YA-friendly manner.

Chapter 4

Writing the Almighty Hook

· ·

In This Chapter

▶ Developing ideas into strong story premises

▶ Writing the hook for your book

· ·

*W*riting isn't all ideas and execution. It's decision-making, too. To be published in today's competitive marketplace, your decisions from initial idea onward must culminate in a novel that can find a place in the market even as it stands out as something intriguingly different and well written.

In this chapter, I show you how to develop a teen-friendly idea into a market-friendly premise for a young adult novel, and I explain how to express that premise as a one-sentence hook that distinguishes your novel for editors, agents, and readers and becomes your touchstone throughout the writing process.

Understanding the Importance of a Hook

If you want a publisher of young adult fiction to sign your novel, you must be astute not only in how you craft your book but also in how you position it for the marketplace. Writing a moving novel about young love and clueless parents isn't enough; oodles of those are already out there. You must put your young lovers and lame parents in uncommon circumstances and use your great writing to march them through an original plot. That's what makes a book stand out from all the others crowding bookstore shelves. Your hook is your place to proclaim that difference.

A *hook* is a one-sentence description of your story that tells people the following as succinctly as possible:

✔ What your story's about

✔ Where your story fits into the current market

✔ Why your story is a fresh approach to its subject matter

✔ Who your audience is

Above all, the hook leaves readers wanting to know more. An effective hook accomplishes these goals in fewer than 50 words, preferably closer to half that. Anything longer is unruly and risks that readers of that hook (typically editors and agents) will lose sight of the most important points.

Note that the hook *implies* your story's fresh approach, marketability, and audience; those points are not made explicitly. The hook does not literally say, "The audience for this book is older teens" or the like. Also note that a hook is not a mini story summary. You craft one of those for the second paragraph of your *query letter,* the cover letter that accompanies your sample chapters when you submit your story to editors and agents (see Chapter 13).

Here are examples of strong hooks using three well-known YA stories:

✔ Convicted sneaker thief Stanley Yelnats is sent to a hellish correctional camp in the desert where prisoners dig holes all day, every day, and where bumbling Stanley finds a treasure, his first real friend, and a new sense of self. (*Holes* by Louis Sachar; 40 words)

✔ A group of World War II-era English schoolboys crash-lands on a deserted island with no surviving adult and wages an epic battle between civility and savagery. (*Lord of the Flies* by William Golding; 26 words)

✔ Seventeen-year-old Bella moves from sunny Phoenix to dreary Forks, Washington, where she falls for a stunningly beautiful boy who turns out to be a vampire with epic enemies. (*Twilight* by Stephenie Meyer; 28 words)

Another term for *hook* is *elevator pitch,* a nod to the idea that if you're on an elevator with an agent or editor, you have until the car reaches the ground floor — about one minute — to pitch your story. Hence the brevity. Some writers call hooks *tag lines,* although in-house publishing staff use that term to refer to the tiny bits of text that run on the front of a novel or a marketing piece, such as "They came in peace. They left in pieces." The tag is a selling tool that's tacked on like, well, a tag. Don't confuse *hook* with *premise,* which refers to your story idea and doesn't deal with marketplace positioning. Your premise (what your story is about) is one element of your hook.

This section discusses the importance of crafting a hook early in the writing process. In the same way a pool player calls the ball and pocket prior to taking his shot, you should call your story and audience for editors and agents (and for yourself) before you start writing your novel. That way, you can write your novel with confidence that what you're writing is not only well-crafted but also fresh and thus marketable.

Agent Erin Murphy: Making quiet books loud

"Too quiet" — it's a rejection phrase that seems impenetrable and impossible. What does it mean? How do you fix it? Your story is about characters more than plot and has a conflict that's more emotional than external; you can't describe it in one hooky sentence. Is there hope for it?

There is hope, indeed. If you take those characters of yours and put them on a larger stage, you may have a story about relationships and emotional truth that also has a girl whose mother is running for president (*The President's Daughter,* by Ellen Emerson White) or who has just found out that she's the princess of a small European nation (*The Princess Diaries,* by Meg Cabot). If you set a quiet story in an accessible setting with teen appeal, you may have Heather Hepler's *The Cupcake Queen* or Kristina Springer's *The Espressologist,* the latter of which also adds a dash of Jane Austen for good measure. Take a school-based romance and set it in a swanky French boarding school, and you have *Anna and the French Kiss,* by Stephanie Perkins. All these story choices provide quick, appealing descriptions, interesting titles, and opportunities for eye-catching covers. They stand out from the crowd.

Sometimes you may need to up the stakes. A girl examining her sense of self, her relationships with her parents and friends, and her hopes for the future becomes something much more profound when she's trying to decide whether to live or die (*If I Stay,* by Gail Forman). *The Sky Is Everywhere* gets extra oomph from the love triangle; if author Jandy Nelson had simply written about a girl named Lennie grieving over her recently deceased sister and falling in love at the same time — well, it would have been terrific in Jandy's hands, but the tension of having *two* boys in Lennie's life, and the profound mistake that she makes because of it, knocks this gorgeous but quiet novel over the top. The bits of poetry Lennie leaves behind like bread crumbs add to the book's appeal and give the marketing team something extra to work with, and yet they also resonate with meaning. Perfect.

If you tend to write quiet stories, it's okay to find your story and voice first. But then push yourself to make them noisy. Raise the stakes. Put them on a larger scale. Give readers more to worry about, more to hope for, and more to imagine and relate to. Great voices find their audience no matter what. If we didn't believe that, we'd all go crazy. If you can make your quiet story just a little bit louder and give it a leg up in the process, why wouldn't you?

Erin Murphy is the founder of Erin Murphy Literary Agency, a leading U.S. children's book agency representing writers and writer-illustrators of picture books, novels for middle-graders and young adults, and select nonfiction. Erin began her career in editorial, eventually becoming editor-in-chief at Northland Publishing/Rising Moon Books for Young Readers. She founded her agency in 1999. Find out more about Erin at `http://emliterary.com`*.*

Calling your shot for others

Your hook is your opportunity to declare your story's original spin and get people excited about it. Following is a list of folks for whom you're writing that hook and what they'll do with the information:

✔ **Publishers:** You use your hook to pitch your manuscript to editors during submission. But the hook doesn't stop there. Editors are the fronts of vast operations. When editors are intrigued enough to pursue your manuscript, they use your hook — or a variation of it — to pitch your story to editorial committees, marketing staff, and sales reps. Eventually, the hook makes its way to book buyers via sales reps and marketing materials. Salability is an essential factor in an editor's decision to buy, or *acquire,* a manuscript, and calling out the details that make your story different from others tells everyone what's marketable about it.

✔ **Agents:** Deliver a strong hook in the first paragraph of your query letter, and you'll convince agents that your story can stand out in the busy marketplace. Based on this belief, the agent may request the full manuscript and discover that you have great writing and execution to back up your different angle. The agent then agrees to represent you and the story and sets out to convince editors to do the same.

Your hook is the first thing editors and agents see of your project. Most of the time, editors and agents accept only query letters (which feature your hook in the first paragraph) for submissions. For more on the role of your hook in positioning your project during submission, see the how-to's of crafting query letters in Chapter 13.

✔ **Readers:** Your young readers get your hook in some form or another. You put it on your website and in your personal marketing materials when the book is published. Editors, who have a deeper knowledge of what's selling and to whom, may use your hook as-is or recraft it for your book's front jacket flap copy, and then reviewers pick it up and disseminate it to librarians, teachers, and consumers.

✔ **Everyone else:** You'll be asked, "What are you working on?" and "What's the book about?" somewhere around a million times in your career. Don't reply with your plot summary or even with a one-liner about your premise (the very core idea of your story); reply with your hook. The hook tells people why your story is special as well as what it's about. Then bust out your business card or promotional bookmark so your questioner can rush straight to the bookstore with your title in hand.

Though the industry's focus on the marketplace requires you to consider your market position before you even start writing, don't think you must write a high-concept story to get a book contract. *High-concept stories* put a mass-appeal idea ahead of characters, often to such a degree that the characters seem incidental to the story. You can sell a character-driven story that explores personal growth; you just need to find a unique and compelling way to come at that story. Otherwise, your story will be labeled *quiet,* a term that says nothing about the quality of your writing but that screams volumes about your ability to stand out in bookstores. Writing your hook early forces you to articulate your story's unique quality, which forces you to have a unique quality in the first place. A hook is a great way to see whether what you have is, indeed, different after all.

Calling your shot for yourself

As soon as you settle on your main character, conflict, and theme, writing the hook for your project is a wise idea. This approach isn't just about establishing your market position; it's about boosting your writing process. Formulating a concise description of your story helps you shape its elements and stay focused through months (or years) of writing.

Think of your hook as your mission statement: "I'll write a story about this character in this situation with this outcome and with this message or lesson." No matter how long writing the novel takes or how many subplots strike your fancy, establishing a solid hook early on keeps your story moving forward on a solid trajectory. Otherwise, losing focus is too easy, and you may wander all over the place with the plot. Unfocused plots are a big reason for agent and editor rejections. Let your hook be your beacon in the mist.

Post your hook above your computer and refer to it during the day-to-day drafting, during the editing and revision, during the creation of your submission materials, and even during the development of your promotional strategy and marketing materials.

Writing a Great Hook in Four Easy Steps

A great hook is both informative and tantalizing. It describes your story, positions it in the marketplace, and makes people eager to read the full manuscript. This section walks you through the steps of writing an effective hook. To show you this process at work, I build a hook as you read along.

As you write your hook, keep in mind three guiding principles:

- ✔ **Make sure that character and conflict get top billing.** Your main character and plot are the elements that most distinguish your YA novel from other books, so every other element of your hook is subordinate to these. Above all, tell the world what's different about these two items.

- ✔ **Be specific.** Details distinguish your story and define its audience, so include age, race, era, or any other standout details as necessary.

- ✔ **Keep it short.** The shorter your hook, the better you can focus attention on specific elements, so be selective about what you include. What do you want editors and agents to remember most about your pitch? Put that element front and center and then strip out the rest.

Whether your story is character-driven, plot-driven, or high-concept, you can write a great hook that earns you a "send me the full manuscript" request from agents and editors.

Step 1: Introduce your character

The first thing to do when drafting your hook is to introduce your main character. You don't have to state her name, but doing so personalizes her. Revealing her age defines her further and also defines your audience. After all, young readers like to read about kids their own age or a little bit older. You can replace the age with the character's grade in school if that's more illuminating to your storyline.

Give your character a setup, such as her role (cheerleader, peasant, socialite, geeky sister of the Big Man on Campus) or her persona (nerdy, über-smart, stuck up, rebellious) if those are distinguishing. A story about a boy fitting in at a new school, for example, sounds more interesting when you know that this boy is the school's first male cheerleader.

Using Step 1, here's the start of a sample hook:

> Privileged sophomore Brandi . . .

Step 2: State your theme

Though you don't want to preach to young readers in the story, your hook should suggest what your story's underlying message is. Do this by stating your theme, which helps the readers of your hook understand the potential audience and gives them insight into the main conflict.

Universal themes are those issues and concerns that most teens face as part of the transition from childhood to adulthood, regardless of generation, location, or race. Examples include falling in love for the first time and accepting or rejecting faith. (See Chapter 2 for more on theme.)

You can overtly state your theme, or you can imply it within the character setup and the description of the core conflict. Building on the example from Step 1, here's a sample hook-in-progress:

> Privileged sophomore Brandi avoids social suicide . . .

Most people understand that someone who's "avoiding social suicide" is grappling with issues of friendship, social status, and peer pressure. I could've stated the theme more overtly by using the words "gives in to peer pressure" instead.

Don't be generic about your theme. Use words and phrases that add zip or evoke feelings, such as "dumped" or "rejected" instead of "suffers the pain of love lost."

High-concept books typically don't mention a theme at all because the character's journey isn't their selling point, whereas character-driven stories need a solid statement of the theme.

Step 3: Assert your core plot conflict or goal

Show readers that you're offering a new look at a universal teen theme or subject with your statement of the conflict. This step is where your story stands out the most, so drive home your hook. This is where quiet premises get noisy and compelling.

Here's the sample hook with the conflict included:

> Privileged sophomore Brandi avoids social suicide by refusing to tell on a friend — but she then must spend a month of Saturday detentions with the biggest losers in the school.

Step 4: Add context

In Step 4, you work in details depending on their relevance, with your goal being to add pizzazz and/or context that pushes the reader to want to know more. This step is where your facts get rounded out, suggesting the complexities and intriguing potential of your particular story. It's also where you personalize the hook formula. Move the elements of your hook around a little. Start with the theme instead of the character or try leading with the plot. Look for words that provoke reactions in your readers. Take your hook beyond a statement of fact and turn it into something tantalizing.

Here are the kinds of details to consider adding to your hook:

- ✔ **Time:** The year, the era, and current-event references can all distinguish a story. A World War II story of a boy who loses his dad during military conflict is different from a Desert Storm–era story with the same theme.

- ✔ **Location:** Give the place context, too. A story set in rural Montana is different from one set in New York City.

- ✔ **Circumstances:** Another way to provide character setup is to tip off readers about extraordinary backstories that define the character and plot, as in these examples: "Following his release from a state mental institution, Joe . . ." or "After a beat-down meant to kill him, Joe . . ."

✔ **Category and genre:** Whether you include your genre and category statements in your hook depends on what you're using your hook for. When you're submitting materials to an agent or publisher, you don't need to waste precious word count by stating your category and genre right in your hook; you note those elements elsewhere in the query letter. You probably don't need to do so on your website, either. There, you can put a cover image and the genre designation ("middle grade historical fiction," for example) right next to the hook, so you don't need to include those items in the actual hook.

If you do need to state the category and genre directly in your hook, try something like this: "[Book title] is a middle grade sci-fi tale about [insert your hook here, starting with the character setup you create in Step 1]."

✔ **Words reflective of your tone:** Your hook is more than a statement of the facts; you must tantalize or tease. You can do that with your word choice. If your story is spooky, underscore that through threatening words and dashes followed by unsettling twists. The hook for a silly or lighthearted story should replace standard words and phrases with those that evoke lightheartedness. Don't go crazy with your wording, but do hint at the mood and circumstances. What's the spirit of your book? Classic? Dramatic? Adventurous? Playful? After you work in details and choose words that reflect your tone, you'll have your final hook.

Brevity is desirable. Add context to your hook only if it's vital or particularly surprising or intriguing. Whenever possible, reduce two- or three-word phrases to a single, evocative word.

Here's the sample hook I built in Steps 1 through 3: "Privileged sophomore Brandi avoids social suicide by refusing to tell on a friend — but she then must spend a month of Saturday detentions with the biggest losers in the school." That's a solid and intriguing hook, and at 30 words, it's concise, too. But it can get a boost with a little extra context. Here's my hook after I reworked the language to be more provocative and to suggest that the character's emotional journey involves social status versus sincere friendship:

> When stuck-up sophomore Brandi refuses to rat out a girl in her clique, she must survive a month of Saturday detentions with the school druggies — who happen to be the girls she fingered for the crime. (36 words)

I added details that intensify the distastefulness of her plight (would you rather hang out with "losers" or "druggies"?) and that make the conflict sound even more exciting. Clearly these girls have good reason to make Brandi's next four Saturdays true nightmares.

This is where you should stop to evaluate your story's marketability. Are you offering something *really* different? Does the conflict seem dramatic enough? Have you put your story on a large enough stage, with enough at risk, offering circumstances that really stand out? The time to make big changes in your story's core premise is now, not after you've received rejection letters from agents and editors. Crafting your hook early helps you vet your premise before you write the story, determining whether a market exists for your project and figuring out how you can make your story stand out.

Here are three final tips to make the hook-writing process smoother (and more fun!):

- ✔ **Look to the Library of Congress.** Study the Copyright in Publication (CIP) data summary on the copyright pages of your favorite young adult novels to get a feel for crafting concise statements of a story's main elements. CIP summaries are created to tell librarians and library patrons what a book is about. They call out the features that distinguish this title from all other books of the same theme and topic. Here's a behind-the-scenes secret: Editors or their assistants write suggested CIP copy as part of the CIP application process, and their description often gets used in almost unaltered form in the final CIP data. So again, your hook statement may have a life far beyond your initial pitch.

- ✔ **Get that movie guy's voice in your head.** Don LaFontaine made the words "In a world . . ." synonymous with movie trailers before his death in 2008. Thanks to recording more than 5,000 trailers and hundreds of thousands of TV ads, promotions, and video game trailers, his voice is one of the most well-known in American pop culture. Try channeling Mr. LaFontaine when you write your hook. I used it to write the jacket flap copy for countless published novels in my days as an in-house editor. Just be sure to dial it down a few notches. You aren't *really* Don LaFontaine, nor are you a used car salesman. Don't get adjective-happy, which makes you wordy and gives the hook a feeling of melodrama, which doesn't reflect well on your writing. Stick with statements and abrupt cut-offs to tease.

- ✔ **Try to trim your hook down to between 20 and 25 words.** It's hard, but the exercise is worth the effort. Even if you can't whittle it down that low in the end, the hook you do end up with will be focused, and each word will have earned its place.

Exercise: Write your hook

Using the four steps from the previous sections, develop your hook statement.

      Step 1: Introduce your character: _____

      Step 2: State your theme: _____

      Step 3: Assert your core plot conflict or goal: _____

      Write the results of Steps 1 through 3 in a single sentence:

Step 4: Add context. Experiment with details and words that evoke a tone reflective of your story's tone or purpose. Move the elements of your hook around a little if need be. Start with the theme instead of the character or perhaps lead with the plot. Here's where you personalize the hook formula.

Planning a series

If you have visions of a series dancing in your head, here are a few things you need to know:

The market: A young adult series can be lucrative if it takes off, but it can be a hard sell to publishers because of the financial risk of investing in multiple books. They want distinct hooks and characters for series, and having a recognizable brand-name author at the helm is a big plus. You may not be able to flash the brand-name author card, but you can still get a series deal if your hook and characters are distinct and strong.

The hook: Be able to articulate what makes your series and the individual stories within it different and marketable. Find out as much as you can about competitive series to determine whether yours has a fresh enough spin. Successful series are as much about positioning as they are about well-crafted, entertaining stories. The more succinctly you can state your hook, the better.

The overview: You have several important decisions to make as you strategize the big picture for your series:

✔ **The nature of your storyline:** You may use the same characters and a similar plot structure throughout your series for consistency, but beyond that you must decide whether the series is *sequential,* with each book taking up where the other left off, or *continuous* (or *episodic*), with events happening as if they're part of an unending high school experience (and possibly without referring to other episodes in the series).

If you choose episodic, figure out how to keep the characters interesting across the series while moving them through a complete adventure in each book. If you choose sequential, figure out how your characters age and develop over the course of the series. Each character should have a character arc for the series as a whole, with each book offering distinct forward movement in that development. (Be careful not to age your characters out of your audience age range.)

✔ **Your series arc:** What's your common theme or plot thread through the series? Each book must have a satisfying reach on its own, even as it fits into the overall series arc. Set up a *series bible* to keep track of the details in your fictional world: Allot a page for each character; draw maps to keep track of places; create calendars to keep track of timelines, dates, and major events — whatever you need.

✔ **Your point of view:** The narrator you choose distinguishes your series. If you choose a different narrator for each book in the series, be aware that you risk forcing young readers to connect with a new narrator each time.

The first book: Write the first book before you try to pitch your series to agents and editors. They want to see that you can write a novel that'll win over enough readers to justify multiple books. You can't sell a series on an idea alone unless you're an established, marketable author.

> **The proposal:** A series needs a proposal that presents the series hook, positions the series in the marketplace, and offers the entire first book along with synopses of two or three other adventures to come. If your series has a main thread to be resolved over its course, describe how you'll address, sustain, and resolve that thread. And remember, being able to articulate how your series fits into the marketplace is vital. You must convince publishers that your project is distinct and salable. See Chapter 13 for more on writing a proposal.

Using Your Hook to Shape Your Story

Your hook is your story's foundation, and you're about to build a raging megalopolis on top of it. Characters and motivations, actions and consequences, obstacles and triumphs, settings and senses, dialogue and narrative voices — a novel is complex. You have a lot of details to figure out. Let your hook be the springboard into that figuring process by probing your hook with a series of questions. Your answers will shape your story.

The first question to ask with your hook in hand is "What if?" As in, what if the character you name in your hook were to encounter the conflict you present in the hook? What would he feel, how would he respond, and how would that response make matters worse? For example, using the hook for *Lord of the Flies*, you'd ask, "What if a group of English schoolboys crash-landed on a remote island with no surviving adult?" They'd be scared, probably. And then they'd get organized. Then they'd work together for rescue, and then argue, and then form alliances, and then fight, and then, well, the ball would be rolling. Ideas about plot and cast and every element of the story bubble up for your consideration. Applying what-if to your hook kick-starts your brainstorming.

But shaping a story takes more than a single question and answer. Here are some other things to ask yourself as you develop your idea into a young adult novel chock-full of conflict, growth, and entertainment:

- What problems does your character encounter?
- Why does your character persevere instead of giving up?
- What are the risks and the benefits of sticking it out?
- What's the point of your character's journey?
- What message (if any) do you want young readers to walk away with?
- Who helps your main character? Are those people willing assistants? What do they get in return?

The more answers you generate, the more specific your questions become.

Getting great ideas for YA fiction

Every story starts with an idea. Here are some places to get great ideas for stories that appeal to young readers:

✔ **News and current events:** Watch or listen to newscasts and read newspapers and news magazines. In addition to headlines, read personal interest stories, news of the weird, best-of lists, and so on. Clip, print out, or otherwise save stories of interest. They may not spark specific ideas now, but they could be just the inspiration you need later on.

✔ **Real-life teens:** Listen to young people. What events do your teens share at the dinner table? What are their interests? Who and what do they complain about, and what do they do about it? Don't know any teens personally? Then go where teens go and eavesdrop. Got a mall near you? Teens are there. Fast food joints? Buy yourself a soda and have a seat, because they're there, too. Same with coffee shops near high schools.

✔ **The Internet:** Does eavesdropping on the neighborhood teens make you feel like a stalker? No problem! Plenty of sites on the Internet focus on teen interests. You can eavesdrop from your own house.

✔ **TV, film, music, and teen magazines:** This research you're doing is your chance to watch TV and swear to your spouse that you're working. See what's popular in teen programming, watch their movies, and listen to their songs. Read teen magazines, which cover the things their readers care about. Remember as you do this that coolness is a fleeting thing. What's cool one day is seriously dorky the next, so by the time your book comes out, that cool thing likely won't be cool anymore. Also, be aware that entertainment *reflects* current teen interest; it doesn't represent what actual teens are saying and doing.

✔ **Your own teen years:** What did you worry about most when you were young? What do you remember most? When you laugh with your friends about your teen years, what story do you tell? When you regret your teen years, what incident comes to mind? How and what did you learn from the events that stand out? If you kept a journal or diary back in the good old days, now's the time to read it.

TIP

Answer your questions with pen or pencil in hand or with your fingers on a keyboard. Q&A is part of the writing process, too. When you record your answers, don't stop with just one, and certainly don't stop with the most expected or logical answer. Come up with wild answers — lots of them. Unexpected answers can lead to wonderful directions to explore in your story.

Chapter 5

Creating Teen-Friendly Characters

● ●

In This Chapter

▶ Giving young characters youthful traits

▶ Empowering teen heroes and heroines

▶ Revealing personality through action

▶ Tying character arc to plot development

▶ Writing good villains

● ●

A sk any teen or tween about the novel he's reading, and chances are he'll start with the words, "It's about this kid who. . . ." For young readers, the main character is everything.

The teen lead in your YA fiction must be interesting enough to capture other kids' attention. Then he must be sympathetic enough to make readers start caring about him, then conflicted enough for readers to worry about him and then cheer him on. Above all, your teen lead must be the one to change his life and make everything all better. Teen readers want a teen hero.

In this chapter, you discover how to create sympathetic, believable YA characters by mastering teen traits, channeling their views of the world, blending their flaws with budding heroic qualities, and putting them in charge of their own fates. In your story, Mommy won't be coming to the rescue.

Casting Characters Teens Care About

Young adult fiction, by definition, involves young adults. The main character is a young adult, the secondary characters are predominantly young adults, and the target readers are young adults. This section helps you create youthful characters that young readers can believe in and care about.

Calling all heroes

Your goal with your main character (or *protagonist*) is to move the plot forward and in the process transform that character into something better or wiser, thereby giving life to the story's themes. The reader, too, should be better off for having read this character's tale. To accomplish this, all protagonists, regardless of their age or the genre, have to share three attributes:

✔ **A need or want strong enough to make the hero struggle onward, no matter what obstacles frustrate his quest to achieve it:** This need or want is the character's *goal*. In teen novels, the need/want must be something other teens can relate to. After all, shattering the glass ceiling at the office has no meaning for readers whose career arc is still in the squeezing-lemons-at-Hot-Dog-on-a-Stick phase — if they're even old enough for a work permit. Examples of teen-friendly needs/wants are parental or peer approval, salvation of other characters in physical or emotional peril, or winning a competition against other teens.

Within this need/want attribute is its opposite: the fear of failing to attain that Big Want. This is an important factor because the more undesirable you make the consequences of failure, the greater your hero's fear will be, increasing the tension in your story. Tension makes readers turn pages. I talk about raising the stakes to heighten tension in Chapter 6.

✔ **A key flaw:** The protagonist's *flaw* is that undesirable trait he keeps tripping over as he tries to attain his goal. Another way to look at his flaw is as his *vulnerability*. Maybe he's afraid of heights, or painfully shy, or too self-centered. Achieving success is darned hard when you're in your own way. Hard . . . but not impossible, thanks to the character's core strength.

✔ **A core strength:** This is the personality trait that will overcome the key flaw. The core strength must be evidenced in the character in one form or another throughout the entire story. Simply pulling it out of your hat for the climax feels contrived. Maybe your characters didn't notice this strength or it was just budding, but it was there. For example, if you want to set up a character's extreme act of compassion, the hero may rescue an abandoned animal early in the story and nurse it to health, or he may stop his bike so as not to run over an insect hobbled by a broken wing, or he may surreptitiously give a favorite toy to a needy kid he meets at the park. Small moments like these set the stage for the core strength to blossom at the end of the story.

Perhaps your hero's want is to be popular, his flaw is glory-hogging on the basketball court (earning him not admiration but further alienation), and his strength is a moving compassion for underdogs like himself. In this scenario, his compassion for someone else finally overcomes his need to set a point record when he passes the ball to a teammate with even more at stake for the game-winning basket. Both characters become school heroes, and your main character has made a key transformation. That's an example of a successful *character arc,* which I focus on later in this chapter.

Having your characters act like the teens they are

As you'd expect, teens have their own way of doing things. That rebellious-ness, or perhaps naiveté, derives from their age and the fact that they're still grown-ups-in-the-making. Your story is part of their journey into adulthood. Here are traits you must build into your teen lead so he's convincingly youth-ful as he goes about his business of transforming:

✔ **He must think like a kid.** Your young hero should do things that real kids do or *would* do if they could (like eat a whole box of Pop-Tarts for breakfast) and demonstrate an age-appropriate outlook and sophistica-tion level (like complain of Nazi-esque persecution when his mom says, "What are you doing eating a whole box of Pop-Tarts for breakfast? That's what I bought the cantaloupe for.").

Teens are complex and truly fascinating individuals with their general lack of worldliness; their competing loyalties to family, friends, school, and self; and their almost palpable self-consciousness caused by the physical changes they're undergoing. Teens may exaggerate their emotions and seem to have grandiose notions of self. They may overdramatize things, judging themselves and others harshly, erroneously, and quickly. Worse, they may act on faulty judgments, totally thrashing the situation. Young people can pay a high price for not stopping to analyze themselves or the situation — or perhaps for being unable to do so. Luckily, a key part of growing up is maturing, and a big part of that is developing sympathy and empathy for others. Your teen lead should mature in some tangible way by the end of your novel, moving one step closer to thinking like a grown-up. I talk more about teen mindset and sophistication levels in Chapter 9.

✔ **He must dream like a kid.** Your protagonist's dreams and needs should be in line with those of a person his age. Chapter 2 covers themes and issues important to each age group in tween/teendom. Be sure readers can identify your character's Big Want by the first chapter.

The want or dream should be

- Simple enough for your character to imagine

- Important enough for him to strive for

- As achievable as it is difficult

✔ **He must be the age of a kid.** Young readers want to see themselves in their books. They want to experience conflict and overcome it vicari-ously, finding out how to navigate life from the safety of their reading nooks. So your protagonist must be the age of your target audience or slightly older, because kids are happy to read up. They aren't so keen to read about someone younger than they are.

Make your character's age clear right away, preferably on the first page. How else will readers be able to picture your character performing the action that opens the book? If it feels awkward to state his age directly, work the age reference into the character's circumstances, such as sitting for his senior portrait, or talking about his learner's permit or driver's license, or being banished from a sophomore-only lunch table for talking to a freshman. Or you can compare his age to someone else's age, such as his one-year-older brother, the high school senior prom king. Don't deliver age as a dry fact. Where's the fun in that?

✔ **He must be a hero-in-the-making.** The teen star must be capable of resolving the key conflict of the story; grown-ups can't do it for him. Young readers want their young heroes to save the day because it makes them feel empowered, too.

For a teen character to be a convincing hero in the resolution of the story, he must exhibit heroic qualities early on. That means providing small moments where he demonstrates his core strength in some way. Readers must get the feeling that this kid, when push comes to shove, can step up to the plate and hit a dinger.

✔ **He must be a good kid at heart.** To be sympathetic despite his flaws, your teen lead must relate to others from a moral center of good intentions, basic respect, and some empathy for others. He must show heart. Yes, I know these are teens and their centers are still pretty mushy, but that's good! Their flux is useful as you set up the character arc and push your main character to establish, recognize, identify, and accept his core flaw and strength. Don't worry if your main character has a rough edge — as long as you give the kid a good heart, his flaws will make him believable, and his mistakes will prove him relatable. Have him show all the emotions that would wrack a real person who struggles and triumphs.

✔ **He must be willing to risk it all.** When you manage your tension right, you have something serious at stake — something your protagonist can't bear to lose. Yet at some point, he'll knuckle down and risk that very loss to overcome the final, biggest obstacle of the story and attain his goal. Suppose your fame-hungry freshman b-baller gives up his last chance to set that first-year point record by giving the game-winning shot to a senior during the final game of the season. Your hero makes a personal sacrifice to let a senior with no hopes of college ball get one last chance at his own basketball glory. In your version of the story, does the teammate make the shot?

Exercise: Create your main-character thumbnail

A *character thumbnail* is the foundation for your main character. Use it to establish your protagonist's core attributes. The more concise you can be as you fill in the attributes, the more clear and attainable these attributes are likely to be for you. Create a thumbnail for all your key cast members, not just your star.

Name and age: _____

Need/want: _____

Consequences of failure: _____

Key flaw: _____

Core strength: _____

As you move through this chapter, you'll flesh out this thumbnail into a full character profile.

Selecting a jury of peers

Friends and love interests are central to a teen's life. In fiction, they're called your *secondary characters*. Yes, Mommy and Daddy may score juicy secondary roles in some YA plots, and the hottie history teacher may make a cameo or two, but this is teen fiction, so the bulk of the action and interaction should be about and among teens. Even in a fantasy story where your young hero vanquishes immortal bad guys alongside grown-up soldiers, the characters he turns to for camaraderie and romance are typically folks his own age.

Note that I'm talking about the supporting cast here, not the villains or other creeps who make the hero's life miserable. They get their own title *(antagonists),* have their own considerations, and thus warrant their own section later in this chapter. See "Writing Believable Baddies" for details.

Fleshing out your secondary characters

Like your main character, secondary characters should have driving needs or wants, key flaws, and core strengths. Don't slack off with this crew. Flat stereotypes like the Fat-but-Witty BFF may slip into place easily, but they can't perform the full duties of an effective secondary character. Those duties are to

- Provide place and plot context
- Provide factual information
- Offer opportunities for revealing the main character's emotions
- Underline or deliberately undermine the main character
- Provide character contrast or confirmation
- Add depth and texture to the story, enriching the reading experience

Using the supporting cast to reveal the main character

Secondary characters are great tools for showing instead of telling. They give the main character opportunities to reveal things that would otherwise have to be worked into the narrative.

Consider this scenario: A tenth-grade girl and her friend are out running Sunday morning, training for the state cross-country finals. The main character trips on sidewalk cracks in the predawn shadows but keeps going. Her buddy offers to buy her a crash helmet because she can never stay on her feet. The main character replies that she just has to avoid breaking her skull for three more weeks. She's going to end this season with a trophy if it kills her. The buddy shoots a sidelong glance at her friend and says, "Too bad. Tristan Hot-Dude-That-You're-Obsessed-With will be working at the sports store today, and, well, you know, last night when I was closing the store with him, he told me he's seen us running every morning and wants to join us. In fact, there he is right now. Hi, Tristan!" The main character then trips mightily and lands face-first in a bush.

Thanks to the secondary character's input in this scenario, readers discover that the girls' commitment to winning has them up earlier than any other human on a Sunday (setting, context, and goal revelation), that the main character is klutzy but still focused (personality building), that the big race is in three weeks (fact), and that the heroine is awkward about Tristan and his appearance totally blows her focus on her goal (plot advancement, increasing conflict). The best friend accomplishes her duties as a secondary character while revealing that she is confident with Tristan and has a flair for drama. She could've easily called up the main character the night before to convey the news. This secondary character's other appearances in the story would reveal whether her bomb-dropping tendency is a flaw or a strength. Is she setting up the protagonist for failure or preventing her from chickening out? That depends on what the secondary character's personal goal is.

Because secondary characters don't get as much screen time as main characters, you have to do many things with them simultaneously. Instead of just having them talk with the protagonist on the phone or in the safety of one's bedroom, put both characters in situations that reveal their personalities and relationship through action and in settings that allow them to reveal moods using props, as I do with the bushes and sidewalk cracks in the running scenario. If you were to flesh out that scene, you could reveal physical traits of both characters. Perhaps you'd compare the length of their strides or the way they carry their bodies as they run. Again, the focus is on the action even as you reveal something else entirely. This is showing instead of telling, and it's making your secondary character earn her *I ♥ my BFF* button.

Steering clear of stereotypes

Stereotypes are the stock characters everyone's familiar with, like the snobby cheerleader captain, or the cocky, dim-witted varsity jock, or the nerd with a protractor in one pocket and D&D dice in the other. Usually stereotypes are what editors are referring to when they use the term *flat characters* in rejection letters. Stereotypes move through the story with all the depth of paper dolls, doing exactly what you'd expect them to do, with nary a surprise in sight.

Writers use stereotypes as shortcuts, relying on familiarity instead of doing the work necessary to flesh out the character. This tactic undermines the novel. A book peopled with characters whom readers already know doing just what readers knew they'd do is a disappointment even to kids.

If you use stereotypes, abuse them — that is, use the stereotype to set up expectations in readers, only to defy those expectations by having the character do something different. How's that for insidious fun? This is a great tool for teen fiction because so many teens are image-conscious, constantly judging each other and feeling judged. Play on characters' misinterpretations of each other and the images they're trying to project. Characters may be hiding certain traits (such as the brilliant blonde cheerleader who doesn't mention her calculus prowess because her friends are more interested in the football game), and they may choose to advertise other traits (like the nerd who adopts the geek-chic look, knowing that looking smart will get him a tutoring gig with that hot popular chick). What happens when the hidden traits come out and mess up those carefully constructed images?

Give your readers complex people who do unpredictable things. That's exciting reading! Setting your readers up for surprise sets you up for surprise, too.

Exercise: Create secondary-character thumbnails

Draw up character thumbnails for each secondary character to push them beyond stereotypical friend/family roles such as the fat-but-witty BFF (see the earlier section "Exercise: Create your main-character thumbnail" for general info on thumbnails). Include a section on the history of that character's relationship with the teen lead, the current state of that relationship, and the purpose of this character's inclusion in the story (for example, "to help the protagonist overcome shyness so he can date the girl of his dreams" or "his kidnapping gives the protagonist a reason to fight his way into the enemy's stronghold despite the dangers").

Although the thumbnails should cover the secondary characters' goals, you needn't include the consequences of failure; the story is about the main character completing an arc, not the secondary characters. The secondary characters' goals may be part of a subplot, or they may not play into the plot at all, but your knowing them gives secondary characters a reason to behave as they do, making them believable characters instead of convenient tools.

If a new character happens to pop into your story as you're writing it, let him hang out a while to see whether he fits in. Secondary characters have a way of arriving before you even knew you needed them, providing support or vital nudging to get your protagonist around his obstacles. Just remember to go back later and work the new character into the beginning of the story if that's appropriate.

Offing the old people

There's a really good reason young adult literature is filled with orphans, absent parents, and inattentive caretakers: Old people try to take control. They insist on solving kids' problems, and readers don't want that. Kids want to read about kids empowered to solve their own problems because that makes readers feel empowered, too.

YA fiction keeps grown-ups out of the decision-making and problem-solving parts of the plot. Leave that to your young protagonist and her peers. Don't let grown-ups control the plot; delegate them to supporting roles.

If you want an adult character who is present, attentive, and eagle-eyed, then turn him into an antagonist, with your teen lead going out of his way to avoid that person. Think of it as a rebellion of sorts as the teen struggles to take control of his life, to prove himself. That's a very valid teen theme, and it doesn't require you to rub out all the adults like some literary Al Capone.

Be wary of the adult minor character who clearly knows everything but only trickles it out. Those guys are just illogical pains in the keister. *If you know what's wrong and how to solve this, then tell us already!* Playing coy frustrates readers and reminds them that an author is pulling the story strings. Let the kids — readers and characters, both — figure it out for themselves.

Bringing Your Characters to Life

Young readers don't fall in love with character profiles; they fall in love with walking, talking (albeit totally imaginary) *people*. It's time to breathe life into your cast. This section tells you how to let readers know what your characters look like, how they move, and what their attitude toward the world is without pulling the plug on your great action to do it.

Revealing character through action

Show, don't tell is a pithy writer mantra that advises you to reveal character qualities through action instead of relying on *exposition* (narrative statements, descriptions, or summaries). This idea is particularly important for YA fiction. Kids don't relish long bouts of exposition about someone's hairstyle, eye color, and personality. Here are two ways you can use action to reveal character qualities:

✔ **Body language:** Body language is an excellent *show, don't tell* tool. It reveals things about the character, underscores what she's saying, and sometimes deliberately contradicts what she's saying. Using body language is a dynamic way to approach a scene. For example, someone who's lying may turn her head or body away from her accuser, or she may place an object between herself and that person.

Just as many writers eavesdrop to enhance their characters' dialogue, you should eavesdrop with your eyes to enhance your characters' nonverbal dialogue. Spend some time studying body language in everyday interactions.

✔ **Prop manipulation:** A lively way to reveal a character's mood is through prop manipulation. *Props* are your character's tools for interacting with a place. How she handles objects gives readers great insight into her psyche. Punching pillows, slamming snooze buttons, yanking loose threads . . . what a fun way to convey a character's mood! And you can give great attitude tip-offs with actions such as digging a staple out of a desk while Teacher Man lectures her, or slow-sipping a Slurpee while Big Bro revs his engine at the curb and yells, "Hurry up!" Prop manipulation is powerful, teen-friendly stuff.

Be sure to think creatively about your setting and the props that are available in the locations you choose. Setting is a powerful but often overlooked characterization tool. Unusual settings lead to unusual props and unusual behavior — and fun reading. Chapter 8 goes into depth about how your setting choices illuminate and influence your characters.

Try putting the same prop in several settings and let the character react to it each time, showing that character's tendency to behave a certain way over the long haul. Then have her handle the prop differently at some point to demonstrate that her experiences have changed her.

Revealing character through dialogue

In Chapter 10, I give you the full rundown on writing natural, realistic teen dialogue. Here I give you ways to use dialogue as a characterization tool, letting your characters reveal their personalities and moods through their word choice and delivery style. Consider the following:

✔ A character who is inherently intelligent may talk in a slow, thoughtful manner that addresses multiple sides of an issue. One who is well-educated may use impressive vocabulary. One who is from a high socioeconomic class may use complex and impressive grammar.

✔ A character who is cool, casual, or of a low socioeconomic station may fragment his sentences as he speaks or get lax with his grammar.

✔ An outgoing character may blather on and on — often revealing too much in the process.

✔ A naïve character may lack self-censoring mechanisms and inadvertently blurt out things that he would've been better off keeping to himself.

✔ A shy, secretive, or reluctant character may speak only when spoken to and answer only in short blurts.

✔ A character who plays his cards close to his chest may hedge when he talks, mix his messages, or deliberately mislead.

✔ A rude, intolerant, or impatient character may interrupt people.

✔ A character who lacks confidence may talk in questions, mumble, whisper, stutter, or let his sentences trail off.

✔ A character who's self-confident and independent may make statements or deliver commands when he speaks.

Every character should have a usual, most comfortable way of talking, and readers will form opinions about him based in large part on his dialogue. There will, of course, be temporary changes to a character's speech habits depending on his circumstances (such as when he's talking to a teacher versus when he's chatting with a friend). And some characters' speech habits may shift over the course of a story as the character evolves or works through his issues. Of course, any one of these delivery styles could be a ruse, with the character feeling just the opposite. Let readers make that call by judging what your teen says against what he does and how he does it.

Getting physical

Select unusual and evocative physical traits and then convey those by using physical action instead of description. Reporting a character's hair and eye color is nothing more than reporting her eye and hair color. Far more revealing is the quality of those eyes (shifty, innocent, alert) and the state of that hair (greasy, tangled, smelling of shampoo). Not only do those details give readers something to picture (or smell), but they also give insight into the character.

Choosing physical traits

Here are some things to consider as you look for unusual physical details for your characters:

✔ **Social judgment:** Kids care about what others think about them. That's a huge part of teen angst. Consider how you want your character to be perceived and influenced by the world. Fat Kid has a different world than Skinny Kid. White Kid has a different world than Hispanic or Black Kid. How will your character's world manifest in her physical presentation?

✔ **Personal history:** A kid's past determines how he carries himself, his facial expressions, and his clothing and mannerisms. Is his expression always angry? Is he always hunched over, hugging his folder to his chest? Does he walk tall, feeling confident because of his past — or perhaps defiant against it? Are his arms covered by scrawly tattoos he's scratched in himself? Are piercings visible . . . or present but *not* visible to the general public?

✔ **Fashion sense:** How a person dresses says a lot about her personality. Consider giving your character a standard item of clothing, such as a leather jacket or a cami or maybe a ball cap that her dad gave her — something that reflects a certain style or attitude.

✔ **Role model influences:** A kid who idolizes his dad may copy Dad's appearance. Role models, celebrities, and sports icons affect a teen's fashion and physical demeanor.

✔ **Personal likes, dislikes, and bugaboos:** Character interests can manifest themselves physically in ways that influence the plot and the character relationships. For example, a character whose favorite color is black may wear all black, leading to others' mistaken belief that he's part of the school Goth crew. A macho straight boy may always wear something pink to defy homophobia in his school.

✔ **Setting factors:** A girl dresses and fixes her hair differently for school than she would for church or for a slumber party in her cousin's garage. For a twist, the character can deviate from expected protocol on purpose. Fuzzy slippers at church? That would surely tick off her preacher dad.

✔ **Socioeconomic factors:** Money matters, as does social standing. Depending on which side of the tracks a kid lives on, he may have gnarly teeth or bleached ones. He may walk as if his knees were permanently locked because of uncomfortable pleated slacks, or he may walk like a child with a full diaper because of baggy jeans belted below the hips. (Yeah, you know that style — at the merest hint of normal walking, those jeans are going *down*.)

✔ **Faith, race, and ethnicity:** Reaching beyond the obvious skin coloring and facial feature opportunities, faith, race, and ethnicity offer opportunities for unusual physical details that are ripe with symbolism and event-sensitive meaning. Use ethnic or faith-based jewelry, for example, or clothing and personal decorations such as Mehndi decorations (henna tattoos) or ashes on a Catholic's forehead during the first day of Lent.

✔ **The character's goal:** Your character's goal and role in the plot can influence physical traits. Antagonists are often pictured as unattractive or even abnormally attractive. Religious kids who are being set up for a fall from faith may dress primly early in the story. Beware of stereotypes here, though. If you use stereotypes, use the images to set up expectations and then defy them. Physical traits can be a powerful bait-and-switch tool for storytellers.

Choose physical details that illuminate characters rather than just let readers visualize them, and strategize unusual opportunities to reveal those details. Make your descriptions short and memorable, and patiently pepper them in as scenes move along. Don't try to paint an exhaustive picture. Give your characters room to fill in the blanks the way they want. Engaging the imagination is a major thrill of reading, after all.

Showing physical traits

After you choose your characters' physical details, you can use one of the following four techniques to convey them:

✔ **Show the character in action.** *Show, don't tell*, remember? Get that body moving — let readers find out that he's tall from his long strides or that she's a lefty from her battle with righty scissors. Use body language and props to reveal physical details as well as personality ones.

✔ **Describe the character.** Hey, it's not totally illegal. In fact, description adds nice variety when combined with the other techniques. Just keep the description short and the details interesting.

✔ **Describe the character via associations.** Compare and contrast traits among characters. Example: "The girl towered over me, and her dark skin made me look like Snow White's eighth dwarf, Whitey." That's a zippier approach than simply describing your character as pale and short.

✔ **Have another character describe him.** Example: "Joseph Mulgrew, get your skinny little keister over here. I swear, if you was a fish they'd toss you back. Hurry up, boy!" Or: "You're not wearing those ripped pants again. It's all I can do to keep you clothed, child. As a baby you just ran around naked and wild . . . at least we're spared that travesty now."

The beauty of flaws: Creating a not-so-perfect character

Nobody's perfect, especially teenagers. Their days are all about messing up and learning from their mistakes — that's how they learn and mature. Believable teen characters, therefore, have flaws and internal contradictions to lead to mess-ups and conflicts galore. Teens may judge, assume, overstep, exclude, disrespect, and put their own interests ahead of others'. They may say one thing and do another, believe one thing one day and the opposite thing the next, and contradict themselves left and right. Mix that in with those teens who've learned to be more assertive and thus more willing to disrupt and displease, and you have all kinds of angst and conflict at your fingertips.

Author Karen Cushman: It all comes down to character

The most fun I have with my books is dreaming up interesting, compelling characters, inventing a world for them, and letting them loose. The actual writing is much less fun. What little plot I have in my books grows from character.

I have to know as much as possible about my characters before I know what they'll do or say. A lot of the character development that I do is unconscious, but I tried to re-create some of it for you here:

✔ **Voice:** I like to hear my characters talk to me, so I start with the voice. Is it humorous and ironic, like Birdy's? Naive but wise like Alyce's? Sad and angry like Rodzina's? Complaining and confrontational, as are Lucy and Matilda? The voice of the character helps me know how she'd behave in different situations. How do I decide on a voice? I close my eyes and listen. It works.

✔ **Attitude:** Then I want to know how my character behaves. What is her stance in the world? Is she acquiescent? Challenging? Compromising? Is she quick to anger, or does she long for peace? How does she act when confronted with a difficult decision or person? How does she react to someone else's difficulty? What does she think important? True? Impossible? What brings her joy? Gives her pain? What does she really, really want? Are her desires and reactions consistent? If not — real people are not always consistent — what is the reason?

✔ **Change:** I think about how my character changes from beginning to end. Why does she change? What precipitates it? Is it a minor change in attitude or perception or something major? How is it reflected in the story? Matilda Bone's change is apparent in her actions, Lucy Whipple's in her decisions, Alyce's even in her appearance.

✔ **Physical description:** A character's appearance grows from the story. I wanted Meggy and her father to have something in common (besides their similar peevish temperaments). Therefore, they both have clouds of dark hair and deep, dark eyes. Catherine is different in desires and attitudes from other medieval maidens; so, too, is her appearance. She is not the ideal blue-eyed blonde but instead is brown-haired and gray-eyed. Her different appearance is a metaphor for her overall difference. Rodzina is a survivor — sturdy and tough; so, too, is she physically. In *Alchemy and Meggy Swann*, Meggy yearns for transformation. I wanted there to be some important change for her to want, not just fewer freckles or curly hair, so I researched disabilities and decided upon a disorder that left her with a clumsy, ungainly, painful walk.

✔ **Name:** Characters' names usually come unbidden. Will Sparrow's name popped into my head. It seemed right for him and then led me to his physical appearance — a boy named Sparrow should be small and brown like the bird. Alyce in *The Midwife's Apprentice* has many names as her name changes to herald her changes from abused child to midwife's apprentice. Lucy Whipple sounded to me like a classic New England name; I made her California Morning to reflect what she is fighting against.

Every writer has her own method for creating characters that live and breathe on the page. Do what works for you. Remember, when delineating character, as in the rest of your writing, show, don't tell. Don't list your character's attributes or faults but let us discover them there, on the page, word by word and breath by breath.

Karen Cushman has created some of the most memorable characters in young adult fiction, including Alyce from the Newbery Medal Book The Midwife's Apprentice, *Catherine from the Newbery Honor Book* Catherine, Called Birdy, *California Morning Whipple from* The Ballad of Lucy Whipple, *Meggy from* Alchemy and Meggy Swann, *Will Sparrow from* Will Sparrow's Road, *and the stars of* Matilda Bone *and* Rodzina. *Find out more about Karen's characters and award-winning books at* www.KarenCushman.com.

Alas, flawing your protagonist can be one of those easier-said-than-done things, because writers fear doing anything that may make a hero less likable. Such writers play it safe, keeping the hero as middle-of-the-road as possible so as not to put anyone off, and their stories wallow in the doldrums at as a result. There's just no conflict. These same writers may find it a total joy to flaw secondary characters because the writers aren't so stuck on keeping the supporting cast likable. The writers let their secondary characters do things that tick people off, prompting those people to do things back and creating fantastic conflict; they let their secondary characters say things that tick people off, prompting those people to say things back for more conflict; and they let their secondary characters show up where they're not wanted, which ticks people off, prompting those people to react, creating even more conflict. Do you see the common thread here? A flawed character pushes buttons and in doing so worsens the conflict — and conflict is what pushes a plot forward. That's why secondary characters steal scenes.

Flaws don't render protagonists unlikable, not if those protagonists operate from a moral center. Rather, flaws give your protagonist a heavier presence in the story by landing her in the heart of the action. Remember, if your teen lead is a good kid at heart, with good intentions, basic respect, and empathy for others down deep, she'll remain sympathetic. Flaws keep things unpredictable and create conflict. They're an intrinsic part of the internal character arc, giving your hero something to fix. In fact, really dig into this: Work the flaws into the plot, with their resolution coming along with the resolution of the plot. Flaws equal conflict, and conflict is plot gold — and great fun for readers.

Don't confuse flaws with *physical challenges*. A stutter is not a flaw, but the lack of confidence that accompanies (or perhaps causes) the stutter is. Your character will overcome his confidence issue during his character arc.

A great way to pinpoint your character's key flaw is to first identify his goal in the story and then figure out what would foil that goal. For example, a boy who wants to show his patriotism by enlisting as a drummer in the Confederate Army can't very well do that if he lacks the discipline to practice his drumming. *Lack of discipline,* now there's a plot-driving flaw.

Backstory: Knowing the secret past

Knowing the events that molded your main character into the young adult she is on Page 1 helps you to know the best setting for introducing her and the best way to shake up her world, starting her on her journey through your story. The pre-Page 1 events that set up the character and the circumstances are called *backstory*.

Backstory may be a character's personal history, family history, or cultural history. This history matters for characterization because you can understand and predict what people will do if you know what they've been through. Having a solid backstory is particularly helpful for writers who don't want to outline their entire story but who still need to understand the flow of the plot and which benchmarks to aim for. You don't know exactly what your character will do, but you can make pretty good guesses and write with those in mind and then roll with the surprises as they crop up.

Your audience doesn't get the same backstage access. Readers only *meet* the characters on Page 1; readers don't and shouldn't *know* the characters. That's what the novel is for. Telling readers about a character's past generally leads to a backstory *dump* — a big halt in the current action for the sake of explaining the motives behind that action. Dumps can kill any momentum you've built up. They're telling instead of showing.

That's not to say that showing your character's history via flashbacks is preferable. Inserting flashbacks simply to expand the characterization is momentum-crushing, too. And it's unnecessary. You're writing for teens here, not Dr. Freud — you don't need you to analyze your character's childhood. Flashbacks are tools for illuminating plot, not character, and even then they have severe restrictions. Chapter 6 talks about *sprinkling*, a technique wherein you insert small glimpses of the past here and there, often as statements or quick references in those brief narrative moments between lines of dialogue. Sprinkling reveals isolated and carefully selected facts from the past when they're pertinent to current events and character outlook or behavior. There's an exception to every rule, and sprinkling lets you have the best of both worlds: essential backstory details without devastating backstory dumps.

Exercise: Create a full character profile

The preceding sections encourage you to think deeply about who your young characters are, what makes them tick, and what makes them feel and look their age. Now it's time to expand your brief list of each character's core strength, key flaw, and biggest want or need (your *character thumbnail*) to flesh out your characters' personalities. You can do this for as many characters as you like, but start with your protagonist. Not only does this *character profile* help you get to know your characters, but it also scratches any itch you may have to write their backstories into the novel. You write the backstory here.

Following is a list of key factors that influence and illuminate your characters. Add any other items you consider character revealing. Other items you may consider include likes and dislikes, things the character is good at, things she's bad at, things that embarrass her, things that make her proud, vices, favorite phrases, nervous habits, hangouts, and so on.

Nicknames: _____

Attitude/outlook: _____

Race/ethnicity: _____

Faith: _____

Family history/relationships: _____

Role models: _____

Key friendships: _____

Social status: _____

Academic performance: _____

Fashion sense: _____

Special talents/hobbies: _____

Formative events: _____

Don't rush the character profile. If you need to write a few pages to cover the family dynamics, do it. If family members play a part in the story, you need to know how the lead will interact with them. You may even want to write a scene to witness a character's formative event for yourself. Just don't fall so in love with the scene that you want to include it as a flashback. Profiling is about *your* getting to know your characters; readers get to know the characters through the events of your story.

Want to get to know your main character even better? Invite him to dinner. Take him shopping for the meal, letting him pick out the first course and surprising him with dessert. Set him a place at the table. Imagine what he'd tell you about his day, what info you'd have to pump him for, and how he'd behave at the table — mannerly? Annoyed by an adult? Impatient? How would he react to your surprise dessert? There's nothing like sharing a home-cooked meal to find out more about a person.

After you've finished your character profiles, read them through a few times to internalize them, and then close them in a notebook, put the notebook on your shelf, and let your characters just act. You're done raising them; now it's time to set them loose.

Fictional characters tend to act the way they want to act after you set them loose. This is often a sign that a character has come truly alive. Strive to be open to the curveballs your characters throw at you as the story progresses.

Putting Your Characters to Work

A lot goes into creating rich, youthful characters, but there comes a time when the planning must end and the action kick in. As soon as your character steps onto the page, the plot is in her hands. What she wants, what she does, and where she goes all drive the plot forward, transforming your star from one state of maturity or awareness to another . . . and your readers, too. This emotional growth is called a *character arc,* and every teen protagonist needs a satisfying one.

In this section, you find out how to introduce your characters, write a satisfying character arc, and empower your teen characters as masters of their own fates.

Making the introductions

The opening pages of your YA novel introduce readers to your characters and their circumstances. Keep two guiding principles in mind as you do that:

✔ **Establish your main character in the first scene.** Your protagonist must connect with readers immediately to get them vested in her desire to attain her goal. Open with your star in a setting that illuminates her personality, attitude, and outlook; that sets her up for the initial conflict that will launch the plot; and that offers opportunities to reveal key physical traits, including her age. Scene I is the first stop on her character arc, and you need to present her goal and the flaw that will stand in her way.

Your tools for these revelations are action, dialogue, body language, setting location and props, and snippets of well-placed description (see the earlier section "Bringing Your Characters to Life" for details).

✔ **Don't introduce too many characters at once.** It's overwhelming to meet a bunch of people all at once — or worse, to be fed a bunch of names and information about people who aren't even on-scene. You can't characterize each one distinctly and memorably in the blink of an eye, so readers think they must memorize a list of names because they don't know who's vital to the story and who isn't. That's story setup, and like backstory dumps, I want you to treat them as toxic. Take your time with new characters. Your audience can meet them as needed.

Using character arc to drive your plot

Change thumbs its nose at people who sit around waiting for it. Your teen lead needs to make things happen in order to better her circumstances or attain something she wants. In the case of Suzanne Collins's *The Hunger Games*, Katniss wants to protect her baby sister, and to do that she must survive the killing competition. Every action Katniss takes in the game arena is about more than winning the competition; it's about returning to her sister. That packs a more powerful emotional wallop, and that's what drives the plot of *The Hunger Games*. Each new event in the story challenges the teen lead further, pushing her beyond her original boundaries toward a new level of awareness of herself and the world around her.

Growth doesn't always have to be transformative. Growth can simply be shoring up your position against whatever is thrown at you. This is just as meaningful as the kind of growth that has someone changing who they are or how they view the world.

The Twist-and-Drop Test: Bringing a character back to the beginning

You don't have to nail your character in the first draft. Few writers do — even prolific best-selling authors. Your first draft is your introduction to your character. What's important is that when that draft is complete, you evaluate what you've done and see where you can make things better on the second pass. The Twist-and-Drop Test is one way to judge that.

When you're done with the first draft, pick the protagonist out of your final scene, twist around, and then drop him back into the first scene to see whether he handles that scenario differently. If he handles it well this time around, the conflict would never take hold and the novel wouldn't even be necessary. This tells you he's changed successfully as a result of his journey through the book. If he doesn't act differently when dropped back into that opening scene, he

probably hasn't completed his arc and transformed in a meaningful way.

If you need to, write the test scene so you can see how your teen lead performs. Who knows? You may use that scene for your final scene, bringing your story full circle. I did that in my debut novel. In the opening scene of *Honk If You Hate Me,* a store clerk asks the teen lead, "Aren't you that Monalisa Kent girl?" Mona cuts her off, denies it, and makes a quick exit. In the final scene of the book, a clerk in another store asks Mona, "Aren't you that Monalisa Kent girl?" and this time Mona looks the clerk dead in the eye and says, "Yes, I am." She's made peace with her fame, come to own it and be proud of her efforts. She's undergone a successful character arc.

The best character arcs are unveiled slowly, step by step with the plot, and with a feeling of discovery. Readers want to get to know your characters the way they get to know people in real life — a little bit at a time. For more on character arcs and plot, see Chapter 6.

Granting independence to teen characters

Teens yearn to be masters of their own fate, and so do teen characters. You have to trust and let your characters reveal how the plot will play out. Even if you're an outliner, be open to surprises, or your story may feel forced or unnatural or just plain unsatisfying. Here's how to get the best from your characters — the best conflict, the best mess-ups, the best epiphanies, and the best resolutions:

   ✔ **Cut the apron strings.** You've met your character now. Let your hair down in the next round. Quit trying to protect her, and let her loose. Remember that the best characters do unpredictable things. Your job is to be encouraging, to recognize a good call when you see it and roll with it. You can't do that if you're protecting your characters. I know they're kids and you want to keep them safe, but just as with your own kids, you have to give them room to fail. Cede some control. You're a storyteller, not a puppet master. Think of how your character would react to a situation, not how you'd like her to react, and then go with what she tells you.

✔ **Practice tough love.** Take some chances with a character. Show bigger flaws and greater emotional ups and downs, and put more at stake for her. Don't keep her so middle-of-the-road. Make her earn her keep as the protagonist. If your character isn't strong or is passive, empower her! Make her active, let her pass judgment and then act without thinking. If her arc isn't strong enough, give her bigger challenges (see Chapter 6 for the full rundown on plot). Or put more at stake. Give her more to lose. Give her more and more-damaging flaws, and play them up throughout the book.

Writing who you aren't

You're a grown-up and yet you're writing for young adults — maybe even as if you *were* a young adult. And maybe you're compounding that challenge by being a girl writing about a boy, or vice versa. Don't be intimidated by this. A common trick for writing characters who aren't like you is to look for people who intrigue you and then borrow from them. Even better, pick and choose elements from multiple people to form a composite, lest you be sued or disowned (neither is fun). Inspiration can come from famous people (current or historical), famous fictional people, and people you know, such as friends, relatives, neighbors, coworkers, and old classmates. Then there's your own memory of your own teen self; writers often work bits of their own personalities into their characters.

When writing a gender you are not, start with this understanding: You aren't writing a Girl or a Boy; you're writing a Person. If you approach your character with this attitude, you're not as likely to step right into gender stereotype. That said, it's true that boys and girls are different, especially during puberty when kids' bodies are suddenly manifesting those differences in drastic, hormonally charged ways. This is YA fiction, and you need to address gender differences in your characterizations.

I'm going to tread the fine line of stereotype here, but when it comes to boy characters and emotion, less is usually more. Too much emotion, and they sound sappy or girlish. When it comes to emotions in teen/tween girls, less is usually not enough. Don't make them hysterical, but do understand that girls tend to be more demonstratively emotional.

Here are a few other gender differences that may help your characterizations:

✔ Girls tend toward multitasking. Boys work on one, maybe two tasks at a time.

✔ Boys learn by doing. Kinetic and tactile, they're stimulated by taste, touch, and smell. Girls use their eyes and ears to learn.

✔ Boys tend to be more active, and girls are more verbal.

✔ Boys tend to be more outwardly aggressive, and girls practice mental and emotional aggression.

✔ **Hide the safety net.** Don't let your teen cower in her room the whole book. Shove her out the door and then lock it behind her. Choose settings that make her uncomfortable and force her hand. Make her uncomfortable by making yourself uncomfortable. Setting interactions deepen characterization. (Find more on setting in Chapter 8.)

Writing Believable Baddies

An empowered teen protagonist is nothing without someone to struggle against, and that someone is called the *antagonist*. An antagonist may be a rival or evil nemesis, or a faceless institution, or even a friend or family member who talks your main character out of doing something or in some way acts against your character for his own reasons. An antagonist opposes the protagonist in some way for some reason. An example of antagonists from the Classics shelf would be the fake duke and dauphin in *The Adventures of Huckleberry Finn*. This conman team feigns friendship with Huck and escaped slave Jim only to exploit both of them, throwing up serious barriers in their quest for freedom, right down to selling Jim to a farmer. A contemporary issue-story may pit a teen against one or both parents. A teen romance may have a rival for the cute boy's love, and a crime novel may have a criminal villain.

You should know your antagonist as soon as you know your protagonist, designing goals, flaws, and strengths that will certainly clash. Without those, you may as well just go to the bad-guys store and buy yourself a blow-up villain. (I hear the Evil Cheerleader is on sale.)

Giving the villains goals and dreams

Antagonists must be as deeply drawn as your main character if they're going to be distinctive and memorable. You don't want a cardboard cutout villain in a novel you've worked so hard to populate with rich, youthful characters.

The best antagonists are those who hinder not because they're stereotypes with jobs to do but because they're pursuing their own dreams and struggling with their own inner conflicts. Or maybe they're doing all the wrong things for all the right reasons. Good antagonists are layered, unpredictable, and even sympathetic characters.

It's entirely possible for an antagonist to do terrible things without seeing himself as a villain. People have different moral philosophies, after all. Maybe he thinks harming one person is okay because he's acting for the greater good. Or maybe he just has a permissive value system and doesn't see what he's doing as wrong. A bad guy who doesn't think he's bad can come in many different forms — all of which enrich your antagonist and thus the entire story.

The main conflict of your book will most likely stem from the clash of the antagonist and the main character. Make sure you can articulate each one's goal and why those goals can't happily coexist. Ultimately, the antagonist won't achieve his goal because his strength can't overcome his flaw, with both getting trumped by the hero's core strength.

Seeing the good in the bad

You give your young audience a richer reading experience if you can generate at least a little sympathy for your bad guy, even the super baddies. After all, the Evil Overlord was once a wee sweet baby, too. Something happened to corrupt him. Look at Gollum in *The Hobbit*. As evil as that creature is, your heart also feels bad about his psychotic subjugation to the One Ring. He was once a hobbit called Sméagol, flawed and therefore primed to succumb to the power of the ring. Gollum was victimized at one point and there's sympathy there, helping to make him one of the all-time memorable antagonists. In his case, wicked won out . . . and readers do, too.

A good bad guy needn't be despicable; he may simply have conflicting or intrusive goals that pit him against your protagonist. A well-meaning dad, for example, may want his son to join the safe, financially rewarding family business, whereas the son wants to be a rock star. Such antagonists can be suave as they go about their business, blatantly confrontational, or clueless to their antagonistic ways.

A moral center makes for a sympathetic character. When possible, have your antagonists act from places of kindness, as with the dad who thinks his son's rock 'n' roll dreams are financially unsafe and thus foils them. Readers will understand the motives even if they don't agree with them. That gives kids something to chew over when the book is done.

A bonus with the sympathetic antagonist is that he can be convincingly reformed. If it's natural to your story, consider letting him see the error of his ways thanks to the hero's good example. This can be a rewarding ending for your reader. Don't force it, though. Sometimes reform just isn't realistic. Teens are usually barely capable of saving themselves, so saving someone else may be expecting a lot. A contrived happy ending is a disappointing one.

Of course, some stories call for bad guys who are wicked through and through, from start to finish, and there's just no way around it. If you're creating a sinister villain, make him worth fighting against. Make him smart and unpredictable and always forcing the hero's hand. Or make him deceptively charming, allowing him to rise to power and to lure people in. He may be operating from an evil center, but he's intriguingly coy in how he pulls off his villainy.

A great ploy is to give your villain a reluctant hand in the story's positive resolution. It's Gollum, after all, who leads the hobbits to Mount Doom, where he accidentally destroys the Ring and himself along with it.

Making an example of an antagonist

If you can create as rich an antagonist as you do a protagonist, your young readers will come away from the book learning as much from him as they do from the star. An antagonist usually embodies traits that teens struggle with themselves, showing them what would happen if they were to give in to bad impulses and emotions. The antagonist helps them see the badness that lurks within them, judge it, and then vanquish it. Teens need to feel validated in their refusal to give in, strengthened by their virtue. When the teen lead conquers or outwits the antagonist, teen readers conquer, too.

Exercise: Write a character profile for your antagonist

Create a character profile for your antagonist (see the earlier section "Exercise: Create a full character profile"). Include elements such as his biggest heartbreak, his formative events, his modus operandi, his capabilities and expertise, his motivation and personal rage. This character didn't just materialize out of nowhere; he has a history, too. Find out how he came to be who he is in this adventure, and see whether you can't work up some sympathy in your hardened author heart for him. If you can, that sympathy will come through for readers. Fallen heroes make wonderful villains.

Chapter 6

Building the Perfect Plot

*W*riters who plot successfully have this in common: They're a pushy bunch. And hurrah for that. They understand that well-crafted plots push their story forward — or more specifically, push their main characters forward — and in the process push the readers through the pages of the book. It's a win-win deal, with readers getting the riveting read they want and the main character (usually) attaining the goal or transformation she wants — albeit with a few bumps and bruises along the way.

In this chapter, I use both *p* words, *plot* and *pushiness.* You can't have one without the other. Here you craft an effective plot in seven steps that push the main character through a series of escalating challenges toward the final resolution of her main conflict. If you're an outliner, you can use these seven steps as the headings for your outline. If you prefer to let the story unfold as you write it, then these steps give you an essential understanding of how your plot should fall into place as it flows from your pen. Also in this chapter, I cover the role of pacing and tension in plotting; the distinction between character-driven stories and plot-driven ones and why you should care; and the pros and cons of prologues, flashbacks, and epilogues, three popular but perilous plotting tricks.

Choosing the Approach to Your Plot

Every young adult novel, no matter what its target audience is, delivers a sequence of events that are all tied to one main conflict, with the lead character progressing through those events toward a resolution of that conflict. That's your *plot,* also called a *storyline.* Characters (and readers) gain new insight from the struggle. In teen fiction, that insight generally involves maturing and understanding the world a little better, and it always empowers the teen lead with the solution. How the plot pushes your character forward is up to you. Your story may be plot-driven or character-driven, depending on where you want to place your emphasis (more on that in this section). Your story also needs solid pacing to keep readers turning the pages.

All this pushing business may sound violent, but you can't be namby-pamby in your plotting. Change is hard for people, teens in particular. Change is thrust upon them every day, and it's uncomfortable. Your job is to inflict that discomfort on your character to elicit the transformation or to push him through the action when it would be much easier for him to simply duck and cover under the nearest desk.

A character's emotional, psychological, and social growth through the course of a story is called his *character arc*. You can't have a strong and complete character arc without strong plotting. Plot and character development are complementary, not separate elements. Because of this interrelationship, many of the points I bring up in this chapter are also explored in Chapter 5, which is about creating teen-friendly characters.

Acting on events: Plot-driven stories

Plot-driven stories put the action first. They typically have an episodic feel to them as the characters move from event to event, with those events generally happening thanks to outside forces. Think armies attacking or plagues striking or little green men swooping in from Mars. These stories don't dwell much on how characters feel about events, but they do contain a lot of reacting, strategizing, and preempting. In fact, plot-driven stories tend to be very goal-oriented. The focus on action can move the story forward at a quick pace, and who doesn't love that? "It's a real page turner" is the kind of praise that great plot-driven stories elicit.

Not surprisingly, these often action-packed stories tend to appeal to boys big time (more on boys and books in Chapter 2). Adventures, fantasies, and mysteries/crime stories/thrillers are often plot-driven. Historical fiction may be plot-driven as well, when the heart of the story is a historical event.

The danger of chasing a quick pace is that it's easy to fall back on stereotypical characters while you tend to the action. Not good. Stories with rich, unpredictable characters are far more satisfying to read than those with rank-and-file stereotypes who behave exactly as you expect them to. Don't shrug off your character work, even if action is yo' daddy. Chapter 5 shows you how to spot stereotypes in your manuscript and give them the old heave-ho should they dare show their one-dimensional faces.

Focusing on feelings: Character-driven stories

Character-driven stories spotlight your main character's emotions and psychological development over the events in the plot. In these stories, *what* happens isn't as important as *how* the character reacts emotionally to what happens. Contemporary-issue books, chick lit, and multicultural stories tend to be character-driven. Often, character-driven stories fall under the coming-of-age theme.

Because of their emphasis on emotions and internal growth, character-driven stories easily fall prey to telling. The writing maxim *show, don't tell* means to let your readers interpret actions and motivations based on their own observations of what characters do and say. Don't tell your readers how everybody feels; that's boring. You may as well tell your readers to close the book and take a nap.

Don't be afraid of action! Embrace it as a very un-boring way to illuminate your characters' thoughts, moods, and emotions. Plot events are great characterization tools. They give characters opportunities for powerful "Aha!" moments, they push characters to do things they normally wouldn't do in a million years, and they definitely qualify as showing, not telling. Chapter 9 has more info on showing instead of telling.

Keeping the events flowing in a character-driven story also prevents your character from falling into a morass of emotional wallowing and self-analysis, which slows down the pace . . . and frankly annoys the heck out of most people. Stories should compel readers to turn the page, making them itch to find out how the character will react to each new development.

Seven Steps to the Perfect Plot

You can break every story into three parts:

- ✔ The beginning, which presents the conflict and the goal
- ✔ The middle, where the story plays out to a climax, with the stakes and the tension rising along the way
- ✔ The ending, where the conflict is resolved and the goal is usually attained

But here's where math takes a back seat to art: The three parts of a story play themselves out in seven distinct steps. Doesn't add up? Just watch. These seven steps take you through the entire plotting process, from identifying the character's goal straight through to an effective, satisfying resolution of that goal. It's a perfect plot in seven steps.

Author Jean Ferris's pointers for powerful plots

When I first started trying to write for publication, people gave me all sorts of advice. "Write what you know," for instance. That would have been good advice if I'd actually known much about anything. Or, "Write about your father." My father had quite a dramatic life, but his story wasn't mine to tell. Or, "Write about your mother," and later, "Write about your mother's Alzheimer's." I'd lived that. I didn't want to live it again through writing.

Finally, I was given two pieces of advice I could use. The first (and best) piece of advice: "Get your main character up in a tree and then throw rocks at her. That's how you plot."

Huh?

But then I got it. The essential requirement of a plot is conflict. The primary character has to encounter an initial impediment to getting what she wants (the tree) and then obstacle after obstacle (the rocks) that continue to thwart her. The story must contain suspense regarding whether she'll achieve her objective. Readers must have doubts that she'll dodge the rocks and get herself down from the tree at all. The higher the tree and the bigger the rocks (and the more of them!), the better. That equals more suspense and more doubts, which means more page-turning by your readers.

The problem for the writer, of course, is how to get the character out of that tree and how to get her to avoid the rocks — or to survive their impact — without making any of it seem too easy, too predictable, or too improbable. But that comes later. You have to get her feet off the ground first.

That second piece of advice? "Write about something important to you. It'll keep you interested long enough to write a whole book." This has turned out to be true. The best results seem to come from the subjects I feel most passionate about. I've carried that advice in my hip pocket all these years. Right next to a rock. A passionate writer should always have one of those at the ready.

Jean Ferris has written more than a dozen acclaimed novels for teens, including Love among the Walnuts, Once Upon a Marigold, *and* Eight Seconds. *Find out more about Jean at* www.jeanferris.com.

If you're an outliner, this list of steps may be right up your alley. If you're not, it can still serve as a general guide as you draft your story page by page. Are you the kind of writer who wants to map out the structure of the plot first and fill in the details later? Or do you like to fly by the seat of your pants, letting your characters tell you what's what as they figure it out for themselves? Flip to Chapter 3 to see which way your pen leans.

After you master these steps, you can start tweaking and massaging them to suit your personal style. That's more than okay; it's what's supposed to happen. That's how people write surprising new novels. These seven steps are your road map to the perfect plot, but the vehicle you drive down that road is entirely up to you.

Step 1: Engage your ESP

When you're planning your story, spend a few moments reading your protagonist's mind. Your goal as you poke around in there is to find out what he wants more than anything. Maybe he wants a family or the independence that a car represents or to cast the One Ring to Rule Them All into the Cracks of Doom to end the Dark Lord's siege once and for all.

Whatever the desire is, it must matter to your main character, big time, to the point that the fear (or the consequences) of failing to get that want is as powerful as the want itself. Whether the story is character- or plot-driven doesn't matter; when you know what your character really, really, really wants, you have his number. Hint at or flat-out reveal this want in some manner at the beginning of your novel, right there in Chapter One. Then spin every event in the plot to somehow play into this want, pushing your character further into fear and desperation.

While you're in your character's head, find out his strengths and weaknesses. Every lead character should have at least one core strength and one big weakness *(flaw)* to make him believable. Knowing his core strength and flaw helps you plot a story that pushes the character to grow in a meaningful way. Spend some time understanding the basics of your character (a process I discuss in Chapter 5) before you put that character through his paces.

Step 2: Compute the problem

Time for some math: want + circumstances = problem. *Circumstances* are the obstacles that hinder your character's attainment of his Big Want. The obstacles can come in any form — you can set constraints on your character or impose social pressures or set loose some evil white-bearded overlords who lust after rings with super whammy powers. When you figure out what or who you want your character to work through in order to reach his goal, you have your problem, or *conflict,* which must be resolved in the ending.

Reveal your conflict in the beginning of your story, preferably in Chapter One or by Chapter Two at the latest. Withholding your conflict from your readers only makes them wonder why the heck they're reading about that protagonist. Offer the reason up front and get them vested in the character's efforts to overcome his problem.

You can use circumstances to cause problems for characters by dangling temptation in front of a teen who's clearly flustered with his status quo, by putting Joe Normal through something extreme, or by putting Joe Abnormal through something truly center-of-the-road and seeing how he deals with that.

Step 3: Flip the switch

It's time for the event that sets everything in motion: the *catalyst*. This is a major plot moment, one big enough to put the ball in play and to give your main character a good kick in the pants. Perhaps your teen is sitting in the audience at his mom's wedding and decides to sabotage his new stepdad. Or maybe the class bully gives your protagonist a monster wedgie in front of the entire cafeteria. Or maybe the butler kills the maid in the study with the candlestick, and your character is the only witness to the crime . . . and the bloody butler knows it. Don't dillydally; unleash your catalyst within the first chapter or two of your book.

Step 4: Dog pile on the protagonist

This step is where your character takes action that only worsens his problem, over and over and over. In other words, you put the poor kid through the wringer. When he gets knocked down, he'll struggle back up only to get knocked down again and then smothered by a bunch of goons. Dog pile!

Standard plot structure calls for three knockdowns, progressively more painful and harder to recover from. Think, *when it rains, it pours.* Don't be wishy-washy about plotting. If you don't keep the pressure on and the stakes high, you may end up with a *sagging middle* — which is as sluggish as it sounds. As your character struggles to solve his problem but only exacerbates it, intensify his desperation to overcome each obstacle in his path, and make the consequences of failure even more undesirable. This strategy cranks up the tension and pushes readers to turn the pages with gleeful anticipation. No sagging in sight. After the third pummeling, your character faces his ultimate test: to get up and remain standing once and for all.

Place these obstacles in your character's path throughout the bulk of the story — that is, throughout the story's official *middle*.

Step 5: Epiphany!

In the *epiphany,* the character's flaw is exposed to or realized by your character (see Chapter 5 for details on flaws). This step is the tail end of the story's middle, happening at the verge of the climax and leading to the story's resolution.

Step 6: Final push

This is it — the official climax, the resolution of the conflict, the attainment of the goal, the final battle for the character's almighty Want. Your character figures out how to overcome his flaw and his story problem and then makes one final effort, using that core inner strength of his (see Chapter 5) to overcome the biggest obstacle. This *climax* is the highest point of interest, when the conflict is most intense and the consequences of the character's actions become inevitable.

Note that I didn't say, "Your character asks a grown-up to solve his problems for him." In teen fiction, you empower the teen with the ability to fix things. Your teen readers are attracted to the hero because they want to see that fixing their own broken stuff is possible. Remember, teens are reading not only for entertainment but also to experience the tough stuff of life from the safety of their own cozy reading nooks.

Step 7: Triumph

Your character succeeds in his final effort and reaps the rewards. Huzzah! Balance is restored and order reigns once again. It's entirely possible, of course, that your ending is bittersweet, with no victory laps in sight. Nobody said endings have to be happy, but they do need to offer a point of satisfaction for your readers, a sense that a journey has been completed. The triumph in that situation may be a new understanding and a new way to move forward in life. The resolution must be emotionally satisfying. The character's arc, started in Chapter One, should be complete.

The winding down of events after the conflict's resolution is called the *denouement.* This is where you tie up all the loose ends, or at least the ones you're interested in tying up. (You may want to leave something open to interpretation, and that's okay as long as you tie up all the subplots that figure directly into the main conflict. More on that later.) All that magnificent tension you worked your readers into has been released, and now relaxation settles in. At the risk of taking a how-to book about writing for teens to a place where only adults are allowed, think of the denouement as that cliché B-movie cigarette-in-the-bedroom moment. Yeah, you know what I mean. *Ahem.* That's denouement.

Want to do something unexpected with your ending? Have your character fail to attain his goal but make that failure a good thing. Or have him succeed in achieving his goal only to discover that success wasn't actually the best thing for him. People don't always want what's good for them, after all, and young people need to be exposed to that reality, too.

Exercise: Plot your trigger points

Use this exercise to plan your plot. If you usually steer clear of outlining, start this exercise but stop after stating your catalyst (Step 3). Even non-outliners need to know their protagonist's want/goal, his flaw, and his strength, and they need to know what catalyst sets the story in motion even if the rest of the story remains open to the character's development.

1. **Want/goal and flaw:** What does your character want more than anything? What personal quality/habit/mindset must your character overcome to get his want or goal?

2. **Conflict:** What is the problem throughout the novel, the conflict that the character struggles through?

3. **Catalyst:** What gets your character up that tree? What event sets everything in motion?

4. **Obstacles:**

    Obstacle 1: Name the first obstacle to overcome.

    Obstacle 2: Name the second obstacle to overcome, with higher stakes.

    Obstacle 3: Name the third obstacle to overcome, the do-or-die moment.

5. **Epiphany:** State your character's core strength. What event or situation makes him realize he has this strength?

6. **Climax:** How does your character's strength get him over that last hill?

7. **Triumph:** Has your character achieved his want? State how he will have grown as a result of his success or failure.

Tackling Pacing and Tension

Some teens savor character-driven stories; others prefer plot-driven ones. But ultimately, both groups want the same thing: for you to push them through the pages. They long for riveting reads they can't put down. You know what I'm talking about. Just when you think, "Okay, it's time to go to sleep. I'd better put down my book" — Bam! A new thing happens in the plot, and you absolutely, positively must know how it plays out. That's what keeps readers up all night. That's strong forward momentum — strong pacing.

A story's *pace* is the speed at which it moves forward. That speed is influenced by how quickly the plot events unfold and the rhythm that your chapter and sentence structures create. For example, a plot that unfolds in many short chapters, each filled with several short scenes, has a quicker pace than a plot that plays out through long, uninterrupted chapters. You may slow things down with longer text blocks or speed them up with short text blocks and more dialogue. You can even throw in a dramatic punch with a chapter that's just a single line all by itself. Heck, you can cut it all the way down to a single phrase if you're feeling bold:

> **Chapter 10**
>
> Sarah's dead.

Now that would be a real pace tweaker.

When all is said and done, regardless of whether you're writing a plot-driven or character-driven story, a well-paced plot must continually reengage readers, luring them deeper and deeper into the story.

Pace is a rather abstract element of storytelling, and managing it effectively requires balancing many different elements. But it's really worth the effort. The more you play with these elements, the more variety your pace will have and the richer your story will be. I show you how to change up the pace in this section. I also talk about tension, a close relative of pacing.

Picking up the pace

When you want to speed up the pace, you can spring an event on a character and write his reaction in a staccato succession of short statements, as in the following:

> Clark froze with the blow to his stomach. It was surprise more than anything. This wasn't right. This pain, it shouldn't be like this. Hot. Sharp. And the blood.
>
> Blood?
>
> Clark fell to his knees, clutching his stomach. Red seeped between his fingers as his attacker fled into the tunnel. Clark should've known they'd have knives.
>
> He should've known.
>
> He should've been ready.

You can also speed up the pacing by running a sequence of events together:

> A car pulled up in the driveway. *Oh no. Mom!*
>
> Chris grabbed the trash bag and tossed it through the open window and then bolted into the kitchen, where he shoved the bottles under the sink and swiped the counter with the sponge and yanked open the good-china drawer and shoved in the bottle caps and then slammed it shut and leaned against the fridge. When Mom walked in, his arms were crossed over his chest, and he was whistling.
>
> "How'd it go, baby?" she asked.
>
> "Eh. Typical sick day. Totally boring." He shrugged and then shuffled off to his room. *Home free.*

Other methods for increasing the pace include using more dialogue (see Chapter 10) and skipping over mundane activities like putting on one's socks and then one's shoes and then tying those shoes before going out the door. Just walk out the door!

Slowing the pace

Although you want to keep your story moving forward, it needn't always zoom at Mach 10 — not even in action-driven novels. A nonstop rush is hard to write and utterly exhausting to read. Sometimes you need to slow things down to give readers a break from the intensity.

To slow the pacing, you can take your time with the rhythm of your sentences and transition into the next moment of action. Or you can pause on a detail, perhaps a prop, as in this example:

> When he got attacked that day in the subway, he hadn't expected the old man to be carrying a hunting knife. Old men carried canes, he knew that much, or umbrellas, to block out the sun on hot days. They carried newspapers, too, usually tucked under their arms and slightly smudged from their fingers. And hats, always they had hats. But knives? Never. Old men never carried knives. It was just wrong.

Just when your pace has settled into its breather, come in hard and fast with something new and even more intense. A well-paced story doesn't let story breathers turn into naptime.

Other methods for slowing the pace include interrupting the action with a flashback (see "Flashbacks" later in the chapter) and adding more and longer narrative blocks, being careful not to lapse into long descriptions or summaries that fall under the heading of Telling Instead of Showing. After all, even your pauses should be dynamic in their own right. You can also pause the grander action to spend time on a small detail, such as the loving washing of a young sibling's hair or the meticulous pruning of a prized plant.

Creating tension

Pacing is tied to *tension,* that feeling of absolutely having to know what happens on the next page. The more tension your story has, the stronger its pacing will be and the harder it'll be to put down. Tension isn't in the actions so much as in the fear of the consequences, so tension can be just as high in character-driven stories as plot-driven ones.

Author Kathi Appelt talks tension: Raise the stakes, honey!

I have been a writer my whole life, from writing on walls as a toddler to writing professionally as an adult. In that lifelong career, I have written articles, picture books, nonfiction, poetry, essays, short stories, a memoir, and even a song or two. But for years and years, the novel was a form that absolutely eluded me.

For a long time, I told myself that I didn't need to write a novel. After all, I had plenty of published work to stand on, and I had plenty of ideas for new works. But I was kidding myself, because in my heart of hearts, it was a novel that I wanted to write. But I couldn't crack the form. I had drawer after drawer, boxes stacked upon boxes of half-finished novels. It seemed like I could create wonderful characters, interesting landscapes, and great, colorful details, but my characters, despite their goals, just didn't seem to make much progress. I'd get about halfway through and then my story would lose steam and whimper into oblivion.

Turns out the essential element missing from my work was tension. In order for a reader to care about your story, the stakes have to be raised. You can have a character overcome incredible odds and obstacles, but if there's nothing at stake, then there's no reason to pull for that character.

Consider this example. Say we have a great guy named Phillip who is a cross-country racer and whose goal is to win the regional track meet. We'll put Phillip at the starting line and pull the trigger on the starting pistol. *Kapow!* Off he goes. If we use a basic plot, with three obstacles of increasing difficulty, we can first have Phillip develop an annoying blister on his heel. But because Phillip is tough, he runs through the pain. Next, it starts to snow. Now Phillip is having trouble seeing the track because of the snow, and his blister is getting worse, so the odds against his winning are increasing. Finally, he stumbles and turns his ankle. The entire pack is well ahead of him, and Phillip is trailing badly.

I'll leave it there. Whether Phillip wins doesn't really matter. But what's missing from this story is the *why* of it. Why is it so important that Phillip win this race? You see, there's nothing wrong with this plot, nothing wrong with the obstacles, nothing wrong with the character. But we have no idea what the stakes are and why it matters so much to Phillip to win that race. Is a college scholarship at stake? Is he racing to prove something to his family, something about honor, about perseverance, about stamina? Is he racing to win enough money to buy medicine for his little daughter? What will be irrevocably lost if he doesn't win? Why is it so important to Phillip?

And that's the key word — *important*. The stakes have to be so important to the main character that if he doesn't achieve, acquire, or overcome his goal, we the reader will care. If not, then it's just a race.

Winning or losing doesn't matter unless the stakes are high. Raise 'em, honey. Otherwise, nobody will care.

Kathi Appelt is a National Book Award finalist for her middle-grade novel The Underneath *and the author of more than 20 award-winning books for kids and teens. She serves on the faculty of the Vermont College of Fine Arts' MFA in Children's Writing program. Check out her website at* www.kathiappelt.com.

Here are three ways to increase tension:

- **Increase the pressure.** You create tension in a story by making the consequences of failure too unbearable for your protagonist to even contemplate. Your main character must have something very important and intensely personal at stake. When you have a lot to lose, the fear of losing trumps the fear of not getting what you want.

- **Force the issue.** Tension also comes from the nature of your conflict. Your character battles internal conflict as the plot pushes him out of his comfort zone. He battles external conflict as people or circumstances get between him and his goal. Don't be nice to your characters; make the obstacles bigger. Put the characters through their paces and make them earn their goal. Exploit their fears, their angst, and their dreams.

- **Strain the circumstances.** Regardless of genre and theme, young adult fiction is a matter of circumstances. For serious tension, put normal kids in extreme or abnormal circumstances and see how they react and how others react to them. Or put extreme or abnormal kids in normal circumstances. Teens love to see normal juxtaposed with abnormal as they deal with their dueling desires to both fit in and stand out. From discomfort comes tension.

The tauter the story tension, the more rewarding the read.

Managing Your Subplots

A great way to add interest to your teen fiction is to work in a subplot or two. *Subplots* are minor storylines that complement your main plot, adding depth and texture to the overall story. They often involve the main character but not always; they could be subplots of the romantic interest or of a parent or other family member. If you're not careful, though, subplots can distract both you and your readers. Here are some hints for managing subplots to their maximum benefit:

- **Round them out.** Subplots should have their own beginnings, middles, and ends, and they must contribute to the main plot in some way.

- **K.I.S.S. overcomplicated plots goodbye.** As my dad would say, Keep It Simple, Stupid. Don't get buried in subplots. Giving the main plot some elbow room is fine. In fact, in teen fiction, simplicity is often preferable because you don't want to overwhelm your young readers any more than you want to overwhelm yourself. Stick to one or two subplots at the most. If that seems like too much to deal with, cut them altogether. You don't *have* to have subplots.

- **Put the plots on a collision course.** Your subplots should dovetail with the main plot by the story's end. They can parallel the main storyline, closely resembling it or diverging in significant ways in order to highlight the main plot. Sometimes, they may even intersect with the main plot. This approach gives your entire story a sense of cohesiveness.

✔ **Keep your motives pure.** Subplots are meant to enhance your main plot, not make up for its flaws. If you find yourself adding more subplots because you're afraid you don't have enough happening in your story, stop and examine your main plot. The storyline may not have enough at stake, and maybe your character is just skating along without much challenge. Get tough with her and with yourself. Put bigger obstacles in her way and make the consequences of failure truly unpleasant. That should take care of the problem.

✔ **Give yourself permission to leave a thread hanging.** The general rule with subplots is that you must resolve them all by the story's end, usually in conjunction with the resolution of the main plot. However, you can make an exception to that rule. Leaving something unresolved on purpose is okay. Sometimes life is messy. Sometimes friends don't make up, and sometimes delinquent dads don't make good. Sometimes, a subplot can't be fully resolved.

What's important is that your protagonist accepts the situation and walks away from that intentional loose thread with an insight he didn't have before and an ability to move forward with his life despite the messiness. If he never makes up with his dad, so be it. The resolution of such a subplot may be more abstract, with the main character reaching a state of peace or acceptance with that lack of resolution. Ultimately, this is your protagonist's story, and your readers' satisfaction lies in his completed character arc, not his dad's.

A subplot can seem to be its own little story but ultimately dovetail with the main storyline in a way that enriches the overall themes. Suppose your main story features a nerdy girl with zero fashion sense who undergoes a transformation with the help of her ultra-hip older sister, who chips in out of sheer embarrassment. Or so readers think. A subplot for that story may involve the sister's very important relationship with her popular boyfriend — a relationship that comes to a screeching halt at the end of the story when the sister dumps her Mr. Popular because he treated her baby sister cruelly. Thus, it turns out the older sister helped out of love, not embarrassment. She just had a poor way of expressing herself through the process. The story ends with the main character having a more appreciative opinion of her older sister.

You can use subplots to manipulate your story's pacing and tension by cutting away from the main story at a juicy moment for a subplot-related scene. That said, wield this tool kindly. Readers can get frustrated if they hit a tense point in the main story but then get put on hold while the author switches to a subplot in order to stretch out the tension. Be thoughtful about how long you're making the readers wait to find out what comes next. Whenever you're tempted to employ this technique, ask yourself whether the benefit outweighs the risk.

Pulling Off Prologues, Flashbacks, and Epilogues

Prologues, flashbacks, and epilogues are three nifty tricks of the writing trade, but much like Houdini's legendary escapes, including them in your act introduces an element of danger. Prologue and flashback techniques are related to each other in that they serve the same general purpose: to fill in backstory. All three techniques provide information outside of the main narrative. In this section, I talk about the benefits each one offers and guide you around the potentially hazardous parts.

Prologues

A *prologue* is a kind of story introduction that some books offer readers before they dig into Chapter One. Prologues may set a mood or give necessary context for the fictional world readers are about to enter. They may establish a mystery that compels readers to turn the page in search of the details (details that may not be revealed in full until the final chapter).

One prologue form that's especially common in fantasy is the presentation of a legend that somehow informs the main themes and goal of the story. J. R. R. Tolkien's famous prologue for *The Lord of the Rings* acts as a bridge for readers, conveying them from the finding of the Ring of Sauron in the book *The Hobbit* to the Ring's more complex adventures in Middle-earth, which are the focus of *The Lord of the Rings*. Prologues aren't limited to fantasy, though. Historical fiction makes common use of them, too, and they can crop up in just about any genre.

Don't confuse a prologue with an *epigraph,* which is an opening quotation that touches on the story's main theme but stands complete and separate from it. An epigraph is something for readers to chew on in the back of their brains as they read the story. The epigraph may be a quote, a song lyric, a poem, or just about anything. (See Chapter 12 for info on quoting somebody else's work.) A prologue isn't a foreword, either. In a *foreword,* someone who isn't the author comments on the book or the story as an entity, perhaps talking about the book's history or its relevance to culture or to the readers. A *preface* has the same job as a foreword, only it's written by the author.

Pros of prologues

Prologues are great ways to give readers information that's essential to understanding the story's current events but that doesn't fit into the main telling for some reason. Prologues are also lovely for creating ambiance, which you may try if you want to creep out readers before they venture into a story of things that go bump in the night. When you use a prologue that way, you create a reading experience instead of just delivering info.

A twist on that approach is to put readers in the know while depriving your main characters of that same information. This strategy creates a juicy disjunction in awareness. Imagine a prologue that gets you all tense about the sinister evil that lurks in the dark basement of an abandoned house, and then you flip the page to Chapter One, where the Smith family pulls up to the house in a suitcase-laden station wagon and Dad proclaims, "Welcome to your new home, Johnny!" As the parents unpack and little Johnny runs excitedly from room to room, they have no idea about the evil seething below their feet — but you do. That's fun storytelling.

Cons of prologues

Here are some of the drawbacks of prologues:

- ✔ **Delaying the story:** The prologue's position at the book's front puts it between the reader and the story, and therein lies the danger: It serves as a turnstile that readers must shove through before they can get to Chapter One, which contains the most vital material in the book. You probably planned to hook your readers in Chapter One with revealing action, intriguing characters, and a compelling promise of what lies ahead. But by using a prologue, you force that prologue to do some hooking, which essentially means the reader must start the book twice.

- ✔ **Encouraging info dumps:** You may info-dump in the prologue, trying to set up the story before it happens. As in, *Psst! Hey, reader, let me tell you something about the character before you start.* You have plenty of time to slip kids some background info after they come to care about your protagonist and the problems ahead of her. If readers don't care about her, they won't give a fig about the things that happened in her past to make her who she is today.

- ✔ **Frustrating readers:** A prologue that shows some undefined evil attacking an undefined person with undefined results can very easily anger readers, who see your obvious withholding of information as manipulative rather than inviting.

- ✔ **Being skipped:** Readers may skip over the prologue altogether and go straight to Chapter One, which nullifies your purpose entirely. You can't control that, but you do need to understand that it happens, especially with impatient and often reluctant teen readers.

How to use prologues safely

Prologues can be very useful, but they can also be huge barriers that keep readers out. You can minimize the risk if you ask yourself why you're feeling the urge to use a prologue in the first place:

- ✔ **Are you trying to create a mood?** If that's the case, then sure, use a prologue, but you better grab teens' attention (follow the principles I cover in Chapter 7). The prologue will be your Line 1, Page 1, Do-or-Die initial contact with readers. The prologue must be entertaining in its own right, and it must propel readers into your first chapter.

✔ **Are you trying to slip some background information to the reader?** Hold on to that information for now. You can slip it in after readers start caring about your protagonist and the problems ahead of her. I talk about "sprinkling versus splashing" in Chapter 8 in regard to setting, but the principle is the same for backstory: Splashing backstory onto the page can stop young readers cold. Instead, sprinkle it in those brief narrative pauses during dialogue, sprinkle it in the dialogue itself, and sprinkle it in brief expository snippets here and there. Sprinkling background info in the body of the story should always be your first choice over delivering it in a prologue. If you don't lure your teen readers into your story right off the bat, it won't matter if they know the backstory or not.

✔ **Are you trying to tease?** This is a tempting reason to use a prologue, but if you withhold too much, your prologue may frustrate readers instead of teasing them into Chapter One. Instead, tell readers exactly where the characters are, who's there, and why. Withhold nothing but the ultimate outcome of the events in the prologue. That's plenty of tease.

Flashbacks

Flashbacks are scenes that interrupt the current story in order to show past events. Sometimes they explain character motivations and histories. Sometimes they fill readers in on past happenings that directly influence current ones. Sometimes they simply deliver information that can't be worked into the regular story.

The most well-known type of flashback is an entire scene of the past, with dialogue and an emotional core that's exposed using sensory details (more on sensory details in Chapter 8). For the most part, when people talk about flashbacks, they're referring to this kind. A less-intrusive and thus less-noticeable flashback is the quick reference to events or details from the past, as in the following:

> Thinking of that old car made Mike smile. He could practically smell the polished bench seat now. He and Grampy used to drive it to church every Sunday, just the two of them, no one else. Not Cousin Lucy, not Cousin Joey, not even Grandma Emmajean. Then, after Grampy died, Mom went and sold the car. Mike hadn't been to church since.

Pros of flashbacks

Flashbacks are useful for slowing the pace. They're also great for revealing emotional elements of a character or for helping characters remember events that bear on the current plot development.

Cons of flashbacks

The flip side of slowing down the pace through flashbacks is flat-out disrupting the story. That sabotages any tension or forward momentum you've built up. Full-scene flashbacks are particularly susceptible to this risk thanks to their length and depth.

Flashbacks risk being big backstory dumps, with writers turning to them to fill in gaps of knowledge for readers. Using flashbacks this way is dangerous because not only have you jammed down the brake pedal, but you've also thrown the whole car into reverse, sending your readers backward in time and out of the moment you've worked so hard to write them into. You may never recover the readers' emotional investment after such a maneuver.

How to use flashbacks safely

A flashback isn't a tool of convenience; it's a strategic writing device that must warrant the intrusion. Your flashbacks must offer insight or information that can't be worked in by other means and that's necessary to help readers understand what's happening in the "now" of the story.

Here are tips on using flashbacks effectively:

- **Use flashbacks (especially the full-scene kind) sparingly and with caution.** Keep them focused and brief; no running off on tangents. Let flashbacks accomplish their goal in an entertaining or emotionally resonant manner, and then scoot yourself right back to that main story that kept your readers so deeply engaged. The quick reference-style flashback is great for this kind of emotional hit-and-run.

- **Give full-scene flashbacks smooth transitions.** Signal an upcoming flashback with an item or a sensory memory trigger, such as a smell that sends the character back in time. Or give the flashback its own chapter. Changing the tense is another trick — for example, you may make your flashback present tense when the rest of your story is past tense. Transitions give readers a heads up that something different is coming.

   Clarity is a must. When the flashback actually starts, be clear about the who, what, where, and when of it. You've already interrupted the flow of your story; don't let confusion sneak in like an unwelcome stowaway.

- **Save your flashbacks until after Chapter One.** Throwing them in right away is often a sign that you're trying to provide backstory, which is something you should sprinkle into the story only as needed. Don't give readers a paragraph or two of great scene-setting action and then cut away to a time long ago that explains where the characters are and why they're here. Stay as firmly in the present as you can.

- **Above all, make sure those full-scene flashbacks show instead of tell, which is your frontline defense against info dumps.** It's hard to plunk down a big blob of background information when you have a full scene going on, complete with dialogue and sensory details.

If you find yourself moving material back and forth between a flashback and a prologue, unsure which makes you happier, that may be a sign that a back-story dump is in progress. Brainstorm other ways to give that character context. Chapter 5 has lots of ideas. You may ultimately decide that a prologue or flashback is the only way to accomplish your goal — hey, it's a perfectly valid device — but just be sure you're convinced of that "only."

Epilogues

An *epilogue* is that extra bit of narrative that's tacked on to the end of a book, right after the final chapter with its resolution of the final conflict. An epilogue may be a scene, some out-of-time commentary by the narrator, or something entirely different from the main text, such as a poem or a song or a faux news article about the characters or events. Generally, an epilogue provides extra information that furthers what readers knew at the end of the story or makes them question their interpretation of events. Although epilogues aren't common in young adult fiction, they do show up now and then. *Harry Potter and the Deathly Hallows*, the final book in J. K. Rowling's famous series, has a famous epilogue.

Pros of epilogues

You can use epilogues to throw curveballs at readers, forcing them to question what they thought they knew at the end of the story. That can be wicked fun for both you and your readers. Epilogues can also tie up loose ends or fill readers in on what's become of the characters after the main events of the story.

Cons of epilogues

Epilogues can ruin that perfectly good sigh of satisfaction readers get following the plot's resolution in the final chapter. A perfect plot and character arc leaves readers feeling complete; swooping in with more information may kill that buzz. Knowing the ultimate outcome of an event or a relationship isn't always desirable.

How to use epilogues safely

Here are some tips on using epilogues effectively:

✔ **Ask yourself whether the information you want to include in your epilogue is truly extra or whether you're actually ending your main story within the epilogue.** Resolve your main story within the main story structure instead. That's what your final chapter is for. The epilogue is bonus material.

✔ **If you do choose to include an epilogue, consider doing something entirely different with it.** For example, step out of the main story's point of view, directly address the reader, or include a poem or news article or something else that makes the epilogue distinct from the story's narrative style.

✔ **Keep the epilogue short.** Although epilogues can be quite long in adult fiction, I recommend brevity for young adult fiction. Don't go giving readers the idea that something new is beginning. And don't be caught kicking a dead horse: When your story's done, it's done. Let it go.

✔ **Make sure an epilogue is truly warranted.** Readers often enjoy wondering what will become of everybody. Do the young lovers live happily ever after after all? Does the aspiring football player go on to become an NFL star? Did the main character really die on that last page, or was he only faking it? Sometimes inquiring minds *don't* want to know — they want to linger over the possibilities.

Chapter 7

Creating Teen-Driven Action

· ·

In This Chapter

▶ Opening and closing effectively

▶ Making and keeping plot promises

▶ Shaping scenes and chapters with teens in mind

· ·

As if being a teenager weren't hard enough — hormones going crazy, friends with hormones going crazy, teachers nagging you like crazy, parents with no patience for your blooming brand of crazy, and mirrors with daily surprises that surely have no other purpose than to drive you wall-to-wall crazy. No wonder everyone thinks teens are legally insane. But then all this other stuff is coming at them, competing for their attention: homework and television and video games and after-school activities and summer jobs and the Internet and, oh my, that total hottie in fifth-period algebra who made eye contact *twice* in one week. If you want teens to pick up your book and stick with it to the end, you have to earn your face time with them. You do that by serving up action they can really get crazy about.

In this chapter, you discover strategies for fleshing out your perfect plot with engaging, teen-friendly action. You open your book with action and close it with a twist. You weave individual scenes into powerful chapters that move your teen lead toward her goal. Above all, you empower that teen lead by resting the outcome squarely on her shoulders.

Grabbing Teens' Attention

You can't pussyfoot around when you're trying to grab teenagers' attention with your fiction. You gotta hook 'em on Page 1, Line 1 by embracing your fiction firsts. As much as that first kiss, that first boyfriend, and that first time (wink, wink) matter to teens, all the firsts in a story matter to readers as well. The first line of your story catches their attention. The first paragraph lures them in with its narrative voice and tone. The first page establishes the main character, the setting, and the key concerns. And the first five pages contain the first disaster and establish the main problem or goal and theme. When you get all those right, you nab your readers' attention, and they willingly spend their precious time with your story.

In this section, I reveal how to open your novel so readers are reeled into your story.

Opening with action

The first page of your novel is make or break, so open with action that's dynamic and engaging and that reveals something about your character. Notice I didn't say you should "open with a bang." Although that well-known advice is right about demanding attention, it doesn't often translate into something useful for writers. Folks think they have to blow up something or start with a fist to someone's teeth or crash a car into shrubbery during the Driver's Ed Class from Hell. Sure, you can open with an explosive event if doing so suits your story and genre, but that's not the case for the majority of teen fiction.

For your opening, think *dynamic,* not dynamite. Instead of opening with a bang, your first scene should show your character performing an action that tells readers something about who he is and gets them interested in knowing more. If you give teens an opening that's both dynamic and engaging, they'll give you their attention and their commitment to read on. This section describes what you need to know to master dynamic, engaging openings.

Divulging revealing details

Action that offers readers something to care about is more engaging than action that simply goes boom. Your first scene should show your character performing an action that reveals his personality, behavior, and desires. Provide action that helps readers get to know and care about your character as he hurtles headlong into his first obstacle.

Dynamic, revealing action is stuff like a short boy meticulously filling a syringe with clear liquid from a vial and then slowly, almost lovingly, injecting himself in the thigh with what turns out to be growth hormone. Clearly, this is a boy who's willing to go to extremes to get what he wants. Not only do teens sit up and take notice of revealing action like this, but they also commit to reading on. Mission accomplished!

Starting with events underway

You don't have to show things before they got wonky. Open when the job is already going downhill, when the friendship is already showing signs of cracking, when the day is already officially, irretrievably bad. A dynamic opening can start any time, any place, not just at the beginning of the day, the school year, the friendship, the job, and so on.

Starting with events underway offers more than just action; it offers something to care about. Do you think teens would rather read about Annie turning off her alarm, rushing through a shower, and then racing through the door of American History to find a note tucked under her desk? Or would they rather read about a teacher reaching over Annie's shoulder during class to pluck from her hands a juicy note about Brad Conroy's butt? Her racing around has a lot of movement, but readers will be more engaged by the action that reveals her interest in Brad's posterior and leaves her in horror that the entire class will hear about it.

Have a little fun with your opening action. The events must reveal something about your character, but they needn't tie directly into the main conflict of the story. For example, a story about a girl who dreams of being a prima ballerina may start with an action sequence that shows her pounding her way through a typing test despite having broken her finger on the way to school. The typing test isn't what matters here. What matters is that readers see that this girl is no quitter, at least not when physical pain is involved. Readers can discover her big dream later in the chapter, after you've established her character strength via the typing test. (Or perhaps pushing through pain is a character flaw, if that ability is going to her into trouble.)

Engaging the reader with dialogue and narrative voice

Opening your book with dialogue is one way to kick things off, but it's dangerous. In fact, this technique is so dangerous that some writers swear it off like poison on toast. Here's why: When the first words in a book are a line of dialogue, they have no context. Readers don't know who's speaking or why, where, or how the words are being delivered. The words just float, attached to no particular character and sounding like nothing particularly describable. It's hard to call that engaging.

However, if done right, a line of dialogue can be just as engaging as a narrative opening. The trick is confining the dialogue to a single line and being sure that this single line is worthy of being a first. The spoken words themselves must be distinct and revealing in both voice and sentiment, and they should suggest action of some sort. "Hanging in there, Joe?" is unworthy of being a first. This replacement would be worthy, though: "Out of the way, buddy, or you're getting this two-by-four right in the kisser." That voice has flavor, and the words suggest action and reveal that the speaker has a very casual manner when dealing with serious things.

You need to stop with the talking at this point and add narrative that gives your line of dialogue the context it so desperately needs. Your readers must know who's speaking, where he is, and who he's speaking to. Here's one way to do that:

"Out of the way, buddy, or you're getting this two-by-four right in the kisser."

I dropped so fast my hard hat flipped off. Owen had already hit me twice that week with boards from the roof, so I knew he meant business. "A warning this time?" I muttered. "Gee, I'm honored."

"Shut it, loser."

Working construction with my cousin was a rotten way to spend my last summer vacation.

After you catch teens' attention with your opening lines, readers start paying attention to the way you deliver your lines — your *narrative voice*. Narrative voice is what the narrator says and the way he says it. It involves word choice, sentence structure, tone, and point of view. Chapter 9 offers techniques for giving your narrative voice a distinct personality and making it teen-friendly. For now, be aware that in the opening passages, your reader responds to your voice as much as anything else.

Tell 'em how it is: Giving key info

The first five pages of your manuscript must introduce the main character and his key want or goal, establish the story's setting (in a process called *world-building*), and unveil your plot via a catalyst that sets the whole story in motion — all in a way that young minds find intriguing and entertaining. A tall order, yes, but you can do it. Think *who, what, where, when,* and *why* (although you may withhold the *why* to give the reader something to guess at). The *how* will come as the full plot unfolds. Take a look:

- ✔ **Establish your main character.** Your opening action introduces your teen lead in such a way that readers know his greatest want and his key flaw. The opening should also provide hints of his personal strength, which will come out in full force at the climax of the story and lead to the plot's resolution.

  By the time teens are done with your first five pages, those readers should relate to, sympathize with, or worry about your main character — hence the importance of building characters with age-appropriate emotions, psyche, interests, and maturity levels (something you master in Chapter 5). When you get your lead in a tight spot, his internal journey of change begins.

- ✔ **Establish your setting.** Surround your characters with your fictional world in the first five pages, filling in the details about the place, time, and social context of your story's action. You needn't be exhaustive here, but you do need to use the conditions of that time and place to create a solid *sense of place* — a tangible ambiance or mood — and let readers understand how that place influences the character and plot.

Opening with action in diaries and journals

You can open with action even if you tell your story in diary or journal form. Simply open with an entry that delivers some action from the day in review. That's what happens in Karen Cushman's Newbery Award–winning *Catherine, Called Birdy*. In that novel, Cushman starts with action, tells readers how it is, and makes a promise about what's to come:

✔ **Revealing action:** In the first three entries of Catherine's journal (all brief enough to fit on Page 1), Catherine covers being commanded to write in a journal, getting tangled in her spinning, and being cracked upside the head by her father twice before dinner instead of the usual once. This reveals Catherine's cheeky ambivalence toward the journal she's writing, her utter ineptitude with the skills required of female gentry in 1290 England, and her messy relationship with her father. The story's opening is both dynamic and engaging.

✔ **Key info:** The next three entries, which fall on Pages 1 and 2, have the villagers sowing hay while Catherine spins some more, gets tangled some more, spins and gets tangled further, and then takes a break to try embroidery, only to have to pick out her stitches after her mother sees what she's created. A couple entries later, she strikes a deal with her mom that says she doesn't have to spin anymore if she keeps the diary. Clearly Catherine wants release from the ridiculous unpleasantness of her privileged life.

✔ **Promises:** By Page 3, Catherine tells readers that "something is astir." Her father is eying her as he would eye a horse he was looking to buy — or sell. There! Did you catch it? The promise! Catherine's about to get the change she wishes for, but it's a change of someone else's making, and she doesn't like that any more than the life she already has.

In the first five pages, Cushman delivers dynamic action without any explosions. Readers get an introduction to Catherine's life and her distaste for it, and they get a promise: Catherine is going to keep this journal as her father tries to marry her off, sending her into a whole new phase of life. Throughout it all, the opening pages hook readers with their spunky albeit cranky narrative voice.

Resist the urge to open your book with a description of the setting, no matter how important the setting is to your particular story. Teens aren't the most patient readers, and often they're reluctant (as in *Gee, thanks, Mom, a book for my birthday. Silly me for wanting that video game*). You need to hook teens before they get bored or lured away by more exciting things. If you're trying to create an ambiance right away or show how this character or situation couldn't exist in any other environment, you can incorporate the setting material into the action (head to Chapter 8 for details). Build your world without bogging down your initial pages with big descriptions of the where and when.

✔ **Unveil your plot.** For a strong start to your story, unleash the *catalyst* (commonly called the *first disaster*) on your character within the first five pages or certainly by the end of the first chapter. Waiting longer gets risky. Teens want to get to the crux of the matter as soon as possible. Get your character in that closet where she overhears what she shouldn't have overheard and decides to act on it. Have her snubbed by the "in" group at school and decide she's going to exact revenge or show them up or get them to accept her. Have her be denied something she wants and swear she's going to get it come hell or high water. You're presenting your main conflict, which sets the plot in motion and begins your character's internal journey of change. (See Chapter 6 for seven steps to building the perfect plot.)

Don't open your book with a big backstory dump. *Backstory* is the information that explains why your teen lead is where she is in life and how the time, place, and social context affect her present circumstances. That information may very well be important, but it's not for Page 1, Line 1. Grab the readers first and then inform them. See Chapter 6 for ways to work vital backstory into a prologue or flashbacks or ways to sprinkle vital backstory into the story a little later on.

Readers needn't start with a complete picture. They're embarking on an adventure of literary discovery, so give them something to discover. You can hold back some information to give them something to piece together. Don't get carried away with this, though. You build tension by making readers wonder what will happen next, and well-informed readers are in better positions to make guesses about what's ahead. That's *interactive reading,* and teens love it.

Making promises

All the work you do with the first line, first paragraph, first five pages, and first chapter amounts to this: You're making a promise to your readers. You're telling them what they're reading for and what your character's goal or want is, and you're hinting at the obstacles she'll encounter along the way. If you want kids to keep reading past those first pages, you have to promise them something in return. Intrigue them with your promise and then deliver on that promise in the rest of your story.

Your story's hook is your promise in a nutshell. (If you didn't write your hook, go to Chapter 4 and do so.) The hook states your promise not only to your readers but also to yourself — "*this* is the story I want to write, no matter how busy I get or how many tangents call out to me" — and to editors when you submit your manuscript.

Pushing Readers' Buttons with Scenes and Chapters

A fantastic way to pump up the action for teen readers is to mercilessly manipulate those sweet, trusting kids with your chapter structure. The way you *structure* your story (or slice it into parts and chapters and scenes), directly affects the pace, making your readers feel anxious, rushed, or relaxed, all at your whim. That's serious power.

On the practical side, chapter structure is a necessary organizational tool for you and for your readers. It creates an internal logic and flow, and it helps everyone stay focused. Imagine a novel without chapters: one long procession of events, page after page, paragraph after paragraph, until (finally!) "The End." You'd be lucky to avoid wandering off on tangents, and your readers would be completely overwhelmed. Definitely not a teen-friendly sensation.

How you divvy up your story into scenes and chapters is your call, but keep in mind that teens have a notoriously short attention span. Frequent breaks create lots of white space in a book, providing visual breathers and making the book more welcoming. Also, the more breaks you have, the more opportunities you have to write engaging openings and mini-finales, which I discuss in "Mastering transitions" later in this chapter. Finally, frequent endings make readers feel like they're really zipping through the story.

White space is the empty space surrounding the paragraphs and images on a book page. Readers see this space as visual breathing room and generally feel more comfortable when there's more of it. Pages with long text blocks and minimal white space can be intimidating. A teen thumbing through a novel in a bookstore factors the amount of white space into his or her decision to buy. In Chapter 10, I talk about the role of white space in dialogue.

Knowing a scene from a chapter

In order to slice up your story, you need to know where to place the knife. In this section, I provide general rules to help your chapters and scenes feel satisfying and complete.

Crafting a chapter's contents

Every chapter in your story should have a specific plot goal that propels your character one step closer to the resolution of his overall conflict. When you string your chapters together, you have your full plot, beginning to end. Think stepping stones across a creek. A chapter that doesn't support your character's journey renders him one soggy lad.

Author Gary Soto: Building a plot, complication by complication

Novels live or die by their believable complications. Also, I find in my novels that movement — literal movement — is important. Staying in one place leaves readers yawning. Keep the characters moving but with purpose. The reader will tag along to find out what happens.

My own young adult fiction is regional by nature — and by *region,* I mean my hometown of Fresno, California. I may start a novel with atmosphere in order to provide a sense of place. Let me share with you the first paragraph of *When Dad Came Back,* a work in progress:

> The August sun weighed heavily on the backs of gardeners. A dog's shadow crawled away, whimpering. Snow cones leaked like faucets. The color green deserted lawns, and roses shed petals to reveal their thorns. No breeze stirred the stiff laundry on clotheslines.

A load of poetry, I see. A nice touch, but I've got to get the story going or lose the reader. It's already time to move forward. Enter the main character, 13-year-old Gabe Mendoza. In the following paragraph, Gabe, shocked by the heat of the day, is even more shocked at a figure approaching. He stops when he confronts his father, absent from his life for seven years and now homeless and in bad shape. So it's established: The father has arrived in town (Fresno), and Gabe is immediately troubled, as his mother will be when she gets wind of her ex seeking to rekindle a relationship with their son. Should Gabe give his father a second chance and accept him back into his life? Or should he tell his deadbeat father to stay away? It's a painful debate for Gabe, one that gnaws at him, and just by the fact Gabe's conscience is wrestling with the dilemma, the reader grasps the boy's sensitivity.

Okay, we have the initial problem. But I need something else, a secondary problem, a complication that ignites the reader's imagination and makes him root for Gabe, a sort of underdog. So appears Frankie, a wannabe gangster two years younger than Gabe. Frankie is practicing his trade with a crew of three other boys. A bully at heart, he's testing the streets, especially in the streets where toughness matters. Frankie taunts Gabe on several occasions, eggs him on, calls him this and calls him that. Gabe does his best to avoid a confrontation until Gabe responds to an insult to his mother, which results in a bloody fistfight in a strip mall. But it all starts with Gabe physically moving away from his father and encountering Frankie.

But wait, there's more! Frankie's family, rotten to the core, is involved in theft. We move to their garage, stacked ceiling high with stolen goods. It's not only stolen goods, but a puppy that has been snatched by one of Frankie's older brothers — stolen so the puppy can be raised viciously to protect their loot. In short, the reader knows the dog is mistreated. The reader can't accept that. And Gabe can't either.

A YA novelist can be painterly, yes, but he must use tension created by plot complications and the movements — swift and purposeful — of the main character to keep young readers riveted.

Gary Soto is the author of many much-loved middle grade and young adult novels, short stories, plays, and poetry collections, including Accidental Love, The Afterlife, Mercy on These Teenage Chimps, *and the acclaimed* Baseball in April and Other Stories. *Find out more about Gary at* www.GarySoto.com.

Sometimes a chapter is a single event experienced from beginning to end. Other times, a chapter is broken down into several different events (scenes) that together achieve the single chapter goal. After you accomplish that goal, through one scene or many, the chapter is complete.

Use this list to ensure your chapter includes all the necessary ingredients:

✔ Your character has a need or goal that ties into the overall plot.

✔ The character takes action on that goal but encounters conflict.

✔ The conflict mucks things up further for your character.

✔ The character is stuck with a new or worsened problem (a *setback*) to deal with in the next chapter.

In this manner, your plot progresses chapter by chapter until it hits the climax, when things finally improve for your character.

Keep in mind that writing is not a paint-by-numbers project. I guarantee you'll find books with chapter structures that look nothing like the ones I describe. Sudden changes in chapter length can create dramatic tension, as in a two-word chapter that simply says, "Sarah's dead." Deviating from expectations is a great way to create drama and manipulate the story's pace, as I show you in Chapter 6.

Staging the scene

A scene is a single event with its own conflict that, when combined with other scenes, contributes to the overall goal of the chapter. This progression of scenes within a chapter is called *scene-sequencing*.

As with chapters, a scene has a main character with a need or goal, the character takes action on that goal and encounters conflict, and then the situation is worsened at the end, leaving him with another problem to deal with in the next scene. The big difference between a scene and a chapter is that a scene sticks to its own specific issue, and it doesn't try to move the character into a whole new phase of the plot. That's the chapter's job. When a scene is complete, readers know more or are more emotionally affected, but the character may have to address another issue or two in one or more scenes before he's ready to move on.

Tension comes from having something personal and important at stake. If you use scene-sequencing to keep raising the stakes one notch at a time, you continually amp up the tension in your novel.

You may cut to a new scene because of a change in venue. Scenes usually take place in one location but not always. For example, a character may nag her sister from one room to another, or a kid may be chased on bike around town. The chasing or the nagging is the event that defines the scene.

The first-paragraph survey: Critiquing your plot progression

Back in my college days, I learned a speed-reading technique called *surveying* that bolstered my reading speed and comprehension. Using my fingers to pull my eyes along the page, I scanned the first sentence of each chapter to get a feel for what I was about to read. If there were headings and subheadings, I surveyed those, too. Then I'd go back and whiz through the meat of the chapters, filling in the details of what I'd already figured out from my survey. This technique worked for nonfiction, textbooks, how-to's, and, yes, fiction. Years later, as a children's book editor and then a published YA author, I realized that surveying can help fiction writers critique their plot progression. I call it the *first-paragraph survey*.

You apply the first-paragraph survey to finished first drafts. The technique reveals flaws in the progression of your plot or character arc. These flaws are important to discover because plots that stutter, stall, or wander off on tangents lose their readers. Forward momentum is crucial to a strong story.

Apply the first-paragraph survey by reading the first paragraph of each chapter in your manuscript. See whether your plot is escalating in tension and your character is being pushed to her brink. Each chapter opening should at least partially reveal the situation that plays out in the chapter. Ideally, you'll find that each chapter is a clear next step from the previous one. If you encounter a chapter that isn't a clear next step, you've probably discovered a scene that doesn't forward the plot or the character arc. If you encounter a chapter that feels like a repeat of the action in the previous one, that's a signal that your plot may have stuttered or stalled.

As you slice and dice your plot, don't be afraid to cut out something completely. Excise or rewrite any chapter that doesn't show clear forward movement in characterization and plot. Killing scenes or chapters you love is hard, but everything in your book must earn its keep. Your story doesn't have any room for your pets. Teens are objective readers and have no such attachment to your individual scenes and chapters.

You can see the first-paragraph survey at work in Chapter 8, where I explore how Phillip Pullman's *The Golden Compass* uses setting to push the plot through his book. You can apply the first-paragraph survey to scene sequences within chapters, too. Your goal is the same: to make sure every scene pushes the character toward the goal of the chapter. If it doesn't, cut it out and don't think twice about it. Your allegiance should be to your plot and your character, not to individual incidents, scenes, or chapters.

Sometimes multiple scenes are necessary within a chapter to let multiple characters have their say. Switching from one point-of-view character to another can be a reason to start a new scene. (More on POV in Chapter 9.)

Don't take this sequencing strategy as meaning you must have a linear structure for your stories. You don't. Sometimes nonlinear structure is much more fun. Shuffling the order of events around or deliberately skipping events and then referring back to them later (or not at all) can make a story wonderfully unpredictable. Some readers enjoy filling in the blanks and deciphering twists.

Just be sure you're bumping them around for a distinct purpose and that the order fits the theme or style of the story. Readers may enjoy a challenge, but they don't enjoy a meandering mess.

Exercise: See the scene

Make each scene prove its worth on paper before you commit it to the page. Write a scene synopsis first, noting your scene goal, how it will contribute to the chapter goal, and why the book absolutely will not be complete without this scene. If you're an outliner, fill this out:

- ✔ **Character:** Name the POV character.

- ✔ **Scene goal:** How does this scene contribute to the chapter goal?

- ✔ **Action:** What action will your character take to accomplish his scene goal?

- ✔ **Conflict:** What will foil your character's effort?

- ✔ **Setback:** What's the new problem for the next scene, or how is the old problem worsened?

Another way to wrap your brain around the role of conflict in a scene is to think of the "action + *conflict* = setback" sequence as "action + *reaction* = setback."

Here's a filled-in sample:

- ✔ **Character:** Freshman Jill, the aspiring cheerleader

- ✔ **Scene goal:** This final scene in a three-scene sequence has Jill trying to teach herself cheerleading skills but failing. Unlike the two scenes before, this scene makes her failure public.

- ✔ **Action:** Jill tries to learn to do a handspring in the privacy of her best friend's backyard.

- ✔ **Conflict:** Jill's best friend catches her neighbor, who happens to be the school's "Morning Update" cameraman, filming Jill when she flips herself onto the laundry line and then hangs there, awaiting extraction.

- ✔ **Setback:** Jill must now find a way to convince Camera Boy to delete the humiliating video.

You can adapt this list for chapters, too, changing "scene goal" to "chapter goal" and asking yourself how the chapter goal contributes to the overall story goal.

Mastering transitions

No scene or chapter is successful without a smooth transition into and out of it. Your goal with a transition is to take your reader from what has happened to what is about to happen in a dynamic and entirely seamless way. You certainly don't want your character to wallow around in that space between events, whiling away the time with mundane stuff like brushing teeth and sleeping and doing homework. No one wants to read that. A smooth transition skips the minutiae and instead jumps readers from one activity of interest to another with the help of dynamic openings and mini-finales:

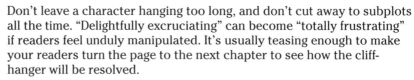 **Dynamic openings:** A strong novel re-engages readers with every new chapter and scene. Just as you do in the opening paragraphs of the book, start your chapters and scenes with a promise about what's to come, revealing the situation that will be played out. Drop your readers into the middle of the action and let that action reveal something about your character's current state of mind. For example, instead of making readers wait for the bus and ride into school with the main character after he has a conflict at home, just start a new scene that opens with him punching his school locker.

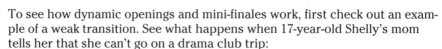 **Mini-finales:** A strong novel pushes readers from one chapter or scene to the next with endings that leave readers craving more. I call such endings *mini-finales* because they have all the drama of a satisfying ending — the unpredictable twists, the painful denials, the intrigues, the surprises, and the unexpected challenges — without the final resolution that readers get in the book's grand finale. Mini-finales get to use cliffhanger endings, where you let one character hang by his metaphoric fingertips as you turn to some other character or event entirely. This delightfully excruciating tease tactic works wonders with your tension.

 Don't leave a character hanging too long, and don't cut away to subplots all the time. "Delightfully excruciating" can become "totally frustrating" if readers feel unduly manipulated. It's usually teasing enough to make your readers turn the page to the next chapter to see how the cliffhanger will be resolved.

To see how dynamic openings and mini-finales work, first check out an example of a weak transition. See what happens when 17-year-old Shelly's mom tells her that she can't go on a drama club trip:

> I nearly dropped my backpack in shock. "But why not?"
> "Because I said so."
> "That's not a reason."
> "Well, it's the reason you're getting. I'm tired of explaining myself to you. Heaven knows you don't listen." Mom tucked the newspaper under her arm and picked up her coffee. "I said you're not going, and that's final." Then she strolled out of the room.

Like a big dope, I just stood there and watched her go. I couldn't believe it. I, Shelley Smith, drama club president, wasn't going on the ski trip of the century because my mommy said no.

I stood there a minute more before a plan struck me. I would go on the trip. I'd just get my dad to sign my permission slip. He'd be home early enough for me to call Mrs. Stanton with the official okay.

The clock over the sink said four o'clock. Another hour and this whole thing would be settled. Dad would make it better. He always did.

I sat down at the counter with my algebra book and flipped to the chapter on sine and cosine. Might as well get some homework done while I wait.

Not that I had to wait long. Dad's key rattled in the door at 4:35. He was early. Yes!

By the time he reached the kitchen, I was already dialing Mrs. Stanton's phone number. "Dad, you gotta help me. I have about thirty seconds to call Mrs. Stanton before she books the lodge for the drama club ski trip and I need you to sign the permission slip."

This example falls prey to the mundane accounting of passing time and fails to inject new energy through a location change. Now here are those same events, only with a scene break that skips the time between parental conflicts, a mini-finale that sends readers into the next scene wondering what Shelly will do to fix the setback her mom dealt her, and a dynamic opening that starts the new scene in the middle of the action:

I nearly dropped my backpack in shock. "But why not?"

"Because I said so."

"That's not a reason."

"Well, it's the reason you're getting. I'm tired of explaining myself to you. Heaven knows you don't listen." Mom tucked the newspaper under her arm and picked up her coffee. "I said you're not going, and that's final." Then she strolled out of the room.

I just stood there and watched her go. I couldn't believe it. I, Shelly Smith, drama club president, wasn't going on the ski trip of the century because my mommy said no.

* * *

When Dad pulled into the driveway an hour later, he nearly ran me over.

"Shelly! Good grief, what are you doing sitting in the driveway?"

I raced to his window. "Ooh, that woman!"

"What woman?"

"Your wife."

"My wife? You mean your mother?"

"Yeah. Her. That woman. Did you know she won't let me go on the drama club ski trip? I swear, it's like ruining my life is her new hobby now or something." I bent down and looked him dead in the eye. "You've got to do something about this."

"Do you mind if I get out of the car first?"

"No time for that." I flipped open my cell phone and started dialing. "I have to call Mrs. Stanton this second. She's booking the rooms tonight."

"Shelly, close the phone. Now." He sighed and started rolling up the window.

I grabbed hold of the glass and tried to stop it. No way was I going to get shut out twice in one day. "But Dad—"

You see where this scene is going. The girl's efforts to fix the problem from the previous scene are about to cause another conflict in this scene, leading to yet another setback. Both scenes contribute to the chapter's overall goal, which is to deny Shelly this trip. By inserting a scene break in between the two events, I've skipped the boring stuff and provided dynamic ins and outs. That makes for a more lively pace and reading experience.

Leaving Teens Satisfied

A great YA novel ends with the same careful attention to its readers' needs that it shows in Chapter One. Chief among those needs is character empowerment. Letting your teen protagonist resolve his own story is essential. And you must make that resolution believable and teen-appropriate. You must also deliver on the promise you made to your readers way back in the first chapter — often with a twist that they won't see coming. That's how to leave teen readers satisfied.

Empowering your teen lead

One of the few indisputable laws of YA fiction is that the stories must empower their teen leads with the resolution of their own conflicts. Kids read to learn about themselves as much as anything else. They want to feel empowered to make their own decisions in their own lives and to accomplish their own goals and satisfy their own wants. Watching characters solve their own problems and reach their own goals makes readers feel validated, supported, and inspired. Seeing a teen triumph is fun for your readers. There's nothing fun about watching a grown-up swoop in and save the day.

This Law of Empowerment explains all the orphaned kids and distracted or absent parents in YA fiction. Authors kill off the old people to give the kids the spotlight. I go into YA's proclivity for parenticide more graphically in Chapter 5's tips about casting your novel.

Teen empowerment needs to happen right from the beginning. Your plot should grow from your teen character and be teen-focused. It should be about decisions and consequences, two very scary but important concepts for teens to master as they transition to adulthood, and it should put the solution to the teen lead's main conflict in his young but increasingly capable hands. Teens are your cast, teens are your readers, teens must be your heroes.

Keeping it real

Teen-friendly action calls for events that suit the main character's maturity and abilities. A teenager who sneaks into a nuclear missile silo and figures out the shutdown sequence moments before the missile launches strains believability. Even the most brilliant of teens would be hard-pressed to pull off such a feat, and readers know that. Your audience must believe in the match-up of the action and the teen characters in order to feel satisfied by the story. Readers aren't about to cut you slack. You'd just be another grown-up who doesn't *get* them. If you're going to make your teen a hero, devise an ending he really can pull off.

Keeping your promise

Here's one of those rare indisputable fiction laws: You must keep the promise you make to your readers in Chapter One (see the earlier section "Making promises" for details). Failure to do so leaves your readers dissatisfied, if not completely ticked off. I mean, they've read an entire novel in hopes of seeing you resolve a specific conflict for a character they've grown to love, and then you don't? Liar! You have a duty to deliver. You must complete the character arc you set into motion with that very first catalyst, and you must tie up the loose ends of the subplots that supported Mr. Teen Lead's journey. How you do that is up to you and your creativity. Just do it.

Delivering a twist

Predictable is a very bad word in fiction. It's a complete bummer to read through a whole novel, investing yourself emotionally in a character and his tribulations, only to reach the end and have the story play out exactly as you would've guessed. That's an "Oh. Yeah." ending. Nobody wants that. Readers want an "Oh yeah!" ending. You can dish that out in the form of a twist that simultaneously fulfills and defies readers' expectations.

An ending that has nothing to do with any of the elements preceding it isn't convincing. A good twist has a certain logic because it evolves from the events in the story. Readers can actually go back and point to elements that subtly foreshadow the unexpected ending. When you *foreshadow*, you plant veiled hints about what's ahead. The hints seem innocuous and may be repeated throughout the story, but the foreshadowed item suddenly becomes a story-changing element upon which the resolution hinges. Because the ending isn't the one you led your readers to expect, they're also surprised.

Say you have a story about a kid who fixes up old cars in his garage. This kid meets a girl who also likes cars, only she likes shiny modern ones. A parade is coming up, and the budding couple must decide which car to enter into the parade. You could write their love story in a way that pits his classic style against her modern one, with the reader expecting one of the young lovers to give in so that they can ride off into the sunset together in one of the cars. When the ending comes, they do ride off into the sunset together, but they're not in either car; they're on his cousin's moped, which has appeared many times in the story but never in a way that called much attention to itself. That twist both fulfills and defies reader expectations.

Louis Sachar's *Holes,* winner of both the National Book Award and the Newbery Medal, delivers a truly whopper twist. I won't reveal that twist here because a spoiled ending is a bigger bummer than a predictable one. But I will say that the ending gives new meaning to old events, which is a very powerful way to say "so long" to your readers.

Another way you can get both the familiar and the unexpected in the same ending is to bring your story full circle. Write your character as he is at the end of the story into a scenario that mirrors the opening scene of the book. For example, if your character finds a wallet in Chapter One and keeps the cash inside, then that character could find a valuable necklace in the final chapter and choose to return it, demonstrating her hard-won maturity.

It's hard to beat the thrill of hearing a reader say of your ending, "Whoa, I never saw *that* coming." As the writer, you're the master manipulator right down to the last word. Wield that power mercilessly.

Chapter 8

Setting Is More than Somewhere to Be

It's one thing to look at a photo of a forest. It's another thing entirely to be in that forest with the muted crinkle of damp leaves under your sneakers, the gentle breeze fluffing your hair, and gnats dodging up your nostrils and flitting at your eyeballs and inciting you to spastic fits of air-slapping until finally you smack your own cheek. There's looking at it, and then there's living it.

Teens want to live it. Bring on the damp crinkle and the caressing breeze and the stinging slap in their fiction. Bring on the setting.

Too often in YA fiction, writers shortchange setting as they focus their energy on creating fast-paced plots with tight dialogue, strong characters, and no-muss sentence structure. They drop their characters in a location — a room, a park, wherever — and then it's "Onward, ho!" to the action and the dialogue. Where's the sense of place? Where's the feeling that this scene could happen nowhere else but *here?* Where's the full reading experience? Reading such manuscripts is like watching a movie for which the special effects crew has forgotten to generate the blue screen's background, leaving the characters walking and talking in front of a vast blue nothingness. That'd be a pretty big boo-boo in a feature film, wouldn't it? So, too, in a novel.

Setting is a powerful tool that enhances your characters and plot, making your entire story more meaningful and satisfying. It's not enough to simply put characters in a room with a view — or in a forest with trees, for that matter. You must give environmental details that engage readers' senses and that characters can react to or manipulate. Your readers deserve the sensory engagement that comes from hearing the crunch of frosty grass under a character's bare feet or feeling the sudden whispery kiss of a spider's web that dangles from the eaves. Without setting, you'd just have a girl walking across a lawn and an old house.

In this chapter, you lob setting into play, using place, time, social context, and setting props to deepen your characterization, advance your plot, and make readers feel like they're inside the story rather than just watching it. And you do it in a way that tickles teens as surely as those gnats just tickled your nose hairs.

How the Where and When Affect the Who, What, and Why

Setting establishes the time and place of your story's action. But more than that, it involves the *conditions* of that time and place, the physical and social state of your where and when. Packaged together, these conditions can create a *sense of place* — a tangible ambiance or mood — that's far more meaningful to young readers than a simple X on a map. Keep reading to find out how place, time, and social context work together to shape your setting.

Place

Place is the physical location of the action. It may be geographical, such as a Southern California beach, a farm in Iowa, or simply "on campus." Or it may involve manmade structures such as a building, a bedroom, or the back seat of the prom king's 1958 Chevy Impala. Place is anywhere characters can physically *be*. Physical details such as lighting, temperature, and weather are part of your location, as are fine sensual details like the slick leather of the Impala's upholstery and the roiling thump of its 502 blower motor.

Your location affects the plot and influences the mindset of your characters and your readers. Choosing a physical location that is wide and airy, for example, can inject a sense of freedom into a scene, slowing down the plot and relaxing the tension. By contrast, a tight, confined location can feel oppressive and make the character crave escape, setting up the plot for a burst of action and a change of pace. Strategic use of location can pay great dividends in your plotting, pacing, tension, and characterization.

Time

Every story has a calendar and a clock. Time of day, season, or year . . . past, present, or future — your choices with time influence what young characters do and how and why they do it. Consider your mood in the morning versus at night. Your energy level is different, and your ability — and desire — to interact with other people almost certainly changes. The same can be said of weekend versus weekday, summer versus winter, the beginning of the school year versus the last week of school.

Characters' behaviors and mindsets are heavily influenced by time, and you should use that to your advantage. If your young character needs time to process big news, crank the thumbscrews by launching her into a Monday with a whole week of classes, oral reports, tests, and homework ahead of her, giving her zero chance to process. If she needs separation from an abusive father, set the story in winter when she's snowed in and there's no hope of leaving, short of her best friend's carjacking a snow plow to rescue her. Use time to force issues. Your readers will love it.

Social context

Every setting provides a *social context* that involves the people dynamics and what's going on at your chosen place and time. Think male wigs here, curly powdered ones upon heads sporting wooden dentures and uniformed chests draped with muskets and other Revolutionary War accoutrements. Think hippie love beads and bellbottoms marching on the White House, or backyard keggers with all the cool kids and a single wide-eyed science nerd, or simply the dining room of a middle-class family in 2012 Tulsa, with Mom spooning mushed peas between a baby's squinched lips on one side of the table and Uncle Joe and Teen Big Brother on the other side, their faces twisted in major gross-out.

Your time choices may invoke concepts such as

- The culture of an era
- A community's response to a historical event
- The rules of a social class or interaction between social classes
- The fickle subculture of a small group, such as a family, a school, or a circle of friends

Your social context drives the actions, thoughts, and feelings of the characters and thereby turns your plot left, right, and — if you play your cards right — completely upside down.

Info dump alert! Be stingy about sharing the history of your setting with young readers. History dumps put the skids on pace and can come across as lectures. Leave that to the high school history teachers. Generally, it's more important that readers get a feel for the setting than the history behind it. When history is necessary because it advances your plot or illuminates your characters, keep it brief and sprinkle it around as much as possible. (I explain how to sprinkle later in the chapter.)

Setting Up Your Characters

Setting is a powerful tool for characterization. Used strategically, it can influence and illuminate a character's thoughts, words, and actions.

Manipulating their minds

Setting offers juicy opportunities to expose a character's thinking — and to manipulate it ruthlessly. Deliberately juxtapose settings to rattle your character and make him rethink what he thought he knew. Pull that kid out of his element for important emotional moments and then let him work out whether to scramble back to that comfort zone or formulate new understandings of his world. Or move him for good to a setting that's clearly an ill fit and flat-out force him to confront his bugaboos. Setting manipulation can spark fantastic psychological fireworks. Consider a story that sends an orphaned Quaker boy to live with his slave-owning uncle in Antebellum Virginia. Psychological fireworks, indeed!

Similarly, setting can reveal a character's emotions. Where is he happiest? Where does he go when he's in despair? Imagine a 15-year-old boy finding solace in the songs of mockingbirds on an isolated, flower-enshrouded mountaintop. Now imagine that same boy hunkered under a freeway overpass, enshrouded in the sounds of the traffic, the vibrations of the ground, and the fumes of a world too busy to notice him. One character, two very different ways of coping, with setting to thank for the difference.

Setting can bear a character's soft underbelly and force epiphanies. For the full ins and outs of characterization, check out Chapter 5.

Putting words in their mouths

Choose your settings with an ear for adding zip and depth to dialogue. You can tell a lot about a person by the words that pass her lips — and nothing gets those words flowing better than a setting that challenges her. Tromping through biting snow drifts, stepping on a sticky wad of gum, walking through a screen door she didn't see . . . any one of these setting-induced unpleasantries can put curses in the mouths of saints. An annoyed teen can really cut loose.

Social context can be just as vocally inspiring, with your character reacting to changes in the dynamics of her social group or simply talking in jargon that reveals the community she grew up in.

Character word choice isn't limited to dialogue, of course. Characters who narrate their own stories fill their narratives with words that reflect their region, social context, and time period. The same goes for a protagonist's internal thoughts, or *interior monologue*, in a third-person narration. Chapters 9 and 10 cover dialogue and narrative voice in detail, really digging into how a character's *where* affects his words.

Kicking characters in the pants

Characters need a sense of place to know how to behave. Your setting's social context influences your character's value structure, helping him determine when something is acceptable and when things must change.

If that awareness isn't enough to make him act when you need him to, you can nudge him along with location changes and place-related props or give his social context a good tweak. For example, you can put a dingy, mud-caked window screen between him and a loud fight outside, forcing him to make a choice: Ignore the fight or leave the safety of his house to watch it — or maybe even put up his dukes and dive in. Whichever choice he makes, there will be consequences, and your plot will flow from there. Your manipulation of the setting can be the kick in the pants young characters need to move them into the next phase of the plot.

Tying Your Plot to Your Place

Setting's job doesn't have to stop with prodding your main character through the scenes. It can drive the whole darned plot. It can be a primary motive for the action, with you speeding up or slowing down the pacing and relaxing the tension by moving characters to different locations or changing the elements around them. Writers of action-adventure stories need to understand this, but setting changes can be an equally powerful tool to someone seeking high drama, say, in historical fiction, where the events and social context of a time period force characters to action. With such stories, your setting choices determine the very structure of the story.

Phillip Pullman's *The Golden Compass* is a superb example of how you can bring all the elements of setting — time, location, and social context — to bear on the plot, using location changes to propel the action forward. In that book, setting offers a motive for the action, with the main character actively seeking a new physical environment. Part I of Pullman's story has its star, 11-year-old Lyra, yearning to go to the icy North. The plot moves forward step by step with her physical progression Northward:

- ✔ **Chapter 1:** Lyra is inside a pompous, stuffy room in Jordan College, breaking rules in search of excitement.

- ✔ **Chapter 2:** Lyra hides in a cramped closet, stifled by the hanging scholar robes, overhearing stories of the North and forming her dream to go there.

- ✔ **Chapter 3:** Lyra moves up to the rooftops of Jordan College and gets a view of the world beyond the college's walls, as characters from the North come to Jordan and kidnap children to take them Northward. Her friend is kidnapped, now turning her desire to go North into need.

- ✔ **Chapter 4:** Lyra gets the opportunity to travel North and she takes it, traveling for the first time in her life, from the college to the grand city of London.

- ✔ **Chapter 5:** Lyra gets stuck in London and feels caged by daily life inside stores and grown-up apartments and restaurants. She finally runs out into the night, escaping to go North.

- ✔ **Chapter 6:** Lyra meets up with the Gyptians and embraces their nomadic life aboard riverboats, completing her journey to the North over the next few chapters, taking readers to Part Two of the book, with Lyra in the North for the climax of the story — which is tied intricately to a physical phenomenon of the North called the *aurora borealis*.

Whether you tie your plot and your setting to the same wagon or just use setting changes to push the story forward, you can craft your time, location, and social context to directly affect your storyline.

Not every story involves an epic journey through many locales. If your story demands just one or a very few locations, that's okay. Just use the tips in this chapter to make those locations as rich and influential as they can be.

Choosing the Best Setting for Your Teen Novel

Where you choose to set your story determines much of what happens in it and how it happens. Set yourself (and your characters and plot) up for success by choosing the right setting from the get-go. That means always choosing a setting that advances your characterization and storyline and enriches the storytelling.

Never settle for knee-jerk settings simply because they seem like the natural places for the characters to be. Don't put your character in his bedroom for no other reason than you need a retreat for him, and don't put him in a class-room because, well, a kid's gotta go to school, doesn't he? That's settling for a knee-jerk setting. Instead of going with your knee, engage your brain. That is, brainstorm creative alternatives that offer juicy possibilities for sensory setting details and unexpected dialogue and action. Throw out that bedroom retreat idea and come up with other places a boy can go when he's over-whelmed, like rock-skipping at the lake (look out, Guy in Boat!), a curb at the Gas 'n' Go with some buddies and a Slurpee, under the back porch, in the tunnel slide at the park, or in the doghouse with beloved Ruffers at his side.

Be provocative. Don't drop your characters just anywhere and rely on the action and the dialogue to do the work. Put your characters in unexpected set-tings that provoke surprising dialogue and unpredictable action. That makes things exciting for your readers — and for you.

Successful "surprise" settings must also be believable. Have valid reasons for putting the characters in that setting so it supports and enhances the story rather than distracts from it. Always ask yourself what makes *this* the best setting for the events at hand.

Here are some things to mull over when you're working out the setting, either for a scene or for the whole story:

- **Time:** If you don't want to deal with a school setting, have your story take place during the summer. If you let it happen during the school year, you must account for the fact that a large portion of your teen characters' awake time is spent in school.

- **Familiarity of the place:** Maybe the school setting itself isn't what's ailing you. It could be that you're just bored by the familiarity of that setting and need to freshen it up. Or maybe you're choosing the wrong place in the school. Is math class really the most dynamic choice for your scene? How about ducking your characters into the janitor's closet, or putting them in the nurse's office, or having them fetch something from the teacher's lounge? Or hey, how about working in the cafeteria? There's major teen angst in forced hairnet wearing. These are ways to let a character go to school without boring yourself — and your read-ers. If you really do need a classroom setting, Home Ec. provides great props and gets students more engaged in activities than does an English Lit. lecture. Or try a science room, where a lab session can be far more dynamic than a seated review of the periodic table.

✔ **Characters:** Do you know your main character well enough yet to predict how he'll react to your setting decisions? Test his mindset and personality. Put him in a setting that's loud and see whether he likes the ruckus or whether he cringes, wanting to flee. Knowledge is power: If he cringes, then you know that you can ratchet up his angst at your whim by simply adding more sensory stimuli or moving him to a crowded location — and vice versa, of course. You've got his number now.

✔ **Audience:** Setting can manipulate your audience along with your characters. Exploit that. For example, if you want the readers to feel anxious and flip through the pages quickly, you may try risky, scary settings. Just make sure they're appropriate settings for your age group. Twelve-year-olds probably don't need to be reading about raunchy rave parties, as tantalizingly risky as that may be to them.

✔ **Your story driver:** Is your story plot- or character-driven? *Plot-driven* stories focus on the action, with events taking priority; *character-driven* stories give primary consideration to your protagonist's thoughts, decisions, and emotional journey. If your story is character-driven, tease and expose the character by choosing settings that push his buttons. If it's plot-driven, the setting variety should reflect the ins and outs of the storyline. But even plot-driven stories need strong characters, so keep your characters growing through interactions with the setting.

✔ **Plot:** How big of a role do you want the setting to play in your story? Maybe you just want the setting to pull the readers in for a richer reading experience. That's okay for some stories — you don't have to go all-out all the time. Decide up front just how big of a job you want to assign to your setting.

Consider your genre. If you're writing a historical novel, you'll probably need to give the social context serious attention and convey the time and era thoroughly by touching on it in every scene and having your characters interacting with props unique to that era. If you have an action-adventure tale in the works, give special thought to how the setting can advance your plot.

✔ **Story structure and narrative voice:** Your target age group determines your narrative voice and sentence style (see Chapter 9 for more on that), so your audience's narrative voice needs to influence your handling of setting. Maybe you want short, declarative statements instead of a more formal voice and thus want shortcut settings, places kids are familiar with so you don't have to explain them. That may well send you to the bedroom or the classroom; just be sure you freshen up those settings with interesting prop manipulations and unusual details (see the later section "Freshening up common settings" for tips). You're going for familiar, after all, not generic.

Above all, mix it up. Use multiple settings if you can, avoiding monotony by moving your characters around. And don't just move them from building to building; try moving them outside when they've been inside, and see how they react to that change. Imagine a teen girl and her mom always bickering inside, and then move them outside for some forced gardening together. How would that setting change affect their dynamic? Would it push them to the edge (with sharp pruners in hand!), or would their enmity diffuse as the fresh air and physical distraction worked their magic? Contrasting settings can underscore characterization and be a factor in adding a moment of drama to a story.

Making the Setting Come Alive

You chose your setting for a reason — mine it so readers can experience that sense of place for themselves. Give them the sounds and smells, the textures, temperatures, and sensations that distinguish that location by having your character hear them, smell them, and feel them.

In this section, I explain how to put all five senses to work in your writing, and then I give you an example to show how it's done.

Engaging the five senses

When revealing setting, don't rely solely on sight; doing so can lead you to long descriptions, which can function like off switches for young readers. Strong, effective settings engage all the senses.

Show, don't tell is the general writing rule that says not to tell readers something when you can show it through action instead. Showing is dynamic storytelling that delivers a richer reading experience for your audience.

Here are three ways to engage the five senses in your fiction:

- ✔ **Battle the elements.** Every location has physical characteristics, such as lighting, temperature, and noise level. Have a character react to those elements in ways that convey to readers how the elements make him feel.

  Don't just write that it's cold in the snowy field; have your teen protagonist hunching his chin into his jacket, or blowing warm breath into his cupped hands, or poking his nose with a mittened finger to see whether it's totally numb or if maybe he can still incite a sharp jolt of pain. You want the sensations of that place, and having your characters react to the elements is one way to convey that.

Don't rely on adjectives to convey your sensory details. Build the quality of those details into your other words. Adjectives such as "cold" and "snowy" become unnecessary when you bring in mitten-and-jacket-related action to convey the sensory details.

Be creative with your sensory details, and work several together for greater effect. Sweat trickling down a boy's back as he trudges through a cornfield may evoke the feeling of heat, but it's generic. Go deeper. Work several elements together to get more bang for your buck: A boy trudging through a cornfield is so preoccupied with holding a jacket over his head to shield his scalp from the sun that he trips on a dirt clod and falls into the stalks, getting scratched and muddy. Now, not only is he hot, he's having a terrible, horrible, no good, very bad day to boot. Imagine the words *that* would put in his mouth.

✔ **Manhandle the props.** Props offer your characters opportunities for tactile interaction with the setting — which means major opportunities for sensory details. Splintery chopsticks can be flung in frustration, pianos need their keys plunked, flowers must be sniffed, guest towels must be squeezed for softness. Every interaction with a prop is an opportunity to pull the readers deeper into your story by making them feel *there*.

✔ **Write scenes about the setting.** Your story is about a character and how he overcomes a challenge, yes — but it's also about the circumstances that define that character. Remember, his perception of the setting illuminates his mindset and influences his personality. You can get sensory with your storytelling by writing scenes that seem to be about the setting even though they're really delivering information about the characters and plot. Think of this as a legal bait-and-switch, one that makes for fun storytelling.

Don't worry that in pumping up the setting in your story you're sacrificing action. All three of these sensory engagement methods call for boatloads of action. If you use these methods instead of just reporting the action to your readers, you're putting them in it. That's a great way to hook and keep teen readers.

Get a feel for sensory details. Describe a room in your house without naming the room (living room, bedroom, and so on). Without your directly stating it, how will your readers know the following?

✔ The temperature in your room

✔ The room's age

✔ The time of day or year

✔ What and/or whose room it is

✔ What's beyond the room's walls

Engage as many senses as you can, using the three sensory engagement methods I describe earlier. Remember to work several setting details together for richer effect.

Sample scene: Two girls on a bus

Here's a scene that applies three sensory engagement techniques: battling the elements, manhandling the props, and writing scenes that appear to be about the setting but really aren't. In this scene, two teen girls ride a city bus home from their after-school jobs. The girls' dialogue is interrupted by the vibrations of the bus, the sounds of its doors and the traffic around it, and props inside and outside of the vehicle, with the characters reacting to those elements. One girl is talking to the other while an old lady sits nearby, with the bus hitting potholes:

> The old woman's grocery bag jiggled on the seat next to her. A carton of eggs was visible through the translucent plastic.
>
> "He *said* that?" Rachel shook her head slowly at the news of my job offer. "That boy needs to get real."
>
> "I know, seriously," I said. The bus rumbled through an intersection, with the egg bag jiggling forward as if on tiny legs. "I told him no way."
>
> "But you need that job."
>
> "Like a hole in the head, I do." A big pothole and the bag jumped. I shoved my Fedora back, away from my eyes. It was stupid, buying a too-big hat. So what if it was half price? "I'd rather babysit the Miller Monsters every day than clean some rich boy's bathroom once a week. If I was meant to be a maid, I'da been born with a feather duster instead of a hand."
>
> Rachel snorted then grabbed at the pole in front of her as the bus swerved. A red Mercedes ripped by us, its horn blaring. Rachel jumped up and stuck her face out the window. "Look where you're going, idiot!" she screamed. "Where'd you buy your license, Wal-Mart?" She sat back down. "Stupid jocks with daddy's cars."
>
> The old woman's wrinkles deepened. Rachel flashed her most angelic smile. The egg bag teetered at the edge of the seat.
>
> "I'd take the job," Rachel said. "Babysitting sucks rocks."

Can you see where that bag is going? Another pothole, and those eggs are scrambled. The point of the conversation is to show how poor these girls are, how one has some pride peeking through while the other lets it all hang out. But I've written the scene about a public bus. That setting serves up a great opportunity to show that their life is uncomfortable. Readers get shaking and harsh horns and screams and wrinkly scowls. The action in this scene revolves around the bus and the characters' reactions to it, but readers discover a ton about the characters' personalities and their lots in life.

Researching your setting

It's important to know enough about your setting to be able to render it realistically. Of course, the easiest way to know your setting is to choose one that you've experienced personally. But this isn't always possible — you can't very well have firsthand knowledge of life as a page boy in the court of King Edward VI. If the all-important sensory details aren't coming to you from personal experience, then research is a must:

- ✔ **For physical locations:** Consult maps and read resources that describe the area and its physical traits. Push yourself beyond the topographical details, seeking out the area's typical architecture, the region's birds (and their birdsong), its insects and wildlife, and so on.

- ✔ **For time and social context:** Consult news stories or historical accounts about the era or culture. The more primary sources (journals, diaries, memoirs, personal correspondence) that you can consult, the better. Be sure to keep young people's perspective in mind as you note the details. What were young people's lives like in that time and place? How were they different from your readers' lives? Get the full rundown on using primary and secondary sources to research YA fiction in Chapter 3.

Allot a section of your writing notebook to setting and write down details you discover during your research. Taking notes reinforces the details for you, rendering them a part of your creative process as you write. Plot and characterization ideas will almost certainly pop up. This section of your notebook can also be a great reminder for you during later drafts, which may come months or even years after your initial setting research. (Chapter 11 explains the process of building a story through multiple drafts.)

Be a character in your own setting so you can later imagine your characters there. Close your eyes and imagine yourself sitting at a window in a house during that time and in that location (preferably use the house your character will live in). Look out the window. Imagine that view in the different lights of day and all four seasons. Now move to the other side of the window. How does each of those seasons feel now? How do they smell? How do they sound? Now leave the house in whatever transportation is available. If it's a vehicle, take a window seat and peer out along the way. See the buildings you pass, the plants, the animals, and people. When you get to town, go window-shopping. Shopping or trade is an essential part of life for everyone, in every age and era, from markets to malls. Which shops do you encounter? What do they look like? Which shops have the most foot traffic? Go into the shop doors and ask the salespeople for help. Enhance this exercise by firing up music of the area, age, and culture. You'll find plenty on the Internet that you can sample or stream.

Author Jennifer Donnelly: Finding stories in places

I don't much like the word *setting*. It sounds theatrical, contrived, showy. I like the word *place* a lot better.

Place is incredibly important. It isn't just something you drop in behind your characters, like a stagehand lowering some fake scenery. Place is a character in its own right. The place where your protagonist grew up, the places she runs to or from — these places all work upon her as surely as her mother, her best friend, or her boyfriend does. These places shape her, define her, save her, or doom her. And just like your flesh-and-blood characters, place needs to come alive in your pages. It needs to speak to the readers. It needs to help explain why.

To capture the feeling of a place, you have to be relentless in your pursuit of it.

When I researched Paris, past and present, for my novel *Revolution*, I smelled, touched, listened, watched, and tasted my way through the city. I inhaled deeply in crypts and graveyards, taking in the scent of minerals, rain, and loss. I listened to market people coaxing and heckling and flirting, to mothers scolding their children. I touched old stones and old bones and heard

them whisper. I walked for hours, watching the faces of the people I passed, watching the light. I forced myself down into the catacombs, though I suffer miserably from claustrophobia.

Eventually, I knew how it felt to my character to stumble around in the catacombs, terrified. To see the guillotine at work in the Place du Trône. To light up the black 18th-century Parisian sky with fireworks. To fall in love at Sacre Coeur.

I didn't get everything I wanted. I never do. But I got what I needed, I think — a magpie's cache of sights, sounds, and smells that allowed me to take my readers out of a subway car in Queens, a Starbucks in St. Paul, a beach chair in Miami. Out of the 21st century. Out of themselves and into the Paris that filled my heart — and broke it, too.

Jennifer Donnelly is the author of several award-winning novels for adults and young readers, including the Carnegie Medal Winner and Michael L. Printz Honor Book A Northern Light *and the genre-melding historical drama* Revolution. *For more about Jennifer, go to* www.jenniferdonnelly.com.

Weaving the Setting into Your Narrative

All fiction writers strive to craft fast-paced plots, engaging characters, and believable dialogue, each delivered in an entertaining way. But YA fiction writers have the added task of crafting sentence structures and a narrative style that are accessible to young readers, and you have to fit your setting descriptions into the style you've chosen. Chapter 9 gets down and dirty with the process of synching sentence structure and narrative style to target audience, but here are five strategies aimed specifically at wielding setting with teen accessibility in mind.

Keep in mind the Rule of Three: Try to trigger three senses per chapter. For readers, a rich setting is the difference between watching characters and being there with them, so if you can engage many senses with your writing, you're golden. Scenes are more meaningful and satisfying that way.

Sprinkling versus splashing

Stopping your story to splash setting onto the page can be hazardous in teen fiction. Splashes can stop young readers cold. Sometimes, yes, you may need to pause your plot work for some setting details — a little descriptive moment — either because it fits the overall style of your narrative voice or because, simply, it's time for a breather. But in general, splashing means stopping, and stopping is rarely what writers want. Instead, sprinkle.

Work in the setting here and there, as if flicking wet fingers at your pages instead of pouring water on them straight from a spout. Even teens who aren't intimidated by a few lines of description are likely to skip over big splashes in search of the story thread. Providing details about time and place as you go keeps settings accessible and interesting to teen readers.

A *narrative beat* (see Chapter 10) is that bit of narrative material that separates two lines of dialogue. More than just "he said/she said," a narrative beat gives readers a breather in an exchange of dialogue. You can sprinkle the setting into a beat as action. In the following example, the beats are the parts not enclosed in quotation marks:

> "I can't do this!" I flung my math book at the trash can but missed and dented the wall. Great. Now I'd have to fix that, too. Stupid metal mobile homes. "I quit!"
> "Quit what, school?"
> "Yeah, school. I quit!"
> Dad shrugged. "Okay. Pass the salt."

Karen Cushman's Newbery Medal–winning middle grade novel *The Midwife's Apprentice* demonstrates the power of sprinkling in its opening chapter, which is just four and a half pages long. That chapter opens with a short passage about an orphaned girl who crawls into a rotting, "moiling" dung heap for warmth. That chapter ends with that same warm dung heap. In between, sprinkled references to the heap's foul safety transform this setting detail from sewage to sanctuary, helping readers see past the girl's filth to her savvy survival skills. The character is established via the setting, without any disruption to Cushman's direct narrative style. And frankly, a dung heap off the beaten path is a far more striking way to open a story about a homeless girl than simply having her begging in the streets. The readers, the character, and the story all win because of Cushman's setting choice.

Stacking the sensory details

A concise way to work in setting is to stack sensory details upon each other. That way, you can tag several senses at once, quickly and effectively, without disrupting a youthful, direct sentence structure. This isn't a matter of describing several details outright, one after another, but rather of using props and actions that imply multiple sensations simultaneously.

Linda Urban's *A Crooked Kind of Perfect* uses direct sentences in a first-person narrative of a 10-year-old girl. The story is told in mostly action and dialogue, and sometimes her chapters are just a few sentences long. The text is concise, with little room for flowery setting material. Yet Urban still works in several senses by stacking the references upon each other, as in this sentence: "Miss Person puts her glass of ginger ale to her forehead, like she's trying to soothe a headache." Readers feel the pain of the woman's head and the coolness of the glass — two senses in one shot, without a lot of hoo-ha. That's effective stacking.

Keeping it young

When possible, wield your setting in a way that conveys youthfulness, even if you're writing in a formal, more traditional style. Do this by

- Having young characters handle props in youthful ways, such as touching what they shouldn't

- Behaving inappropriately for the location, as in playing hide-and-seek in a church

- Reacting to sensory stimuli in immature ways, such as bouncing around and rubbing furiously at goose bumps while waiting in the cold

There's often irreverence, lack of consideration, lack of self-consciousness, or plain unbridled curiosity in the way young characters interact with the environment around them. With maturity comes more measured behavior.

Phillip Pullman employs youthful prop manipulation in the opening paragraphs of *The Golden Compass*. There, 11-year-old Lyra moves around the scholars' retiring room examining a massive table set with meticulously polished place settings. Whereas an adult might tuck her hands behind her back so as not to break or in some other way disrespect anything, young Lyra reaches forward and flicks a wine goblet to make it ring. With that one brief, child-like gesture, readers see that this girl is not going to be intimidated by grown-ups and their airs. She is practical and curious and a girl of action; when she wants to know something, she acts to find out. This is a great quality for a budding heroine, and it's conveyed by giving the setting and prop an active twist of youth.

Giving the setting a job

Some writers treat setting as a character, with moods and tasks to accomplish and failings and, in some sense, a will. This is a great way to get teen readers to connect with the setting, as if it's another member of the cast.

In Ysabeau S. Wilce's fantasy *Flora Segunda,* Flora's house is a full-fledged active entity, with 11,000 rooms that shift location at random, although it stops short of having a conscious will. When she steps through a doorway or into the elevator, Flora emerges wherever the house puts her. Non-fantasy stories may not be able to go that far, but they can sure take a similar path. In my novel *Honk If You Hate Me,* the town seems to rest above a mysterious heat source, in effect sizzling like a hamburger patty on a grill, and the characters act accordingly. When the protagonist accomplishes her goal, the town stops simmering. In Louis Sachar's *Holes,* the desolate wasteland in which the juvenile delinquents are sentenced to dig is not personified, but it still has a very definite job: to punish the boys.

Even if you want to stay far away from personification, consider giving your setting a job in your story. Make it act up in a specific way that forces your protagonist to respond as if to a member of the cast, as if he feels the setting is actively out to manipulate the situation. Because it is! With you pulling its strings, of course.

Now, although you should avoid stopping for long passages of description, that doesn't mean you should *never stop for description.* There will always be exceptions to writing rules, because writers are always creating stories that break molds, and setting sometimes calls for its own time in the spotlight. Kathi Appelt's National Book Award Finalist *The Underneath* is one of those mold-breakers. Poetic and flourishing, that novel spends a huge amount of time on setting. But even then, Appelt doesn't just put on the brakes for big setting splashes. Her passages show the setting in action: ancient trees imprison an immortal snake within their roots, the river keeps cat siblings apart, and the raised porch that creates "the Underneath" space hides the animals, keeping them safe as if a force field separates them from the evil beyond the hidden space. In this novel, the descriptive passages present the setting elements as characters with specific jobs.

Freshening up common settings

Teens spend the bulk of their waking time at school or in their rooms-cum-sanctuaries, so YA fiction writers inevitably set scenes in one or both locations. There's a certain shortcut in that maneuver, because all teen readers will be familiar with those settings. Problem is, familiarity easily translates into b-o-o-ring. There are other go-to settings in YA, such as the coffee shop or the library or the kitchen.

Challenge yourself to choose less-expected locations or to freshen up the common ones, giving them a spin or adding details that make them exceptional and interesting. Make them earn their place in your book. Here are three ways to go about freshening:

✔ **Do the unexpected.** Make a teen's room sterile and spotless instead of messy, which would reveal qualities about the character. Or give it unexpected furniture, such as blow-up chairs. Focus on unlikely details in your common locations, like an unusual picture in a living room or a banana placed front-and-center on a desk during a class whose teacher requires spotless desks (true story, by the way, from my college days; just wish I'd been brave enough to use a pineapple).

If you have a car, make it smell like, say, strawberries, or something else out of the ordinary. Or inflict a crack across the floorboard of the car, right behind the front seats, where the backseat passengers' feet will rest. (That's another true story — me riding in a car with a crack across its middle. I was in junior high, getting a lift home from a softball game with my friend and her mom. I could see the road passing underneath my feet! I imagined the crack splitting wide, dropping me onto the freeway as the theme from *Rocky* blared on the radio, staticky but still triumphant. My friend and her mom acted for all the world as if the crack didn't exist.) Young readers will take note of unexpected setting details — especially ones that play off each other like the *Rocky* theme and that gaping maw at my feet — and they'll remember.

Sometimes the most memorable setting details come from your own experiences. Think about a room or other location from your childhood that still gives you a warm fuzzy when you recall it. What made it so exceptional? Consider the furniture in the room, the smells and textures, the noises you could (or notably could *not*) hear in there. Now think of a place that made you uncomfortable and that gives you the willies even now. What details prevented you from feeling at ease? Develop the habit of looking for out-of-the ordinary items in locations that are particularly meaningful to you and consider working them into your stories. The details that stick with you are likely to make an impression on your characters and your readers, too.

✔ **Act against stereotype.** You can freshen up common YA settings by going against location stereotypes. A library where people talk and shout, for example, can make a rule-following character uncomfortable. Or how about a bedroom that the character's mom decorated in, say, old lady wicker furniture or something else very non-teen-friendly, robbing it of its sanctuary status? You can do the same with social context and time, finding ways to defy stereotypes about them. Settings that defy stereotypes help keep your story dynamic for young readers.

✔ **Use running prop gags.** Have some long-term fun with setting details and props, such as a stereo dial that keeps falling off, or neighbor kids who are always at their window across the alley from the protagonist's bedroom, or an oddly deep well on a pioneer farm that requires the characters to crank and crank and crank *and crank* the handle to lift up the water bucket. The gag doesn't have to be funny, just distracting enough to get your characters' attention. Young readers will love watching how the gag perturbs your characters — or doesn't. Sometimes no response is just as useful as an extreme one.

The most effective prop gags are those that reveal something about your characters or their situations, thus earning their places in the story. Throwing something in purely for laughs can score some giggles, but generally a novel filled with things that don't further the story feel scattered or random.

Freshening up common YA settings is fairly easy in quirky novels. In my novel *Big Mouth,* I had the school be sponsored by a ketchup company that insisted that the entire campus — walls, lunch tables, and all — be painted red. This affected the plot, setting up a student rebellion called the Mustard Revolution. Edward Bloor gives school a similar tweak in his novel *Story Time*. He turns the school into a test-taking lab, with characters attached to treadmills and drinking brain-enhancing smoothies to prep them for standardized tests. But historical novels and contemporary dramas can use these tricks, too. These techniques work for all genres of teen and tween fiction, and they do so in a manner that can fit even the most spare and direct narrative style.

Chapter 9

Crafting a Narrative Voice Teens Will Listen To . . . and Love

- -

In This Chapter

▶ Injecting personality into your writing

▶ Getting off your soapbox and into teens' heads

▶ Synchronizing your language with your audience's maturity level

▶ Showing instead of telling in your narrative

- -

Narrative voice is a defining feature of young adult fiction. The perfect YA voice doesn't just project a distinct personality; it also instantly connects with an intensely opinionated group of humans who exist in a constant state of angst thanks to raging hormones and the strain of navigating social minefields on a nanosecond-by-nanosecond basis. Phew! The mere thought of attempting such a connection may send shivers down the spines of parents of teens, but it needn't give you the willies.

Connecting with teen readers is actually quite easy when you know the tricks of the trade. That's what this chapter is for. Here, you discover how to create a distinct, teen-friendly voice by mixing and matching the elements that make up narrative voice — point of view, word choice, and how you string those words together — all with a twist of teen psychology.

I'm Not Talking Dialogue Here: The True Meaning of Narrative Voice

The term *voice* can be misleading thanks to its knee-jerk association with dialogue. But narrative voice isn't dialogue. *Dialogue* is what your characters say, and I've set aside Chapter 10 for that. *Narrative voice* is what the narrator says. Most importantly, narrative voice is how that narrator says what he says.

Author Jane Yolen: The distinct voice

Editors and writing teachers always talk about writers finding their voice, as if it is lost somewhere. But they are talking about three things when they say this: the author's voice, a character's voice, and the narrative voice.

The author's voice is about the chosen words, how we report the various senses, how the world we have invented becomes real. The character's voice should be different enough so that even without a tag (George said, Mary shouted) the reader knows who has spoken. And the narrative voice . . . well, that's how the story rolls out.

But in each case, what makes that voice distinctive is word choice, the lyrical line, the emphatic beat, the rhythm and rollick of the sentences.

Here are three tries at the same story, each done with a distinctive voice:

Example 1

Once upon a time, in a New England village, there were three men who loved the same woman. One was a carpenter whose outside was as hard as bark, though inside he was soft as the pith of a tree. One was a baker whose mind and heart were pliable as dough. And the third was the minister whose soul was open to God and closed to man.

Example 2

The village of Seven Oaks had a single road running through its heart. Houses leaned over the road like gossips at the fire. Most of the gossip concerned the three men who loved Maggie Mars: the carpenter, the baker, and the minster.

No one in Seven Oaks knew who had the inside track. Not even Mistress Mars.

Example 3

Maggie Mars leaned over the bowl in which an apple peel floated, waiting till the peel settled to the bottom.

"Peel away the future's mask.

"Show me the name of my true love at last."

She watched as the peel curled into the letter O.

Not Nick Tree, the carpenter, then. Nor the baker, Peter Breed. Nor even Lemuel Pearl, the minister. She tossed the water out the door and chewed on the peel, wondering who might be her true love. The only man in the village whose name began with an O was Otis, the pigkeeper. She shuddered. Surely not.

Read them aloud and you will immediately hear the differences. One is not better than the other, but each brings the reader to a different and distinct place. That's the power of voice.

Jane Yolen has been called the Hans Christian Andersen of America and the Aesop of the 20th Century. She is the author of more than 300 books for young readers and adults, including fantasy and science fiction novels, historical novels, poetry, and children's books. Her books and stories have won the Caldecott Medal, two Nebula Awards, two Christopher Medals, the World Fantasy Award, three Mythopoeic Fantasy Awards, the Golden Kite Award, the Jewish Book Award, the World Fantasy Association's Lifetime Achievement Award, and the Association of Jewish Libraries Award, among many others. Visit www.janeyolen.com.

The *narrator* is the entity telling the story. That entity can be all-knowing and unnamed — called an *omniscient* narrator — or it can be a character in the story, called the *point of view character* because the story is told from his or her point of view.

In this section, I explain the importance of narrative voice and then reveal the elements that go into creating an engaging narrative voice.

Getting a feel for narrative voice

You often don't know people's personalities until they open their mouths and say something. At that point, you can judge their word choice and the way they deliver those words. Perhaps they use words incorrectly, suggesting a lack of education or a low socioeconomic background. Maybe their delivery is overly earnest and loud, with more guffaws than necessary, making you feel like they want not just your attention but the whole darn party's. They could be run-on talkers, or spare talkers, or those startling people who somehow manage to talk in exclamation points! Or perhaps what they say and how they say it reveals imminent mental breakdown.

Narrative voice in fiction works in the same fashion. You may make some guesses about a story based on its cover, sure, but to really know a story's personality, you must open the book and judge what the narrative says and how it says it. Here are examples of two very different but distinct teen-friendly voices:

Example 1

We were so bored, it wasn't even funny. I was all, "Guys, come on, let's go do something already," but they just kept looking at me like, "Yeah, right," as if I was some, like, I don't know, some kind of freak or something.

Example 2

Dallin eased open the misshapen door, a sliver of moonlight slicing the darkness beyond it. Breathing. A light rustle. The peace of sleep. He closed his eyes and pressed his forehead against the coarse wood. He could easily slip in. He could leave the rebellion behind, lock it out for good this time and creep back to his pallet like nothing had ever happened. His brothers wouldn't question it, finding him there in the morning, nor would his mother. Family. Safety. The temptation was strong.

Seeing what goes into narrative voice

Several elements come into play as you create your YA narrative voice, and every author mixes and matches them differently. Here they are:

- ✔ **Point of view:** Obviously, a 16-year-old girl would narrate her story differently than a 13-year-old boy would. Whether you choose first person, third person, or omniscient, your point of view influences every other aspect of your narrative voice.

- ✔ **Sensibility:** YA writers must master something that writers of adult fiction don't need to consider: a youthful sensibility. Young people are learning to be self-aware rather than self-centric, and their appreciation of others' places and fortunes in the world is still maturing. You must step away from your adult sensibility and see the world as youngsters see it, letting that view influence your phrasing and sentiments.

- ✔ **Word choice:** Individual words are the bricks and mortar of narrative voice. Energize your story with dynamic words, stir readers' emotions with evocative ones, and torpedo clichés with fresh turns of phrase. Further distinguish your voice with regional words and phrases, casual "colloquial" wording, or distinctly formal word choices.

- ✔ **Sentence structure, paragraphing, and punctuation:** The way you string words together determines the depth of your voice. Sentence variety adds a rhythmic quality that you can manipulate with punctuation for a richer voice.

Here's the essential rule for creating a teen-friendly narrative voice: Your voice must suit your target audience. There's no fudging that. Twelve-year-olds have a different maturity level than 17-year-olds, so you'd better know exactly who you're writing for. (Flip to Chapter 2 for help identifying your audience.)

Pinning Down Your Narrator and Point of View

The big boss of narrative voice is *point of view* (POV). Your narrative sensibility, your word choice, and how you string the words together are all determined by who you choose to narrate your story and how that narrator perceives and judges the events.

Imagine a 16-year-old girl narrating her quest to become the most popular girl in school by hooking up with the captain of the football team. Now imagine her 13-year-old brother narrating her efforts. Now try an anonymous all-knowing narrator who can get in the head of the football player she's stalking. And now try the football player himself. Each narrator offers distinct opinions about the events, and they'll use their favorite words along with deliveries and tones that reflect their personalities and prejudices. The way your chosen narrator mixes and matches these elements determines your narrative voice.

In young adult fiction, it's common for a teenaged main character to narrate the story as he or she experiences it — a first-person point of view. But "common" doesn't mean "always" or even "most of the time": Third-person point of view is just as plentiful in teen fiction, with readers outside that main character's head, looking over his shoulder. And then there's second-person and omniscient, both of which appear in teen fiction. Each point of view has pros and cons. In this section, I describe different points of view you can employ in your novel.

First-person POV

In the *first-person* viewpoint, you write from inside the head of your narrating character, using the pronoun *I*. For example, "Dr. Finch's eyes were fixed on me, and I was sure he'd decided I was rude and stupid like Mama said and that I should just leave already." Choose this POV if you want a particular character's speech inflections and vocabulary to define your narrative voice. The narrator needn't be the character at the center of events, although in teen fiction he usually is; the story may be recounted by a best friend or side-kick. Either way, this narrator filters the events for your readers, deciding what to comment on and lobbing judgments.

Here are the pros and cons of first person:

- ✓ **Pros:** This POV is popular in YA fiction because teen readers can relate to narrators their own age. Also, being inside the narrator's head makes readers feel as though they're experiencing the action and emotions themselves.
- ✓ **Cons:** The downside with first person is that you're limited to what the POV character can actually see and think.

Second-person POV

Choose the *second-person POV* when you want to address the reader directly, using the pronoun *you*. Although not a common POV in fiction for adults, second-person shows up often in YA fiction thanks to the popularity of diary formats and old-fashioned narratives such as Kate DiCamillo's *The Tale of Despereaux* (which periodically steps out of the story to address the reader by name: "But, reader, he did live."). You can find young adult narrators who talk straight to readers throughout the entire story (as in contemporary stories that have a confessional feel to them) and stories that treat the reader as the main character (as does Charles Benoit's *You*).

Here are the pros and cons of second person:

- ✔ **Pros:** Technically, the "you" in the diary format addresses the diary itself, not the reader — which essentially turns readers into voyeurs. Oh, the delicious violation of reading someone's diary! Unfettered access to the narrator's most intimate revelations brings readers as close to the narrator as one can get. Definitely a pro.

- ✔ **Cons:** It's mighty hard to lose yourself in a story if the narrator keeps reminding you that you exist. That's called a *self-conscious* narrative — which isn't a compliment. Those old-fashioned second-person narratives risk jolting readers with every reminder or keeping them at arm's length throughout. And frankly, people tend to bristle at the idea of being told how they think or feel, especially teens with their I'm-Sick-of-Adults-Telling-Me-What-to-Do-All-the-Time mentality. (More on that later in "Making Sense of Teen Sensibility.")

Sometimes a very casual first-person narrator throws in some *you*'s, as in "It's not like I can just bust right in there, you know, and get all up in their faces. Church folks don't operate like that. You got to be smooth with that crowd." In cases like this, the narrator is addressing a sort of universal *you,* not the reader directly. You're not likely to confuse anybody with this vocal tick. However, those same casual narrators sometimes address readers directly and randomly, as with "It's not like I had a choice. I mean, what would you do?" This approach risks knocking readers out of the fictional world you worked so hard to draw them into. It's safest to avoid *you* altogether unless you've made a conscious stylistic choice that you intend to stick with throughout your entire story. Used randomly, *you* is a distraction.

Third-person limited POV

Generally referred to as *third person,* the *third-person limited* POV lets you eat your cake and have it, too, allowing you to see the story through a single character's eyes *and* describe things outside of that character. Third-person narration uses the pronouns *he, she, it,* and *they,* never *we, you,* or *I.* Here's an example:

> Becca watched Elton board the bus. She thought about running to him for one last kiss — a long, deep kiss that tasted like berries and sunshine and promised Forever. But she didn't. She stayed right where she was. She wouldn't say goodbye.

Here are the pros and cons of third-person limited:

- ✔ **Pros:** Third person is a popular YA POV because it allows readers to connect with and follow one character throughout the entire story. Everything that happens is filtered through that character's perspective.

> ✔ **Cons:** The risk with third person is that readers can feel a step removed from the events and emotions. Sitting on someone's shoulder just isn't the same as being in her head.

Third-person omniscient POV

Most people call *third-person omniscient* simply *omniscient,* although technically it's a form of the third-person point of view. Third-person omniscient uses the pronouns *he, she, it,* and *they.* Choose this POV when you want to write about events that take place away from your main character's direct experience, happening anywhere with anyone at any time. Here's an omniscient POV:

> Aunt Shera explained to Dain all about hazelwood and its virtues in ancient wands. As the shadows lengthened, the two talked on. Dain was glad to have his aunt share his excitement about his wizard training. He loved casting spells, he loved concocting potions, he loved getting high marks and making his family proud.
>
> Cleatus knew no such love. In fact, he kept his wizard training entirely to himself. If he told his father he could make things disappear with a mere flick of his wrist and a whispered phrase, he'd catch a cuff to his ear for lying. No, wizard training wasn't news for the dinner table, not in this house. For Cleatus, wizard training was his way out.

Here are the benefits and drawbacks of omniscient:

> ✔ **Pros:** Omniscient, written from the perspective of an anonymous godlike entity who knows things that none of the characters can know, is the most liberating POV because you're no longer limited to what your narrating character can see and think.

> ✔ **Cons:** You can get into your characters' heads only via internal thoughts: "Aslon hefted the sword. *Too heavy,* he thought. He laid it back down." Another drawback is that jumping from one character's perspective to another's and then to another's in a single scene can get confusing. And injecting new perspectives as additional characters arrive on scene can be jarring. It's a good idea to establish a small core of characters whose points of view are crucial to telling the story.

The unreliable narrator

You can throw readers a curveball by using an *unreliable narrator.* Also called *fallible,* this kind of narrator misleads or in some other way tells readers less than the truth. This creates a layer of tension between reader and narrator as you force the audience to evaluate your narrator's claims.

Using multiple points of view in YA fiction

Some call it *head hopping*, some call it *third-person multiple*, some call it flat-out confusing. Telling a story through multiple character viewpoints isn't common in teen fiction, and people have strong opinions about why that is. Many writers and editors worry that young readers feel overwhelmed when faced with keeping track of multiple narrators. They say it's asking a lot to expect teens to emotionally connect with that many narrators. It's also a lot of work for the writer. Mastering a single, distinct narrative voice is a full plate; creating three, four, even five distinct voices for the same story is a tall order.

Not that using multiple points of view is impossible to pull off, as Donna Jo Napoli demonstrates so well in her novel *Zel*. Napoli's twist on the old Rapunzel tale has three narrators telling the story, with two of the narrators using third person and the third narrator using first person. You can use multiple narrators in teen fiction — doing it well is just really challenging.

There are certainly reasons for using multiple points of view. For one, you can inject tension into your story by having two characters report the same event completely differently — with neither one lying. People see, hear, and experience life differently, and multiple viewpoints let young readers examine that.

If you believe multiple viewpoints are integral to your story — such as when you have a murder witnessed by five different characters and want to give each character a chance to speak up — then using several narrators could be well worth your efforts. Here are some tips:

- ✔ **Make clear breaks when switching from one POV to another.** Switch at the end of paragraphs, at the end of scenes, at the ends of chapters and parts. Switching mid-paragraph or mid-scene can disorient readers.

- ✔ **Be diligent about making the voices distinct from each other.** Distinguish the voices through word and phrase choices, sentence styling, or sensibility.

- ✔ **Be sure that each character adds something that the other characters could not — information, important opinions, and so on.** If you find that the voices sound the same or that the characters are simply rehashing the same material from different vantage points, then perhaps using multiple POVs isn't right for you or for that story.

Above all, don't choose multiple viewpoints simply because you think it would be fun to try. With so much at stake, you must have a story-driven reason for putting everyone to the extra effort.

An unreliable narrator is usually a first-person narrator, although a third-person narrator can fudge the truth, too. He may mislead readers intentionally, as in the case of lying to avoid blame, or he may twist the truth out of bias or prejudice. His lack of credibility may not be so conscious: He could be at the mercy of a mental issue or drug use, or he could be, quite simply, really slow on the uptake and unable to process what he sees well enough to report it reliably. Whatever the reason, an unreliable narrator has compromised credibility.

There are several ways to let readers know your narrator has credibility issues. You can tell them up front that the narrator is a liar, as Justine Larbalestier does on Page 1 of *Liar;* you can let them infer it themselves from the narrator's behavior, from his claims, and from the way others react to him or her; or the riskiest option, you can wait until the end of the story to reveal to readers that they've been duped.

There are pros and cons to using unreliable narrators:

- ✔ **Pros:** Some readers enjoy the guessing game that comes with wondering what the real scoop is. This creates interactive reading (a plus with young readers!) as the audience evaluates every statement the narrator makes.

- ✔ **Cons:** Some readers see this as an annoying narrative trick. One of the accepted conventions of fiction is that readers can trust the narrator to report everything he knows, with the caveat that he may have limited access to information or may misinterpret or refuse to see the truth of a situation. Regardless of his limitations, readers trust that he's being as honest with them as he is with himself. They can feel betrayed or manipulated when that unspoken agreement is violated.

To win over readers with your unreliable narrator, keep the narrator sympathetic so readers will *want* to believe him even while they fear they can't. The tips in Chapter 5 help you build a narrator whom readers can root for. You can show evidence that he's been wounded by life or has goodness somewhere in him, have him embody traits that teens struggle with themselves and can thus sympathize with, or put him in situations that allow readers to feel bad for him even as he jerks them around.

Exercise: Developing your narrative POV

As you weigh the point of view choices for your fiction, it's helpful to try out your options, getting an idea about which POV feels most natural to you and which offers the best storytelling options for your story. Using the following scenario, write a couple of paragraphs or even a full scene using each of the four POVs I cover in this section: first person, second person (straight narrative or diary format), third-person limited, and third-person omniscient. (Bonus points if you attempt to write from the unreliable narrator's POV.)

> Tom, a tall, lanky freshman with an unusually strong and accurate arm, dreams of being the school's first freshman quarterback, scoring a college scholarship, and then going pro. But first he must go through the Ballard High Bandits summer tryouts. He walks into the locker room on Day 1 and encounters the current quarterback—a 6'2", 220-pound senior. Write Tom's initial reaction.

Past or present? The right tense for you

Consisting of just four words, "Past or present tense?" seems like a clear, straightforward question about technique. But these four words can really get writers' hackles up.

Proponents of past tense hail it as the conventional choice, making it more familiar — and thus more comfortable — for writers and readers. Their argument is that the natural feel of past tense lets readers sink past the storytelling into the story itself: "A smell drifted from the pot. I held my breath. How did I get myself into these situations? I sat down and draped a napkin across my lap."

The other side of the argument declares that present tense is more immediate and thus more engaging. Present supporters love the sense of urgency the present tense injects into a story: You're in the midst of the action, with anything and everything still possible — even the worst-case scenarios — so the suspense is high. The downside is that present tense can be more challenging to write. For one thing, it's not as common in general fiction as past tense, so it can feel less familiar and natural. On top of that, detractors complain about an inherent awkwardness in having a first-person narrator describing his physical actions as he's doing them, interrupting the rest of his thought process for something no one actually pays any attention to in real life. However, smooth transitions between the actions and the narrative elements that they interrupt can mitigate that: "A smell drifts from the pot. I hold my breath as I sit down and drape a napkin across my lap. How do I get myself into these situations?"

So how do you know which tense is right for you and your story? Luckily, teen fiction gives you plenty of room to choose. For one thing, teens are open to unconventional approaches, so present tense is common in their fiction and you're free to choose it with confidence that your readers will go there with you. Plus, teens aren't likely to have formed distinct opinions about tense and won't be digging in their heels out of sheer principle. So if you're feeling the urge to give present tense a whirl, you can. It may be just what you need for an action-driven story, one where sitting on the edge of one's seat is an integral part of the experience. By contrast, if you want to spend some time on scenery or sense of place, or if you want a more pensive tone or formal style of voice, past will likely be your tense of choice.

Sometimes your choice isn't so clear-cut. If you're not feeling a distinct pull one way or the other, experiment. Trying out both tenses is easy to do. Simply write a scene or two in both tenses and see which version serves the story best.

Whichever tense you settle on, your primary charge is to be consistent. Tense slips are easy for writers to make but hard for readers to overlook. Young or old, readers don't like being jolted out of the story. Don't give them a reason to get their hackles up — stick to your tense.

After you've completed each approach, consider the following: Was one POV more natural to write than the others? Which version reveals more about Tom's personality? Your comfort with the POV isn't always the primary factor in your decision about which one to use for your novel. Comfortable is safe, and safe doesn't always make for the most dynamic story. Weigh all the factors in your POV decision.

Making Sense of Teen Sensibility

Young people process and react to events or behaviors in a less sophisticated manner than most adults do. You can inject a youthful quality into your narrative voice by phrasing things to reflect that less mature perspective. To tap into that perspective, you must understand two things: teen sensibility and the teen tendency toward hyperbole. Take a look.

Self-awareness and the teen psyche

A common pitfall for teen fiction writers is sounding too mature for their characters, too self-aware or analytical of other characters' behavior. As in, "I've got no more patience for John. I know the guy needs someone to talk to, but not me, not today." These words and delivery feel young enough, but the *sensibility* — how the speaker responds emotionally or intellectually to a situation — is too adult.

Some teens are very astute about human nature and do puzzle over it, absolutely — their thoughtful brooding can help you inject nice tension into your story by letting readers be privy to your protagonist's thoughts while limiting fellow characters to what they can see. But many tweens and teens don't focus on why they or others behave as they do; they just judge, act, and then react to the consequences. A teen's maturation process propels your protagonist through his character arc, and self-awareness is the insight he gains at the end, when he's completed his internal journey. Until then, shift your thinking to the less-sophisticated teen sensibility, phrasing the text so it focuses more on how the events are affecting the protagonist than the other characters involved: "I blow past John. He can talk to my locker, for all I care." Use quick judgment and action, letting the chips fall where they may.

Character arc is the emotional growth of the character through the story. Each new conflict or obstacle challenges the character further, pushing him beyond his original boundaries toward a new level of awareness of himself and the world around him. Flip to Chapter 5 for info on character arc, internal journey, and other juicy characterization stuff.

When handling the teen psyche, be aware that teens are highly allergic to preaching. Nothing screams, "Hello! I'm an adult telling you how you're supposed to think!" more than a lecture. Bye-bye, teen readers. Instead of pushing your theme so hard, focus on the plot and the characters. The theme will come through, with the protagonist's successful completion of his arc embodying your message. Your readers will get it. Trust them.

Also keep in mind that teens have age-based rules about behavior, and they don't tolerate dissension in the ranks well. Sixteen-year-old boys who play hopscotch on the playground after school are convincing only in deliberately quirky stories. Sixteen-year-old boys must do things that readers believe 16-year-old boys do — or the boys must have a really good reason for breaking rank. Your characters' behavior must always match their age and maturity level. Don't risk sounding like a clueless adult. The credibility of your voice is at stake.

Embrace your inner drama queen

One way to convince teens that you understand how they think is to embrace their overly dramatic mindset. You've noticed, haven't you, how many teens tend to overreact and get way too dramatic about the events at hand? For them, things aren't bad; they "suck, big time." And Mom doesn't get mad; she "freaks out" or her "head explodes" or there's the classic, "She's gonna kill me!" Teens get blamed for everything (just ask them), and no one has ever in the history of the world felt the way they feel right now.

A big reason teens react strongly is that they don't have the experience to put minor events in perspective. And adults, for their part, can forget the ways in which small, subtle cruelties can hurt. As you craft your fiction, keep in mind that teens' over-the-top reactions aren't always ploys for attention — teens take the events seriously. You should, too. Failure to do so risks making you sound condescending in your narrative.

Teenhood often involves extreme emotions and grandiose notions of self. Tap into that. Let the things that happen to your teen protagonist rattle her cage, and let her be dramatic about them and judge herself and others harshly, erroneously, and quickly. The words and phrases you choose can suggest a grandiose view of the situation, its extent, its implications, and its impact on the protagonist herself. When you're striving for a youthful narrative voice, *hyperbole* (making extravagant statements) is your friend.

Cracking the door open for teenage drama doesn't mean throwing that door wide for stereotypical characters or hokey dialogue that over-emotes to make up for a flat plot. These are official traits associated with the term *melodrama* in literature, and you don't want to stray into that territory with your fiction. You still need to support your characters with a strong plot filled with tension that stems from high stakes. (Chapters 6 and 7 cover those in depth.) You can't count on exaggeration and hyperbole to add all the emotional zing — that's what gives melodrama its bad name. Wield the teen tendency to overstate as but one tool for injecting a youthful outlook into your narrative voice.

Word Choice: It Pays to Be Picky

To create a distinct narrative voice, you must choose your words carefully. Your phrases, too. A story bulging with bland words and empty clichés may fill pages, but it has zero personality.

Make it your goal to use a rich, active vocabulary. That means energizing your story with dynamic words like *bolt* instead of *run* or *perch* instead of *sit* and stirring your readers' emotions with evocative verbs that do double-duty, such as *slumped,* which conveys both mood and action. You can also explore specific styles of voice, such as the vocabulary of particular regions or formal versus colloquial styling.

Above all, absolutely, positively, no matter what else you do, strive for fresh turns of phrase instead of clichés. Rendered nearly meaningless by overuse, clichés will smother your voice.

I cover age-appropriate word choices, clichés, and style of writing next.

Say what? Using appropriate words for your audience

When you're choosing among 5-cent, 10-cent, and 50-cent words for your YA fiction, there aren't as many restrictions as you may think. Big words appear in tween and teen fiction all the time. What's more important is that you adjust the length and style of your sentences for younger readers, not that you shorten their words.

That said, do try to balance these factors as you choose your words:

- ✔ Your style (a formal voice would likely use more elevated words than a colloquial voice, for example)
- ✔ Your point of view and genre
- ✔ Your target audience's sophistication level

A journal narrated from a 13-year-old girl's first-person point of view, for example, isn't likely to include words like *fathom* and *parse.* Those are too sophisticated. The words you choose for first-person narration should be words a kid that age would use.

Need a little guidance matching vocab to age range? Type "grade vocabulary lists" into your Internet search engine, and you'll get a slew of websites that list common vocabulary words for each grade level. Some kids may have a greater vocabulary range than their peers for a variety of reasons, but this gives you a useful reference point for the general age range.

Sending kids to the dictionary

Some authors like to include meaty 50-cent words to challenge readers, deliberately sending kids to dictionaries to increase their vocabulary. That's a worthy goal. My only caution with that strategy is to avoid going overboard. You want kids to be excited by a new word or two, not feel pummeled by a wagonload, and you certainly don't want to keep sending them out of your story.

Give kids a chance to figure out word meaning from the context in case they don't want to go in search of their dictionaries — or heaven forbid don't own one. The point is to enrich their vocabulary. If they can get that from the context, more power to them.

Flinging f-bombs

It's common for teen fiction writers to become obsessed with four-letter words: *Dare I include profanity? Or is that the kiss of death? Real teens cuss in real life. . . .* Believe me, it's a very common quandary.

If you're considering the *f*-word, you must also consider a *g*-word: *gatekeeper.* Before YA novels land in teens' hands, they almost always pass through parents, teachers, or librarians. They certainly pass through editors and booksellers. These are the gatekeepers for young readers, and generally speaking, cussing clogs their filters. Sure, teens cuss, and yes, it'd be "real" to write that into dialogue, but how many parents want to drop the *f*-bomb right into their kids' hands?

There's a now legendary case of a Newbery Medal–winning book that upset many parents and librarians with its use of the anatomically proper term "scrotum" on Page 1. Although that's not usually considered a cuss word, *The Higher Power of Lucky* faced a censorship uproar, with critics decrying the use of that word in a novel for 9- to 12-year-olds as purely for shock value. Imagine if it had been the *f*-word. Know that if you swear in a novel for young readers, your book may not reach its intended audience. You must balance that risk with your need for authenticity.

You can make a case for foul language in 12-and-up YA when it's organic to the character or situation, such as with warring gangs in a dicey 'hood. Gatekeepers may accept bad words there because they're already letting the kids read an *edgy* story — a story with generally taboo or rough subject matter. But even in edgy stories, you can usually avoid four-letter words or unsatisfying substitutions like "Golly gee, man!" by simply rewriting *(recasting)* your sentence or scene to avoid the need to swear. Let your characters fling cutting insults or act out physically in a confrontation — throwing things, shoving, flipping the bird, and so on. You *can* avoid "f— you." If your book doesn't need cussing to exist, don't endanger its existence by cussing.

Overusing slang

Teens throw around slang the way toddlers throw food — with messy, mindless abandon. It's tempting, then, to try to re-create that quality of teen life in your fiction. I cover *slang* — informal words and made-up expressions of the moment — in Chapter 10's discussion of realistic dialogue, but for now, if you find yourself tempted to sling slang, hold your fire. It's too easy to sound like an old person trying to be a jive hipster, and that's just painful. More important, though, is the fact that slang can date your book the instant you write it. Slang comes and goes more quickly than reality show stars. In all but the rarest exceptions — like, say, books that are meant to embrace or self-consciously re-create a particular moment in cultural history — you can just as easily write your novel without it.

For that matter, don't refer to technology in your novel if you can help it. Or music groups or TV shows, either. Talk about gone in the blink of an eye! Worse, what's cool one day could be the epitome of geekdom the next, so your efforts to make your characters hip could backfire in a truly ugly way. One of my early jobs in publishing was digging old paperbacks out of the publisher's archives and reissuing them for the new generation. A vital part of that task was reading through the books in search of references to momentary Hot Things like records and VCRs and OMD and EBN-OZN, all of which had to be nixed before the book could reprint. What's an EBN-OZN, you ask? I rest my case.

Getting fresh with your phraseology

A frequent flaw in the manuscripts crossing editors' desks is clichéd writing. Characters *roll their eyes, talk to brick walls, hope against hope,* and *couldn't care less*. Falling back on this kind of shorthand is easy because everyone understands the ideas behind these stock phrases, so you know kids will get your point. But when young readers don't have to think very deeply as their eyes roll over the words, they don't get engaged. They can easily sink into passivity, which is just a breath away from *bored* — a word that should make you shudder.

An engaging narrative voice uses fresh turns of phrase to keep things interesting. Be bold. Show teen readers respect. Challenge them with more vivid expressions. As much as you may joke about the teen psyche and recognize that you have reluctant readers in your audience, you must also remember that teens can be very sophisticated readers.

To pop yourself out of a cliché mindset, allow yourself to give in to the clichés in the first draft. When a scene is spilling out of you, the last thing you want to do is interrupt it! The second draft is when you get tough. Start by flipping open a good thesaurus. No, you're not looking for word-for-word substitutions. Instead, skip down to the slang part of the thesaurus entry (sometimes labeled "nf" for *nonformal usage*) to remind yourself that there are other *ways*

to say something, not just other words. This can open your mind to an unexpected way of saying something, which may prompt you to recast the whole sentence. Or maybe you'll rewrite a whole paragraph or a whole scene or even give your character an entirely different personality. Consider this first draft sentence:

> Kirk couldn't care less about math, so he rarely did homework for his algebra class.

"Couldn't care less" is cliché and doesn't do more than convey my point. Bland voice alert! Looking up "unimportant" in the thesaurus leads to this:

> Math cut no ice with Kirk, so he just blew off his algebra homework.

Better. It has a certain regional flair now . . . yet it's still not particularly revealing. Readers now know Kirk doesn't like math and won't do it, but his personality is still off stage. Latch onto the attitude that peeks up in the phrases "cut no ice" and "blew off," and push this thought a step further. What was it, exactly, that he hates about math? *How* would he blow something off?

> Kirk had 45 algebra problems to simplify that night. $15x + 9 + 5x - 2 = \ldots$ Ah, screw it all. He did the simplest thing and left the book in his locker.

Now that has personality. Readers get a feel for the math that's torturing him, and then he does his knee-jerk teen drama thing and ditches the math book entirely. This gives you a richer peek into the character's personality, and it's far more engaging than the original line with its stock "Kirk couldn't care less about . . ." phrase.

Exercise: Creating a word bank

Some writers type up lists of evocative words, called *word banks,* for each book they write. If you have a story heavily focused on water, your word bank would include words with watery context that you can use even when you're not talking directly about the water: *soggy, slick, mist, glossy, flow, wave, undulate, drown,* and *refresh,* for example. Stories with physical violence should make use of words, phrases, and actions that are intensely corporeal, violent, or harsh: *rip, drop into my seat, stomp up the stairs, bruised fruit, twist to see behind, knock, sharp, thump, crack, rigid.* A steady stream of theme-invoking vocabulary enhances your narrative voice, generates a distinct *tone* (the attitude or mood of a story, such as spooky or pessimistic), and — bonus! — adds depth to your themes at the same time.

To create your word list, look up three to five words related to your theme or subject matter in a thesaurus. Peruse the entries and select synonyms that are active, unusual, interesting in the mouth, or evocative of a mood. Type those words into four columns labeled "Verbs," "Adjectives," "Nouns," and "Phrases." Print your word bank and post it near your desk for inspiration when you're cranking out scenes.

My novel *Honk If You Hate Me* takes place during the ten-year anniversary of a fire that altered the fate of the main character and her entire town. My word bank for that novel was filled with words and phrases that evoked the imagery of fire. Here is part of that word bank, which ultimately filled up one side of an 8-1/2" x 11" sheet of paper. The four words I started with were *fire, flame, burn,* and *heat*. These and similar words are embedded in the narrative and dialogue throughout the novel.

Verbs	*Adjectives*	*Nouns*	*Phrases*
glow	sweltering	blaze	flare up
spark	roast	blaze	warm as toast/ warmed over
warm	toasty	rager	hot as hell
bake	sunshiny	beacon	hot enough to fry an egg on
broil	red hot	burn	like a furnace
flicker	stuffy	firecracker	slow cooker
stifle	sticky	rocket	boiling/melting/ flash point
suffocate	sizzler	cherry bomb	in a flash
choke	hottie	fizzer	burned out, totally fried
fume	stoked	flare	totally burned me
reek	gutted	fire pit	spontaneous combustion

Allow yourself half an hour for this exercise. You'll probably find yourself looking up more than your original three to five words as each entry opens up your mind to new possibilities. It's like brainstorming, only with vocabulary instead of ideas. Go with it! You may not use every word in your bank, but the words will be there to inspire you along the way.

Showing a little style

You can inject personality into your narrative voice by employing one of these overall styles of wording:

- ✔ **Formal:** This style puts proper words in their proper places at the proper times, grammar-wise. It's often the choice for omniscient narration, especially when you want a more classic feel for your voice. Contractions can help you avoid sounding stilted in your properness. For example, "She warned him to stop racing about. Their mother wouldn't appreciate a phone call from the hospital."

- ✔ **Colloquial:** This is often considered the "real life" way of talking, with casual turns of phrase, lax grammar, and roundabout sentences. It's common in teen fiction, especially with first-person POV. Example: "She wished he'd quit running already. Getting all crazy like that would just land him in the ER again, all busted up and looking lame in some backless nightgown. Oh yeah, Mom would love that." That's someone talking without conscious care for sentence structure. It has an organic feel, as if this character is sitting next to the reader, rattling off the story as it comes to her. Contemporary "real life" teen fiction frequently uses colloquial styling.

- ✔ **Regional:** This style invokes the dialect of a particular region, such as the Southern United States.

Writing dialect does *not* mean getting all funky with your spelling. Droppin' the *g* is really jes writin' an accent, and most o' the time, writin' accents is plain distractin'. See?

With regional styling, it's more important that you capture the unique turns of phrase and rhythms of the region. For example, "Go on, now" and "do tell" and "I lit out after her" send you to the South. Combine such distinct phrases with narrative clues like crab apple trees in the yard and nearby bayous and the like, and you'll create a world. Consider this: "It's all about Mama and her being a teacher and all." You could write that as "It's all 'bout Mama and her bein' a teacher and all," but why? Page after page of apostrophes can be obnoxious. Version 1 of the Mama line suggests a folksy region, and surrounding it with similarly styled dialogue and narrative details that suggest a specific place would yield a smooth flavor that's far more satisfying than tweaked spelling.

You'll have the best luck with regional styling if you've actually spent significant time in the region in question, but the Internet can help you get a feel for a particular area's wording style. For example, Internet searches for "regional slang" reveal that "pop" dominates the Northwest, Great Plains, and Midwest, while "soda" is the word of choice in the Northeast, greater Miami, the area in Missouri and Illinois surrounding St. Louis, and parts of northern California. Do specific searches for your region of interest and read local newspapers, blogs about local happenings, and the like to get a feel for the regional lingo. If you need insight into the phrases of a particular historical period, look for articles and books of the time, or read articles and books written *about* the time. (For tips on consulting primary and secondary sources, see Chapter 3. For more on dialect, head to Chapter 10.)

Syncing Your Delivery to Your Audience

You can tailor your narrative voice for your target age group by syncing your delivery to their sophistication level and attention span. You're in control of your sentence structure and paragraphing, and you decide when and how to punctuate. There are rules, yes, but there's also plenty of room for you to do it your way — that is, the way that most successfully engages your identified readership. This section shows you what I mean.

Sizing up sentence structure and paragraphing

Sentence structure injects major personality into your narrative voice, and paragraphing can affect the pace of your story. Here's how:

- Short sentences can sound matter of fact or abrupt, and they can quicken the pace, creating a sense of energy and excitement. Short paragraphs propel you through the pages with a stronger wind behind you.

- Long, complex sentences can sound poetic, knowledgeable, and confident, allowing your narrator more time to chew on a thought and thus conveying more maturity. Longer paragraphs enhance that quality.

In this section, I explain how to use paragraphing and sentence structure to engage your audience. I also give you a few tips on adding complexity without falling into a pattern or muddying the content.

Matching length and complexity to your audience

As a general rule, the younger your audience, the simpler and more direct your sentences and the more frequent your paragraphing.

Here's an example of effective delivery for 8- to 12-year-olds:

> Hunting ghosts was a louder job than Darin expected. Oh, he'd figured on some blood-curdling screams. And a few boos. And maybe some jangling chains.
> He hadn't figured on his little sister.
> Or her constant whining.

He should've. Katie always wanted to be part of everything. It didn't matter to her that Darin didn't want her to be part of anything. And what Katie wanted, Mom made happen, so now Darin was hunting ghosts with the whiniest, bossiest kindergarten monster to ever walk the earth.

No wonder the ghosts were so hard to find. They were terrified.

This example shows that you can get great sentence variety in a young, declarative delivery, and you can even slip in some longer sentences as long as they're direct and active, which is a key factor in those middle-grade novels that don't skimp on the sentence complexity but still keep the narrative voice young.

Older teens in the 12-and-up range, especially the 14-and-up group, can handle more-complex sentences. Offer them more clauses and longer paragraphs, with a little more punctuation:

Hunting ghosts was a louder job than Darin expected. Oh, he'd figured on some blood-curdling screams, and a few boos, and maybe some jangling chains or a creaking coffin or two. He hadn't figured on his little sister — or her constant whining.

He should have. Katie always wanted to be part of everything, even though Darin wanted her to be part of nothing. But what Katie wanted, Mom made happen, so now Darin was hunting ghosts with the whiniest, bossiest kindergarten monster to ever walk the earth. No wonder the ghosts were so hard to find. They were terrified.

A pox on passive voice! Staying active

Want to kill a perfectly wonderful story? Use passive voice. It's deadly. You get *passive voice* when the action in your sentence is performed on the sentence's subject, as in this example: "The key was lost by Vance." That's passive . . . and majorly yawn-inducing. Imagine a book full of that! Vance, the subject, needs to be doing the action himself: "Vance lost the key." There, that's active — and far more engaging, especially for teens and tweens.

Passive voice is unwelcome because it makes readers feel distanced from the story. They never fully sink in. And the sentences can get pretty confusing, too — especially when you start with *subordinate clauses* (phrases with verbs and nouns that can't quite stand alone) and make readers root around for the main action: "With all the screaming and craziness of the rioting crowd, the key was lost by Vance." Egads! This sentence has riots and screaming people and all kinds of action, so it should be a great moment in the story. But it's not a great moment because the action is suffocated. Don't make young readers work that hard. Active construction would do the job wonderfully: "It was a total riot — screaming, shoving, unbelievable craziness. No wonder Vance lost the key."

Passive construction can sneak up on you. Consider this: "The key was lost." Without the subject in there (Vance), you may not catch this passive setup. But the effect is the same: a distanced reading experience. The occasional passive sentence won't kill you, but if your critiquers complain that they can't get into your story or that the pace feels slow, go on a hard target search for passive construction. Rewrite any questionable sentence as a direct statement ("Vance lost the key") and then stand back and consider the entire paragraph it appears in, tweaking the sentences in the paragraph for variety while keeping them active.

Varying the sentence structure

Regardless of your target audience, you want to vary your sentence structure. Don't start every sentence with "He did this . . . He did that . . . He did another thing. . . ." YA writers can easily slip into such patterns. Yes, these writers get the short, direct sentences they want, but the lack of sentence variety creates a highly distracting staccato delivery.

Sometimes start with a noun, sometimes state a thought, sometimes make an observation. Variety helps you avoid monotony and keeps readers engaged. Plus, when you deliberately break away from variety for extended, focused passages of only long or only short sentences, the effect is powerful. Such moments add significant personality and drama to your narrative voice.

Keeping subordinate clauses in check

Like passive voice, overusing subordinate clauses can make readers feel at arm's length. A *subordinate clause* is a group of words that has a verb and a noun but can't stand alone as a sentence. Writers like to use subordinate clauses to give the main action context. You're not a criminal if you use subordinate clauses once in a while. The problem comes when you use them too often. Frequent appearances of the word "as" in your manuscript can be a red flag that you have this habit. Check this out:

> As she ran by the coat rack, Tessa grabbed her jacket. "Rain, rain, go away!" she shouted as she pulled up her hood. She raced across the street as the first drops fell.

If you're doing this, you're probably *trying* to be good. Writers often turn to this "as" construction to avoid making a bunch of direct statements in a row, which can have a staccato affect. They're striving for longer sentences. Only, they're going in the wrong direction, burying one action inside another, sentence after sentence, paragraph after paragraph. If you find yourself doling out *as*es like candy on Halloween, go back to working in more direct statements, with active verbs. And when you do use long sentences, don't rely solely on "as" clauses. Instead, mix it up a bit with "then" and "and" constructions, as in this fix:

> Tessa grabbed her jacket from the rack. The forecast called for rain. "Rain, rain, go away!" she shouted from the open doorway. A fat raindrop smacked her forehead. Tessa pulled up her hood, stuck out her tongue at the clouds, and then bolted across the street. Prince Charming awaited.

No *as* construction, a mix of short and long sentences, lots of direct statements with dynamic verbs — this is immediate and thus more teen-friendly.

Putting punctuation in its place

To contribute to your variety and sense of rhythm, consciously build in pauses with commas, periods, dashes, colons, and semicolons. Readers need these breathers. Imagine listening to a person who never takes a breath — your pulse will quicken and your breath will go shallow. The result is a rushed feel, a voice that's hurried and probably tense (which is why skimping on punctuation is a trick for quickening the pace and increasing the tension, which I cover in Chapter 6). As insignificant as a dash or a comma may sound, its judicious placement can create a very dramatic moment or just plain give your reader a break. Here are several versions of the same passage, repunctuated for different dramatic effects:

✔ **A straightforward delivery:**

> He hadn't figured on his little sister or her constant whining.

This is a direct statement. Nothing fancy-pants about it.

✔ **An aside:**

> He hadn't figured on his little sister, or her constant whining.

The comma-separated phrase at the end reads like an additional fact, tacked on as an aside.

✔ **An important point:**

> He hadn't figured on his little sister. Or her constant whining.

That period turns one thought into two, calling out the whining as something worthy of its own sentence entirely. It must be important.

✔ **An interruption:**

> He hadn't figured on his little sister—or her constant whining.

The dashed phrase creates an interruption, and interruptions always feel important.

As for exclamation points, rarely use them. They backfire easily, making it seem as if your narrator or characters are always screaming or hyped up. This is the bad kind of drama, where you're forcing the emotions instead of letting them build naturally from the situation. If you pick the right words and shorten your sentence structure at the desired moment, your emphasis will come across without exclamation points. Save exclamation points for choice moments to get the most bang for your buck.

Show It, Don't Tell It

You'll probably hear the adage *show, don't tell* a million times in your writing career — as well you should. It's a really big deal. *Show, don't tell* means you need to let your readers interpret actions and motivations based on their observations of what characters do and say. Don't interpret for readers. Don't tell them how an action was done ("angrily") or why it was done ("they'd always talked to each other like that"). Show the characters behaving angrily by speaking words that are harsh or abrupt. Show the characters talking to each other in several exchanges that demonstrate how they "always" talk to each other. Lead readers to your desired interpretation, but don't interpret for them.

Showing instead of telling enriches your overall storytelling, and you'll hook and hold young readers as a result. Not only does showing draw the reader into the story as a participant, but it also enhances the emotion in the manuscript because it makes you convey the characters' emotions in a multitude of ways, not just through direct statements. And the characterizations often get a boost, too. Check this out:

> "Um . . . I . . . um . . ." Shawna stammered. It was never good to hem and haw around Mrs. Dunston when trying to think up a believable lie. She had an unbelievably sharp sense of smell, only it was specifically honed to detect lies. Like the way a shark can smell when there's blood in the water, Mrs. Dunston could smell a lie from a mile away.
> "Don't even think about lying, young lady," she commanded while turning to face Joe. "Joe, tell me *exactly* what happened."

That's telling. Here's the showing version:

> "Um . . . I . . . um . . ." Shawna stammered.
> "Don't even think about lying, young lady." Mrs. Dunston turned and pinned Joe to the wall with a firm finger to his chest. "You. Tell me exactly what happened."

The second exchange is much shorter and more dynamic, and the pace is snappier. Plus, letting Mrs. Dunston's forcefulness come through in her pinning of Joe allows you to remove the italicized emphasis from the word "exactly." Showing the characters in action relaxes their dialogue, deepens their characterization, and lets readers engage with the story more directly as they form their own opinions.

Dialogue is a good indicator that you're showing instead of telling. It's usually more interesting to hear characters reveal their personalities through their words instead of just reading descriptions about them. Plus, lines of dialogue add variety to your paragraphing, giving you yet another tool for creating a distinct, teen-friendly narrative voice. I talk about dialogue at length in Chapter 10.

Adverbs aren't illegal, but you'd do well to consider them so. *Adverbs* are words that tell how something is said or done. The most obvious ones are those ending in *-ly*, such as *quickly, rudely, flabbergastedly,* and the like. Don't tell your readers how something is said or done; just have your characters say it or do it.

If you're finding it hard to abandon adverbs, try this: Look at the adverb and verb you've paired up and consider the visual you're trying to convey to readers — and then pick a single verb that evokes that visual. For example, in the sentence "He walked slowly," you probably want readers to picture some-one who trudged along. Then use "trudged"! A single evocative verb trumps a generic verb-and-adverb combo any day.

Even though you're trying to show characters in action, don't get caught up in the minutiae of an action. Here's an example with unnecessary action:

> As she ran by the coat rack, Tessa reached out, grabbed her jacket, and slung it across her shoulders. "Rain, rain, go away!" she shouted as she pulled up her hood, tied the string under her neck to keep it shut, and then raced across the street as the first drops fell.

Save your breath. If the character pulls up her hood, it's a pretty good guess that she put the jacket on. Readers aren't dumb. They can make the leap. Let them. And give your voice some pizzazz in the process.

Chapter 10

Talking Like a Teen

*T*alk may be cheap in the real world, but in young adult fiction, it's made of gold, wrapped in C-notes, and sprinkled with diamonds with a bow on top. The reason for its extreme value? Simple: Teen readers want to hear directly from the teen characters in their books. Nothing makes them feel closer to the action. And you, as the mastermind behind those characters, are the caretaker of that bond. The dialogue you write must be able to entertain your young readers, intriguing them, informing them, comforting them, and, depending on which characters are moving their lips, sounding like them. All with your being a grown-up. How's that for an easy day at the office?

Crafting successful dialogue for young adult fiction starts with two understandings:

✔ **Strong dialogue is realistic but not real.** Real teenspeak is a mess of *um*s, *like*s, *you know*s, tangents, and runaway trains of thought that, when transcribed onto paper, are pretty much impenetrable. Young readers won't work that hard, nor should they have to.

✔ **Strong dialogue is inseparable from the narrative that surrounds it.** Dialogue and narrative are a team. Dialogue that sounds natural to the ear strikes a rhythmic and emotional balance between the words inside the quotation marks and the words outside them.

This chapter helps you strike that balance in your YA fiction with clear, engaging dialogue that pulls off three vital story needs: revealing things about your characters and your plot, pushing that plot forward, and sounding convincingly young to flesh-and-blood young people. To do that, I've filled these sections with techniques that'll, like, have you, you know, confidently talking to and talking like a teen in, um, like, no time at all.

Telling Your Story through Dialogue

Dialogue is a potent storytelling tool because what characters say and how they say it opens windows into their worlds. Speech reveals personalities, moods, relationships, even the plot twists that rock those worlds. And because characters are the headline attraction for teen readers, their words have that straight-from-the-horse's-mouth credibility. Of course, you and I know who the real boss is. By applying the techniques in this section, you can manipulate your characters' mouths to reveal exactly what *you* want at the precise moment you want it.

Character and mood: Letting your teens talk about themselves

Folks may praise straight talk in real life, but in fiction, the less-than-straight keeps things interesting. Here are eight ways you can manipulate the dialogue to make your characters reveal things about themselves:

✔ **Mix their messages.** How many people actually say what they mean or what they truly believe or what they really, really want someone to know? People hide and hedge when they talk — and so should your characters.

If you want, you can deliberately tip off readers when a character is being dodgy, which is an insidious kind of fun. You can confirm hunches for readers or deliberately seed distrust by writing dialogue that contradicts the speaker's body language and behavior. For example, if a girl says, "No, really, you're still my best friend ever," to one friend while texting another, readers have to decide whether actions speak louder than words. That makes for nice, interactive reading. You can create ambiguity, too, making the story more complex and perhaps adding an undercurrent of darkness to what should be happy. For example, a young boyfriend may say, "I love you with all my heart," right before punching his girlfriend in the face. Let readers wrestle with that mixed message.

✔ **Adjust the delivery to reflect a character's confidence.** Want to show a teen who lacks self-confidence or is too dependent upon others? Have her talk in questions: "I do it like this, right?" By contrast, a character who makes statements may be self-confident and independent: "I do it this way." And a character who commands when he speaks simply oozes confidence: "Here. This way." Of course, any one of these deliveries could be a ruse, with the character feeling just the opposite. Teens have been known to put on a tough-guy act. You get to decide whether to play it straight.

✔ **Let characters blabber or be abrupt.** When you want to show outgoing, open personalities or a sense of willingness in a character, assign him long chunks of dialogue, maybe without even letting the other person get a word in edgewise:

> "Oh, sure, come with me into the back, love. I've got what you need. Size six, right? People are always asking for size eight, so we're out of that, but I can tell the six will do you fine. Here, can you hold this box? Not as heavy as it looks. That's right, that end up. Now where did I put . . . ?"

In contrast, short bits of dialogue are for shy, secretive, or reluctant characters:

> "Yeah, we got some. Somewhere." Sigh. "I'll check. Wait here."

✔ **Put their feet in their mouths.** Let your teens blurt things out, inadvertently revealing bits of plot, personal secrets, or just more info than they want known, for whatever reason. Teens have fewer self-censoring mechanisms than adults do — they talk first and think second. And their tact is definitely still under construction. The next time you write a scene in which teens converse, let them blurt something out and then react; have them give voice to their judgments and then try to talk their way out of those spastic confessions.

✔ **Interrupt them.** A classic way to reveal mood in dialogue is through interruption. You can demonstrate a huge number of moods this way: anger, impatience, excitement, and resignation, to name a few. You pull off an interruption in written dialogue by letting one character cut another off, using an *em-dash* (—) to signal the break-in and following that immediately with the words that interrupt:

> "I didn't mean—"
> "Stop. Just stop." John yanked his letterman jacket out of her hands. "I'm done with the lies."

For best effect, don't immediately follow the em-dash with a narrative statement about the interruption, as in the following:

> "I didn't mean—"
> John interrupted. "Stop. Just stop."

Describing the interruption blunts the impact. Let the interruption play itself out.

✔ **Fragment their sentences and add hesitation.** Break up dialogue with *ellipses,* those three dots that trail off sentences or indicate a stuttering of some kind in the middle. Ellipses can indicate a character who's gathering his thoughts or somehow hesitant about what he's saying:

> "You could . . . oh, I don't know . . . try being nice to her, maybe?"

You can also use ellipses for agitated or rushed talkers who can't hold their focus:

"I saw him go that way! He was just . . . just . . . just go after him, will you?"

- ✔ **Expose their brains.** Each character chooses words and strings sentences together in ways that reveal that person's educational background and innate intelligence. Colloquial, formal, erudite, ignorant . . . the words that tumble from your characters' lips tip off readers about individuals' schooling and Mensa status. (See Chapter 9 for info on choosing words and styling your sentences.)

- ✔ **Use a different voice for each character.** Here's where writing character thumbnails or full profiles (Chapter 5) for secondary characters pays off. When you know the personalities and background of everyone in the conversation, you can sculpt distinct verbal tendencies (such as interrupting or running their mouths) for each character, creating flavorful and distinctive dialogue.

You have a lot of tricks up your sleeve; pull them out when things get heated. Conflict can be scary, so some writers shy away from verbal tussles, but don't be intimidated. Characters who argue are filled with emotion, and those emotions can easily get the better of them, leading to all-out conflict. Yank on heartstrings or make blood boil by writing exchanges that combine interruption with fragmenting with mixed messages with blurting. Verbal conflict isn't just about causing distress; it's another clever tool for revelation. Plus, it can allow one character to lead another to awareness or somehow influence her attitude or behavior — which leads to character revelation and growth, pushing the plot forward in the process.

Worried that a conversation feels one-sided? Rewrite it from the other character's point of view. Rewriting allows you to understand how *all* the characters feel about what's being said and about the situation in general so you can accurately portray everyone's social nuances and moods in the official version.

Delivering information: Loose lips reveal plot and backstory

Dialogue is a dynamic way to convey plot and backstory facts and for pushing the plot forward. But be warned: Dialogue that's included simply for fact delivery won't sweep any teens off their feet. You need to sneak in the facts and give the story a nudge forward without boring anybody in the process.

There's no law against having one character tell another one the facts. In some situations, fact-delivery can be useful, such as when characters are plotting to break into their school or lead an army into the Dark Wizard's fortress. It's just that a chat focusing on facts can come across as your feeding info to the audience rather than your characters' engaging in a natural back-and-forth. And you're all about authentic conversation, right?

Here are some tactics for delivering facts in a way that spurs the characters into action, pushing the plot forward:

- **Frame your facts as concerns.** If you're writing an adventure tale, you may write, "There's no way we can cross that. Shoot, Torrie, that rope was everything. Now how are we going to cross?" This line focuses on the character's concern for the success of their entire adventure. Contrast it with this line of dialogue, which focuses on the facts of the challenge: "We have to cross the chasm to get there, and it's fifty feet wide. We need a rope to cross it." Both versions get the point across, but the first carries more tension and emotion because the character is voicing a big-picture concern rather than explaining the facts. Here's another example, from a contemporary YA romance. The first version is heavy on facts:

   > "I'm afraid Todd is cheating on me. He disappears several after-noons a week and won't tell me where he was."

   This revelation isn't as energetic as the second version, which focuses on how those facts impact the speaker:

   > "Todd's not coming. He finally realized I'm a total loser and he's going to stay away forever and I'm going to grow old and lonely like Miss Eugenia and no one's coming to my funeral and that just sucks."

   Now that's concern, run through a teen's grandiose, self-obsessed mind without a filter in sight.

- **Tell characters something they don't know.** People don't usually tell each other what they already know, as in, "Remember? Dad lost his job three months ago because he can't speak up for himself." That never sounds realistic.

- **Tease readers with bits.** Give readers part of the facts in the dialogue but not all of them. I talk about sprinkling plot facts and backstory into the narrative in Chapter 7. Dialogue is a great venue for sprinkling. You can make readers wonder about what you've left out to entice them to stick with the story.

- **Blurt out the facts.** Not only does speaking before thinking reveal char-acter personalities, but it reveals plot facts, too. Blurting is a wonderful tool for pushing the plot forward because characters are forced to deal with the revelation once it's out there.

- **Extend one character's statement of fact into a full and entertaining conversation between characters.** Go ahead and lay those facts on read-ers in full, only do it in an entertaining way that starts the scene at one point and escalates it to another. For example, you could have a charac-ter say the following:

   > "Shelley's not home. I think she's gone to that park down by Joey's house. Only, Rachel trains her dogs there. If she sees Joey and Shelley together, it won't be good. We have to get down there!" Luke ran down the driveway.

This dialogue does its job — delivering the facts and nudging the plot forward to the next phase — but that's it. Not a lick of entertainment in it. Blah. Instead, get those facts across winningly through a back-and-forth conversation, with the characters using sentence fragments and cutting each other off and discovering things and reacting to epiphanies:

> "Where'd Shelly go?"
> "The park, probably."
> "Thanks a lot. There's only a million parks in town."
> "Not by Joey's house."
> "Joey's house? No way. Please tell me she didn't go there."
> "What? It's just a park."
> "Rachel trains her dog there. If she sees those two together . . ."
> "Aw, man, you're right. We have to get down there."
> Luke didn't answer. He was already running down the driveway.

✔ **Frame it as gossip.** Whether you're writing a contemporary story, historical fiction, a fantasy, or a futuristic adventure, teens love talking smack, dissing, and spilling the beans about other people (so do grown-ups, really, but for the most part they know what discretion means). Teens haven't fully internalized that lesson about locking their lips and throwing away the key. Tact is certainly not their friend yet, nor do teens shine at anticipating consequences. Sometimes, teens just plain like being up in somebody's business. Gossip in dialogue is a treasure chest of revelation and story advancement.

Choosing the setting: Their "where" determines their words

Setting is a powerful storytelling element, and it certainly makes its mark on dialogue. Where you set a scene shapes what the characters in the scene say and how they say it. They fill their dialogue with words that reflect their region, social context, and time period. Characters in a blustery outdoor setting, for example, talk in a very different way about their chores than they would if they were sitting at the school desks during a film, speaking behind their hands. Kids in California during the Gold Rush would speak differently about their chores than kids on a California beach during the 1960s. You can read about the power of setting in characterization in Chapter 8 and as an influence on narrative voice in Chapter 9. Here, I want you to realize that your setting choices determine the kids' spoken words and affect the actions they take in the narrative beats surrounding it.

Move characters to a different location for their conversation if you have a scene that seems to fall flat, that doesn't have the tension you want, or that just has characters sitting at a table talking back and forth, leaving you with few opportunities for narrative beat action beyond "he turned to her and scowled." The shake-up can be just what you needed to jog the emotion loose.

Find out just how important the location of the conversation really is. Write a conversation between a couple of teens. Then write a second version, keeping the same goal for the conversation but changing one key thing about the setting. For example, try setting the first version in a private place, where the characters can shout and get wild, and then move them someplace public, such as a fancy restaurant in which they must whisper and are frequently interrupted by waiters. Or set the first version in class, where half of the discussion must take place through note-passing; then move the conversation to the baseball dugout, with the characters running off for an at-bat or a turn at shortstop and then returning to resume the conversation. How much does this affect the content or the wording they choose? Adjust the weather, temperature, and lighting conditions accordingly, and let the characters interact with props as they try to maintain their trains of thought.

Author Deborah Wiles talks dialect in dialogue

I'll never forget the back-and-forth I had with a copy editor over a line from my first book, *Freedom Summer*. My young narrator says, "Mama helps my plate with peas." The copy editor kept changing "helps" to "heaps," even after I had explained that this was typical Southern speech. Finally, I sent the manuscript to my editor with a huge, handwritten "HELPS! HELPS! HELPS!" on that particular page. And the book went to print with the just-right word in that sentence.

Dialogue is the primary way I capture character and the flavor of a time and place. I'm a Southern writer, and I remember what it's like to watch moths dance around a porch light at night, and to smell my grandmother in Cashmere Bouquet after her afternoon bath, and to eat boiled peanuts with my brother, so I have my characters talk about these sorts of specific details just as naturally as they would talk about the weather.

Every time my characters open their mouths, they give the reader a glimpse into who they are. Comfort tells us how to behave at a funeral,

and you get a sense of her. Ruby reads the dictionary out loud to her chickens. John Henry tells his friend, "I wanted to swim in that pool! I want to do everything you can do!" and we know how angry he is — we don't have to be told. There is an energy in dialogue that pushes the story forward and hooks the reader.

In dialogue, characters offer up their hearts. Sometimes those hearts break. Sometimes they are angry, sometimes they are joyful, sometimes they are curious, or scared, or silly. I try to remember that every emotion has a corresponding action, and that action is often best expressed in dialogue that offers up a unique character in a specific time and place.

Deborah Wiles is the author of picture books and novels for young readers including Each Little Bird That Sings, *a National Book Award Finalist, and* Countdown, *book one of* The Sixties Trilogy: Three Novels of the 1960s for Young Readers. *She teaches and writes from Atlanta, Georgia. To find out more about Deborah Wiles, go to* www.deborahwiles.com.

Even Old People Can Sound Young

Teens don't talk like grown-ups . . . but grown-ups can talk like teens! Embrace these four guiding principals as you defy your age to create young-sounding, youth-pleasing dialogue.

Rediscovering your immaturity

Youthful dialogue uses less-sophisticated words and phrases than adult dialogue, and it spins conversations as if they revolve around the teen who's speaking (even if they don't). Remember, teens tend to be a self-absorbed lot. With this teen mindset engaged, your character would be more likely to say, "I can't stand school" than, "School is boring." He may grumble, "I can't suffer his rules any longer," instead of "The King is a cruel man." Or he may complain, "My dad never listens to me," instead of "My dad is hard to reach." The shift in focus can be subtle, but it's an important one. In Chapter 9, I talk about teen sensibility and hyperbole in narrative voice. The principles are the same for dialogue: A teen or tween talks about what *he* wants to do and how things that others do affect *him*.

Teens and tweens may also talk in exaggerations, revealing grandiose mindsets. They say "I'm a total loser" or "Everything's ruined now" or "I'll never be able to show my face" because they're still learning to put things into perspective. For teens and tweens, everything feels immediate and full of impact. Their feelings tend to be easily triggered, whereas adults have learned to buffer and blow off. (On their good days, anyway.)

The actual words spoken must be simple, too. In the narration, you usually have a little more leeway to use bigger words, and you can get spicy with verbs. But although "lounging" and "percolating" can be perfect in narrative, they'd be more convincing as "laying around" and "all bubbly" in teenspeak. Kids don't generally break out the 50-cent words in normal dialogue.

Go ahead and bust out big words and formal diction in dialogue when you want characters to mock formality, show off superior intelligence, or try to impress someone. There's a time and place for everything, including fancy talk.

Relaxing the grammar

Writing realistic, youthful dialogue often means ditching stiff, proper, grown-up delivery and embracing casual syntax instead. Some teens string their words together in a footloose fashion — and throw in a little bad grammar while they're at it. Consider: "You need to stop doing that" or "Stop running in the hall." At best, those lines are dull. There's certainly no youthfulness in them. Instead, a teen may say, "Don't be doing that" or "Quit with all the running." You may need to toss a blanket over your signed copy of *Elements of Style* before attempting this kind of anarchy, but it really will make for more natural teen dialogue.

Listening to kids talk — at the dinner table, at the mall, wherever — is a great way to study how teens put words together. Later, read your dialogue aloud to judge whether it jives with what you're hearing.

Even formal historical fiction benefits from more-relaxed syntax for the younger characters in the cast. Give them run-on sentences, dialogue that doubles back on itself, incomplete sentences, and improper grammar, as in the following examples:

Example 1

"He laughed and took the whip from my hand and said 'Run on home, Rudy,' like I wasn't already out of knickers and needed someone minding me. Gah. I swear on Mama's grave, Old Tate is the Devil hisself."

Example 2

"Nay, mistress, I would never. Not ever, I wouldn't."

Getting casual doesn't mean trying to use teen jargon, or *slang* — those informal words and made-up expressions that distinguish one generation from another. Consider this exchange between two teen boys: "Dude, that flick was sick." "I'm sayin', bro! Way killer." (Translation for fellow old fogies: "sick" is "cool," not vomitous or snotty.) These are the words of youth, yes, but they tend to call attention to themselves in written dialogue — and they easily sound contrived when usurped by adults. Also, slang will date your book ("groovy," anyone?), which is only desirable if you're writing historical or futuristic fiction. For info on slang, pop over to Chapter 16.

Ditching the fake teen accent

Too often, adults try to mimic teen speech by using italics to recreate teens' distinctive way of emphasizing: "It was *soooo* bad" or "I *so* did not want a ton of homework" or "John was a *total* pain. The *worst*." You might as well be trying to write the Southern drawl or the Texas twang. (As for filling the pages with exclamation points to convey that youthful zest, don't even get me started!!!) It's nearly impossible not to distract readers with such font shenanigans. You want your young readers focusing on what's being said, not critiquing your teen accent.

Italicized words may be a red flag that you're not doing enough with your *narrative beats,* those lines of narrative that break up your dialogue, where you should be indicating your character's body language or his actions as he talks (check out the later section "Taking breathers with beats" for details). Narrative beats can take the burden of emotion off the dialogue. The following example uses italics to convey the character's pain:

> "It was *so* bad," he said. Then he rushed from the room.

Version 2 ditches the italics and gains emotional impact by inserting violent narrative action between two lines of simply stated, relaxed dialogue:

> "It was bad." He pulled a rose from the vase and rotated it slowly in his fingers. Then he turned to the sink, jammed the rose down the garbage disposal, and hit the grinder button. "She can find another sucker," he said. He pushed past his mom and ran upstairs. The disposal was still grinding.

Of course, using one or two italicized words doesn't mean you have a problem. Just watch out when you're starting to see a handful or more. That's not emphasis; that's a crutch.

Cussing with caution

Swearing is a valid tool for writing dialogue, but because your audience is young, you must approach profanity in dialogue with caution (I call for the same caution in Chapter 9's discussion of narrative voice). Yes, real kids cuss in real life. Swear words serve as conversation fillers; they add emphasis; and they inflict shock, insult, and emotional injury, which is all very useful in real life. But dialogue isn't "real." It's a realistic representation, and representations can be manipulated to avoid profanity.

Gatekeepers are the parents, teachers, librarians, and booksellers who will put your book into their children's, students', and young customers' hands. Gatekeepers are just as wary of swear words in dialogue as they are of swear words in the narrative. The *f*-word is the *f*-word, whether it's in quotes or not.

You can usually rewrite your scene to have the character's actions convey the emphasis or inflict the damage. Characters can break things. They can punch. They can jump up and down while cheering instead of saying, "That's *f*-ing fantastic!"

When all is said and done, you're the boss of your story. If you decide that cussing in the dialogue is natural to the story and vital to the character and the moment, then that's your call to make. Profanity does show up in YA novels, usually for older readers. Just proceed with caution and a full understanding of potential potholes.

Developing an ear for teenspeak

Writers are praised as being great observers, but they're also aces at eavesdropping. Inspiration for teen dialogue is all around you if you just sit back and listen. Hang out where the kids hang out in your area and listen to how they talk to each other. But don't just study what the kids say; focus on how they say it. What verbal tactics do they use when they're arguing? Does their arguing differ from how adults would argue? Does one kid stick to the issue in dispute while the other jumps from insult to insult until something hits a nerve? Do they sit there fuming after the argument, passing the time in tense silence as they wait for their moms to pick them up? After all, storming out may not be possible if they're not drivers yet. How do they talk when they're all snuggly? Are they oddly loud then, as if they want others to pay attention to their public display of affection? Compare that to how you'd behave as an adult in the same situation. Turn yourself into a student of everyday teenspeak and actively look for hints to a kid's background, mood, and idiosyncrasies.

Do be careful as you do all this research, though. A grown-up lingering on the fringes of teendom can seem creepy. Put on some headphones with the volume off and fake rockin' out. You still may seem creepy, but at least it wouldn't be in a criminal sense.

If you're not in the mood to hang with the kids, you can find inspiration in TV shows and movies, too. Although do remember that the characters on screen are uttering dialogue written by a grown-up who's trying to sound like a kid, too.

You can find fictional dialogue worth studying in your fellow YA writers' novels. Read YAs with an ear for how those authors make their dialogue convincingly youthful. What tricks do they use? What's their dialogue tag style? How do their young characters alter their speech when talking to adult characters? The more you read strong dialogue, the better your chances of writing strong dialogue.

Exercise: Ready to do some eavesdropping? Find some teen hangouts near you. Locate the teen watering hole or plunk yourself down in the food court of the local mall. You're bound to find young people grouping there. If you're a teacher, you have your focus group right in front of you. Next passing period, listen to them chatter instead of taking roll or organizing yourself.

Version 1: Transcribe the conversation you overhear. Just type the meat of the conversation, though. Filter out the *ums* and *likes* and the social pleasantries. Stay on topic. Let your hands rest during the extraneous comments and tangents. See whether the teens ever get back on topic — they may not, which is a lesson in itself. Take home your transcribed lines, imagine a backstory for each kid who spoke, and then fill in some body language and narrative beats. Work out the obvious slang that would date this conversation and iron out the emphatic teen accent. There! You have dialogue, complete with rich surrounding narrative — and a firmer understanding of the relationship between "real" and "realistic" teen speak.

Version 2: Apply the same eavesdropping principles to one side of a phone conversation. Most teens have cell phones and are happy to talk in public so others know they have friends, so this scenario should be easy to find. Take home your transcribed lines and fill in the other end of the conversation, putting the two speakers in a setting where they can be face to face.

What the Best Dialogue Doesn't Say

Sometimes, it's not how you say something that matters; it's what you don't say at all. Dialogue in teen fiction is most natural when it leaves out all the filler that plagues real-life conversations, when it omits direct answers to questions, and when it doesn't get bogged down by backstory.

Censoring the babble

Realistic dialogue is not a transcript of real speech. Everyday speech is meandering, boring, and sometimes flat-out incoherent when typed onto a page. Seriously, it's a total mess. See for yourself. Here is everyday speech with the babble unfiltered:

> "I don't know, it's like — whatever. You know? Who really cares about tryouts? I don't. It's just the same stupid 'Oh, I'm so popular and everybody loves me' garbage every year and, like, I'm sick of it. It's just so, I don't know . . . I'm just tired. Can we go? Can we just leave? I'm so tired."

Here is the fictional dialogue version, with the Babble Censor engaged:

> "I don't know why I even bother. It's just a popularity contest. 'Oh, look, my dad drives a Mercedes, and I can shake a pom pom!' Big joy. I'm done with it. Let's go."

Strong dialogue doesn't include all the civilities of everyday conversations, either. No "Hi, how ya doing? . . . Fine. What's up? . . . Not much with me, but did you hear what happened at school today? . . . No, what?" Strong dialogue skips the niceties and gets right to the point of the exchange: "Stop with the locker. Did you hear about Jackie? Knocked up! Seriously. And it's all over school. She ran out of U.S. History crying. I'd hate to be her. Trudie's having a field day with it, though."

Dodging the question

Strong dialogue isn't afraid to leave questions unanswered. Have your characters dodge questions instead of answering them directly. Have characters talk past each other, around each other, and flat out refuse to respond. This runaround reveals characters who are preoccupied, who have something to hide, or who are trying to manipulate a person or a situation. For example:

> "Have a good day, baby." His mom kissed the top of his head before swiping a slice of his toast and heading for the door. She froze in the open doorway, toast in one hand, keys in the other. "That's weird."

"What?" Michael spooned in another mouthful of Wheaties.

"I could've sworn I parked the car in the driveway last night." Michael snapped up straight as his mom stepped onto the porch and clicked the garage door open with the key remote. "They say the memory is the first to go . . ."

In a silent flurry, Michael scrambled away from the table, grabbed his backpack, and rushed to the door. "Can't be late!"

He bolted down the steps, leaving his mom facing the empty garage. "Where . . . Oh no. You didn't. Michael, where's my car?"

But he was already rounding the corner.

"Michael! Where's my car? Come back here! Michael!"

Is Michael guilty of grand theft auto? His blatant evasiveness certainly teases that possibility. And how the heck will he return home? Mom's question will still be hanging in the air when he does. Withholding answers in your dialogue is a powerful way to build tension, enrich conflict, and wreak havoc with the plot in truly wonderful ways.

Avoiding info dumps

Strong dialogue doesn't dump info like some load in the road for readers to scale if they're committed to their journey. That is "telling" instead of "showing," and it can be a fatal roadblock in your story. Young readers want (and need) information, but they don't want to run up against a solid wall of it.

Instead, reveal backstory and plot information in small bits, without dumping. Try delivering it in an exchange. For example:

"Joe, stop. Give me a look at that eye. Your dad did that to you?"

He swatted her hand away. "You act like that's something new. Heck, he knocked out five of my teeth before kindergarten. Here, hold this." She juggled the hot dog he shoved at her. "Taxi!"

A lot happens in this little snippet. You get a glimpse at this character's backstory before he shuts readers down by cutting away to the taxi, a move that pushes the story forward even as readers try to imagine a past as abusive as he suggests. It may take many pages, many scenes, or many chapters before Joe gives readers a deeper look at his traumatic past. Such patient storytelling is far more intriguing than a block of text with Joe explaining that his dad always hits him, has since he was little, that it makes him sad but what's the use in talking about it, that none of the teachers he's told in the past have done anything, and so on. My quick exchange of dialogue covers all that clearly and richly. It's dynamic, leaving room for questions and unfinished business, so you know this is going to play out in the story ahead.

Using summarized dialogue

Sometimes conversations need to happen between characters, but readers don't need to hear those conversations — when two characters make plans to meet up later, for example, or when a parent tells a kid to do his chores. Those exchanges may take care of necessary business, but they aren't interesting to read. You can summarize dialogue in the case of mundane exchanges, when things are repeated so often that readers don't need to hear them again, or when you just need to keep the pace moving and a conversation would bog you down. Check this out:

> Mom was tinkering in the kitchen when I bolted past with my car keys. "I'm going to Mark's house."
>
> "You need to put away your clothes first."
>
> "I did put them away."

> "Shoving them under your bed doesn't count. Go put them away *in the closet.*"
>
> "Aw, shoot. Fine. But then I'm going to Mark's."

Now for the summarized version:

> I almost made it out on the first try. Mom stopped me at the door, though, with orders to put my clothes away. I tried to tell her I'd already done it, but she said shoving them under my bed didn't count. It was another ten minutes before I was on the road. Who knew if Mark would still be there?

Although summarizing dialogue may seem to go against the *show, don't tell* rule, it's preferable to boring a reader or slowing the story. Just be sure you're not summarizing dialogue that furthers the story, adds tension and/or emotion, or escalates conflict. That's what dialogue is for!

Don't linger on the past. Instead, mention it and then show that past informing the present. Keep touching on the past, drawing it out more and more through the book until it's all finally revealed and the character has had his say. The result is a satisfying read across the full novel.

Info dump alert! If your characters say, "As you know" or "Like I told you" or "Remember?" you're probably telling with your dialogue.

Getting the Balance Right: Dialogue and Narrative

Strong dialogue doesn't stand alone — what you do with the narrative surrounding it determines whether it hits a homer or languishes in the on-deck circle, forever swinging but never connecting. In this section, you team up your dialogue with narrative beats that inject rhythm and emotion, with action that enhances rather than just moves, and with white space that punches up the drama while giving young readers the room they need to kick back and enjoy the story.

Taking breathers with beats

In real-life conversations, speakers stop now and then to breathe. They give their words a moment to sink in, or they pause to add dramatic emphasis, or they need to physically move, perhaps smooching their sweetie or devoting brief but full-bodied attention to a hairpin turn in a racing video game. Authentic written dialogue does the same thing in moments called *narrative beats*. Here's a patch of dialogue with the narrative beats italicized:

> "Want this?" *I held up my half-eaten burger. Ricardo wasn't the kind of guy to get all weirded out about spit. Food was food.*
> "Nah," *he said.* "I'm on a diet."
> "What diet?"
> "It's called the seafood diet." *Suddenly he grinned.* "I *see* food, I eat it!" *He grabbed my burger and bit off half in one bite.*
> *Clearly, I wasn't the kind of guy to get all weirded out about dorkiness. A friend was a friend.*
> Life at Horace Walker Middle School wasn't a place to be picky about friends. Fact was, I was lucky if I made it through the week without being locked in my own locker, or stuffed in the cafeteria trash can, or locked in the janitorial supply closet. Friends didn't come easy there, so I took what I could get. And Ricardo was what I could get.
> "Here," *I told him,* "might as well have my fries, too."

Beats are the bits of narrative that surround the dialogue, supporting it or expanding on it some way. The *dialogue tags* (the "he said/she said" stuff) count as beats because they illuminate who is speaking and sometimes how. The paragraph of narration that isn't italicized in this example qualifies as *exposition,* being separate from the act of speaking. It's as if the narrative steps away from the conversation for a moment to address the story in a larger way. Don't worry — there won't be a test on this difference. The point is that you realize how narrative beats work in tandem with the spoken words to create strong, revealing dialogue. What I hope you also see in that example is that effective beats contribute rhythm to a written conversation.

Rhythm is part of what makes dialogue sound natural to the ear, and a big part of rhythm is variety. As with every other element of fiction writing, you want the craft to be invisible so readers can sink into the story. So when you work beats into the rhythm of the conversation, construct the beats in a variety of ways so they'll blend in.

Here's an example that lacks variety, depending too heavily on dialogue tags with clauses tacked on. It suffers from a distracting staccato quality as a result:

> "You! Stop there!" a voice called out as I reached the halfway point in the tunnel.
>
> "I'm not going back!" I shouted as I increased my pace down the dark corridor.
>
> "Stop! Now!" the voice called out again, getting closer.
>
> "I'm not giving up now," I muttered, breaking into a run.
>
> "Stop, or I'll shoot!" the voice repeated as it closed in.

Here's a more active and varied version:

> "You! Stop there!" a voice called out as I reached the halfway point in the tunnel.
>
> I increased my pace. "I'm not going back," I shouted. The gypsy had said the side tunnel was about here, and finding it meant freedom. It was so dark, though. I put my hands out to feel the wall as I stumbled forward.
>
> "Stop!" The voice was getting closer.
>
> I broke into a run.
>
> That's when I heard the click of the gun.

Adding variety to the narrative beats gives the second passage great rhythm and opens up opportunities for creating tension and generating emotion (more on those points in the next two sections). The result feels more like a fleshed out scene than simply a verbal exchange between an escapee and his pursuer.

Making the action count

Narrative beats offer wonderful opportunities to enhance the dialogue and the overall story, yet too often writers fill them with dud action. Characters brush hair from their eyes, for example, or they turn to look at the other speaker. Sure, technically that's action, but it's innocuous. You want action that takes its job seriously, revealing, illuminating, deliberately undermining, and pushing characters into action.

The action in a beat can add information to the scene, as in the preceding example of the prisoner fleeing down the dark corridor. Or it can tell readers what inflection to give a line of dialogue, taking the pressure off the dialogue to provide all the emotional context. Check out this example:

> Beth looked at him. "I want to go, too."

You don't know how to read this, do you? Is Beth whiny? Is she desperate? Is she resigned or hostile? There aren't any clues in the action I've tucked into that narrative beat. You may be tempted to solve this by using italics to add emotion, as in the following version, but that's melodramatic and wholly unnatural. It puts all the pressure on the dialogue to convey the girl's desperation.

> Beth looked at him. "I *really* want to go."

This next version incorporates revealing physical action into the narrative beat, taking the pressure off the dialogue and giving readers insight into Beth's determination:

> Beth darted ahead of him and blocked the doorway. "You're not leaving without me."

Let the word *look* be a red flag for you. It's a legitimate verb, yes, but using it can easily become a habit in narrative beats, causing you to miss opportunities to contribute to the plot or the characterization. You'd be surprised how often characters are looking or staring or smiling or frowning in manuscripts submitted to publishers.

The Stop Looking Test calls out action words you should *not* be using in your narrative beats and reveals a tendency toward generic actions in your beats. You apply the test by counting the number of times you use specific words. You can use a text counting program (found online) to do a merciless word count and see what tops your list besides *the* and *that,* or you can pick some of the common baddies and search for them in your manuscript with your word-processing program's find-and-replace feature. Here's a list of generic verbs that crop up in narrative beats with surprising frequency:

look	smile	stare	gaze
frown	laugh	turn (to)	feel
mean	thought	sat	stood

Or perhaps you have pet nouns and phrases, such as "fresh breeze" in a story involving sailing. A word-counting program can reveal those pets.

Skeptical that a word count can reveal anything useful about something as subjective as dialogue? Let me tell you about a writer friend of mine, whom I'll call Stewy (hey, I like the name). I had Stewy put the first draft of his YA manuscript to the Stop Looking Test — which revealed that he'd used the word *look* 398 times. His manuscript was only 352 pages. Stewy also found that he'd used the word *face* 121 times, *glance* 118 times, *smile* 83 times, *nodded* 82 times, *turned to* 82 times, *scowl* 32 times, *frown* 17 times, and, because he was writing an epic fantasy in a formal voice, *visage* and *countenance* 5 times each. Clearly, Stewy was trying to add action and narrative beats to the characters' conversations, but as this test reveals, he needed to learn that conversations are about more than the expressions on the participants' faces. He also had a tendency to nudge the dialogue along by having characters repeat or rephrase what others just said, as in, "Wait. What do you mean, *evil?* How is he evil?" The Stop Looking Test revealed that he used the phrase *What do you mean?* 12 times, *What are you saying?* 3 times, and *wait* 9 times. That's heavy-handed information delivery, a no-no I address earlier in this chapter.

This test was a major turning point for Stewy. Addressing nothing else but his dialogue and its supporting beats in his revision, he took the next draft of his manuscript to an entirely new level. In fact, I'm proud to say that a signed copy of that fantasy, Stewy's publishing debut, occupies a place of honor on my bookshelf.

He said, she said: Doling out dialogue tags

Dialogue tags, also called *attributives,* are signposts that tell your readers which character is speaking during a conversation. Strong dialogue wields its tags in a low-key manner, with the effect of pointing its finger instead of smacking readers upside the head. That means, most of the time, sticking to the old standby "said": He said . . . she said . . . Tommy said . . . the scary man in the double-knit cardigan said. "Said" has earned its keep in fiction, being a soft word that readers' eyes can slide over, letting them register the speaker's identity without being distracted from the dialogue itself.

You may be tempted to declare "said" boring and go for more active attributives, such as *uttered* or *bemoaned.* Indeed, those are active verbs, but they're also distracting. Leave information about mood or the manner of delivery to the exposition in the narrative beat or to the dialogue itself.

Here are a few other tips for choosing your tags:

- **Be judicious.** You don't have to ban all non-*said* attributives, but if you do stray from the old standby, do so only occasionally. *Replied* and *asked* are common, slidable words, as are *cried* and *shouted,* but don't go crazy. Keep the list minimal.

- **Use speaking verbs.** You can't *smile* a line of dialogue. Nor can you *laugh* it. You certainly can't *guffaw* it. And there's no way to *hiss* dialogue that contains no *s*'s. If you're going to use tags other than *said,* stay in the realm of the possible.

- **Lay off the adverbs.** Adverbs such as *quickly, angrily*, and the like tend to hang out with attributives. Those *adverbs* — words that describe how a line of dialogue is delivered — defeat the purpose of all your hard work in crafting emotive dialogue and action in the narrative beat. Adverbs are "telling," and as such, they're functional but not engaging.

- **Purge unnecessary tags.** A manuscript crammed with "he said/she said" can feel choppy, so purge some. The rhythm will get a boost when you omit some dialogue tags entirely and replace them with narrative beats that clarify who's speaking. Check this out:

  > Hector stopped his ascent when his hands reached the top rung. The ladder swayed but didn't slip. His eyes were just above the roofline. "You're not going to watch from up here, are you?" he said.

"Best view in the house," Constance replied. "C'mon. It's like you're right there in the sky with the fireworks."

"That's what I'm afraid of," Hector said.

"Not everything is life and death, you know," she said.

"Maybe not," he said. "But I'm going to live long enough to tell you which things are. Come get me when the fireworks are over. I'll be under my bed." Then he climbed down, slowly, rung by excruciating rung.

Now here it is with some of the tags replaced by narrative beats:

Hector stopped his ascent when his hands reached the top rung. The ladder swayed but didn't slip. His eyes were just above the roofline. "You're not going to watch from up here, are you?" he said.

"Best view in the house." Constance patted the roof shingle next to her. "C'mon. It's like being right there in the sky with the fireworks."

"That's what I'm afraid of."

"Ay dios mio, Hector. Not everything is life and death."

"Maybe not." He chanced a look at the loose gravel below the ladder. "But I'm going to live long enough to tell you which things are. Come get me when the fireworks are over. I'll be under my bed." Then he climbed down, slowly, rung by excruciating rung.

The result is a smoother telling that uses body language and prop manipulation to let readers know who's speaking. This enriches the characters and overall storytelling. To aid in identifying the speakers during the tagless back-and-forth in the middle, I've added Hector's name to Constance's dialogue. This kind of name-calling is a useful trick, but go easy on it. Using character names within dialogue is okay now and then, but it can sound stilted when you do it too often.

✔ **Don't tack on phrases all the time.** Consider the following:

"I'm gonna catch you," he said, running to his left.

"No you won't," she cried, jumping over a rock.

"Watch me," he shouted, dodging behind a tree.

"Yuck!" your readers will say. (No, that one they'll *bemoan*. Most definitely.)

Welcoming teens with white space

You can enhance dialogue by what you *don't* surround it with. *White space* is that empty space surrounding the letters, words, paragraphs, and images on a page, and it's important to YA writers because kids regard this visual elbow room with a sense of relief. Pages with long text blocks and minimal white space can intimidate the heck out of young readers, but you can welcome teens in with plenty of white space.

Teenagers (and adults for that matter) are known to make book purchases based on a quick thumbing of the book in the store. They're gauging the amount of white space and dialogue in the book.

Publishers are conscious of the white-space factor and so design young adult fiction with wide margins and large, roomy fonts whenever possible. You can do your part by using more and shorter passages of dialogue to increase white space. Or when you're feeling especially manipulative, you can increase your paragraphing (that is, the frequency with which you cut away from one paragraph to start another) to create shorter blocks of text, more empty indents at the beginning of paragraphs, and more empty blips where paragraphs end before reaching the right-side margin.

You have more freedom with paragraphing than you probably think. The only "rule" is that you should break to a new paragraph when you move on to another idea, but that's only applicable for nonfiction books, anyway. In fiction, where you're telling a story rather than organizing facts, the paragraphing is an element of the storytelling, and you can do whatever the heck you want to do with it.

You can cut away for dramatic impact, for instance.

Or to make a point.

Or to increase the pace.

Or, heck, for the simple rhythmic joy of it.

Paragraphing is a storytelling tool that goes far beyond white-space manipulation. Here are some tips for paragraphing your YA fiction, with the needs of young readers front and center:

- ✔ White space is very welcoming to kids, so start a new paragraph when the one you're writing seems long. Older teens are more tolerant of long paragraphs, but don't get carried away. Even grown-ups like their white space.
- ✔ To increase your pace, use a succession of short paragraphs.
- ✔ Want to shift your point of view from one character to another? Start a new paragraph.
- ✔ Start a new paragraph when you move on to a new action, incident, phase in the scene, or featured character.
- ✔ Give every new speaker in a conversation a new paragraph.

Sometimes authors allow characters a long turn to talk. Perhaps the character is telling a story and the other characters are listening with rapt attention and zero interest in interrupting the flow. If you try this, consider chopping up the long hunk of dialogue into several small paragraphs to make it more welcoming to youngsters. When the speaker doesn't change, each new paragraph of dialogue has opening quotes, but the line preceding it doesn't have closing quotes. Save the closing quotes for the absolute end of that speaking turn. I must warn you, though, that a long speaking turn isn't kid-friendly. Consider cutting away from a long speech for a narrative moment — such as action, or setting observations, or dialogue from another character that encourages the long talker to go on. Then go back to him and give him the rest of his turn.

And here are a couple of paragraph formatting tips (consider this a preview of my submission formatting advice in Chapter 13):

- ✔ Don't add an extra line space between paragraphs in your manuscript. Those between-paragraph spaces may be the norm in blogs and Internet articles, but they're not acceptable in fiction manuscripts. They drive editors nuts. (Yes, I know this very book uses extra line spaces between paragraphs. I can't help that — the *For Dummies* designers are a stubborn lot. Something about "a consistent look for all the books in the series," blah, blah, blah . . . I'll justify the extra line space in this book by saying how-to books follow different rules than fiction, but you know the real reason.)

- ✔ While I'm talking formatting, indent the first line of every new paragraph. Five character spaces is the generally accepted depth of an indent — which is what you usually get when you hit the tab button on your keyboard. Adjust the tab settings in your word-processing program if it doesn't do this automatically or if the spacing seems uncomfortably long or too short to be easily noted by scanning eyes.

Weighing your balance of dialogue and narrative

Satisfying teen fiction establishes a balance between the dialogue and narration. If you have too much dialogue, the burden of conveying emotion falls too heavily upon the spoken words. If you have too much narrative, you risk turning off those young readers who thumb through the books with an eye for white space and dialogue. Yet again, the YA author must walk the line between the story's needs and the needs of young readers.

Gauging the effectiveness of the balance

Judging whether you've achieved a balance between dialogue and narrative isn't a matter of counting the words between quotation marks; it's a matter of weighing the effectiveness of dialogue and narration as a unit. As long as you engage your readers, it doesn't matter if you have far more narrative than dialogue. Trouble lurks in blocks of overly descriptive narrative that lack tension and sit on the page like big lumps.

Strong dialogue is as much about the exposition that surrounds it as it is about the talking, so even if your text includes a lot of narration, you may have more conversing going on than you thought at first glance. Here are two books that include a lot of narration to good effect:

- ✔ **The Book Thief:** Markus Zusak's *The Book Thief*, targeted to ages 12 and up, is almost 600 pages, with probably two-thirds of each page being narration rather than dialogue. This setup may intimidate younger readers, who tend to feel comfortable seeing white space and dialogue on their pages. The thing is, *The Book Thief* has a lot of friendly white space thanks to frequent paragraphing, and its conversational narration makes even the narrative bits feel like dialogue, establishing a satisfying balance.

- ✔ **The Hunger Games:** Suzanne Collins's *The Hunger Games* is skewed even more heavily away from dialogue, which makes sense considering her teen lead spends much of that book avoiding people (a wholly understandable impulse since those other characters would rather stab her in the throat than chat about the weather). The paragraphing, abundant action, and tension make that book's dialogue/narrative balance satisfying.

The reverse, a book that's two-thirds dialogue on each page, can feel balanced if the narrative that does appear offers dynamic and revealing actions that challenge readers — perhaps deliberately contradicting the spoken words or teasing about feelings that the speaking character is trying to hide. Narrative should somehow add subtext or additional tension to the story.

Exercise: Start with Dialogue

In this exercise, you build a scene from nothing but spoken words. Follow these steps:

1. **Write a conversation with just the dialogue, letting the words unfold naturally.**

   Don't try to inject emotion or tension into the words. Just let the characters utter what needs to be uttered. Don't even add dialogue tags. Consider this a stream-of-conscious writing moment.

2. **Add narrative.**

   Go back and underscore the emotion with body language and physical actions, taking the setting and props into account to reveal mood (as I discuss in Chapter 8).

3. **Insert dialogue tags.**

   Go back and insert dialogue tags where you feel like you need a narrative beat for rhythm or where you see more than three lines of back-and-forth dialogue that has no surrounding narrative. Readers need clarification regarding who is talking so they don't lose track.

Now you have a full scene that should be evenly balanced.

Doing a Little Mind Reading: Direct Thoughts

When you want to give young readers insight into your protagonist's state of mind without revealing those details to other characters in a conversation, you write the protagonist's thoughts as if he's talking to himself. This is called a *direct thought*. It helps to think of direct thoughts (sometimes called *interior monologue* or *internal dialogue*) as those comments that sit on the tip of your character's tongue without actually being uttered:

> I picked up the recipe and read the next ingredient: coconut. *Over my dead body.* I trashed the recipe and then stirred more vanilla into the batter. Coconut should've been outlawed by the Geneva Convention.

The last line in this example isn't italicized because although it's an opinion that certainly reveals the character's mindset, it isn't internal dialogue that's one lip shy of spoken. This is called an *indirect thought* because it doesn't offer the direct wording of the thought.

A direct thought is a form of dialogue (hence the *internal dialogue* moniker) that's not surrounded by quotation marks. Those are saved for spoken dialogue. It's totally your call whether you set direct thoughts in roman font or italics. That said, they're usually italicized in YA fiction as a handy visual cue for young readers. You can omit the speaker attribution if you go with italics. Thus,

> Aslon hefted his sword. *Too heavy*, he thought. He laid it back down.

becomes

> Aslon hefted the sword. *Too heavy.* He laid it back down.

Most of the time, the fewer words, the better. There's no formal ruling on the italics, though. An alternative style forsakes italics altogether and assigns a dialogue tag:

> This is going nowhere, he thought.

You don't need the tag for direct thoughts if you use italics, but if you think a tag is necessary for a rhythmic beat, by all means include it. Note that just like spoken dialogue, direct thoughts are written in present tense even when the rest of the book is written in past tense.

Sometimes writers run into problems trying to distinguish between direct and indirect thoughts in a first-person narrative. Think of indirect thoughts as "narrative insights" rather than direct transcriptions of the thought. I've italicized the direct thoughts here, with the roman parts being indirect thoughts:

- ✔ **First person:** The new kid gave me the creeps. *Not on my watch, buddy.*

- ✔ **Third-person limited:** The new kid gave her the creeps. *Not on my watch, buddy.*

- ✔ **Omniscient:** The new kid gave her the creeps. She couldn't imagine who he thought he was, coming in there like he owned the place. *Not on my watch, buddy.*

Feel like you're doing some mind reading? Good. That's what direct thoughts offer readers: a chance to read the character's mind. If only you could do that in real life.

Part III
Editing, Revising, and Formatting Your Manuscript

The 5th Wave   By Rich Tennant

"The margins on your book proposal are sooo even, Ms. Holly, and the type so black and crisp. I'm sure whatever the book's about is also good, but with centered headlines and flush-left columns like this, we'd be fools not to publish it!"

In this part . . .

Y ou've completed draft one of your young adult novel. Now what? Draft two!

Oh, stop with the groaning. Revision is important — it's how you take your manuscript to the next level, where you tweak it and buff it and shine it up like a new penny, making all that hard work on draft one worth it. Finding the shine may take two drafts, or it may take four, but as every successful writer can tell you, it will definitely take more than one. This part is all about the revision process — what you can do on your own, when to call in the cavalry, and how to clean the whole thing up for submission to agents and editors.

Chapter 11

Editing and Revising with Confidence

In This Chapter

▶ Evaluating your own manuscript

▶ Seeking outside input and weighing criticism

▶ Revising constructively and fearlessly

• •

*E*xpect to write several drafts of your YA fiction. That's part of the writing process. And expect your first draft to be as homely as a mud fence. That's part of the process, too. In its early stages, creativity is messy. Even celebrated masters churn out frightful first drafts that barely resemble their final, polished gems.

This reality can be discouraging, I know, but take heart. Ungainly early drafts don't mean you've ruined your great concept. Rather, they mean you took the first step in turning that concept into a strong story. The manuscript will evolve. This chapter is about that evaluation process and the rewriting that results. I tell you how to assess your story through a combination of self-editing and outside critiques, and then I explain how to formulate a specific revision plan and act on it with confidence.

Self-Editing, Where Every Revision Begins

You can't rewrite, or *revise,* your manuscript until you know what specifically needs revising — and you can't know that until you've analyzed your finished manuscript and then brainstormed ways to improve its weaknesses and enhance its strengths. Even if you plan to have others read and respond to your finished draft, you need to self-edit the manuscript first. The time to show your manuscript to others is when you can't see obvious changes anymore.

The read-through: Shifting your mindset from writing to editing

Effective self-editing requires as much objectivity about your manuscript as you can muster. That means doffing your writer's cap and donning your reader's beanie so you can read your manuscript as an outsider would. Here are some tips for making that switch:

- **Set aside your manuscript for a while.** The length of that "while" is your call. Some writers feel they can come at a story with fresh eyes after a couple of weeks. Others need a couple of months to feel like they're outside the story instead of immersed within it.

- **Mimic the book-reading experience.** Get as close to a printed-book feel as possible. Print out your manuscript (double-spaced to leave room for notes), punch holes in the side, and mount it in a three-ring binder. Heck, get the manuscript spiral-, strip-, or comb-bound at your local copy shop.

  If you're tech-savvy, you may be inclined to read your manuscript on an e-reader or PDA, which lets you upload your files, insert highlights and notes in the text, and then export the notes as a text file on your computer. Resist this urge. Get away from screen-reading altogether so your reading experience is completely different from your writing experience. Coming at your manuscript with a fresh eye is difficult, so give yourself as much help as you can.

- **Read the manuscript someplace comfy but unfamiliar.** If you've trained yourself to want to write as soon as you step into your writing space, being an objective reader there will be tough. Get out of your writing space when you self-edit. Go someplace entirely different. Imagine you have a full tank of gas, a several-hour block of time, and a brand-new hardcover from your favorite YA author. Where would you go to lose yourself in that special book?

- **Read and make notes but don't rewrite yet.** If you stop and try to rewrite during this phase, you lose your chance to evaluate the overall pacing. Just mark problem places in the margins as you read, circle things that catch your eye, and jot down a list of tasks as they occur to you, general or specific: "work on dialogue; feels stiff overall," "boring exchange; move characters outside the house and have others interrupt," "give Lucy a backpack." For tips on what to look for, see the following sections. A double-spaced manuscript has ample room for line-specific notes, and you can make the general notes in your handy-dandy writing notebook. (More on keeping a master writing notebook in Chapter 3.)

When you're ready to start making changes, go through your notes to prioritize the items and then formulate your plan of attack.

Create a *revision list* that you can work through item by item during several different passes through the manuscript. Prioritize your revision list so that big-picture items (such as character, plot, and setting work) are first, followed by smaller items (such as language tweaks). You want to start big and finish small to avoid revising specific sentences that may be completely omitted when you fix a bigger problem. For more info on rewriting, see the later section "Revising with Confidence."

Self-editing checklist

When you report to your comfy but unfamiliar reading space, refer to this self-editing checklist. The following questions help you determine not only where the story needs improvement but also what those weaknesses indicate craftwise so you can strategize ways to address them. Look back into the craft chapters of this book (Part II) for ways to improve what you find lacking in any of these areas:

✔ **Characters:** Is your protagonist empowered with the resolution of her own problem? Does her core strength overcome her key flaw to influence this outcome? Does she demonstrate that she has what it takes to prevail? Your protagonist has a story to carry, so make sure you can answer "yes" to all these questions.

Do you write against stereotype or offer surprising traits in your secondary characters? Does your bad guy have strengths and ambitions, too? These elements make your supporting cast as rich and interesting as your lead character.

What youthful traits have you given your characters? Are your teen/tween characters grandiose and self-centered enough? Do you rely too heavily on statements to reveal your characters, or do you work in plenty of prop manipulations?

✔ **Plot:** Pay attention to the following elements of plot:

- **Opening:** Do you start in the midst of action that reveals something about your protagonist's predicament, personality, and dreams?

- **General:** Does each scene in each chapter contribute to the chapter's overall goal? Can you cut any scenes? Do you need another scene? Does each obstacle push the plot and characters further?

 Is the power in the teen protagonist's hands and not an adult's? Is the protagonist's epiphany clear and powerful enough? Has the protagonist made enough of a change?

 Have you foreshadowed all surprises and resolved all subplots?

- **Tension and pacing:** Does your mind wander during the reading? Where? Is enough at stake then? Are the consequences of failure dire enough? Are there rich moments of teen drama as the tension increases? Do you force your character far enough out of his comfort zone during crucial moments?

  How much white space do you have? Are your paragraphs large, or do you break them frequently, creating lots of little paragraphs? Have you employed paragraphing and spacing techniques to affect the pace at desired moments?

- **Info dumps:** Do any of your characters use phrases that indicate telling instead of showing ("as you know" or "like I told you" or "remember?")? How much backstory made it into the book? Can you trim any of it?

  Have you included too much minutiae in the actions? Are you reporting characters' moods and motivations instead of letting readers deduce them from character behavior?

✔ **Setting:** Have you let your setting influence what characters say and how they act in each scene? Have you found any slow scenes that may benefit from a new location? Is there enough variety in your locations?

Do the characters interact with props in every scene? Can you specify what that interaction reveals? Do you see opportunities to substitute more-revealing prop interactions?

Does the main character have a retreat? What would happen if you didn't let him go there?

Have you invoked at least three physical senses in each chapter? If there are descriptive passages longer than three or four sentences, can you trim them? Do you need to create more of a sense of place in the revision?

✔ **Narrative voice:** How many 50-cent words does the narrator use? Is that the right amount for your audience? Is it the appropriate amount for your narrator and your narrative style?

If you have a young narrator, is his syntax deliberately improper when appropriate? Does the narrator exaggerate as a teen would? Have you struck a distinct teen tone? Circle and replace all clichés.

Are the narrator's observations youthful enough? Does your point-of-view character have access to all the information he needs to tell the story?

✔ **Language mechanics:** Do you use contractions to add youth to and relax the voice? How about loose grammar? Has too much slang slipped in? Are you overmodifying with too many adverbs and adjectives?

Do you use active, evocative verbs? Can you identify any instances of passive voice? Do you frequently attach action phrases that start with the word *as* to your dialogue tags, making them long and unwieldy?

Are your paragraphs overburdened with commas, semicolons, and dashes, or do the paragraphs incorporate enough simple, brief, and direct sentences? Do the sentences within each paragraph begin the same way, or do you vary them? Do any sentences meander? Do you repeat yourself? Are you going on and on about anything?

✔ **Dialogue:** Does your dialogue work with the narrative around it to characterize and to convey plot developments? Is your dialogue plagued by too much fact-delivery and plot work? Does your dialogue reveal things about the characters? What does it reveal?

Do you let your characters talk past each other or evade questions, creating a more realistic feel? Do your characters blurt things out now and then, getting themselves deeper in trouble? Do they interrupt, fragment, and trail off to create variety, tension, and drama? Do you let characters get upset with each other, or do they play it safe by avoiding confrontation? Do the teens talk about themselves and how everything affects them?

Is your dialogue all statements, or do your characters sometimes talk in questions for variety? Is your dialogue filled with slang that will adversely date your story?

Do you have generic actions between bits of dialogue, or do you present rich sensory moments instead? Does every line of dialogue have a dialogue tag? Do none? Or have you created rhythm by balancing dialogue tags and narrative beats that make the speaker's identity, actions, and moods clear without a speaking verb?

Double-check your word count. Although there's no law about how many words can be in a novel for young readers, middle grade fiction typically falls between 25,000 and 45,000 words, and teen fiction hovers between 40,000 and 60,000. If you're significantly over the range for your category, try to cut scenes or tighten your wording. If you're significantly under the word count, look for opportunities to productively and positively expand the story, such as adding character-building and plot-forwarding scenes, adding more dialogue and white space, or expanding the sense of place. Ultimately, a story takes as long as it takes to be told, word count be damned. Consider Karen Cushman's Newbery Medal–winning middle grade novel *The Midwife's Apprentice*, which has just 22,000 words. Don't put yourself in the position of defending an unusual word count unless you're sure it's the final word count for you.

Calling in the Posse: The Give and Take of Critiquing

When you can no longer see obvious weaknesses in your manuscript, that's the time to call in the posse for a critique. A *critique* is a critical evaluation of your manuscript — concept, target audience, character, plot, voice, setting, word choice . . . the whole shebang. Find out whether others agree that you've done everything you intended to do with the story. You'd be wise to get at least one critique, if not a handful from a variety of sources, because others can see what you've become blind to in your self-editing.

Critiques can come from agents and editors at conferences, from freelance editors, from your buddies in the writing trenches, and from young readers. I leave the conference critiques for Chapter 18 because they're an integral part of the conference experience. Here, you get the skinny on the freelancers, fellow writers, and teens.

You have the right to privately accept or reject any comment made about your manuscript, be it from a critique group member, a paid freelance editor, a publishing editor or agent at a conference, a well-intentioned friend or sweetheart, or a real, honest-to-goodness young reader. At times, the feedback may not apply because it reflects personal preferences and styles. Use several critique sources (including, yes, rejection letters if those are involved) to see whether common items keep cropping up. Those are red flags that you have areas in need of attention.

Participating in a critique group

A great way to get that vital extra pair of eyes on your manuscript is to take part in a YA-fiction *critique group*. You share your manuscript (in part or in full) with other YA writers who agree to critique your story's effectiveness for your target audience and your writing in general, and then you reciprocate by critiquing their manuscripts. (Chapter 2 helps you identify your target audience based on age, gender, and genre.)

Every critique group has its own way of operating. You can meet in person for a read-and-critique *(R&C)* session wherein everyone reads and responds to portions of the manuscript on the spot (this version works best with excerpts of ten pages or less). Or you can attach your manuscript to an e-mail and send that to your group, with the reviewers replying via e-mail for all to see or embedding their comments within the manuscript and then sending it back to you. Or you can post your manuscript in a private online chat group, letting the other members post their responses for the entire group to consider and build upon.

Your group may have regular, scheduled critique sessions, or you may opt for a more open format, with each member submitting material for critique whenever she feels she needs it. I know some writers who share only complete drafts when those are ready, limiting their critique commitments while still enjoying the benefits of outside input.

Whether you join an established group or create your own crew, your critique group should reflect your style of working, your time constraints, and your specific writing needs. In this section, I give advice on finding a group and on giving and receiving feedback.

Finding other writers

You can join an established critique group, or you can form one of your own. I give advice on both in this section.

Joining an established group

Joining a critique group that's been in operation for a while lets you get in with people who've already worked out the kinks of how a critique group works. You can tap in to established groups in a number of ways:

- ✓ **Asking writers you've met:** As you network with other YA-fiction writers at conferences or in your local writers' group meetings, you may hit it off with others who share your tastes and personality. Ask these writers whether their critique groups have openings or are looking to expand.

- ✓ **Checking online writers' forums:** Online writers' forums provide opportunities for joining established critique groups, either by developing relationships with members in the forum or through a formalized critique program.

- ✓ **Doing an online search:** Type "YA critique group" in your search engine and narrow down your choices from there, looking for regions, genres, and group styles that work for you.

Forming your own group

Before you approach anyone about starting a new critique group, have a good idea of the kind of group you want. Do you want to limit the group to your genre or to just middle grade fiction or just teen fiction, or do you want to keep it open to all young adult fiction, any genre? Do you want to meet in person and do on-the-spot critiques, or do you prefer your dealings to be online? Your preferences determine whom you invite into the group, and the potential members get to judge the style and demands of the group before they commit.

To recruit critique group members, make it a point to meet as many writers as you can at conferences and chapter meetings. Find out who's writing what and get a feel for their interests and ability to critique others' works. If you can, find at least one writer who is ahead of you — someone who can mentor you and offer advice — and develop a friendship. But be sincere and willing to give, too. Successful long-term critique relationships are built on trust and mutual interest.

You can also post online to search for group members, contacting your local writers' group or posting notice in your online writers' forum.

I don't recommend going beyond six members for your group. That's a lot of reading and critiquing for everyone to do on top of their own writing and non-writing life stuff. If you'd like to work with just one or two trusted critique buddies, that's fine. When you have as many members as you want, finalize the rules so everyone's clear about the who, what, where, and when.

Not everyone will be exactly at your skill level or slightly above you. That doesn't mean less-skilled writers can't help you hone your craft and whip your manuscript into shape. These writers can give valuable critique insights, and you benefit from helping others improve.

Doing critiques

The most useful critiques come from prepared material and prepared critiquers. Critiquing is very useful, but it's also fraught with challenges, such as being clear, being constructive rather than just opinionated, and delivering commentary with tact. When the time comes for actual critiquing, you need to know how to process the feedback you get as well as how to offer feedback to others in as useful a manner as possible. This section covers the successful give-and-take of critiquing.

Getting a critique

Here are some helpful hints for receiving a critique:

- **Make sure the draft you turn in for the critique is as polished as possible.** Typos and obvious grammar atrocities distract your readers and can affect the content of their comments.

- **Identify and share your own issues.** If you have a specific concern about the material you're sharing with the group, ask the members up front to pay attention to that area as they read. Or if you prefer to test the severity of the weakness by seeing whether readers notice the problem on their own, make sure you ask about it after they share their feedback. They may know ways to enhance that aspect of the manuscript so you won't ever have to worry about it again. Don't simply walk out of the session wiping your brow in relief that no one noticed the weakness. Critiquing isn't about getting a thumbs-up; it's about making you a better writer.

- **Ask questions to clarify the feedback.** The most constructive critiques are those that are specific enough for you to act on. If a critique is too general or unclear, seek more information. Make sure you understand as exactly as possible what the beef is so you can understand as exactly as possible how to address it in revision. "I didn't like that character" is unclear. What turned the reader off? "I didn't like how that character always avoided conflict" gives you something to mull over and to act on (if you agree with the assessment).

- **Don't complain or defend yourself when someone criticizes your work.** Remember, for a critique to be useful to you, you must have an open mind. If you don't agree with a critique or you think it's overly harsh, consider your piece from the critic's point of view. Remember that your group is trying to help you develop and hone your writing skills.

✔ **Don't take it personally.** Try to be thick-skinned and to separate yourself from your work as much as possible. A critique isn't about you as a person. Don't tie your self-worth up with your writing. And remember that critiquing is subjective. What one person thinks is terrible, another thinks divine.

✔ **Be gracious.** It's a pretty safe bet that your critique group is trying to help. Thank them for giving you something to think about. You don't have to announce your decision to act on the input. Just do or don't act.

You may encounter people who really can't give useful insight. If you feel you aren't getting beneficial input or aren't clicking with your critique group members, it's okay to leave and look for another group or for a single writing partner or mentor. Every member of the group needs to be giving as well as gaining, and the environment needs to be positive for all. Otherwise, the group can become a distraction to your writing instead of a boon.

Giving a critique

Your critique of another writer's work isn't just your admission ticket into a critique-group meeting. There's a bonus for you: Giving thoughtful, thorough critiques makes you a better writer. You discover how to diagnose weaknesses in stories and build on strengths, making you better able to self-edit and come up with a revision plan for your own manuscripts — or to avoid the problems in the first place.

When giving a critique, treat your group members courteously and respectfully — and remember that they may be critiquing your work next. Here are some tips for delivering a critique in a constructive and tactful manner:

✔ **Give honest feedback.** Always keep in mind the primary goal of a critique session: to help each other develop and hone writing skills.

✔ **Focus on the major story points.** If you're critiquing in a group setting with papers in hand, merely circle and note minor grammar, spelling, and mechanical issues for the writer to see when she collects the papers after the critique — no need to nitpick publicly. See the sidebar "Critique checklist" for the elements to focus on.

✔ **Indicate what's working as well as what's not working.** Identifying and building on strengths is just as important as knowing weaknesses. Give guidance on how to address the issues whenever possible.

✔ **Don't explain how the story affected you personally and/or offer praise based on that reaction.** Although writers may appreciate such sentiment, it's not what a writer needs most when trying to polish a piece or hone her technique.

✔ **Don't hammer in points already made.** If another reviewer points out an issue you noticed, too, a brief "I agree" is sufficient. However, if you disagree with a previous point, providing another perspective is often helpful.

> ✔ **Be supportive.** Constructive criticism is wanted; unnecessarily harsh words
> are not. Be honest but gentle. Encourage others to do their best writing, and
> help one another get over writer's block or rejection. Publishing is a harsh
> world, and no writer needs yet another avenue for rejection.

Hiring a freelance editor

Freelance editors, sometimes called *book doctors,* are experts paid to point
out the strengths and weaknesses of a manuscript and advise the author
regarding revision points. A great time to bring in a freelance editor is after
you've already revised the manuscript as much as you can based on self-
editing and critique-group input. At that point, bringing in a pro who knows
the YA fiction business, market, and audience can help you make your good
manuscript great.

Deciding what kind of edit you want

Freelance editors may do a *substantive edit*, wherein they read the entire
manuscript and use their expertise to critique the main elements of writing
craft. The editors look for large-scale inconsistencies or problems in plot,
character, concept, and voice. A substantive edit also includes comments
on marketability, audience appropriateness, and general appeal. This kind of
info can also be great feedback early in the process, say, after your first revision, when general shaping is still happening.

Or you may pay a freelance editor to do a *line edit,* which is an intensive line-
by-line, word-by-word examination for clarity of words and sentences, appropriate grammar and punctuation, and consistency (of point of view, of voice,
of tense, of timeline, and so on). Most freelance editors provide this service,
although *copy editors* specialize in it. Think of copy editors as paid nitpickers
blessed with intense focus and an encyclopedic knowledge of language rules.

A line edit is appropriate only when you believe all your elements are in place;
there's no point in editing sentences that you may revise or cut when you try
to, say, rework a character who isn't working.

Finding a freelance editor

You can find freelance editors by asking your writing community or agent for
recommendations; by consulting the SCBWI *Freelance Editors Directory* (available to SCBWI members; www.scbwi.org), the *Literary Market Place* (www.
literarymarketplace.com), or the Editorial Freelancers Association
(www.the-efa.org); or by searching the web. Look for editors who specialize in children's books. An editor's role is to sit between the author and
the audience and make sure that what the author is trying to say is what the
audience hears, which means editors must know young readers well — their
needs, wants, and age issues.

Critique checklist

When giving critiques, tell writers their strengths as well as their weaknesses. This checklist can help you do that. Note that this list is less specific than your self-editing checklist. Critiquing is about pointing out strengths and weaknesses in someone else's manuscript, suggesting fixes if you can. Ultimately, you leave it to the writer to figure out what's causing the weaknesses and to correct them. You can't revise someone else's manuscript for them in a round of critiquing, nor can they revise yours.

Share the following list of questions with your critique group:

- **Audience:** Is the theme or topic appropriate for the intended audience? Does the length match the genre/format/age range of the audience? Do the story and narrative voice have teen/tween appeal? Is the tone preachy? Does the story come at its topic from a fresh perspective?

- **Characterization:** Do the characters seem real with depth and emotion, or are they stereotypes? Are the characters' motives understandable and logical within the story? Does the main character mature by the end of the story? Is the character's goal believable and important enough?

- **Point of view:** Is the point of view consistent throughout the piece? Is this the best point of view for this story?

- **Plot:** Does the story develop logically, or does it make sudden leaps that confuse the reader? Are the obstacles realistic

and worthy of overcoming? Are the consequences of failure dire enough?

- **Pacing:** Does the action progress slowly or quickly? How long does the story setup take? Is the reader drawn in from the beginning? Do the chapters end in mini finales and/or cliffhangers?

- **Setting:** Does the story have an atmosphere that allows the reader to experience what the characters experience? Can the reader imagine the location clearly? Does the character interact enough with elements of the setting? Does the setting push characters out of their comfort zones and increase tension? Does each scene happen in the most useful place?

- **Narrative voice:** Does the text have a distinct narrative voice or personality? Is it consistent throughout? Has the writer avoided stock phrases and clichés? Are the words dynamic? Is the language choice appropriate for the target audience? Does the writer show instead of tell?

- **Mechanics:** Is the sentence structure appropriate for the age group? Are there a variety of sentence lengths? Do any aspects of basic style, such as subject-verb agreement, need work because they confuse the reader? Are there too many adverbs instead of evocative, active verbs?

- **Dialogue:** Does the dialogue seem natural and realistic? Can the reader imagine real people talking as the characters do? Does the dialogue focus too much on plot delivery?

Before you commit your money and your manuscript to a paid edit, address these items with prospective freelancers:

✔ **Their credentials:** Freelance editors who specialize in children's books are often former publishing house editors and agents, and many are writers for children. Get a feel for the editors' literary sensibility. Ask about books and authors they've worked with, and ask for references if you feel that's necessary. Most freelance editors have websites with this kind of information available.

If you'd like more assurance after considering the editor's credentials, ask for a sample edit of a few pages, probably three to five. Understand that this is just a sample of her editing style and content; it's not a "full edit of a partial manuscript" and so isn't exhaustive even for the issues within those pages. A sample does, however, give you a feel for how that editor formulates her commentary.

✔ **Their fee and payment expectations:** Fees and billing methods vary, with some editors charging by page count, some by word count, and some hourly. Most freelance editors require a percentage paid up front, with the final payment due upon delivery. Ask for an estimate based on your word or page count and manuscript. Editors may ask for a sample of your manuscript to judge the sentence complexity, because some writing styles take longer to work through than others.

If a full edit isn't within your budget, ask for a *partial edit*. Experienced editors can tell a lot about a manuscript within a chapter or two and give you great suggestions for revision. The editors won't get insight into your overall development of characters and plot, but they'll be able to comment on the strength of your opening, your balance of action and narrative, your initial characterization, your narrative voice, and the marketability of your concept.

✔ **Type of edit:** Specify line or substantive edit (I explain the difference in the preceding section) and ask what the editors look for in each. If you have special concerns — for example, if you know you have trouble with dialogue — ask for particular attention to those aspects.

✔ **A due date for the edit:** The actual edit may require just seven or eight hours, but the editor may not be able to get to your project for several weeks. And because editing is intense mental work, the edit may be done over the course of several days. Find out the freelancer's timeline and decide whether it works for you.

After you've agreed on all the preceding points, memorialize them in a single letter or e-mail or in a formal Letter of Agreement.

No freelance editor can promise you a book contract. An editor's criticisms, questions, and suggestions are just that: suggestions. What you do with the revision is up to you, and even if you nail every item the editor calls out, no one can predict how a publisher or literary agent will react to the manuscript. Just ask J. K. Rowling, whose Harry Potter was rejected by 12 publishers. Evaluating a manuscript for publication is a subjective process, depending on any number of factors (see Chapter 13 for details). When you're working with a freelance editor, your job is to make your writing and that particular manuscript the best it can be.

Literary agents are great sources for freelance editor recommendations, but they can't require you to use a particular editor's services. Nor can they take payment from that editor for those referrals or charge you for editing your manuscript themselves. These practices are violations of the Association of Authors' Representatives (AAR) Canon of Ethics. For more on agents' roles, check out Chapter 13.

Getting input from teens and tweens

Some writers of young adult fiction want feedback from teens and tweens themselves. The inclination is good — after all, who knows what teens like to read better than teen readers do? — but there are pros and cons to the endeavor:

- ✔ **Pros:** Teens can tell you what sounds lame to their ears, point out parts that hit them as preachy or more adult-sounding than youthful, and let you know whether kids their age even care about the topic you've chosen.

- ✔ **Cons:** Teens and tweens aren't so adept yet at articulating their reactions to a story. It's hard enough for grown, experienced writers and editors to specify what needs improvement. Also, teens are often enamored just with meeting a real-life writer and so may be impressed with *any*thing you set before them. Or they may not feel comfortable criticizing your work to your face. This is why editors and agents don't want to hear, "I read it to a class of teenagers, and they loved it!" in your submission letter. For these reasons, you shouldn't take anecdotal teen reactions to a manuscript as gospel.

In this section, I tell you how to get your manuscript in teens' and tweens' hands, and I provide a few tips on getting useful feedback.

Recruiting teens to read

If you can find a favorite teen reader who does seem to have the ability and inclination to critique constructively, his or her input can be invaluable. You can seek teen feedback in three ways:

- ✔ **Informal feedback:** Pass your manuscript to your son or daughter, your nephew or niece, or that kid who mows your lawn every Saturday. Ask him to put his thoughts in an e-mail, or set up a time and public meeting place (with his guardian's knowledge and presence, too, if that's most appropriate) to chat about his reactions to the story.

✔ **A structured focus group approach:** Formal teen focus groups aren't part of a publisher's marketing model, but you may find them helpful. Here you get feedback from a group of teens. The teens read the manuscript and then meet with you to give their reactions. Group discussion can help build up ideas and suggestions that may not have occurred to an individual in a one-on-one interview. On the flip side, a strong-minded or particularly outspoken individual can dominate and sway the group's opinions.

If you go with a focus group, be sure the readers' parents are involved and/or aware, and be careful how you solicit kids for the group. Consider enlisting your child's Girl or Boy Scout troop, book club, or other group where you personally know the kids or the adults running it.

✔ **Class visits:** A common way for authors to get feedback from a large group of teen readers is through class visits (Chapter 15 talks about visiting schools). Here are two ways to get student feedback on your story:

- **Get an on-the-spot reaction to your story as part of a general class presentation about writing.** Getting feedback isn't your primary task in this case. Rather, you present the students with something they want or need, such as information on becoming a writer or the how-to's of a particular writing skill. This presentation gives teachers a motive for scheduling your author visit (which is necessary if you're making a paid visit). Then, while you're at the school, you can talk about your book, read excerpts, and ask specific questions as part of the presentation. Make note of the students' reactions and questions.

- **Arrange to have the class read all or portions of your manuscript prior to your visit.** You can ask the teacher to make this a class project, letting the kids write up their responses as a for-credit writing assignment. They can even fill out questionnaires for you to take home. Kids are often freer with their criticism when they have the distance of paper and pen.

Working with young readers

Here are some tips for working effectively with young critiquers, regardless of your route to reader input:

✔ Provide questions ahead of time so readers can mull as they read. Off-the-cuff question-and-answer isn't a teen strong suit.

✔ Be specific with your questions. Otherwise, you'll get lots of "I like it" responses. Ask open-ended questions to avoid yes-or-no replies.

✔ Tailor your questions to your audience. Teen readers don't typically have the experience to address technical items such as pacing and tension, but ask teens about the believability and likability of the characters, and you'll get an earful. Young reviewers may have extensive commentary on the concept and themes, your opening action, and your plot resolution, too.

✔ Use simple, clear language. Don't get all jargony.

✔ Encourage readers to clarify or expand their answers.

✔ Point out how much you value reader input. Explain how feedback makes better books for other kids their age.

✔ Tell the kids that you *want* to hear the bad stuff, that they needn't spare your feelings. Then embody this idea by not defending yourself if you're holding a face-to-face session.

✔ At the end of the session, thank each responder and the group as a whole for giving you things to ponder.

Revising with Confidence

Revision means modifying your story to make it better. Revision may entail rewriting parts of your story, adding things to it, subtracting things from it, or rearranging parts of it, all with the end goal of transforming your flawed first draft into a seamless, flowing final draft. This section tells you how to tackle the items on your revision list and experiment with fixes in a constructive, confident, and safe way.

Starting big and finishing small

Revision isn't a single act. Rather, it's a series of passes through your manuscript, each focused on a specific task, until you have a fully revised next draft that's ready for a new round of critiquing. Breaking down a revision into chunks keeps it manageable, helps you maintain your focus, and provides satisfaction as you cross off tasks from your revision list. Start with big-picture items and finish with small stuff, such as punctuation tweaks. The passes may look something like this:

✔ A pass for characters, putting them in more extreme situations or changing the setting of a scene so you can make a character act differently, even if to the same end

✔ A pass for plot to ensure that all the events work together or build upon each other to move the overall plot forward; also use this pass to add foreshadowing elements such as early mentions of key props or character traits that will be vital to the story's resolution

✔ A pass to fix those scenes where you noticed the tension and/or pace sagging

✔ A pass for dialogue, working on the balance of spoken words to narrative actions that reveal things about the character and/or plot; weeding out dialogue tags in case of abundance or adding them in case of a dearth; or making the dialogue more youthful by mussing up the grammar and syntax

✔ A pass for filling out the setting, creating a stronger sense of place

✔ A pass for smoothing the transitions into and out of scenes

✔ A pass for narrative voice and word choice, ditching all those adverbs and dull phrasings that do the basic job but lack real flavor

When you've crossed off all your tasks and finished all your passes, do another round of editing (self or professional) and critiquing to determine whether you need more changes. Make sure all the changes work. Several rounds of revision may be necessary to work out the kinks.

Keep your goals in sight. Digging into a revision means once again immersing yourself in story minutiae. To stay motivated, frequently remind yourself of what you're doing and why. Keep your revision list posted where you can see it and cross things off with a big black pen after you've tackled them. Also, refer frequently to the hook statement you posted before you started the first draft (see Chapter 4).

Taking chances with your changes

The best revisions come when you're willing to experiment. Tepid, fearful revisions leave you with barely improved manuscripts — and they're just not fun. Go for it! If you're not sure whether something will work, give it a whirl anyway. So what if it doesn't work? You can always reinstate what you cut. Sure, you may lose some time when you experiment, but you just may find the fix you need to break the whole revision wide open.

Here are three tips to help you let your hair down during revision:

✔ **Set aside the text you cut.** When you decide to omit a scene or passage, don't delete the material. Instead, cut and paste it into a master "Deleted Material" document on your computer. You can always retrieve it later. You likely won't need to retrieve it, but knowing you can easily reinstate the material makes you bolder about killing your darlings.

"Killing your darlings" is a writing phrase that refers to the act of deleting parts of your story — maybe scenes, maybe passages or words, maybe even characters — that you slaved over and love but that ultimately don't move your story forward. Parting with things can be extremely hard, especially when you like them, but sometimes what you like isn't what's best for the story.

✔ **Save new drafts as new files and label everything.** Good labeling lets you revise without fear. Save a final copy of your first draft and never touch that copy again. In fact, lock it to prevent saving over it by accident. Then open up that document, rename it "Draft 2" or "D2," press *save,* and start your revision work within that new document.

Rename and resave whenever you make substantial changes: "TITLE_ d2_present tense" and "TITLE_d2_past tense." When you're not making substantial changes, you may want to date your revision files in this manner: "TITLE_d3_12022011. (***Tip:*** Don't use month names like "Dec" because your computer will arrange your files in alphabetical order, making a mess of your electronic labeling system.) If you need to, set up subfolders to keep track of the drafts. Good draft management allows you revise confidently because you know you can easily go back to previous drafts.

✔ **Use special editing features in your word-processing program.** Turning on your word-processing program's track-changes or reviewing feature can help you revise with confidence because it lets you keep track of your changes with different-colored fonts and margin notes. You can make notes in the side margins, highlight portions of text you're thinking of changing or deleting, and strike-through and replace sections instead of erasing them from existence. You can "reject" any of these changes later, which reinstates the cut material or undoes your changes. If this feature intrigues you, play around with your program's version of the feature. Or you can simply use your program's text-highlighting function in normal writing mode to highlight sections you want to rewrite later.

Knowing the final draft when you see it

At some point, you must declare that you're done revising and that it's time to submit your final manuscript to publishers. How do you know when you're holding that final draft? Alas, it's a best-guess scenario, but here's the likely state of affairs on that day: You self-edited and solicited criticism on your first draft, you addressed all those critique items to the best of your abilities, and then you ran the manuscript by the critics once again. You repeated this process until the criticisms were minimal (someone can always find *something*), and you don't feel you need to act on them. You've run through the checklists in this chapter multiple times and feel confident that you've addressed all the items to the best of your ability. You can't think of anything specific to add to your now completely crossed-out revision list.

There. That's when you know you have a final draft. You can then submit that draft to publishers in phases (which I talk about in Chapter 13). Submitting to only a few publishers at a time allows you to test-run the manuscript, so to speak. If the agents and/or editors in that first phase reject the manuscript, then read their letters for clues about their reasons for rejection and do another round of revision before launching into the second submission phase. Do this until you score a hit.

Don't skimp or rush when revising. I know you're eager to land that book contract, which means you're eager to submit. But it's a mistake to submit a manuscript that you know needs work — the publishing editor's job isn't to help you with developmental stuff.

Ultimately, revision is about doing the best you can to satisfy yourself as much as possible. Too many people submit knowing that there's work to be done. Don't blow an opportunity by rushing it. If the material's not ready, stay your submitting hand and give your revising hand another go at the manuscript.

Chapter 12

The Finishing Touches:
Formatting and Finalizing

• •

In This Chapter

▶ Checking punctuation and proofreading

▶ Formatting your manuscript

▶ Understanding copyright and securing permissions

• •

You've drafted, edited, revised, and finally decided you have a final manuscript. At this point, you're probably dying to send that manuscript to publishers. Don't. Stay your hand just a tad longer. It's time to do a final cleanup and polishing pass. You're sending this puppy out to word-loving professionals, after all — typos and poor punctuation will not earn their confidence. You're a writer, so you should know the proper positioning of a period in dialogue.

Use this chapter as your checklist while you review your punctuation, proofread the whole story one last time, and format the manuscript so it looks how it's supposed to look when it crosses an editor's desk — which makes you look wholly professional. I also help you judge whether you need to secure legal permission for the use of someone else's work in your story, and I tell you how and when you should secure those permissions.

Paying Attention to Nitty-Gritty Details

When you're writing tens of thousands of words and using countless punctuation marks, it's easy to mess up a few of them. But it's also easy to catch and correct those slips before your manuscript leaves your possession for good. This section is dedicated to helping you do just that.

Patrolling punctuation

Double-checking your punctuation is part of crafting a professional submission package. Here are ten questions you should ask yourself to avoid the most common punctuation mistakes:

- ✔ **Have you put your punctuation inside your double quotes?** Surround written dialogue with double quotation marks, and then tuck all the punctuation related to that bit of dialogue inside those double quotes:

    > "Are you going to the fair?" he asked.
    > "If I don't have to ride with Ben," she replied. "Ben's weird."
    > "Gimme a break!" He strode away. "I swear . . ."

- ✔ **Are your single quotes inside your double quotes, too?** When your speaking character quotes another person, surround that quotation with single quotation marks and then close up everything within the dialogue's double quotes:

    > Kelly snorted. "He's nuts. 'The only way out is in,' he says. The guy makes no sense."

    > "'The only way out is in.'" Kelly snorted. "He's nuts."

    If the material being quoted within the dialogue needs punctuation, keep its punctuation within the single quotes. Then put the dialogue's end punctuation after the single quotes:

    > "How am I supposed to 'Dress for success!'?"

- ✔ **Are you missing your serial commas?** Check all lists of three or more items to make sure you have a comma after every one, including the item that precedes the conjunction (*and, but*, and so on):

    > I packed my bag, pet my dog, and then left.

    > They were red, green, and blue.

    Leaving out that final *serial comma,* the one preceding the conjunction, is common for writers because serial commas are omitted in journalism. In fiction, the serial comma stays unless you stick a conjunction between every pair of items on the list:

    > They were red and green and blue.

- ✔ **Have your semicolons earned their place in your manuscript?** Semicolons aren't common in YA fiction because they're generally used for complicated sentence structures. When you use a semicolon, the sentences on either side of it are mechanically complete on their own, so why not just rewrite the passage so that they *are* two separate sentences? That's easier on kids — and easier on most grown-ups, too. And the truth is that semicolons can come across as signs that you're trying to show off that you know how to use them.

Semicolons do have a practical role in lists, replacing serial commas when the elements of the list are long and complex or involve internal punctuation. But here, too, you can often recast the sentence or paragraph to avoid this complex punctuation mark. Remember, you have a young audience, and simpler is better. Make sure any semicolons that survive this polishing pass are necessary.

✔ **Do you have your possessive apostrophes right?** Here's how to apply apostrophes properly when you want to indicate ownership:

- Add *'s* when you have a singular noun or name:

    The cat's milk spilled.

    It was James's last chance.

- Add only an apostrophe when you have a standard plural noun:

    Both cars' trunks were open.

    The classes' rivalry was vicious.

- Add *'s* when you have a plural noun that doesn't end with an *s:*

    The people's court is in session.

✔ **Are your dashes the right lengths?** *Em dashes* are those long dashes that indicate a break in a line of thought. Use them to add dramatic emphasis or to explain the main clause they're attached to — as I'm doing now. Em dashes have more kick than commas, which is why I adore them. Their close buddies are *en dashes,* which are half the measure of the em and which signal a range, such as 1–4. Don't confuse those little guys with the even shorter *hyphen*, which forms the link in compound words such as *all-out.* In fiction writing, close up the spaces on either side of the dashes, butting them right up against the letters.

You can insert both em and en dashes from your word-processing program's symbols section. You can also use (or assign) a keystroke shortcut to insert the right symbol, or you can change the program's automatic correction options to insert the right kind of dash as you type.

✔ **Are you shouting at readers with too many exclamation points?!** You may overuse exclamation points in your efforts to express excitement or other strong emotions. This makes young readers feel like you're shouting at them. See how many exclamation points you can edit out of your manuscript. Rewrite the surrounding material, letting the emphasis and emotion come from the content and word choice rather than from the punctuation. Fewer exclamation points makes for more authentic, less forced storytelling.

✔ **Do you really need that stuff between the parentheses?** Parentheses are handy tools for inserting extra information or narrative asides for the reader (like this). Parenthetical info may be wonderful in a stylized novel where your narrator really is trying to throw out tidbits to the audience in a winking fashion, but that's not usually the case. Most commonly, a writer is simply trying to include some extra information:

She went out to the buggy. (Her father had purchased it the previous summer.) It would be a long ride into town.

If you're stuffing something between parentheses because it's extra information, then you likely don't need that information at all. If the information is in fact vital, then yank it out of the parentheses and write it into the narrative where it belongs.

✔ **Are your ellipses accurate?** To indicate an omission within a sentence, to join sentence fragments, or to indicate an intentional trailing off of a complete sentence, use *three* dots, tapping your space bar before and after each one:

> "It's too bad this snooze-inducer isn't a hilarious comedy" becomes "It's . . . a hilarious comedy."

> "The dog skidded around the corner, spun wildly in circles, and crashed into a pile of clothes" becomes "The dog skidded . . . spun wildly . . . and crashed into a pile of clothes."

> "If I had my way . . . ," he mumbled.

When a complete sentence precedes your ellipsis, use *four* dots, with the first dot smashed up against the letter preceding it:

> My choice was agonizing. . . . Yes. I'd do it. I'd do it!

Don't let your computer automatically replace your spacious ellipses with tight ones. The dots are supposed to be separated by spaces, allowing your designer to set her own spacing between the dots when she's prepping your book for publication.

✔ **Are your titles capitalized correctly?** The biggest violation of title capitalization is actually a simple two-letter word: *is. Is* may be a small verb, but it's a verb nonetheless, and all verbs get capitalized in book and chapter titles. The same goes for all nouns, pronouns, adjectives, and adverbs. Here are some other title capitalization rules to know:

- Conjunctions, such as *and, or, if, because, as,* and *that,* are capitalized.

- Articles, including *a, an,* and *the,* are lowercased.

- Prepositions, such as *on, over, in,* and *at,* are lowercased in titles. Technically, the words *about, through,* and *under* are prepositions and thus should be lowercased, but because long lowercased words can look odd in titles, some publishers' in-house style calls for capitalizing prepositions that are five or more letters.

- The first and last words in a title are always capitalized, no matter what part of speech they are.

Avoiding basic blunders with easily confused words

Don't undermine your story with errors that you can avoid by memorizing a simple rule, running your computer's spelling/grammar checker, or simply proofreading one last time. It's easy — and quite fair — to say, "Hey, no one's perfect," when a mistake ends up in a submitted manuscript. But these next six blunders are so elemental and so easy to spot that it's downright embarrassing when they reach the hands of an editor or agent:

- ✔ **To/too:** Mixing up these two words falls into the Typos category. Actually, make that Ridiculously (and Unnecessarily) Frequent Typos. Your finger can easily hit the *o* key an extra time, and your eyes can slide over the short word without fully digesting it when you're proofreading. But understandable or not, this word mix-up should never happen in *your* manuscript because you can easily catch the error through a combination of careful proofreading and a spelling/grammar check.

- ✔ **Your/you're:** This, too, is a common typo crime. *Your* is a possessive adjective that indicates ownership, and *you're* is a contraction of the two words *you* and *are*. This is an easy oopsie to spot if you just step away from your writing for a day or two before proofreading and spell-checking. It's so easy to spot, in fact, that its presence in a submitted manuscript makes the writer look lazy or careless.

- ✔ **Their/there:** Here's another typo that can make you look careless. *There* is usually an adverb indicating time or location or a noun indicating a place, but it never indicates ownership. That's the job of the possessive adjective *their*, as in "That's *their* locker."

- ✔ **It's/its:** This mistake shows up often for two reasons: 1) simple typo and 2) confusion about the difference. *It's* is a contraction of the pronoun *it* and the verb *is*, and contractions always get apostrophes, as when "*It is* my car" becomes "*It's* my car." By contrast, *its* is a possessive adjective or possessive pronoun like *his, her,* and *hers*, indicating ownership of something: "He fixed *its* engine." Just as you wouldn't stick an apostrophe in *his* or *hers*, don't stick one in the possessive *its,* either.

- ✔ **Between you and me/between you and I:** This phrase causes all kinds of angst, with people often mistakenly choosing "between you and I." The biggest reason for that choice is that *I* just sounds far more proper than *me*. But proper doesn't make right. If this phrase shows up in your story, type it in two parts first: "Between *you.*" Yes, that makes sense. *You* is the object of the action. Something can be done to *you*. Now for part two: "Between *I.*" No, that's not right because you can't have something done to *I*. Something can, however, be done to *me*. Or heck, just memorize the rule. Much easier.

✔ **Lie/lay:** Confusing *lie* and *lay* may be the most common mix-up in the entire English language. Here's a simplified rundown:

- *Lay* means to put something down, and its variations are *laid, laid,* and *laying:*

    Today I lay my book down.

    Yesterday I laid my book down.

    Many times I've laid my book down.

    I was laying my book down when I tripped.

- *Lie* means to recline horizontally, and its variations are *lay, lain,* and *lying:*

    Today I lie on the sand.

    Yesterday I lay on the sand.

    Many times I have lain on the sand.

    I was lying on the sand when a crab ran up my shirt.

Regardless of whether the mistakes are due to typos or confusion, these errors are easy enough to spot. Run a search for these words in your manuscript so you can review each one in context. If any of these six items is an ongoing bugaboo for you, type up the rule and post it on your bulletin board for easy reference.

Running spell-check

You don't have to depend on your all-too-human eyes to spot spelling and punctuation boo-boos; just run spell-check to flag potential errors. Too many people forget that this function is available in their computers. Or maybe spell-check seems to take forever on your manuscript because you've intentionally relaxed your grammar and punctuation. Be patient. You've had your manuscript this long, and rushing the final few moments can only hurt you.

If unusual names or spellings appear frequently in your manuscript, speed up your spell-check pass by adding those spellings to the word-processing program's dictionary (just click "add" when the spell-checker offers you spelling suggestions). Or add a *custom dictionary* to your spell-checker. You can activate this dictionary whenever you're working with your manuscript and then turn it off again for all your other documents. For example, you can create a custom dictionary called "My Novel" and include words that may be spelling mistakes in documents that aren't your medieval Mars sci-fi story. If this interests you, directions for creating custom dictionaries for your particular word-processing program are readily available online (type "custom dictionary" followed by your program's name).

Making Passes: Professionals Proofread (Twice)

The last thing you should do with your manuscript before sending it out is the final read-through, which has two goals: to catch stubborn typos and to double-check your facts. Even if you've proofread this thing a million times, do it again, because every time you make a change, you risk introducing a typo. Don't brush that off — a single keystroke can accidentally delete lines, full paragraphs, even entire pages. Or more! I've had manuscripts submitted to me with chapters missing right from the middle. Don't risk having editors and agents think you're lazy or careless.

When you do the final proofreading pass, *do not read your story*. Instead, read your words. That sounds impossible, I know, but it's what you should strive for. Here are tips to help you ignore your story while you read:

- ✔ **Read elsewhere.** Get away from the place you wrote it. You're not in writing mode.

- ✔ **Limit distractions.** The final pass is serious business — no TV or e-mail nearby to distract you.

- ✔ **Read it like a book.** Mimic a book-reading experience. Print your manuscript; don't read it onscreen. Set it in a three-ring binder or get your manuscript bound at your local print shop.

- ✔ **Give it several passes.** Check sentence structure and punctuation on one pass, and then flip through to check formatting on another.

- ✔ **Look over the formatting.** Eyeball the white space. Run your eyes down the page to see whether your paragraphs are all indented. Do a pass where you check only your chapter title capitalization and spacing.

- ✔ **Verify the facts.** This is your opportunity to check any facts or figures that lurk in your fiction.

- ✔ **Use a checklist.** Create a list with your most common boo-boos. That way, you can remind yourself to look for those specifically during your final read-through.

- ✔ **Make notes as you go.** If you discover a big issue, such as formatting that you need to readdress, make a note of it and then go back later so as not to interrupt your focus right now.

- ✔ **Read out loud.** Your eyes can skip over words — and probably will at this point. Read your manuscript out loud to hear it. This helps you spot left out or doubled words. Or if you're really brave, have someone read the story out loud to you.

Remember, your focus is on specific words in the proofreading stage. If you're making sentence changes, then you're still in editing-and-revising mode. This final proofreading pass is for mistake-catching, not rewriting.

If you do make the rare substantive change during the proofreading pass, reread the entire paragraph with the change in place. Many errors and typos are introduced in the final moments when you're fixing something else.

Do you hate the whole idea of trying to be an objective reader and patrolling for nitpicky details? Then hire a freelance proofreader — someone who specializes in sniffing out errant typos, punctuation, and grammar. You hire a proofreader in the same way you secure a freelance editor, which I cover in Chapter 11. If you don't want to hire a pro, call in a friend to do a final proofreading read-through. Try to choose someone who hasn't already read the manuscript, thus ensuring that the new pair of eyes is fresh. Or consider paying a sharp-eyed college student to do a read-through and specify that you're not looking for opinion, just typos.

Formatting the Standard YA Manuscript

The goal of standardized formatting is not to drive you nuts, although it can. The goal is to ease your readers through your manuscript with the fewest possible distractions. If everyone does things in mostly the same way, agents and editors can ignore the tiny details and lose themselves in your story. In this section, I cover the standard ways of laying out your manuscript.

Page setup and such: Tackling the technical stuff

Your final manuscript should

- Be on 8.5" x 11" white paper
- Be printed on one side of the paper only
- Be double-spaced
- Use a standard 12-point font such as Times New Roman or Arial
- Have 1-inch margins all around
- Be left aligned and right ragged
- Have your last name, the title, and the page number in the upper-right corner of every page after the first one: Smith/TITLE, 42 (*Tip:* Insert this info as a header and use your word-processing program's automatic page-numbering feature.)

If you do deviate from the norm in formatting, deviate just in small personal details, not in big ways. For example, no violating the font rules and using Comic Sans MS font for your manuscript. Yes, it may emit a youthful bouquet, but it's also super distracting.

If you have text messages or something of that nature in your manuscript, bend the "no distracting fonts" rule for the sake of clarity. Readers need to follow who says what during a text message exchange, and you need to distinguish those exchanges from the regular narrative. In that case, pick a font that's different from your narrative font but complementary, and consider using gray, black, and, if necessary, a complementary shade of blue to distinguish each speaker. You want clarity, not distraction. Lauren Myracle's *TTYL* lays out IM (instant messaging) lines very clearly. Don't include graphics (such as phone-screen backgrounds) in your manuscript, though. That's gimmicky. Leave that for a seasoned book designer when your book is being readied for production.

You may massage the rest of the formatting details a little without incurring anyone's wrath:

- **Scene breaks:** Mark scene breaks with about three asterisks (***) or pound signs (###) or some other visual indicator. Leaving a large white space could signal the break (it does in published novels), but if one of your scene breaks falls at the end of a page, then the spacing flag disappears. Your designer will decide what to do with scene breaks in the final manuscript. For now, keep them as clear as possible.

- **Chapter breaks:** Start each chapter on a new page, with the chapter title several lines down from the top of the page. You can center the title or set it flush left, and it can be bold or not. That's all up to you.

If your story doesn't have chapter titles, then use numbers, as in "Chapter 1." This isn't a permanent designation. Bound books often omit indicators at the top of new chapter pages. But in your manuscript, make things clear by noting "Chapter X" or the title.

Start the first text line of the new chapter flush left, with no chapter indent. That's another visual clue to ease the reader through your manuscript.

- **Parts:** For books that are divided into parts, go ahead and insert a full page labeled simply "Part I: [Title]" or something similar to make sure everyone's up to speed.

- **Front matter and back matter:** Clearly label everything if you have front matter (everything that precedes the actual beginning of the story, such as a prologue) or back matter (everything that follows the end of the book — perhaps an epilogue or author's note or even a bibliography, which is fairly common for historical fiction).

Putting the right stuff on the first page

The first page of your manuscript is your master information page, with your full contact information: name, address, phone number, e-mail address, book title, genre, and word count. The generally accepted format arranges the items in the following manner:

- ✔ **Contact info:** Place your first and last name in the upper-left corner, 1 inch from the top of the page. Single-spaced below that are your address, your phone/fax numbers, and then your e-mail address and website URL if you have one.

- ✔ **Manuscript info:** The category of the manuscript (MG or YA) goes in the upper-right corner, 1 inch from the top of the page, along with the genre. Single-spaced below that is often a copyright line (more on copyright later in "Copyrighting your manuscript"). Below that is the manuscript's word count rounded to the nearest 100 and preceded by "approx." (To get your final word count, use the word count feature in your word-processing program.)

- ✔ **Title and author:** Write the title in ALL CAPS, centered, about 5 inches from the top of the page or halfway down the page. Single-spaced below that is your name in a "By My Name" fashion.

- ✔ **Story:** The story should start about two line spaces below the title. No need to indent the first sentence of that first paragraph. The rest of the story uses regular paragraph indents and traditional double-spacing. Do not insert an extra line space between paragraphs. Include the chapter designation on this first page only if you're using chapter titles instead of chapter numbers.

Don't include a page number on this first page. Figure 12-1 shows a sample first page of a manuscript.

Figure 12-1:
Include all the impor-
tant details
on the first
page of your
manuscript.

Your Name
2 Main Street
City, State ZIP CODE
Phone: 000-000-000
Fax: 000-000-000
E-mail: yname@yournamebooks.com
www.yournamebooks.com

Middle Grade Fiction,
Fantasy
copyright © [year] by
[Your Name]
35,000 words

TITLE IN ALL CAPS
By Your Name

The story begins here . . .

Protecting What's Yours and Getting Permission

Copyright refers to the ownership of a work after it's committed to paper, canvas, computer, or some other fixed form. You can't copyright your idea; what you copyright is the way that idea is expressed. That's considered *intellectual property*, which means *property rights in creations of the mind*.

You can't copyright a title, but in some cases you can trademark a title through the United States Patent and Trademark Office (`www.uspto.gov`). Some states use "unfair competition" law to protect titles that have acquired *secondary meaning.* In that case, an association between the title and the specific work has been established in the public mind.

As the copyright owner, you can give *(grant)* someone the right to use some portion or all of your story for reprint or for other use, such as film or merchandise. That's what people are talking about when they refer to *rights* in a book contract. See Chapter 17 for details on granting rights.

This section is about making sure you understand basic copyright needs and what it means to secure permission to use someone else's work. I explain how to ask others for permission to reprint some of their material if you want to use it in your book — and why sometimes you don't need to ask permission at all. I also explain what you need to know about copyrighting your manuscript.

Copyrighting your manuscript

Here's the deal: *You* own the copyright to your story — not your publisher (who is buying only the rights to publish it) and not your agent (who is only representing you and that work to publishers . . . for a fee, of course).

Now here's the deal with that deal: Although U.S. copyright law automatically protects your ownership from the moment of the work's creation, you or your publisher should formally register the *final published* version of that work with the United States Copyright Office so you can provide legal proof of ownership should you ever become involved in litigation:

- ✔ If you're self-publishing, you do that registering yourself. Visit the U.S. Copyright Office's website (`www.copyright.gov`) for the forms and how-to of it.

- ✔ If you have a publisher, its in-house staff registers the copyright for you *in your name* as part of the publishing process. You never have to lift a finger. Your publishing contract details this, right down to verifying how you'd like your name to appear on the copyright registration.

This is where writers can get confused: Because copyright law protects your ownership of the work from the moment of its creation, you don't need to copyright your manuscript before submitting it to publishers. It's covered. In fact, you never really need to register copyright. It's mostly a legal safety precaution. If it makes you feel better, you can register copyright for your manuscript prior to submission. It's your time and money. Even so, your publisher will register the final published version when it's ready.

It's standard practice for writers to include "copyright © [year] by [your name]" on the first page of their manuscripts. Technically, you don't even need to do that. It's covered, remember?

U.S. copyright law sets the term of the copyright for works created after 1978 at the author's lifetime plus 70 years, after which the work goes into the *public domain* and no longer has copyright protection. At that point, anyone can print or distribute the material for free because all property rights have been extinguished. If you incorporate some public domain material in your novel, you have copyright in your novel, but that copyright extends only to your new and original elements. Adaptation of public domain material does not remove the material from the public domain.

Don't confuse public domain with *fair use,* which is an exception to the exclusivity of a current, active copyright. I talk about fair use more in a moment.

Understanding plagiarism, permission, and perfectly fair use

You may want to quote someone else's work in your fiction. In that case, you must get legal permission from that copyright owner (see the next section for details). If you don't, you violate their legal rights and can be sued. If you reprint someone else's words or ideas and pass them off as your own, you're committing *plagiarism,* which is stealing and can carry serious penalties.

Now that you're trembling, I'll tell you about an exception called *fair use.* Fair use allows people to print portions of someone else's work in certain instances, such as criticism, comment, news reporting, teaching, scholarship, and research. *Fair use* is as much about the quality of what you use as the quantity. Some people mistakenly believe that the fair-use doctrine lets you use a set percentage of someone else's work without getting permission, but The Copyright Act of 1976 (which took effect on January 1, 1978) doesn't actually set a specific number of words or lines that may be safely used without permission.

Legal precedents and other factors help people judge whether your use is fair. In Sections 107 through 118 of Title 17, U.S. Code, copyright law specifies four factors that should be considered in determining whether use is fair:

> ✔ "The purpose or character of the use, including whether such use is of commercial nature or is for nonprofit purposes"
>
> ✔ "The nature of the copyright work"
>
> ✔ "The amount and substantiality of the portion used in relation to the copyright work as a whole"
>
> ✔ "The effect of the use upon the potential market for, or value of, the copyrighted work"

The catch here is that these four considerations can be applied with great discretion case by case. All four are explored and then the results are weighed together in light of copyright purposes and the facts of each particular case. Fiction doesn't readily fall under the fair use's "criticism, comment, news reporting, teaching, scholarship, and research" umbrella, so your best bet is to contact the publisher of the original work. As long as you're not using the material in a derogatory manner, permission will probably be granted.

The United States Copyright Office (www.copyright.gov) has extensive information on its website to help you know what is copyrightable, what isn't, and what's fair use. When in doubt, play it safe by asking formal permission anyway, or seek the advice of your publisher's in-house legal counsel or an attorney specializing in publishing or copyright law.

Asking for the okay

The act of asking permission is generally an easy one; locating the copyright holder is the tricky part. In this section, I tell you how to find the copyright owner and request permission to use material from both printed works and other media, such as song and film.

Getting permission for printed work

If you want to reprint a portion of someone else's printed work, contact the publisher's Rights and Permissions Department, which has contractual permission to negotiate rights and permissions on behalf of the author. Contact information for Rights and Permissions Departments is prominently featured on most publishers' websites. In cases where the author has retained his rights, the publisher puts you in contact with the agent, the estate, or the author directly.

When you contact someone for permission, explain exactly what you'd like to reprint, how it will be used, the name of your publication and your publisher, the publication date, the number of books you intend to produce, and what you'll charge for the book. You may be charged a permission fee for your use, and the permission terms will be either *limited* to a set time or number of printings or *unlimited,* meaning you can use that material in as many printings of your book as you want and for as long as your book is in print.

Based on a true story . . . sort of

Fact is stranger than fiction, which is why real life is so darned inspiring to fiction writers. Building a story around an intriguing real person is great fun, and readers sure like the real-life angle. But that calls up a big legal question: Can you write about a real person in a real situation? Or perhaps more to the point, can you get sued for writing about a real person in a real situation?

The answer isn't clear-cut. (What legal answer is?) *Libel* is the term used for making a false statement about someone in either print or broadcast that damages that person's reputation. That whole notion of damage to one's reputation is a gray area that provides a good living to attorneys who specialize in libel. You do have wiggle room when it comes to public figures: You can legally write about them, and as long as what you say about them is true, then it's not libel — but you'd better be able to prove it.

Writing about *nonpublic figures,* though, such as your next-door neighbor or your old high school flame, carries more risk: You can very well be telling the truth about them, but you may fall into the *invasion of privacy* realm by publishing it. Your risk doesn't lessen if that old flame has passed on from this world, because his or her living relatives can sue you for invasion of *their* privacy. The safest way to write about people is to pick deceased public ones, because dead public figures cannot be libeled and don't have the same privacy issues.

So the answer to whether you can write about real people in real situations is a qualified "yes" . . . but it's mighty tricky to do so with legal impunity. And even if you are legally protected in what you write about a person, they can still *try* to sue you, which is no fun even when you do prevail. Only you can decide whether that risk is a worthwhile one.

 Make sure all your correspondence with the copyright owner is memorialized in writing. Publishing houses and literary agencies usually have permission forms containing all the publication details, which everyone signs.

Getting permission for other media

In an ideal world, the copyright information would be explicitly stated with the material, such as in the liner notes of a music CD. But the world doesn't always work that way. Be warned that music and film rights are often parceled out (distribution, performance, and so on) and resold, making permissions more complicated.

If you want to reprint something that isn't a published piece of writing but rather a song lyric or musical score or film dialogue or photograph, you may have to do some research to make permissions contact. Here's where to look:

- ✔ **The creator or publisher:** In most cases, the owner of the copyright is the creator of the material, so you can start with that name. If you want to use song lyrics, contact the song publisher's permissions department.

- ✔ **The agent:** Artists' agents are also good contact sources. Artists' websites often list their reps — go from there. If you contact someone who's not authorized to give permission, he'll say so and generally point you to a person who is.

- ✔ **The U.S. Copyright Office:** Research the U.S. Copyright Office's online database of copyright registrations (www.copyright.gov).

Note that song titles, like book titles, are not copyrightable. Exceptions to that are those song titles that have become popular identifiers of a music group, as with the most popular Beatles or Rolling Stones songs.

Keep track of your efforts as you attempt to locate the copyright owner. That way, if you can't locate the owner and decide to use the material anyway, you'll be able to show that you made sincere efforts to do the right thing. Your publisher may print some wording on your copyright page that declares you've made every effort to trace the ownership in order to secure the necessary permission and make full acknowledgment for its use. This statement also says that should a question arise, you regret the inadvertent error and will make the necessary corrections in future printings.

Crediting your sources

When using someone else's material, your final consideration is the credit citation. Fee or not, you credit the original source on your copyright page, listing the copyright owner's name, the original source title, the year of copyright, and the copyright symbol, as follows:

- ✔ **Book:** Excerpt on page X from [*Book Title*] by [author's name], copyright © [year]. Used with permission.

- ✔ **Poem:** Epigraph by [author's name] from "[Poem Title]," from [*Book Title*] by [book author], copyright © [year]; reprinted with permission of [publisher, city, state].

- ✔ **Scripture translation:** Scripture quotations taken from the [*title and version of the Bible*]. Copyright © [year] by [copyright holder]. Used by permission of [publisher].

- ✔ **Song:** [*Song Title*] words and music by [artist/musician/lyricist's name(s)] © [year]. (Renewed) by [new copyright holder's name]. All rights reserved. Used by permission.

As you can see, citation wording can vary. Copyright owners generally provide their preferred wording. If you're using material that you've determined is in the public domain, you're not legally bound by U.S. copyright law to include this formal attribution, but professionalism dictates that you give credit where credit is due.

Which comes first, the permission or the contract?

If you decide that your use of someone else's work requires permission, you must figure out the best time to contact the copyright owner. Most of the time, you have to hold off on contacting the owner until you have a publisher committed because you need to name a publication date and a print quantity. That means you don't usually secure your permissions before submitting your manuscript to agents and editors.

You do, however, need to know whether you have material that needs permission should you land that book deal, so be prepared to talk about permissions before you sign your final contract. Depending on the nature of the content that needs formal permission, your publisher may require you to get that permission before the contract is finalized. If you're using a previously published poem as your novel's epigraph, for example, your book contract won't likely be held up for such a detail. You can get that later, while the book is in production. But if your entire story is, say, based on someone else's novel, as in a contemporary sequel to an older bestseller, your project won't be able to move forward without the permissions issues being resolved. Your potential editor can discuss the options with her in-house legal staff should that be the case.

Part IV
Getting Published

The 5th Wave   By Rich Tennant

@RICHTENNANT

"Someone want to look at this manuscript
I received on e-mail called 'The Embedded
Virus That Destroyed the Publisher's Servers
When the Manuscript was Rejected'?"

In this part . . .

Now that the creative work is done, it's time to take care of business: selling your manuscript to a children's book publisher. The mere thought of opening yourself up to rejection by professionals can be unnerving, I know, but it doesn't have to be. To help you submit with confidence, I tell you how to submit, what to submit, and whom to submit to. And if all this submission hullabaloo isn't your thing, I give you the skinny on self-publishing so you can decide whether it's the publication path for you. Either way, you need to do some serious marketing when your book gets published, and this part has extensive guidance for publicizing, networking, and building a platform in the virtual age.

Chapter 13

Strategizing and Packaging Your Submissions

*Y*ou've done it. You've imagined, brainstormed, read, researched, written, and revised, and now you're ready to show your completed YA manuscript to the world. Freeze! You've just accomplished something countless people dream about but only a fraction actually do: You've written a book, from "Once upon a time" all the way to "The End." That's a big deal. Something deeply chocolate is in order — or perhaps you have a less G-rated indulgence. Whatever form your pat on the back takes, allow yourself this moment, because when the celebrating's done, you have to buckle down for a whole new phase of your YA fiction adventure: submitting your manuscript for publication.

Submitting is more than just mailing your manuscript to people who have "editor" in their job titles. Children's book editors often specialize in genres and are driven by personal taste, experience, and vision. The same goes for agents. A successful submission offers agents and editors the same four things:

✔ A book that will connect with young readers

✔ A book that will sell in the current marketplace

✔ A book that the agents and editors are passionate about personally, want to work on for several years, and are willing to stake their careers on

✔ A writer who will deliver many such books in the future

Agents and editors really distinguish themselves with the third point, personal passion. Submitting without knowing preferences merely guarantees you a stack of rejection letters. Who needs that? Focused, informed submission efforts are quicker, more effective, and certainly more emotionally prudent. Work smarter, not harder.

This chapter is about getting the most out of your time and effort to find the perfect home for your manuscript. I guide you in compiling your submission list, telling you where to look for agents and editors and then how to hone the list based on their areas of interest. Then I take you through the actual submission process, which involves crafting and formatting query letters, packaging the manuscript, and following up. And because, alas, rejection is often part of this match-making game, I tell you how to extract revision possibilities from rejection letters and hopefully inspire you to remain steadfast in pursuing your goal: a contract for your YA fiction.

Creating Your Submission Strategy

Determination and enthusiasm will only get you so far when submitting your YA manuscript for publication. You need a plan of attack that will put your manuscript in the hands of the right editor to make your vision a printed-and-bound reality. In this section, I tell you where to look for prospective publishing houses and editors and then how to pinpoint your best bets. I also help you decide what kind of agent you want — if you even want one at all.

Don't begin contacting editors or agents until you believe you've done all you can with that manuscript. Too many people submit knowing that there's work to be done, thinking that the role of the editor is to help them whip it into shape. That's not how you get a book deal. If the material's not ready, stay your hand. Your time will come.

Compiling your submission list

Begin your search for the perfect editor and/or agent by identifying houses and/or literary agencies that handle YA fiction, and then narrow that list down to those with successful track records in your genre and story type. After that, you select an editor or agent within that company who appears to be a likely candidate for loving your work (I go into that more in the following sections).

Consider setting aside a submission research week. Obviously, research takes time, but it pays off in the long run by shortening the submission process, by making sure you don't waste your one-time submission with a publishing house on a no-chance editor, and by avoiding needless rejection letters.

Getting published — or getting credentials — through writing contests

Sometimes there's a back door to a publishing deal: a contest. Publishers occasionally hold writing contests that offer book contracts as grand prizes. New Voices–type contests, such as the long-running Delacorte Press Contest for a First Young Adult Novel, are the most common novel publication contests. These contests are posted on publishers' websites and are announced in the *SCBWI Bulletin* newsletter and in other writers' groups and forums. You can also look for publisher-run contests through an Internet search for "young adult fiction writing contest." Read each contest's rules carefully, though. Some require entrants to hold off on submitting to anyone else while the entries are being considered — which can be a considerable period of time.

Writers' groups and local organizations also offer writing contests, although book contracts aren't the prizes, of course. But that's okay — these contests can be a way to earn a few bucks because some award cash prizes. Another bonus: Some of these contests are for works-in-progress, which means you can start amassing your prize titles even before you've finished that first draft. (Similarly, many writers' groups offer grants for works-in-progress, as with SCBWI's WIP Grants. For info on SCBWI's annual grants, go to the "Awards & Grants" section of the group's website, www.scbwi.org.)

Unfortunately, there are contest scams out there. Hucksters want to collect free money through entry fees, or vanity presses may attempt to entice authors to pay for publication (more on vanity presses in Chapter 14). Here are some guidelines for telling which contests are legitimate:

✔ **Known names:** Stick with established contests held by reputable, well-known entities. Editors and agents will recognize the prize name in your query letter and give you credit where credit is due. Contests posted in general newspapers, on classified sites such as Craigslist, or in the ads in the back of writing magazines won't gain you any credibility with editors or agents, get you any closer to publication, or keep you, your money, and your reputation safe.

If you don't readily recognize the contest holder's name or organization, research it. Don't stop at the organization's own website; do an Internet search of the name to get independent verification and consult industry watchdog sites like Writer Beware (www.sfwa.org/for-authors/writer-beware/) and Preditors & Editors (http://pred-ed.com).

✔ **Fees:** Entry fees, if required, should be nominal, between $5 and $25. That said, large contests may require larger entry fees (although not much larger), and some scammers are happy to take little bits of money from a lot of people, so fee alone is not a credibility indicator. Consider the entry fee with the other elements listed here.

Contests offering opportunities for further paid services such as "coaching" should raise red flags. Don't pay for extra perks or services.

✔ **Categories:** Legitimate contests usually specialize in a single category or genre. Scammers cast wide nets to bring in the most entry fees possible. Enter contests

(continued)

(continued)

that focus on young adult fiction or children's books.

✔ **The fine print:** Legitimate contests post rules specifying the prizes. Make sure you read them and find their terms acceptable. Vanity presses may post fine print that buries the truth: the prize for winning is publication that *you* pay for. There are other items you should watch out for: Do you surrender first publication rights by entering? Can the contest holder publish your entry on its website? Are you promising anything you don't want to promise merely by entering? Know what you're getting into.

Here are some great places to gather likely prospects for your submission list:

✔ **Publication guides:** Usually available in both print and electronic versions, these resources contain not only contact information for agents, editors, and publishers but also descriptions of everyone's interests, specialties, and submission requirements. Examples of publication guides are *Literary Market Place* (LMP), *Children's Writer's and Illustrator's Market* (CWIM), and the Society of Children's Books Writers and Illustrators' publication guide, which is provided in the SCBWI membership packet and available to active members online. You may find these guides on the reference shelves at your local library.

✔ **Writers' groups and online forums:** Ask fellow writers for recommendations based on their experiences and research. Personal anecdotes are valuable in winnowing down your submission list to those agents and editors who share your literary sensibility.

✔ **Spines and copyright pages:** Check books similar to yours for publisher and imprint information, and then go to the publishers' websites and study the imprint profiles and online catalogs.

Imprints are like departments or teams within a publishing house that cater to specific demographic groups, genres, and the like. A children's book publisher may have separate imprints for fantasy books, for historical fiction, and for paperback editions, for example. The editors in those imprints can acquire only the manuscripts that fall within those parameters. Each imprint has an editorial director who oversees the editors within the imprint and develops her own acquisitions. Sometimes an editorial director gets her own imprint to define (it may even be *eponymous,* or named after her), which allows her to choose the mission and personality of that imprint based on her tastes and vision.

When submitting, consider each imprint independently of the others in the house. Although many houses discourage writers from submitting to two editors within the same imprint, you *can* submit to two or even all the imprints at a house (as long as they're appropriate for your work).

✔ **Acknowledgments and dedications:** Writers tend to thank their behind-the-scenes crew in their acknowledgements — and in the process give you prime submission leads. You have an example of an agent or editor's literary taste right in your hands! If a lead turns into a submission for you, mention that helpful book's title in your query letter to demonstrate that you've done your homework. "I admire your book *X* and believe that my manuscript will be right for you" or "I enjoyed *X* and would love the chance to work with you."

✔ **Conferences or writers' group meetings and retreats:** Editors and agents speak, teach, participate in panels and do individual manuscript critiques at these events. Talk to editors and agents after their presentations or sit next to these people at lunch. That doesn't mean stalk, pounce, hard-sell, or try to hand over your manuscript; they never take manuscripts on the spot, anyway.

Your goal is to make a personal connection that you can refer to when you follow up via mail or e-mail as seems appropriate. One way to do that is to simply introduce yourself, thank the editor or agent for the presentation, and then say, "I believe my manuscript is the kind of book you like, and I'd like to submit it to you after the conference if that's all right." You'll be in a position to say in your query letter, "I spoke with you at the conference. Here's the manuscript I told you about." You'll no longer be just a name on a paper. Whenever possible, pay for one-on-one critiques so you can talk specifically about your manuscript. That's the best connection you can make.

Agents and editors often extend open submission invitations to all attendees at an event, for a limited time. The people offering the invitation tell you how to note the invitation on your submission.

Most agencies and publishing houses allow you to submit your manuscript to just one of their editors or agents — yet another reason to select wisely. (Check their submission guidelines on their websites.) The idea here is that one person represents the interests of all, and if the one you submit to isn't personally interested and chooses not to pass your manuscript along to another colleague, then it's not right for the house or agency. The exception to this one-submission-only rule is personal contact. If you make a personal connection with an agent or editor at a conference, you can submit to him even if your manuscript has already been rejected by the agency or house. Accepted industry ethics require you to note in the query letter that colleague So-and-So already passed on the project because "she didn't connect with it." It's best if you can offer a reason you think this new match is a good one, such as "but I think you'll be intrigued because of your interest in baseball stories" or whatever. The point is to give the second agent a reason not to automatically dismiss your submission because his trusted colleague said no.

Identifying the right editor for you

To make a match that'll culminate in a contract and ultimately a bound book with your name on the cover, you must submit to the right editor for both you and your project. That editor will spend one or two years working with your story, investing her time and her own career on its success in the marketplace (as well as your long-term success), and she'll commit to that only if she connects with the manuscript at the outset and shares your vision for what it could be. That's why there's so much talk about "passion" and "connection" and "vision."

Simply addressing your submission to "The Editors" will land your package in the infamous slush pile — if you're lucky. *Slush pile* is industry slang for unsolicited submissions that editors (or more likely their assistants) comb through once in a blue moon. These days, though, most submissions not addressed to a specific editor are simply returned or automatically recycled. Publishers don't have the staff to deal with them. And why should they? Those authors haven't researched the editors to determine whether a match is even a remote possibility. That lack of effort influences their perception of your professionalism and perhaps even your sincerity. With editorial bios and interviews easily accessible on the Internet, there's no convincing excuse for not making that determination.

Much like dating, publishing is about finding the right chemistry. Knowing editors' interests increases your chances of making a match — and of doing so quickly. That means getting to know the person behind the title. Editors' interests are evidenced in their *acquisitions* (the manuscripts they buy), in their publications, and in their explicitly stated wishes. Get online and search for the editors in your target imprints. Here's what you're looking for:

- ✔ **Bios:** Editors' bios are sometimes published on their publishers' website, and they're usually available on blogs and websites of individual writers and groups. You can also find bios in industry publications when interviews or appearances are involved. Those bios list noteworthy books the editors have worked on and the authors they've worked with, giving you a sense of the editors' literary sensibilities.

Read the editor's noteworthy books. Or at least check out the descriptions, reviews, and first pages through an online bookstore. If these books are important enough for the editors to highlight in their bios and interviews, the books are important to you as prime examples of the editors' sensibilities and buying tendencies.

- ✔ **Interviews:** Read all the interviews you can find, which almost always include the direct question "What are you looking for?"

✔ **Deals:** Type the editors' names into the *Publishers Weekly* website (www.publishersweekly.com) to see what they've been buying lately, or follow deal news with the free *Publishers Lunch* e-newsletter, which reports book deals each week (www.publishersmarketplace.com). You can pay for a more in-depth version called *Publishers Lunch Deluxe* or get direct access to searchable deals databases through a Publishers Marketplace membership.

✔ **Appearances:** See whether your target editors are speaking with writers' groups in your area or acting as faculty at writers' conferences. Editors commonly give speeches, teach sessions, participate in panels, and conduct manuscript critiques. Attend if you can. Editors usually state what they're looking for in submissions and may extend submission invitations to attendees, and you may get a chance to meet the editors personally. When possible, pay for a manuscript critique for uninterrupted face-to-face time that's dedicated to your work — if the manuscript and the editor are a match, book deal! If not, you'll know and won't waste your one-time imprint submission on that editor.

✔ **Open calls:** Keep your eyes peeled for "assistant editors" or for veteran editors who've recently switched publishing houses. These folks tend to be in active acquisition mode as they work to *build their lists* (sign up manuscripts to work on and writers to work with). You'll find them making the rounds at conferences and other writers' events and participating in Internet interviews to get their names out and their wish lists known. Sometimes they'll even post notices in SCBWI's *Bulletin* that they're making an exception to the house "no unsolicited manuscripts" policy for a limited time.

When you've identified a likely editor, double-check his or her current employer to confirm that your desired editor is still employed in that imprint. Editors tend to move around from house to house. If you have to, call the publisher's operator. Don't ask to speak with the editor, though. Queries via phone are intrusive no-no's.

After you identify and rank your editorial prospects, send out submissions in phases. Send to perhaps ten publishers and then wait. If you get a bite in the first round, huzzah! If not, you may be fortunate to have several editors forgo the form letters for actual comments about why they rejected your project. This gives you a chance to revise based on the feedback of experts in the trenches before you send the manuscript out in the second wave. If all you get is form letters, so be it. Proceed directly to the next round of submissions. Do this until you get a hit. Of course, you could submit to dozens at once, but if they all reject the submission citing the same general issue, those doors are now closed to a revised version in the future.

Steel yourself. Submitting even to the right editor takes patience and fortitude, because getting a response may take up to six months. *Solicited* manuscripts, which agents submit, get reviewed far more quickly than unsolicited ones because editors want to maintain their good rapport with the agent so as to keep the hottest manuscripts coming. You may send a polite follow-up at 8 weeks and again at 4 months. More on that later, in "Packaging your sub-mission."

Deciding to work with an agent

The desire for expediency is why some writers insist on having agents. Agents have well-established working relationships with editors, know who's looking for what, and enjoy direct access to editors who are off-limits to writers because of policies that disallow *unsolicited* (or non-agented) submissions. Although you certainly don't need an agent, many writers use them to land book deals and thereafter use agents as expert advisors. Of course, that means you have to do a round of agent submissions. Even expediency takes time.

Knowing what an agent can do for you

Agents are experts in both market trends and editor/house tastes, and agents' primary role is to use that knowledge to match up a manuscript with the right editor, resulting in a book contract. Do you *need* an agent? No. But they're great to have in your corner for three reasons:

- ✓ **To get access to the right editor:** An agent knows who wants what and how to reach them. In a perfect scenario, an agent spots your great manuscript about, say, a runaway slave in the Civil War, knows that Editor Ellen is looking for more historical fiction and has a particular yen for the Civil War era, calls up Editor Ellen to say, "I've got exactly what you're looking for," and gets the manuscript to the top of Ellen's reading stack. No wasted mailings to editors who can't stand historical fiction, saving time, money, and effort for all.

- ✓ **To bypass those no-unsolicited-manuscripts policies:** In a practical sense, agents act as prescreeners for editors, so editors know that a submission from an agent has a significantly higher probability of being their next acquisition. Editors give agent submissions priority, often fielding the initial contact as a phone call. The trust is high enough that editors even take part in agent-run *auctions,* wherein agents invite several houses to read and then bid on a manuscript at once, with the manuscript going to the highest bidder. Running an auction well takes a lot of skill, trust, and industry savvy.

- ✓ **To be a partner:** Literary agents are more than just salespeople. You want an advocate for your work, someone who believes in you and your talents, who will go to the mat for you and not only find the best money for you but also help you map out your long-term career and manage your rights. Your agent is your publishing partner.

For all this, the agent gets a percentage of your earnings from both your *advance* (your upfront payment, due upon signing the contract) and the subsequent *royalties* (the percentage of money you make on each book sold; find more on rights and royalties in Chapter 17). This is why it's in an agent's interests to look for projects she thinks will sell from authors who'll have long, productive futures in publishing. Your agent won't make money until you do.

Beware of interminable agency clauses in your author-agency agreement. *Interminable agency clauses* allow an agent to remain the "agent of record" for the full life of the copyright (which is the author's lifetime plus 70 years) instead of just for the duration of any contracts that agency negotiates. That's not right. Your agent should get a commission only for the life of your book's contract with your publisher. If the contract with that publisher is terminated for some reason, the agent should get paid again only if he sells the rights for a new edition to a new publisher. Look out for language that lets an agent "remain Agent of Record in perpetuity" or "for the legal life of the Work" or that states an "Agent's interest in the Work is irrevocable."

Because of the wait time involved in seeking agent representation, writers often submit their manuscripts to editors even as they submit to agents. That way, they're working on both fronts at once. This, of course, requires researching both editors and agents. If you were to land an editor first, you could discontinue your hunt for an agent. However, if you see value in having an agent as a publishing partner and advisor, don't stop your agent search when you land the book deal. In fact, you'll probably find the search easier because you already have a book under contract and have demonstrated that your work is salable. Ask your editor about the agents she works with. If you land an agent first, be prepared to provide your new agent with a list of editors who've already considered your project. The agent won't resubmit to them. Don't worry that you've closed doors all over Publishing World by submitting to editors while trying to land an agent; the agent you finally sign with will know plenty of other editors at the houses you've already tried — and in other houses, too. It's unlikely you'd exhaust all your editorial opportunities on your own.

Identifying the right agent for you

After you've compiled your list of prospective agents who represent MG/YA fiction in your genre, you narrow that list the same way you hone a list of editors: You research them. The Internet is a great resource for this. Keep the following items in mind as you do your research:

- ✔ **Know what you want the agent to do.** Many agents have editorial backgrounds and will help you shape your manuscript prior to submission. Do you want an agent like that? Or do you just want a strategist on your team, one who will take what you give her and find the best place for it? Editorial experience is evident in agents' bios, and their personal statements indicate whether they shape before submitting.

✔ **Know what the Association of Authors' Representatives (AAR) demands.** The AAR is the primary professional organization for literary and dramatic agents. Its members agree to subscribe to a Canon of Ethics — and that's a good thing for you. That canon was adopted to protect authors from dodgy agents who'd take advantage of hopefuls by charging them for editing and then refusing to take them on as clients — or even by charging them for editing and then agreeing to take them on as clients.

If an agent agrees to take you on as a client, any editing he does is free, as part of the submission's preparation. The agent may refer you to an editing service outside the agency, but he can't require you to use that service, nor can he take payment (kickbacks) from the service.

Never pay an agent to read your submission. That's not considered ethical and is against AAR policy. Websites and blogs like Preditors & Editors (`http://pred-ed.com`) and Writer Beware (`www.sfwa.org/for-authors/writer-beware/`) specialize in outing predators who take advantage of hopeful authors.

✔ **Know what others are saying.** Do an online search for the agents' names and read what folks are saying about them in writers' forums. Read the comments that follow blogged interviews, because individual writers often share their anecdotes. Ask your writers' groups for any personal knowledge they may have about your prospective agents.

✔ **Know what agents say about themselves.** Spend time on the agency website, study the agency's policies, and review its client list. See whether the agents are active in industry groups and belong to the AAR. See who has published their clients' work. Read the agents' bios and their interviews on other websites and blogs to see whether you have what the agents are looking for and what they like to publish. This is your chance to get a feel for their personalities and literary sensibilities, to judge whether they're indeed a good match for you. There are many great agents, but not all of them are great for you. Make the distinction.

You don't need to choose an agent who specializes in children's books, but it's better if he does. He'll have more children's book contacts, and he'll have a deeper, more up-to-the-minute understanding of the YA marketplace and the behind-the-scenes goings-on of the key players. Remember, your ideal agent is a long-term partner, not just someone who can negotiate and number crunch.

If you already have an agent for books for adults, discuss getting a *subagent* with her. Subagents specialize in children's books, making the sale for your work and getting a cut of your general agent's portion of that sale. Another option is to have separate representation for your adult projects and your YA novels. Agents may also use subagents for their subsidiary rights (the movie rights, audio rights, and so on). Rights subagents specialize in certain areas of the contract process. See Chapter 17 for info on subsidiary rights.

Query Letters, Your Number-One Selling Tool

For a YA fiction writer, selling a novel starts with a *query letter* — a three-paragraph, single-page pitch letter that highlights the strengths of both you and your manuscript. Children's book editors require query letters instead of proposals, and editors expect to buy completed manuscripts (uncommon exceptions being for previously published authors who've proven that they have the stick-to-itiveness to finish what they've started and the skills to realize what they've promised). In this section, you discover how to write a powerful query letter to sell your novel.

Although querying before you finish the manuscript may seem like a logical way to cut down your waiting time, it's a risky maneuver. Should you get a speedy reply asking for the full manuscript, you wouldn't have anything to send. Most writers send in their material within hours or days of the request for more. Leaving a request dangling is always a little hinky — the agent may wonder whether you're flaky or not as serious about him as you claimed to be in the query, and the last thing you want to do is give agents a reason to narrow their eyes suspiciously. Worse, you may rush out with something before it's thoroughly polished.

Why queries feel like the be all, end all . . . and are

The goal of your query letter is to sell your manuscript to the agent or editor. It's the first thing she'll see, even before flipping to Page 1 of your sample chapters. Sometimes it's the *only* thing she'll see, because some houses and agencies accept only queries for submissions, requesting more material only if a query offers something they want.

Just as the first sentence of your manuscript is vital, so, too, is the first thing that agents and editors see of your project — the query letter. It's as much a writing sample as it is a setup for your manuscript. Therefore, the query letter must be professional, representing both yourself and your story well.

Because the query letter forces you to synthesize your story, name your themes, and state why you think this project has a ready audience even as it stands out from others in its genre, some writers like to write a query letter early in the project, as part of the story development.

Writing a successful query letter

A successful query letter is one that makes the agent or editor want to read the manuscript. The following subsections guide you in crafting that letter, from formatting it to striking the right tone to nailing each part of a standard query. Here are the main three parts:

- ✔ **The opening:** State the hook for your manuscript and indicate why you chose that editor or agent.

- ✔ **The pitch:** Expand on the themes and the general journey of the main character, and position the entire project in the marketplace.

- ✔ **The closing:** State your credentials (your publication history and/or the reason *you* are the person to write this particular story).

Be sure to proofread before you mail that query letter. Do an extra proofreading pass, too, scrutinizing *every* element, especially the inside address and the name in the salutation. A query letter is no place for a typo — or worse, the wrong addressee name entirely.

Striking the right tone

The tone of your query letter should reflect your personality and the tone of the manuscript. If yours is a silly story, let your lighthearted voice come through in the query letter even as you remain solidly in the realm of professionalism.

Don't make grandiose promises or predictions about the project's market potential. Editors and agents know the realities of their markets and evaluate the potential of your manuscript themselves. Your job is to tell them the great features of your story and to present yourself as a professional writer with whom they'll enjoy working. They'll decide whether the story is "exceptional" or "ground-breaking" for themselves.

Paragraph 1: An opening that hooks

You can use the same basic query letter for every agent and editor you submit to. Just tailor the opening paragraph for each person to show that you've done your homework in choosing him or her.

Your opening paragraph should catch the addressee's attention. Skip the civilized pleasantries and go right into your reason for choosing that particular person and delivering your hook. A *hook* is an intriguing one-liner about your story that includes the genre, the main character (especially his age), and the main theme and/or the main conflict in the book. (Chapter 4 is dedicated to developing a tight, intriguing hook.) You can lead off with either the hook or the reason; that's up to you. Some writers prefer to hold their reason until the third paragraph. That works, too — just be sure you get it in there somewhere. Check out these two openings, which switch up the lead-in:

A. Dear Editor X:

What do you give a girl who has everything? Camis, K.P., and an education in real life. In my contemporary YA novel *Party Girl Goes A.W.O.L.*, spoiled 17-year-old Roxy Monroe parties one time too many and gets shipped off to her grandfather's iron-fisted alma mater: George S. Patton Military Academy. Given your deep list of contemporary YA authors, I'd like to send you Roxy's story.

B. Dear Agent X:

I've been following your blog and know that you have a keen interest in contemporary YA fiction. I hope to interest you in my own contemporary YA, *Party Girl Goes A.W.O.L.,* a novel about a spoiled 17-year-old girl who parties one time too many and gets shipped off to her grandfather's alma mater: George S. Patton Military Academy.

If you received an invitation to submit your work, such as at a conference during a face-to-face meeting or through an open invitation to all attendees, open with that: "Thank you for inviting attendees of the X conference on X date to submit. You talked about wanting MGs with high boy appeal, so I'm sending you my MG adventure *Title*." Or "I heard your speech about creating an engaging narrative voice at the X chapter meeting in August. I'm hoping you'll find that my YA novel *Title* has just the kind of gripping voice you're looking for." As you can see, you have plenty of room for individual style, personality, and circumstances in delivering the key information. I'm giving you the mechanics, but there needn't be anything mechanical about your delivery.

Paragraph 2: A pitch that prompts action

Paragraph 2 takes the attention you snagged with Paragraph 1 and builds it up to strong curiosity and then to action: a request for the full manuscript or an eager read-through of accompanying sample chapters. To pull this off, you tease the main storyline without revealing the resolution, connect it to your overarching theme, and then position the project for a specific audience. Although this pitch should fit easily into one paragraph, it accomplishes two tasks:

- ✔ **Setting up the storyline:** Craft four to eight sentences that focus on basic setup. In a story setup, you identify the main character and her age, state her goal, and then tease the interesting conflicts and escalations, leaving the resolution unstated to spark curiosity about how the scenario(s) will play out and resolve. That said, if it suits your project to reveal the outcome — perhaps in a "So-and-So learns that life as a Whatever isn't so bad after all" context — do so.

  I'm purposely not calling this a "mini synopsis" or something similar — you're not out to summarize anything. There's plenty of room for that in the full synopsis, which accompanies your query letter or which you'll make available with the full manuscript when an agent, intrigued by this pitch, requests it.

A million examples of setups are at your fingertips. Choosing books in your genre, study their jacket flap copy or paperback back-cover blurbs, or read their descriptions on bookseller websites. Note how the blurbs state the universal themes even as they focus most intently on the main conflict that distinguishes each story.

✔ **Positioning the story:** Although editors and agents are experts on the YA fiction marketplace, you're the expert on your book. Tell them where your story fits in. State your genre and the age range of your readership (Chapter 2 can help you know that), and then do as many of the following items as you can:

- **Call out universal themes.** Demonstrate that your story has wide appeal by mentioning your core theme. Your story should have *universal appeal,* meaning the theme should be known or experienced by a significant segment of the general teen population. For example, the theme may be betrayal by friends or rejection by a peer group.

- **Mention similar books.** You can help the agent/editor know what kind of story you're offering by mentioning well-known novels that are similar to yours. This also demonstrates that there's a ready place in the market for your story.

Be careful to name names without claiming fame. Don't say you're the next J. K. Rowling — or any other author, for that matter. That comes across as egotistical. Simply say that you were inspired by the other author or that you hope fans of fantastical worlds such as So-and-So's will find your fantasy realm inviting.

- **Highlight fresh angles.** Even as you point out similar titles and universal themes to claim a place in the market, tell the agent or editor what makes your novel different. Emphasize your storyline over your themes because that's where you'll stand out. There are thousands of books out there about fitting in at a new school and earning what you get; there's only one book about a privileged party girl learning to respect hard work and to value teamwork when she's forced to spend her senior year in an iron-fisted military school. Universal themes make a book *accessible* to a wide audience; the storyline makes it *appealing* to them.

- **Plug timeliness.** Mention timely facts to show that your story is right for this moment in time. If you've written about a tormented wimpy kid, for example, point out the increasing spotlight on bullying in schools. Even include a stat or two if you've got them.

If your project is time-sensitive and requires particularly speedy review, state that. For example, maybe the big-deal 200th anniversary of the event featured in your historical fiction is next year, so you want your book out in time to ride the publicity wave. Most agents and editors will try to accommodate that.

- **Note niche markets.** Your story may appeal to a special small but definable and reachable audience — that's a *niche market,* and you should point it out. The editor or agent may not know, for example, that the Midwest has 4-H animal husbandry enclaves whose members may enjoy a story about a girl and her beloved pig. There are many magazines, newsletters, and regional websites dedicated to 4-H news, products, and competitions; those are useful marketing and sales opportunities.

  If a niche market isn't there, don't sweat it — a niche market is by definition a small one, and a publisher isn't likely to offer a contract simply because you can identify a few hundred or even thousand potential readers who may not even follow through and buy the book. Being interested in animal husbandry doesn't make one an automatic buyer of novels about kids and animals.

Here's an example of a pitch paragraph, demonstrating both story setup and market positioning:

> Seventeen-year-old Roxy Monroe is spoiled rotten and proud of it. She's got hot cars, hot clothes, and of course the hottest guy at her posh prep school. But when Roxy's constant partying threatens her chances of graduating high school, she's sentenced to the only school her parents think can tame her: a hardcore military academy. "They made a man out of me," Grandfather Thurmond tells her. "Surely they can do something with you." Now Roxy's life is *Reveille* at daybreak, forced marches, and classmates who think camouflage is cool, weaponry is cooler, and stuck-up party girls are good for just one thing: target practice. Thing is, Roxy has something neither her parents nor Grandfather nor her new Commandant of Cadets ever figured on: a brain. And she finally intends to use it . . . to lead a coup at the academy. Celebrating loyalty, friendship, and the ability to find common ground in the unlikeliest of places, *Party Girl Goes A.W.O.L.* offers a lighthearted, girl-power spin to the popular rich-girl-comeuppance tale.

Paragraph 3: A closing that sells you

The third paragraph of your query letter focuses on you, stating your credentials as a writer and as the crafter of this particular story. If you opted to wait until now to explain why you chose this addressee, go to it. Also kick in with any extra material, such as your special access to your audience or platform items. Don't give a marketing plan — that's not the point of this letter — just list any special things the editor or agent needs to know at this point, such as

- ✔ **Writing credentials:** Note any previously published books (of any kind), short stories, magazine articles, or professional newsletters; a profession related to word-crafting, such as journalist, technical editor, or screenwriter; and any prepublication work-in-progress awards. If you're a member of SCBWI, say so: "I'm a member of SCBWI." If you're not a member, become one — or find another writers' group that appeals to you, due to location, personality, whatever. Membership suggests to editors that you're serious about perfecting your craft.

If you don't have any "relevant credentials," don't sweat it. It won't hurt that you've never been published. You just don't get that extra oomph of credibility.

✔ **Relevant nonwriting credentials:** Acknowledge a profession related to the publishing world, such as librarian, reviewer, or bookseller, or a job that includes interaction with young people (which suggests knowledge of their subculture and reading interests in particular), such as a teacher or youth services professional.

Alas, being the parent of a teen doesn't carry weight here. You're in the trenches with young people, that's for sure, but the experience is too narrow and anecdotal to hail as a professional credential.

Include any relevant (usually exceptional) life experiences that lend authenticity and authority to your story. If you have parenting or other firsthand experience with a person in the circumstances you feature in your story, do mention that. For example, a novel featuring a deaf protagonist gets major credibility points when it's written by the parent, sibling, or friend of a deaf person — or of course *by* the deaf person. Such a writer has insight into the unique world of that protagonist. If you're a twin and have written about twins, mention it. Another example is a pilot who's written about a teen earning money for flying lessons. That's exceptional and lends distinct credibility — it makes you the right person for that particular story — and the editor/agent wants to know it.

✔ **Platform opportunities:** If you have a platform with this audience — say you're a columnist for a local publication with a Latino audience and your novel features a Latino boy and all your columns will plug this book to the publication's audience — note it. You have inroads to that readership, and that's a valuable thing for a publisher to know.

Fill out the rest of Paragraph 3 of your query letter with one or more of these statements (or something similar):

✔ "I hope you'll decide *Title* is right for your list."

✔ "*Title* is complete at XX,000 words. May I send you the full manuscript?"

✔ "Thank you for this opportunity." Sometimes editors or agents extend submission opportunities to all attendees at a speaking engagement. This statement is a great way to acknowledge that.

✔ "This is an X-week exclusive" or "This is an exclusive submission." If you're offering an exclusive, Paragraph 3 is where to say so. (For info on exclusives, see the sidebar "Sending multiple submissions at a time.")

Always end Paragraph 3 with "Thank you for your time and consideration. I look forward to hearing from you" or words to that effect. This sentiment should fit smoothly on the end of your third paragraph, but setting this line as its own paragraph is acceptable. Remember, following the three-paragraph format helps you avoid distraction as you pitch your strengths in an organized manner; it's not about hemming you in.

Don't say that your family or friends have always told you to write this or that all the kids who've read it have loved it. Agents and editors want writers who are committed for the long term, not someone satisfying a whim or a challenge. Offer yourself as the professional writer you are or intend to be.

Formatting the letter

A query letter may be selling something for kids, but it's written to an adult businessperson from an adult businessperson and should reflect that. Accepted standards apply to query letters in the children's books industry, all grounded in the standard business letter format:

- ✔ **General specs:** Keep the letter one page in length, single-spaced, with a 12-point professional-looking typeface such as Times New Roman or Arial. If you're pressed for space, drop down to 11-point but go no smaller. Set your margins at 1 inch all around, with the text blocks being left aligned and right ragged. To avoid distracting from your carefully crafted content, don't get funky with colors or fonts; stick to white paper and black type.

- ✔ **Letterhead or typed heading:** You can put your contact information at the top of the letter (centered at the very top or left aligned under the date) or below your typed name in the sign-off. In either case, include your name, address, phone number, and e-mail address. Also list your website and/or blog if they're related to your writing (this mostly pertains to previously published authors or journalists) or in some way directly tie into the topic of your book or demonstrate your *platform* (think "fan base"; see Chapter 15 for extensive coverage of platforms). The site and blog must be professional in look and content.

  You're not expected to have preprinted letterhead stationery; typed headings are far more common than not in submissions.

- ✔ **Inside address:** Include the editor's full name, job title, imprint, publisher, and then the street address. For a query letter to an agent, list the agent's name, the agency, and the street address.

- ✔ **Salutation:** Address your submission to a specific agent or editor, using her last name, as in "Dear Ms. X:" Remember, "Dear Editor" or "To Whom It May Concern" tells the recipient you haven't done your homework, undermining your professionalism and pretty much guaranteeing your submission a spot in the slush pile or recycle bin.

Your follow-up letter: Responding to manuscript requests

When your query letter results in a request for the full manuscript, accompany that manuscript with a *cover letter* referencing the request and restating your hook. You can't assume the requestor will remember your project, especially if you've taken some extra time to revise it:

> "As you requested, I'm enclosing the full manuscript for *Party Girl Goes A.W.O.L.*, my contemporary YA novel about a spoiled 17-year-old who parties one time too many and gets shipped off to her grandfather's iron-fisted alma mater: George S. Patton Military Academy. Thank you for this opportunity. I look forward to hearing from you."

Use as much personality as you evidenced in your original query letter. That's the voice the requestor responded to, after all.

If there have been updates in your writing career since you originally queried, note those in the cover letter. For example, have you had magazine articles or some other book published? Have you spoken or been invited to speak at conferences or with writers' groups? Have you started a blog or increased your blog stats considerably, expanding your platform?

Also, if you've taken more than a month to send in the requested material, let the editor or agent know you've been polishing; she'd rather you send in your strongest work. If you're doing a substantial revision for some reason (say you had the manuscript professionally critiqued or got feedback at a writers' retreat while awaiting the reply to your query), then set a deadline for yourself to get that revision to the requestor within three months of that request. If you wait more than six months, you may miss the boat completely. By then, the market may have shifted or that requestor may have moved on to another position — or to another house or agency entirely.

Send in only the number of pages requested. Sometimes an agent or editor requests a *partial* instead of a full manuscript — perhaps 30 or 50 pages. If you discover that a chapter will end at 51 or 52 pages, it's okay to round up to the end of that chapter, but don't go further than that.

Lastly, it's a good idea to include a copy of the original query letter so that the agent or editor doesn't have to dig through her files in search of that letter if she wants to review your full pitch.

- ✔ **Body:** You break the main body of your letter into three paragraphs (see the preceding sections for details on these paragraphs). Separate each of those paragraphs with a line space, beginning each new paragraph flush left with no paragraph indent.

- ✔ **Sign-off:** No one's going to whip you with a wet noodle if you use a personally preferred sign-off, but "Sincerely" will do just fine. Insert a couple of line spaces for your signature and then type your name. If you're in a writers' group, list your affiliation under your typed named in this manner: "Member, SCBWI." If you didn't list your word count in the body of the letter, include it here under your name (round it off): "*Title*, MG Fiction manuscript, XX,000 words."

Writing an Effective Synopsis

The purpose of a synopsis is to encapsulate your main plot and main character arc, reporting the following points in just two to three pages:

- ✔ What your main character needs or wants to achieve
- ✔ What threatens her enough to kick-start the story
- ✔ What steps she takes to achieve that goal
- ✔ What challenges she overcomes to get there

That may sound impossible — you just spent several hundred pages doing that, after all. How in the world do you render that much material down to just three pages? You stick to the main events, that's how, filling in just a few lines for each, using direct statements, eliminating setting details, and telling instead of showing — in short, you do the opposite of everything I tell you in Part II of this book!

If you're well short of three pages after you've done all this, you can go back and work in the events of a subplot — but only if that subplot is vital to understanding the main storyline as described in the synopsis. If the storyline is clear enough without mentioning the subplot, then resist the urge to include it. You don't want to make readers of your synopsis sort through nonvital events and characters.

You send this synopsis with your hardcopy query letter, or you embed it at the bottom of your query e-mail, just below your name. (To protect themselves against computer viruses, agencies and publishers don't usually accept attachments to e-mail queries.) Some agencies have query contact forms on their websites that only allow you to write a limited number of words; in those cases, fill their limited forms with your query pitch and save your synopsis for when the agency requests your full manuscript.

Drafting the synopsis

Although writers understand the goal and general mission of a synopsis, they still often battle with the actual crafting of it. Here are three tips for getting the words onto the paper:

- ✔ **Build it from outline form.** Write an outline of the story, listing the main character's goal, the catalyst event, the challenges that escalate the situation (what happens and why the character fails to surmount the challenge), the character's revelation moment, and then the climax and resolution. (Yes, tell how the story ends. A synopsis is not the place to tease; agents and editors want to know the ending if they're reading your synopsis.) Use the seven steps in Chapter 6 to build this outline, or bring your original outline up to date.

After you've listed all the events and their impact on the protagonist's character journey, smooth it all out, turning notes and statements into full sentences and then helping them flow into paragraphs.

✔ **Summarize every chapter, one by one.** Starting with Chapter One, write three to four direct statements about what happens to your main character in the chapter, focusing only on the main actions and central characters. Then remove your chapter numbers and merge your stack of summaries into a running account.

✔ **Have a critique partner draft the synopsis first.** How's that for passing the buck? Actually, this helps both of you. You get a first draft of your synopsis from someone who's not wedded to the details, and your partner gets a valuable exercise in plot- and character-building as she follows the main thread of the story from beginning to end. When she's done condensing, you go in and massage the language to reflect your voice and style. Just be sure to return the favor!

Begin your synopsis with a two- or three-sentence version of your hook to set up the overall concept (I cover hooks in Chapter 4). State the main character, her goal and key conflict, and what she stands to lose if she fails. Then launch into the actual summarizing in the second paragraph.

Tweaking the tone and tense

Synopsis may call to mind a big old boring summary, but you do have wiggle room in terms of tone. If your manuscript is lighthearted, inject a measure of lightheartedness into your synopsis. If the manuscript is young, keep your sentences in your synopsis simple to suggest a youthful sensibility.

Do not let the narrator of your story "narrate" your synopsis. This document is an overview of the plot in your words, from your all-knowing, outside-the-story viewpoint. Make the tone accessible and reflective of your storytelling style, but don't get gimmicky.

Fiction synopses are written in present tense (the *literary present*), as though the story's main action is happening now — even if you wrote your story in past tense. It's okay, though, to break away for a sentence or two to mention a past event that somehow informs the present happenings. I've italicized the description of past events in the following example:

Sarah hates jocks, who always stop and hassle her, wondering if she's the girl *who almost burned down the gym last year. Luckily, Sarah's brother saved the gym — and her along with it. He even saved the spirit banner from the flames.* Now, on the anniversary of the fire, her brother gets to strut down the hall like some superhero while she has to hide behind her locker door until the bell rings.

As long as you keep past tense breakaways short, sweet, and rare, no one will be confused or distracted.

Formatting a synopsis

As with the query letter, your synopsis should be single-spaced, with a 12-point professional-looking typeface such as Times New Roman or Arial. I don't recommend dropping down to 11-point font for this piece, though. Three full, single-spaced pages can be imposing when the font is so small. Set your margins at 1 inch all around, with the text blocks being left aligned and right ragged. Stick to white paper and black type.

The first page contains your name and contact information in the upper left; the title, the genre, and the word count in the upper right; and the word "Synopsis" in the top center. Each subsequent page should have your name, the title, and a page number in the top right corner. This two- to three-page synopsis should be paper-clipped, not stapled. Just tuck it behind the cover or query letter, before the manuscript or sample chapters.

Packaging Your Submission

Now comes the grunt work: packing up your manuscript and shipping it out. As with all other parts of the submission process, there are best ways to go about the big send-off. Here I tell you what to include in your submission, what not to include, and what your final submission package should look like.

What to include

Some publishers and agencies prefer query-only submissions, meaning you just send the query letter, whereas others want materials such as sample chapters and/or synopses, too. Publishers and agencies post their preferences, called *author guidelines,* on their websites. This is also where publishers note "no unsolicited manuscripts" if it's their policy to accept submissions only from agents. Always check for guidelines before querying. Many publishers and agencies require hard copy submissions, although more and more are allowing electronic queries.

Submitting hard copy

If you don't find any submission guidelines, follow these general rules for hard copy submissions (printed and sent via the postal service):

✔ **Send a typed query letter, a 2- to 3-page synopsis, and a sample chapter or two.** Don't waste money sending the full manuscript unless that's specifically requested in the author guidelines. Editors and agents know within the first few pages whether or not they want to see more — in which case they'll request it.

Submit materials for just one title at a time to each agent or editor. If you have manuscripts for several stories, pick your best one and lead with that. When the recipient expresses serious interest in that one, you can discuss your others.

Make sure all pages have your name and the title in a header or footer (and page numbers if appropriate), with the first page of each document having your full contact info: name, title and genre of the manuscript, word count, address, e-mail address, and phone number.

Send only copies, no originals. Most agencies and publishers don't return rejected manuscripts even if you do include a large return envelope, because postal regulations restrict and even prevent certain kinds of mailings. Also, some houses have a policy of simply trashing unsolicited submissions when their website clearly says not to send them.

✔ **Send a self-addressed, stamped postcard if you want to confirm that your submission has reached its target.** The postcard should include your name, the addressee's name, and two blanks in this manner:

Title received on _____ by _____

Writing this card by hand is common, but creating one with your printer contributes to your professional presentation. Paper clip the postcard to the front of your query letter so the recipient will see it, but clip it at the bottom so as not to block your opening paragraphs. This postcard will be returned before the manuscript is read, most likely by the assistant who sorts the mail.

✔ **Include a reply envelope.** Enclose a business-sized SASE (self-addressed stamped envelope) for the editor's "Yes, please send me the full manuscript" reply or for her "Thanks, but it's not for me" reply if that's how it's to be.

✔ **Mark the mailing envelope.** If you're sending a requested manuscript, note that on the outside of the envelope: "Requested Manuscript." If you're a member of SCBWI or another writing organization, note that on the envelope, too: "SCBWI member." This note distinguishes your envelope from the others that come in that day's mail.

Use a paper clip for the materials — no staples, report covers, or binders. When it's time to send the full manuscript, wrap a rubber band around it and put it in a padded envelope instead of in a box. (See, this is why you need your name, title, and the page number on every page.)

Strive for a professional look. Unprofessional submissions have the potential to prejudice the editor or agent.

TIP

Sending multiple submissions at a time

Submitting to more than one editor at a time used to be a no-no, but that's not the case anymore. Just follow these rules for professionalism:

- **Be upfront.** If you're sending submissions to multiple recipients, say so in the query letter. Editors and agents won't hold it against you; multiple submissions are pretty much the norm now. What they *will* hold against you is time lost in considering a project that they had no real shot at because someone else already made an offer. Which brings me to . . .

- **Be respectful: Tell the other editors and agents when a publisher has made an offer.** If an agent or editor offers a contract and you accept, immediately alert the other people you've submitted to. Publishing is a small world, and you may publish with different houses over the course of your career; don't sow sour grapes by failing to notify all parties when a deal is struck.

  If your No. 2 choice made the offer but you really want to hold out for No. 1, you can respectfully alert No. 1 that "I've received an offer on my manuscript, which I am considering. I'd really love to work with you, so I thought I'd let you know that an offer has been made." I'm not telling you to run your own auction (something agents do with multiple editors and which requires precise rules and management skills) or to play one person against another. Be completely aboveboard and communicative; the editors already know you submitted to multiple editors because you told them so in your query letter, and now you're giving the other editor a heads-up that the manuscript is almost off the table. That's fair.

- **Give limited exclusives.** If you have a favorite editor, give her three weeks with the manuscript first as an *exclusive,* during which time you'll show it to no one else. At the end of that time period, you'll be free to send out the manuscript to others. State in your query letter, "I really want to work with you. You'll have a three-week exclusive. I hope you like my book." Stop there. Editors and agents know how a limited exclusive works, and they understand why you've put a limit on it. Keep the time frame reasonably long, three to four weeks.

  If an editor previously read your manuscript and offered revision suggestions, saying, "I'd like to see this if you revise along these lines," unwritten industry expectations dictate that you show that revision to that editor or agent as a short-term exclusive. Time is limited, so editors and agents don't spend time making suggestions to projects they aren't interested in seeing again. That said, if you didn't agree with an editor's recommendations and realized she wasn't the agent/editor for you, you're under no obligation to send any revised versions her way in the future.

- **Personalize each query letter.** Even if you're submitting to many agents/editors simultaneously, you should still tailor the opening paragraph of each letter to let the recipient know why you think she's the right person for this project.

- **Follow their rules.** Be sure to look at the agency or house's submission guidelines. If multiple submissions are unacceptable, the guidelines will state so.

Submitting queries electronically

E-mail queries are becoming more common these days, with agents leading the trend. Check everyone's author guidelines because they get very specific about what to send electronically. Often, agents have an automatic contact window that pops open on your screen when you click "Submit a Query" or something similar, and then you simply type the content of your query letter into that window. Few agents allow attachments of synopses or chapters (to protect against computer viruses that often lurk in attachments), although sometimes agents invite you to insert that material in the body of the e-mail, below your sign-off. Most often the agents or editors base their decisions on the query only.

If the author guidelines don't specify that e-mail queries are accepted, don't assume that an editor or agent will be okay with a receiving a query directly to his or her e-mail address, even if you can hunt that down. E-mail contact is usually reserved for agents and for writers who've been referred by a mutual colleague so as not to overwhelm inboxes. Unless you've met that editor or agent and received specific instructions to use her direct e-mail address, send only hard copy submissions via the postal service.

What not to include

Don't let your enthusiasm trip you up — submit only the items listed in the agent's or publisher's submission guidelines. If no guidelines are available on the agency or publisher websites, then stick with standard submission items (which I detail earlier in this chapter under "What to include").

Don't send marketing plans or proposals — doing market analysis isn't your job. Editors and agents know the market better than you can. They have actual sales numbers at their fingertips, face-to-face feedback from retailers, and sometimes even focus groups. You can refer to other titles in the market-place to position your book (see the earlier section "Paragraph 2: A pitch that prompts action"), but don't comment on the sales viability of your project.

Previously published authors may be tempted to include copies of those other books in a submission, but there's no need to spend the money or part with personal copies that may never be returned. Anyone intrigued by your query letter and writing sample can look up your book with ease on the Internet, seeing the jacket image and reading the reviews and excerpts on your website or through the online booksellers that post those, such as Amazon.com. Editors can even check on the book's general sales figures, believe it or not, thanks to their access to certain book distributor databases. If a previous book had a noteworthy publication, earned awards, or received quote-worthy reviews, include those items in Paragraph 3 of your query letter. Your publishing history is an important credential! The editor or agent will request a copy of the actual book later in the submission process if need be.

Don't include anything gimmicky, either. No author photos, no baked goods (not as uncommon as you'd think, especially around the holidays), and no *ancillary products* (related extras). An author once sent me a vial of home-made perfume related to her story's theme. Only, I didn't know the vial was in the submission envelope when I shoved it into my bag to read at home, along with several full novel manuscripts. The vial was crushed in my car. The scent? Let's just say the manuscript was about a horse and leave it at that.

The skinny on sample chapters

Author guidelines usually tell you whether the agent or editor you're sub-mitting to accepts sample chapters. If the guidelines don't mention sample chapters, submit one or two chapters, up to 15 pages total, depending on whether you have a prologue or a very short first chapter. Some agents and editors ask for up to three sample chapters, or the first 50 pages, but shorter samples are becoming the norm. The askers simply don't need that much material to get a feel for a book. They know right away, within the first few pages, and if they do want more, they request it.

Your real question is which chapters to send. My answer: the first chapters. Those are the ones editors and agents expect to see because those are the first ones *readers* see. That's where you do your hooking. Submitting juicy middle chapters can hurt you because

- ✔ The agents and editors don't have any context for the action and charac-ters in the scene.
- ✔ Those chapters don't have the benefit of built-up tension or emotion. Although those middle chapters are awesome when a reader has worked his way to them, they likely lack oomph to anyone starting the book at that point.

All sample chapters should be on 8.5" x 11" white paper, double-spaced with a standard 12-point font such as New Times Roman or Arial, and printed on one side of the paper only. (See Chapter 12 for details on formatting your manuscript.)

Keeping Your Fingers Crossed

Waiting to hear back on your submission can be a true mental test. Angst-ridden questions can easily take over your mind: "Has she received it yet? Has she read it? Will she say yes or no? When will I hear back? Why is this taking so long?" Don't let your mind be a breeding ground for frustration. Brush all those questions away and leave only this one: "What can I do with this time?" This section answers that question. I have a list of ways to make your wait productive, I give you tips for nudging the process along when nudging is appropriate, and I talk about what to do when the long-awaited news arrives.

Enduring the wait for a response

Agencies and publishers usually specify their response times to submissions in their posted guidelines, but be ready for a 3- to 6-month wait. Some agents and editors may reply only if they're interested in seeing more. Others try to respond to everyone, even if that means using form rejection letters. Form letters stink, I know, but editors can receive up to a thousand submissions a month, and trying to frame their reasons for rejecting a project in a tactful but useful manner adds to response time. In some cases, though, people do take the time to state a reason for the rejection in a personal letter.

After you've submitted, don't just sit and wait to hear back. Dive into your next project the moment you've finished your queries. Just as a watched pot never boils, sitting on your typing fingers doesn't get those editors and agents to respond any faster. Other ways to pass the waiting time include the following:

- ✓ Continue your editor/agent research in case you need to do another round of submissions.
- ✓ Get started on your platform building (which I cover in Chapter 15, along with a ton of other marketing steps).
- ✓ Get familiar with the online young adult book community. (Chapter 15 lists useful forums and YA-dedicated blogs.)
- ✓ Do industry research on your genre and category, or just catch up with the current state of publishing in general. (Check out Chapter 15 for book industry reads.)
- ✓ Read more deeply into your genre.

You may hear back sooner than you think. Agents' and editors' workloads ebb and flow just like yours does, and your manuscript or query may reach them just when they're most ready to read it. And frankly, some people are just faster at responding than others.

If you haven't received a response after two months, send a polite letter asking about the status of your query. If you offered an exclusive but haven't heard back by the end of your specified time, send a letter stating that although you'd still very much like to place your manuscript with that agency or editor, you're going to start submitting the project to other houses, too.

Editor Kate Harrison: Revising with your editor

A lot of authors are surprised to learn how much work there is to be done after their book is sold and before it's published. After all, you've already revised and revised on your own, and the novel that gets sold should be the final version, right? Actually, it's just a jumping off point for the author-editor process. I hear these pronouncements in the media that "editors don't edit anymore," but in fact, I and every editor I know edit like crazy! I sign up a manuscript because I love it, and then my job is to help it become the very best version of itself before I put it out in the world — a version that will ideally reach its audience, sell lots of copies, get great reviews, and win some awards while we're at it! That can mean one round of revisions or it can mean ten rounds — it's really different for every book.

The author-editor relationship requires a lot of trust, an open mind, and a lot of work on both sides, but it's amazing what can come out of the process. I recently spent about a year and a half editing an incredible novel that morphed into almost an entirely different book by the end — some of the characters merged together, names changed, fates were altered, and a soulful romance blossomed. The author was inspiring to work with because he would take a problem I brought up and create his own perfect solution for it. Neither one of us could ever have predicted what this novel would become when I first signed it up, but we couldn't be more excited about it. Sometimes it just takes a bit longer for the story and characters to fall into place, but helping an author get there is my favorite part of the job.

Kate Harrison has worked in children's books publishing for more than 11 years and is currently a senior editor at Dial Books for Young Readers.

Don't cold call agents or editors. Such calls can be awkward, they almost always interrupt work, and they aren't necessary because the posted author guidelines provide specific instructions on how to submit via e-mail or the postal service. If you do a cold call, the agent or editor will assume you either haven't read the guidelines or chose to disregard them — neither of which is professional.

Receiving the long-awaited news

Although you submit via mail or e-mail, your acceptance news typically comes via phone. But it's rarely a call out of the blue. Generally you get a note that asks for the full manuscript, and then perhaps you have some e-mail back-and-forth about revisions, and then the editor tells you she wants to share the manuscript with other editors to get their feedback. This is a serious stage. She may indeed walk to the office next door for a second opinion, or she may be taking your story to her weekly editorial meeting, wherein all the editors of the imprint — and likely representatives of the marketing and sales force — all read and comment on the potential of the project. *Then* you get your phone call.

If the response is "No, thanks," you hear by mail or e-mail. And yes, some editors or agents may never respond. If it's house or agency policy to respond only in the case of further interest, they typically note that in the author guidelines posted on their websites.

Note that not all rejections are final. An agent or editor may write back with a conditional "no thanks — although I would like to see this again if you want to revise along the lines I'm suggesting." Read the next section to find out what to do with that kind of feedback.

Turning "No" into "Yes!"

The writer without a rejection is the exception. Just ask J. R. R. Tolkien. Or J. K. Rowling. Or any other successful writer you can think of. Most of them have been rejected, usually multiple times. Remember, stories and style are subjective, and reliable crystal balls are nonexistent. Often, placing a manuscript comes down to chemistry between the manuscript and the editor or agent. Every reader has subjective tastes and judgments.

This section covers what to do when you get a rejection — how to make sense of it, how to better your chances next time, and when it's appropriate to revise and resend to a rejecter.

Using rejection to strengthen your story (and maybe resubmit it!)

Most editors and agents try to be tactful in their responses. Form letters are a matter of efficiency, not signs of a cold heart. Editors and agents resort to those so they can get through the submissions quickly. Writing a useful yet tactful response to a manuscript takes surprisingly long, so if you get one of those, see it for the extra time and effort it is, and understand that any recommendations in it are offered because that person saw something you can work on. You can decide whether to take that advice, of course.

Sometimes an editor or agent declines the manuscript but asks to see it again if you revise along the lines she suggests. Unless you have a compelling reason not to, do it! This response means that the agent or editor saw a real possibility of taking on your manuscript. Editors and agents don't offer to reread just to be kind — they don't have time for that.

 Don't rush the revision if you plan to resubmit your manuscript. You have several months before any of those requestors even bats an eye. They'd all tell you, very sincerely, to take as much time as you need to get the manuscript right. And frankly, they'd feel dubious if you turned around a revised

manuscript in mere days. They didn't reject your manuscript for surface problems; there was probably some serious work to be done. That said, you should
aim to finish the revision and submit no later than 6 months after receiving the
letter. Editors and agents won't hold a time lag against you (they know that
revising takes time and that sometimes life gets in the way), but the marketplace could shift in that time, as could the very jobs of those agents and editors. Don't wait longer than a year, which editors commonly use as their limit
when they offer open submission invitations at conferences.

What if a rejection letter tells you what was wrong with the manuscript but
doesn't ask to see a revision based on its suggestions? Can you still resend to
that person later if you revise? Yes, you can . . . if you've changed the manuscript significantly. This situation arises sometimes when writers mature,
gaining experience, improving skills, and getting useful feedback from folks
who know their stuff. If that's your situation, then say so when you resubmit
the revised manuscript: "I've changed it significantly since you last saw it
and hope you'll be open to taking another look." Don't keep going back to the
same editor over and over, though. One revision is enough for an editor to
make a final call.

Just because you revise and resubmit doesn't necessarily mean the manuscript will be accepted. You're getting a second chance with someone who
was intrigued, but you still have to make the hard connection.

Reading between the rejection-letter lines

Sometimes an agent or editor takes the time to cite a reason for rejecting,
only to leave the writer feeling confused because the reason isn't specific
enough or uses industry jargon. And sometimes one person's letter flat-out
contradicts another!

Getting feedback but not knowing what to do with it can be frustrating, no
doubt about it. Try to remember that evaluating manuscripts is a subjective
activity — you're bound to get lots of opinions. Your task is to sift through
what you get, see whether there's a common thread in the feedback, and
decide whether you want to address that issue in revision.

To help you with your sifting, I've translated some lines that commonly show
up in rejection letters and suggested specific areas you can tackle if you get
them:

✔ **"I couldn't get into the story."** Your story may have too much setup
at the beginning, or perhaps you're interrupting the action with info
dumps — telling instead of showing. Are you creating enough tension?
Review Chapter 7's techniques for injecting action and forward movement into the story.

✔ **"I never sank into the world."** Check your voice. Is it too complicated or formal? Does it need liveliness, some spunky sentence construction and variety? Revisit sentence structure techniques in Chapter 9. Did the story start at the wrong point of the conflict? See Chapter 6. Have you neglected your physical setting? Review the setting techniques in Chapter 8.

✔ **"The voice isn't strong (or distinct) enough."** Are you picking flavorful words? Looking for original ways to phrase things instead of falling back on clichés? See Chapter 9 for voice techniques.

✔ **"The characters feel flat."** This comment may also come at you as "I don't care enough about the main character to get invested in her story." Revisit your characterization. Are you relying on stereotypes? Have you given readers a reason to care about your character, to root for her or to be fascinated by her? Have you fleshed her out with body language and prop interaction? Is there something sympathetic about her, a core moral goodness? Is her goal important enough — and is the price of failure terrible enough — to cause anxiety for her well-being and success? See Chapters 5 and 7, which cover characters and action.

✔ **"The hook isn't strong (or fresh) enough."** Revisit your concept. How can you reshape your characters or storyline to make it feel new in the marketplace instead of like just another story in that genre? See Chapter 4 for info on hooks. Look for unique places to set your story (Chapter 8), and give your characters unexpected traits, strengths, or flaws (Chapter 5). This can send you back to square one for a major overhaul, but wouldn't you rather know early in the submission process than later?

✔ **"The dialogue doesn't sound natural to my ear."** Your dialogue may be doing too much work. Take the plot details out of the dialogue and work them into the narration. And make those narrative beats count; don't let generic, unrevealing actions hijack those precious moments. Or maybe you have too many dialogue tags or poorly constructed ones, or perhaps you're putting formal grown-up words in kids' mouths. See Chapter 10 for dialogue tips.

✔ **"The voice sounds too sophisticated for a girl/boy this age."** Make sure you're thinking like a kid so you can narrate like one. No overanalyzing people or situations, and don't let a young first-person narrator overempathize with others. Check out Chapter 9's coverage of teen drama and youthful word choice.

✔ **"Too much was going on. I felt confused."** Did you introduce too many characters in that opening scene? Is the writing too complicated, or are you trying to do too much setup in the first pages? Chapter 7 talks about easing readers into complicated fictional words.

✔ **"The pacing isn't strong enough."** Does it take too long for things to happen? Are you including the minutiae instead of sticking to the richest story moments? Revisit scene-crafting and transitions in Chapter 7.

> ✓ **"This manuscript isn't right for me" or "I don't see a place for this manuscript on my list."** Alas, there's no connection whatsoever. No resubmission possibility here. Not so helpful, I know, but at least you have an answer.

Obviously you'd prefer an editor or agent to send you a contract instead of a rejection letter, but if you can determine what was found lacking in your manuscript, you can address those areas during revision and in future stories. Regarding those future stories: Yes, you can submit them to the same editors and agents you tried with past submissions. If you find that they're not connecting with anything you send, however, it may be time to turn to the many other editors and agents out there.

Keeping your ego (and feelings) out of it

So much of acceptance goes beyond your storytelling skill, so don't mistake a rejection of your manuscript as a rejection of you. Publishing is a business. And like every business, it's first and foremost about making money. Editors take on manuscripts they not only feel passionate about but also believe will sell, and scores of factors go into their assessments of what's salable.

That's an unsavory thought to many in the book world, especially to writers, who feel such passion about their craft. And rightly so — without that passion, you wouldn't have spent months or years with those characters and that story. Children's book editors are not devoid of that passion. The halls of publishing are filled with literary aficionados and all-out book-lovers. But those aficionados must keep in mind the business side of publishing: If their publishing houses don't make money, their houses don't stay in business, and if houses don't stay in business, they don't get to publish great books.

Salability is a subjective call, which is why rejection letters say things like "not right for me" and "I don't see a place on my list, but maybe it will be just what another editor is looking for." No single editor has the final word. Getting the thumbs up — and a contract! — is based not only on the editor's reaction to the story you've crafted but also on her perception of the current marketplace, her particular interests, her own career strategies, her imprint and publisher's demands and interests, and, yes, sometimes her mood or situation the day your manuscript rolls in.

Try to keep your feelings out of the submission process. If you're angry, sad, or embarrassed, you won't be able to decide whether to revise or to stick to your current draft and keep submitting. Yes, you're allowed those emotions, but get over them quickly. A working writer must develop a thick skin.

Famous rejects: Five writers who turned "no" into bestsellers

Getting a rejection letter stinks, no bones about it. But "no" is by no means the final word. Just ask these very famous writers who refused to take that two-letter word for an answer:

- **J. K. Rowling:** Twelve publishers rejected Harry Potter, and an agent told Rowling, "You'll never make money selling children's books." But Rowling kept submitting until one publishing CEO's 8-year-old daughter, Alice, begged him to say "yes." He did — to *Harry Potter and the Philosopher's Stone*. Bloomsbury Publishing printed a modest first printing of the book, young readers got their hands on it, and Rowling became a publishing phenom.

- **Judy Blume:** Blume received "nothing but rejections" for two years before hearing "yes." "I would go to sleep at night feeling that I'd never be published," she said. "But I'd wake up in the morning convinced I would. . . . I was determined. Determination and hard work are as important as talent." Blume has since received more than 90 awards for her books, which are among the most widely read fiction for young people, including *Blubber*, *Superfudge*, and *Are You There, God? It's Me, Margaret*.

- **Madeleine L'Engle:** Even though L'Engle was already a published novelist with six books under her belt, she endured two years of rejection by 26 publishers before landing a contract for *A Wrinkle in Time*. Publishers felt the novel was "too difficult for children." That book went on to win the 1963 Newbery Medal and remains hugely popular with young people. Asked how it felt to have such a smashing success, L'Engle said, "Since it was a book nobody wanted, it feels kind of nice."

- **William Golding:** Golding's story about a group of English schoolboys plane-wrecked on a deserted island was rejected by 21 publishers, with one declaring it "Absurd & uninteresting fantasy. . . . Rubbish & dull." *Lord of the Flies* is now a standard in the high school English curriculum.

- **Meg Cabot:** Cabot originally envisioned 16 books in her The Princess Diaries series, but she couldn't get a "yes" on just one. She says the project was rejected "by almost every publishing house in America." Now, 16 Princess books, two major motion pictures, and several other popular series later, Cabot's vision has been realized . . . and how!

Chapter 14

Self-Publishing: Is It for You?

. . . .

In This Chapter

▶ Weighing the pros and cons of self-publishing

▶ Summarizing various publishing options

▶ Demystifying the publishing process and players

▶ Deciding whether self-publishing is right for you

. . . .

The publishing world is in transition. Digital publishing, print-on-demand, freemium . . . it seems as if new formats, methods, and players are emerging every day. The growth is both exciting and overwhelming. One of the biggest shifts in this age of transition has authors taking matters into their own hands — that is, self-publishing. This chapter tells you what self-publishing is, outlines the author's role in the process, and helps you determine whether self-publishing is the right path to publication for your young adult fiction.

What's So Different about Self-Publishing?

In the traditional publishing model, the author's role is to write the manuscript and submit it to publishers until landing a book contract; then the publisher takes over, designing, producing, marketing, and distributing the bound book. Although savvy writers supplement the publisher's marketing efforts to help increase book sales, self-marketing is optional in this scenario. The author gets paid a royalty on each book sold (about 15 percent, with an advance against the royalties) as he moves on to his next project. But here's the rub: What if you don't land that book contract? Or what if you don't want to settle for 15 percent of the sales? What if you don't want to let someone else drive the fate of your book? Then maybe self-publishing is for you.

Self-publishing cuts out the publisher — and the agent, if that's part of trying to land your book contract. Self-publishing puts you in the captain's chair, writing, designing, producing, marketing, and distributing your own book. You fund the expenses and keep all the profits. As with all business ventures, self-publishing has both benefits and drawbacks.

Eyeing the benefits

The reasons for self-publishing's appeal to writers are valid and compelling:

- ✔ **Money:** In self-publishing, you keep all the profits. All the money you make after paying your production- and marketing-related costs goes straight to your pocket, without detouring through your publisher's and agent's coffers. And if you choose electronic or print-on-demand publishing options, you don't have to fork out for warehousing or shipping (more on those options in a bit).

- ✔ **Control:** Not only do you have final say on everything — you have *all* say. This control gives you the freedom to print any type of content, with any type of design, and run whatever marketing campaign you want.

- ✔ **Time:** Your book is available for sale sooner than in the traditional publishing model because you work on your own timetable. No waiting for editors or wending through a publisher's production queue and release schedule with scores of other books.

Realizing the drawbacks

Writers' reasons for concern about self-publishing are valid and sobering:

- ✔ **Money:** You pay all the costs and thus assume all the financial risk. Producing your own book costs several hundred to several thousand dollars, depending on your choice of bound books or electronic books (e-books) and your commitment to content and packaging quality. Professional editors and cover and interior designers don't come free. Marketing costs may extend well into the thousands for professional publicists and campaigns, and even basic marketing items such as websites and promo materials can add up. (I go into detail about marketing options in Chapter 15.) Can you sell enough books to recoup your expenses and then turn a profit?

- ✔ **Control:** You must make all the decisions and thus must educate yourself in all aspects of the publishing process. You can hire freelancers and other experts, but the buck starts and stops with you, so you'd better understand what the hired help is offering and advising.

- ✔ **Time:** Designing, producing, promoting, and distributing a book takes a lot of time — time that you could spend writing.

- ✔ **Stigma:** Like it or not, a stigma lingers around the label *self-published.* Some people will assume the story wasn't good enough to get a "real" publisher. A significant number of self-published books exhibit inexpert or downright poor quality, bringing down the public's perception of the entire category and creating a serious hindrance to your credibility.

Understanding Your Publishing Options

The publishing industry is morphing, but at this time you have three publishing options for your young adult fiction: traditional publishing, print-on-demand self-publishing, and digital self-publishing. This section gives you an overview of all three.

Traditional publishing

In the *traditional publishing* model, a publisher buys the rights to your manuscript and then produces, markets, and distributes the book, paying you a royalty for each book sold. These publishing companies use offset printing methods on traditional printing presses, printing batches of hardcovers or paperbacks that must then be warehoused. The publisher assumes the financial risks, taking a significant share of the profits in return. This approach is a long-established path to publication and the model that I focus on in this book.

Hardcover books have cardboard covers wrapped in cloth and sewed or glued to a block of paper pages. Hardcovers, which are often wrapped in book jackets, have a high perceived value with consumers. *Paperback* books have thick paper covers glued to a block of paper pages. Paperbacks are significantly cheaper to produce, which is why they carry lower cover prices. Although young adult fiction is published in both hardcover and paperback, paperback versions are typically printed and sold in higher numbers.

Traditional publishing can make your life easier. A publisher brings to bear a staff of experts in bookmaking and bookselling, so the quality of traditionally published books is dependably high. These books get stocked in brick-and-mortar stores as well as online because publishers offer bulk deals and sell on credit. And because publishers accept returns of unsold books, retailers are willing to risk buying books by untried authors. Your trade-off for these benefits is minimal control over the book-making process and the packaging of the final product, lower cuts of the profits than you'd get if you self-published, and publication dates that are determined according to your publisher's schedule, which takes into account *all* the books that house is producing, not just yours. See Chapter 13 for info on submitting manuscripts to traditional publishers.

Print-on-demand (POD)

The *print-on-demand* (POD) model is how you get physical, printed-and-bound books without signing with a traditional publishing house. Instead, you pay a POD publisher to handle everything from designing your book to printing and distributing it. A POD publisher prints the book in any number of formats (such as hardcover or paperback), registers the copyright and obtains the ISBN, gets the book listed with online booksellers, and fills orders from customers. The publisher uses high-end laser printers to print books one at a time as ordered. Within days of an order, the book is printed and then shipped to the retailer, customer, or distributor.

Your costs depend on the services you choose. For example, you may use the POD publisher's design templates to lay out the text and cover yourself, or the company can design the book for you. POD companies are able to customize books, such as by pasting CDs onto covers or using higher quality paper, but the writer pays extra for the enhancements.

POD has its share of pros and cons:

- ✔ **Publishing process:** The full-service menu of POD publishers simplifies the publishing process for self-publishing authors, although the companies' staff expertise may not compare to that of traditional publishers.

- ✔ **Cost:** POD books are printed only after they're ordered and paid for, making them pricier per copy than in the traditional model. The flip side is that you don't have to pay for warehousing.

- ✔ **Distribution and sales:** Brick-and-mortar retailers and distributors don't typically stock POD books because POD publishers don't allow them to buy stock on credit, nor do these publishers accept returns of unsold books. Also, with high sales unlikely, retailers don't order enough books to qualify for shipping discounts, so the cost of stocking a POD book is higher for them than stocking books from traditional publishers. This means that online retailers and author websites are the primary selling fields for POD books. Without a strong platform or aggressive self-marketing, books published using POD typically sell only a few hundred copies.

If you're intrigued by POD publishing, start your research with two professional organizations for self-publishers: the Independent Book Publishers Association (www.pma-online.org) and the Small Publishers Association of North America (www.spannet.org). SPAN sponsors a self-publishing Yahoo! group that welcomes newcomers at http://finance.groups.yahoo.com/group/self-publishing.

Digital publishing

Also called *electronic publishing* or simply referred to as *e-books* (electronic books), *digital publishing* allows readers to download electronic text onto a dedicated digital reading device (e-reader) or onto any PDA (personal digital assistant) or computer. E-books are typically distributed via the Internet, usually through online booksellers. As long as a person has a device that can store and display the text, he or she can read the e-book.

E-books . . . free books?

Millions of e-books are available for free on the Internet. How do writers make money if they're giving their books away? Simple: The free stuff is a marketing tool for their paid stuff, that's how.

People like it when you give them stuff. Getting free stuff makes folks want to give you stuff — their money. The business concept is called *freemium* (as in "free" and "premium"), and it works like this: You give people something for free, and then they'll pay for other products that are similar or related to it . . . namely your other books or the rest of a book they've just sampled at no cost. With their low production costs and easy delivery, e-books fit well in the freemium model:

- ✔ **Loss leaders:** *Loss leaders* are products people give away or sell at unprofitable prices with the goal of driving sales of future products. Just as coupons and sales lure you into retail stores where you then buy a whole basket of nonsale items, you can give e-books away in order to build a customer base. If you hook people with your giveaway, they'll come back and buy new books from you because they know you've got the goods. Plus, they'll tell their friends, creating word-of-mouth that will (you hope) increase sales of your for-sale books. This model works if you have multiple novels or perhaps a series with the first volume in the series being the loss leader.

- ✔ **Short-story teasers:** You can give away a short story or novella, something related to your main book, for free. The hope is that this teaser hooks readers, and then they fork over money for your main selection. Your only real cost with this kind of giveaway is the time it takes to write the shorter pieces. Fantasy series lend themselves to this kind of freemium thanks to their deep fictional worlds, which offer many possibilities for ancillary stories.

- ✔ **Limited-time free downloads:** You can build interest and word-of-mouth by offering your e-book for free for a limited time. Make the giveaway period long enough for people to hear about the book, start reading it, and tell their friends about it but not long enough for the entire world to come and download. Also, an end date puts people in the "I gotta buy this before it's gone!" mindset. Your gamble is that those who do download your book for free will love your novel and return to buy your other books.

Digital publishing allows authors, readers, and publishers immense flexibility. E-books can be of any length, and because they're virtual, they don't require warehousing or shipping. Since the introduction of e-readers in the early 2000s, digital reading devices have made great strides in onscreen readability, making them more appealing to readers. Visually, the pages appear onscreen in the same layout as they do in a book. Although you must design and format your text according to the set specifications of each reading device, this formatting can be relatively quick and easy to do.

Consumers have shown their approval by making e-books the fastest-growing segment of the publishing market, with the 2011 Digital Book World Conference announcing that e-book sales reached almost $1 billion in 2010 and Forrester Research predicting nearly $3 billion in e-book sales in 2015.

Because the price of e-readers is going down and the popularity of PDAs and tablet computers is rising with young people, your young adult fiction audience is poised to be a major consumer of e-books. The trick, as with any of your format options, is to make those young people aware of your book so they'll download it. See Chapter 15 for ideas on how to publicize your young adult novel to your unique audience.

Digital publishing can be part of any self-publishing plan thanks to the relative simplicity and low cost of formatting your novel's text. If you choose the POD option and write, edit, and design the book yourself, go the extra step of formatting your electronic text for the main e-reading devices and make it available to an entirely new audience. Traditional publishers do this with the books on their lists. More formats, more readers, more sales.

Knowing the Players

With self-publishing still finding its feet as a publishing alternative, specific players are constantly emerging, merging, and folding. If you decide to pursue self-publishing, you should tap into the self-publishing community online to get up-to-speed with the companies currently offering the most useful, most cost-effective, and highest-quality services. No matter which path your self-publishing endeavors take you on, though, you need to be familiar with five roles in the self-publishing world. I cover them in this section.

Odd tasks you didn't know publishers do

When most people consider self-publishing, they assume that they'll be taking over the publisher's production tasks. And they're right. But that's more complex than most writers realize. Here are six tasks you probably didn't know you'd be taking on . . . and six more reasons for pledging to learn everything you can about self-publishing before you make the final call to do it:

✔ **Ordering ISBNs:** An ISBN identifies both the publisher and the book. With rare exception, you can't sell your books through retailers without one. Publishers buy their ISBNs in bulk from R. R. Bowker, the official ISBN agency of the United States. Because each ISBN is coded to identify the publisher who purchased the number, ISBNs cannot be resold or reassigned. An ISBN purchased through an author services company remains assigned to that company; it does not transfer to the self-publishing author. Therefore, the author services company remains the publisher of record for that book. Self-publishers can buy their own ISBNs (singly or in bulk) directly from Bowker at www.myidentifiers.com. Because every edition of a book (paperback, hardcover, large print) needs its own ISBN, consider buying blocks of ISBNS. For more information, check out R. R. Bowker's question-and-answer section for self-publishers at www.bowker.com, or go to www.isbn.org.

✔ **Filling out an Advance Book Information (ABI) form:** When a book has an ISBN, it can be registered with Bowker's *Books in Print* (the industry's largest bibliographic database) via www.bowkerlink.com. Filling out the Advance Book Information form is part of listing your title in the directory. If you're using an author services company, that company can take care of this step for you.

✔ **Ordering bar codes:** The bar code encodes your ISBN in black bars for retailers to scan, with your numerical ISBN running along the bottom of the bars. Bar codes are obtained from Bowker Bar Code Service after you have an ISBN. You position your bar code on the back cover of a paperback book or on the front flap of a hardcover jacket.

✔ **Determining categories:** Publishers use the Book Industry Study Group's (BISG) industry-standard categories to tell booksellers where to shelve books and to tell readers what they have in their hands. Ever seen something like *JUVENILE FICTION/ Fantasy & Magic* on the back cover of a book? That's the Book Industry Standards and Communications (BISAC) classification. The BISG website explains it all (www.bisg.org). Search for "subject headings list, juvenile fiction" or go directly to the BISAC juvenile fiction listings at www.bisg.org/what-we-do-0-108-bisac-subject-headings-list-juvenile-fiction.php.

✔ **Applying for control numbers:** If you want to sell your book to libraries, you first need to get it cataloged by the Library of Congress (LOC). Normally your publisher takes care of this step, although your publisher gets something called a CIP (Cataloging-in-Publication) instead of a Library of Congress Control Number (LCCN). Publishers with an established history of producing books that are widely acquired by libraries apply for CIP data through the LOC before the book is published and then print the CIP data on the book's copyright page. The publisher eventually sends a copy of the final bound book to the Library of Congress, which adds the book to its collection and uploads the CIP into its database for all libraries to access. But self-publishers don't qualify for the CIP program because of the unlikelihood of wide library pickup. This doesn't lock you out of libraries, though. Individual libraries that decide to carry your book can catalog it locally, or you can apply for a Preassigned Control Number (PCN) at http://pcn.loc.gov before your book pubs. The PCN program assigns your book an LCCN, which you print on your book's copyright page to facilitate cataloging in libraries.

✔ **Registering copyright:** In traditional publishing, your publisher registers the copyright for your bound book with the United States Copyright Office (www.copyright.gov). In self-publishing, you do it yourself.

Author services companies

Author services companies provide publishing services to authors for a fee. Essentially, they're printers that offer extra services such as design and distribution. You may use these companies to print POD (print-on-demand) bound books or to create e-books. Big-name players include Lulu (www.lulu.com) and Amazon's CreateSpace (www.createspace.com).

The distinction between vanity publishing and using an author service company is a blurry one. I talk about vanity publishing in Chapter 1, calling it a dangerous no-no. The big evil is that *vanity publishers* are subsidy printers that offer themselves up as full-scale publishers even though they provide author services for a fee. That is, after they make you pay for manufacturing the book and for their marketing efforts, they take a cut of your profits as if they were a traditional publisher with an actual stake in your book. Not good. Vanity presses may require you to assign your rights to them (instead of just acting as your hired company for manufacturing your book), and they own your book's ISBN (the 13-digit International Standard Book Number that uniquely identifies each book), so they're technically the publisher of record.

When you hire a true author services company, you pay for the services you want and keep all your profits. That sounds simple enough, but the water gets murky when you consider that many author services companies own the ISBNs and may require some claim to digital or e-publishing rights. (***Note:*** ISBNs are coded in a way that identifies the purchasing company and cannot be reassigned if even an ISBN is resold.) In effect, most of the issues that have made vanity publishing unsafe for writers also exist in author services business practices. See? A blurry line — and one that inspires heated debate in self-publishing circles.

Education is the key to going the self-publishing route to publication. Ask for recommendations from your writers' group, research the companies, and explore other writers' experiences through online self-publishing forums. Understand the fees involved from the beginning, know who you're dealing with, and set realistic goals for the final product and sales.

Publisher services companies

Publisher services companies use print-on-demand technology to print and distribute small runs of books for traditional publishers. Think of these companies as small-scale printers. They don't edit, design, or in any way prep the product for printing; they just print the book and ship it out. Because small-batch POD printing is not as economical as printing large batches of books, publishers still rely on traditional offset-press printing companies to print most of their books. Interestingly, many author services companies (see the preceding section) use publisher services companies for their printing and distribution needs, as do some major wholesalers.

Although publisher services companies don't work with individual self-publishers, some self-publishers form their own publishing companies so that they can work directly with publisher services companies, bypassing author services companies altogether (and thus extra fees). The largest publisher services company is Lightning Source, which is owned by the same parent company as Ingram Book Company, the largest U.S. book wholesaler.

Distributors

A *distributor* is a company that buys books from publishers and then sells them to stores and wholesalers. Distributors warehouse your books, fulfill orders, issue invoices, and collect money. If there are returns, the distributor processes them (charging them back to the publisher). Some distributors have sale reps who visit bookstores. Distributers don't market the books, though — that's up to the publishers.

Most distributors are exclusive, meaning you sign agreements to use them and only them. Because you have to pay distributors for their services, they add to the cost of your book. If you want to get your self-published book into physical stores, you need a distributor. When you use an author services company, it'll work with distributors on your behalf.

Wholesalers

Retailers aren't interested in buying their books from a gaggle of individual authors. The logistics would be a nightmare. They *do* buy from established sources: *wholesalers.* Wholesalers don't have sales reps; they merely stock your book and fill orders. The largest wholesalers are Ingram (`www.ingram book.com`) and Baker & Taylor (`www.btol.com`).

Booksellers

Booksellers are broken down into categories such as online and *brick-and-mortar stores* (physical buildings such as the bookstore in your local mall). Here are a few types of booksellers you can access directly or through distributers (see the earlier "Distributers" section):

- ✔ Independent bookstores with on-the-spot owners ordering the books; such owners may be open to self-published authors' approaching them
- ✔ Specialized booksellers such as book clubs, private organizations, and museums
- ✔ Corporate chain stores (such as Barnes & Noble) with specialized buyers at the national headquarters who deal only with distributors and traditional publishers
- ✔ Retail stores with a big interest in books (such as warehouse stores and Walmart), again buying through national headquarters and dealing with distributors and traditional publishers

Libraries and schools are book buyers, too, although they aren't big buyers of self-published books. Knowing where you want your books sold helps you decide which self-publishing option, if any, is for you.

Weighing Self-Publishing for Your YA Fiction

Self-publishing is a serious business endeavor, with your reputation, your finances, and perhaps even your sanity at stake. Every author should consider the pros and cons, the challenges, and the potential based on his own situation and project. This section offers some scenarios in which self-publishing may be a viable path to publication.

Self-publishing works best for nonfiction, for established fiction authors who enjoy name recognition and an established reader base, and for genre fiction (such as romance or crime thrillers) for which authors can easily target readers through genre-related publications, organizations, social media subcultures, and events.

YA self-publishing success stories

The odds of a self-published young adult novel breaking out may not be great, but it does happen. Here are four success stories where authors had a vision, did the work, caught the eye of the traditional publishing world, and inked a book deal.

✔ **Kara Kingsley, author of *Erec Rex: The Dragon's Eye,* middle grade fantasy series, ages 9–12, illustrated by Melvyn Grant:** Kara Kingsley's original plan wasn't to use self-publishing as a stepping stone to traditional publishing, but that's how it worked out, and she's plenty happy with the outcome. When she decided she wanted to publish the first two books in her fantasy series, she set about learning everything she could about self-publishing. Books, online articles — she studied it all. Realizing that time would be a primary challenge for her, she was careful to prioritize her efforts. And then she went for it, using bookstore connections and appearances to sell 30,000 copies of *The Dragon's Eye* on her own. The book even earned a turn as a Borders Original Voices pick. Kingsley came to believe that her books could go further with a large publisher, so she

contacted an agent and soon signed an eight-book deal with Simon & Schuster. The key to her standout success? According to her S&S editor, her sales record helped, but her solid characters and a well-written story sealed the deal.

✔ **Tim Kehoe, author of *The Unusual Mind of Vincent Shadow,* middle grade fiction, ages 9–12, illustrated by Mike Wohnoutka:** Tim Kehoe took eight months to write the story of 11-year-old aspiring toy inventor Vincent Shadow, a character inspired by Kehoe's own successful toy inventing. Then Kehoe decided to go the self-publishing route. He hired illustrator Mike Wohnoutka, whose fantastic artwork helped the novel stand out of the self-publishing pack, laid out the book using Adobe's InDesign software, and printed a few hundred copies. Local bookstores rallied around the book in a big way. Author Vincent Flynn took notice and opened the door of the traditional publishing world to Kehoe. A few weeks after meeting Flynn's agent, Kehoe had two offers from publishers. Little, Brown and Company now publishes Kehoe's Vincent Shadow books.

✔ **Colleen Houck, author of *Tiger's Curse*, YA fiction, ages 12 and up:** Colleen Houck was frustrated. She'd just finished reading *Twilight: Eclipse* but would have to wait months for the next book in the saga. How could she stand waiting? She'd write her own fantasy to fill the time, she decided. And she did. Only, the manuscript didn't fare so well when she started submitting it to agents. After writing the full trilogy but getting only rejections, she decided to self-publish rather than let her story of 18-year-old Kelsey and a 300-year-old Indian curse gather dust. She published the first two books through Amazon, as bound books and as e-books for Amazon's Kindle e-reader. She called bookstores, arranged a signing, got her book into local libraries, put up a website, and took out an ad in a local paper. She priced the first e-book at 99 cents, appealing to Kindle bargain hunters, and ended up on several lists for cheap but good reads. Soon Houck was selling 300 books a month and then 300 a day. Customer requests at Costco led the warehouse store to stock her book; China, Thailand, and Korea contacted her about translation rights; a film producer called.

Then an agent called, and within weeks Houck had a high-profile book deal with Sterling Publishing.

✔ **Amanda Hocking, author of the Trylle Trilogy, YA paranormal fiction:** Amanda Hocking was tired of hearing *no*. She'd submitted her novels about angels, vampires, and zombies to publishers but hadn't landed a book contract. So she took matters into her own hands and self-published two of her novels as e-books in April 2010. Within ten months, she had eight novels and one novella on the market and had sold 900,000 copies. Sales rose from there, reaching into the millions before she signed a high-profile, multi-book contract with St. Martin's Press. Hocking credits her self-pub success to low e-book price points ($2.99 and $.99), aggressive self-marketing through online social media and her own blog, and the enthusiastic support of book bloggers. She also talks plainly about her frustration with the amount of time she had to put into production and marketing tasks when she'd rather be writing, which she cites as the main factor in her decision to sign with a traditional publisher.

Notice something missing from my list? Yep, young adult fiction. YA self-pubbers are hampered by the difficulty of connecting directly with the general teen population. Doing so is difficult even with a traditional children's book publisher behind you. Even if your publisher doesn't send you out on tour, your publisher does give you access to larger promotional efforts and established media outlets, and it can piggyback your title on promotional materials for brand-name authors and create high-quality, high teen-appeal packaging for your book. In self-publishing, these responsibilities fall on the individual author, who must be nimble, market-savvy, information-hungry, and more accepting of smaller sales numbers than a big house is. The average self-pubbed book in any category sells only a few hundred copies; a self-pubbed young adult novel that sells in significant numbers is the exception rather than the rule.

Of course, you didn't choose to write young adult fiction because you thought it'd be an easy get-rich-quick scheme. Self-publishing may be a valid choice for your novel if you're realistic with your goals, wise about your strategy, dedicated in your work ethic, committed to quality, and fanatically obsessed with becoming a self-marketing machine.

The biggest challenge in self-publishing a young adult novel is letting the world know your book exists. Commit to finding out everything you can about self-marketing. Chapter 15 is dedicated to that very task.

Common scenarios for self-publishers

If self-publishing is so darned risky and the breakouts are so rare, why do writers still choose to self-publish their young adult fiction? Here are six scenarios in which you may make the same call — or at least be tempted:

- ✔ **Publishers haven't snapped up your manuscript.** Your manuscript keeps getting rejected, and you no longer believe that a traditional publishing house will publish the project, so you decide to give it a go yourself. You intend to get behind your book in a big way and sell enough copies to make money on the venture. This is the riskiest self-publishing scenario, with the highest investment of your money, time, and effort and thus the most at stake.

- ✔ **You're taking a nontraditional path to traditional publishing.** You want to sell enough copies yourself and create buzz about your book so that a traditional house will pick it up. This isn't a common outcome, but it does happen. You must have sales well into the thousands and/or significant bookseller chatter to attract a publisher's eye, and your book packaging must look professional rather than "self-pubbed." You assume all the costs and promotional duties until the pickup happens, and there's no guarantee it will happen. If this is your strategy, don't wait for publishers to find you. Gather your high sales numbers and bookseller testimonials and seek out an agent or approach publishers directly.

- ✔ **You'd rather do it your way.** You want to retain total creative and financial control and publish without a middleman, and you believe you can sell enough copies to make a profit or at least break even.

- ✔ **You don't want to wait.** It can take a year or longer for a young adult novel to reach bookstore shelves after contract, depending on how long it takes to edit the book with your editor and where your book is placed in the publisher's release schedule. And that's on top of the time the submission phase takes. Self-publishing lets you put the book out on your schedule.

✔ **This isn't your main gig.** Your goal may be to have a self-published novel that supplements your traditionally published books, or you may want to hand-sell your novel as a back-of-the-room (BOTR) offering at your speaking engagements. If you want to hand-sell and don't mind smaller sales numbers, then self-publishing may be for you.

✔ **You just want a book; sales don't matter.** *The New York Times* bestseller list isn't everyone's be-all, end-all. If your dream is to see your name on a book cover and your goal is to give copies to family, friends, and others in your social circle, then self-publishing is a great choice. It's easy and low-cost because you're not concerned with marketing and promotion.

Balancing your goals, your guts, and your wallet

With so much at stake and so much work involved, self-publishing entails more than just printing your book at the local printer. Here are points you should consider as you decide whether self-publishing is your path to publication:

✔ **Your work ethic:** Are you self-motivated? Are you willing to work hard? Are you organized? Are you a multitasker? Do you have the time for this? Are you willing to sacrifice writing time? Do you like being a jack-of-all-trades? Would you go DIY all the way, or would you hire freelancers and consultants?

✔ **Your market savvy:** Do you know your audience and the market? Can you design a cover that will appeal to that audience? Can you target and promote to your audience? Are you a salesperson? Can you get out there and talk up yourself and your book?

✔ **Your financial willingness:** What's your comfort level with risk? How much money are you willing to invest? How much can you stand losing?

✔ **Your motivation:** What's your definition of "successful self-publishing" — a few hundred sales? A few thousand? Bestseller lists? What's your goal? What will it take in terms of money and effort to reach your goal? Are the money and effort realistic for your abilities, life situation, and fiscal responsibilities?

Budget and calculate before you commit to any self-publishing plan. Determine how much you're willing to invest and then shop around to see which services you can buy with that amount. Remember to account for marketing expenses in your budget. Then calculate the number of books you need to sell to break even with your investment. Are you confident you can promote and market aggressively and effectively enough to reach those numbers? If in doubt, adjust your budget, services, or self-publishing plans.

Careful and constructive collaborations

Sometimes two or more creative folks get together and make something wonderful. That can be exciting and rewarding. Getting input, ideas, and perspective from each contributor is energizing. The potential marketing benefits of collaboration can be just as energizing: multiple minds generating ideas, multiple sets of networks to tap into, multiple locales where you can push for local publicity. A team that works together seamlessly and agrees on things quickly can have a wonderful publication experience.

It's important to remember, though, that collaborations are more than just co-creating material and packaging the team. You're entering a business partnership. Too often, writing partners are so excited about the material and the submission process that they don't consider potential breaking points that they should address without rancor at the get-go. For example, do you split your income evenly or according to who does the most work? If one author goes to a conference and sells some books, should she get a bigger cut of the sales of those copies?

Who operates the book website, and who has final say on its style and content if you don't agree? How do you work out different contract wishes? Whose name comes first on the cover? Smart coauthors brainstorm the entire process, considering all the things that may come up and then assigning responsibility. Most important, they memorialize these responsibilities on paper, even if it's just a memo that they're all willing to sign.

Each partner may have her own agent. If that's the case, the agents, too, must work things out among themselves before bringing in the outside pressure of a publisher. Will just one agent negotiate the contract? Which one? Will that agent get a higher percentage? How will the agents reconcile differences in what they each want in the contract?

All parties involved in a collaboration should brainstorm, discuss, and memorialize at the beginning of the project, well before any conflict can arise. A careful collaboration is a constructive one.

You don't have to go this alone. You can collaborate with a coauthor, doubling your resources. Or you can team up with other self-published authors to form a marketing group, stretching your marketing dollars and multiplying your connections. See the information about author promotional groups in Chapter 15.

Chapter 15

Mastering Marketing

● ●

● ●

Marketing is an essential part of being a published writer. After all, if no one knows about your book, who'll buy it? You've got to hawk it to sell it.

The term "marketing" may call to mind images of spiffy ads in newspaper book review sections with your cover image front and center, but marketing is far more than placing ads. That's a specific task of marketing — one called *promotion,* which is the collective term for spreading the word about your book through paid advertising and press publicity. Marketing is bigger than these individual tasks. When you engage in *marketing,* you're researching your target audience and strategizing ways to connect with them, and then you're planning your specific promotional efforts and enacting those plans. Marketing is figuring out who to hawk your book to and the most effective, efficient, and economical way to go about it.

Strong self-marketing authors go beyond any single book, though. They think Big Picture and Long Term, and they ultimately strive to position themselves as go-to authors of great young adult fiction. Their individual novels are components of their overall author branding.

Thanks to the Internet, authors have more control over their marketing fates than ever before. In addition to promoting themselves and their books at appearances and in classrooms, authors are connecting with groups and individuals on social-networking sites and through their own websites, contributing articles and guest blog posts, disseminating sample chapters and creating book trailers, maintaining expert blogs and taping podcasts. . . . Phew! The big challenge, really, is to keep from drowning in the process.

You could easily spend all your time marketing yourself and your books instead of writing them. This chapter helps you define your marketing audience and devise a realistic strategy to target it, decide what to leave to the pros and what to undertake yourself, and arm yourself with the basic marketing tools every author should have and decide how far you want to go beyond them. Best of all, you can begin the process before your manuscript is even finished.

Laying the Foundation

Savvy authors accept that a publisher has limited resources, and they use the Internet to spread the word themselves. These authors establish a base online presence and then promote from there, working the virtual world and the real world simultaneously. The Internet offers even the most introverted authors countless opportunities to generate buzz and sales, all from their cozy writing nooks in the attic. Online marketing can complement and even drive your in-person efforts.

Before you've finished your manuscript, use the Internet to lay the foundation for your marketing efforts. Here's how:

- **Branding yourself:** The Internet lets you create, manage, and promote your image and reputation as a writer to a degree and with an ease never before experienced by the writer masses, especially yet-to-be-published writers. Setting up a website as the anchor for your *brand* (that's you, not your books) and engaging in social media both pay off when your book is ready because your word-of-mouth network is already in place. I talk about branding later in "Creating and maintaining a platform."

- **Learning the biz:** The Internet lets you educate yourself about the industry you're about to enter. Reading online editions of trade publications and keeping in touch with other writers in groups, on forums, and on social-networking sites lets you follow the industry, know the key players, and know how your voice can work into the mix.

   Start with *Publishers Weekly*, the trade journal for the publishing industry. *PW* provides news and articles on publishing trends and reviews of new books for adults and children. Its free e-newsletters offer a steady stream of industry news and insight into bookselling trends. For your particular areas of interest, you may subscribe to the review journals that I list later in "Established reviewers of MG/YA."

   Even as you write your YA novel, you can use the Internet to increase your understanding of the industry so when the book is ready, your industry knowledge is already in place, too.

✔ **Mastering the marketplace:** The Internet lets you keep abreast of *market trends* — that is, what's selling and who it's selling to. Just as you read widely and deeply in your genre, you should read widely and deeply *about* your genre and about children's books in general. Keep up with marketplace news and trends, and when your manuscript and then your book are ready, you'll know the marketplace as well as you know your characters.

As you lay the groundwork for your marketing efforts, be realistic. Despite having a plethora of resources at your fingertips, maximizing every opportunity on the Internet is impossible. Figure out what you can do based on your time, interests, and expertise at the moment.

Even though a good chunk of your industry research can be done online, don't forget about the real world. Go to brick-and-mortar bookstores to see what's on display and to chat with booksellers — especially those who specialize in children's books. Chat with children's librarians to see what young adult fiction is popular with their library patrons. Keep your eyes peeled for newsstand features about young adult fiction, because magazines and newspapers sometimes feature current book trends and noteworthy authors and books.

Working with a Marketing Team

Whether you publish your YA fiction with an established publishing house or self-publish your books, you can have a marketing professional in your corner. Here's a look at what the pros can do for you.

Understanding the marketing department's role

The fine folks in your publisher's marketing department create the marketing plan for each title, fitting it into a grander strategy for the entire list. The department has on-staff experts in publicity (telling the press about your book), promotion (getting word out to the world at large), advertising (creating and placing paid ads), institutional accounts (school and library markets), and Internet marketing. The marketing department provides all the materials and positioning to the sale reps, who physically go out in the field and sell to book buyers.

An author's primary contact in the marketing department is usually a publicist. *Publicists* are responsible for promoting specific titles and authors in the media. They handle mass mailings and schedule interviews for broadcast and print media, author tours, public readings, and book events. These marketing pros spend their days developing media contacts, dealing with reviewers, and pitching articles through press releases or phone calls.

Your job is to work as a team with your publicist. The more involved you are, the greater the potential for book sales. Discuss with your publicist how you can best tap into the network you built while writing your book. Talk about which materials you can expect your publisher to provide to your contacts in national or local media or through whatever venues you can offer. Be responsive, willing, and communicative.

Also be understanding. Publicists can't do it all. They have a bunch of authors and books on their plates and only so much money and time. You must do some marketing on your own, and that's not a bad thing. Even with a marketing department behind you, *you* are your best promoter. You know your project better than anyone, and you certainly have the most motivation.

Calling in reinforcements: Freelance publicists

To help with your self-marketing efforts or to supplement those of your publisher, you may hire a freelance publicist who specializes in children's books. Freelancers strategize publicity campaigns based on your needs and your budget and then implement the campaign to any degree you choose. Here are a couple of ways a freelance publicist can help:

- **Niche and local marketing:** A great role for your freelance publicist is to be the point person for *niche* and local marketing while your publisher handles the main reviewers and media (in fact, few publishers include any niche or local marketing at all in their standard marketing). Niche markets are specific and small, but they matter if you exploit them well. For example, if your YA novel features horses and riding competitions, you may target the equestrian market through equestrian publications by doing interviews, submitting feature articles, or arranging for your book to be reviewed.

- **Blogs:** Your freelance publicist can focus on blogs, which are essentially online journals. Blogs are valuable for spreading the word but can also be a quagmire. After all, anybody can start a blog, and just because a blog exists doesn't mean it has a readership or even credibility. Freelance publicists can help you target the best blogs, each of which has a targeted purpose and audience. Promoting yourself through blogs is a topic all its own; see the section "Creating and maintaining a platform" for info on blogs.

Most publishers appreciate the participation of freelance publicists, viewing marketing as a team effort. In fact, your publisher should be able to recommend good, trusted freelance publicists the publisher already works with. If you look for a publicist on your own, pick one who specializes in children's books, who has worked with reputable houses, and who preferably has handled authors whose names or titles you recognize. To find a freelance publicist, ask writer friends, your publisher, or your agent for recommendations. Some popular book industry blogs like The Book Publicity Blog keep lists of publicists, or you can do an Internet search for "children's book publicists." Whatever your source, be sure to check agencies' client lists, testimonials, and featured campaigns for books and authors you recognize. Many freelance publicists spent large chunks of their careers in the marketing departments of big houses, so check their bios, too.

Communication is the key to making your relationship with your publicist effective. Be available, be open to suggestions, and above all, discuss your expectations upfront. If you're really, really hoping to be interviewed in a certain publication or on a certain show, say so. And finally, even with a pro in your corner, be willing to do your part. Your freelance publicist is not a miracle worker; she can schedule the signing, but you're the one who can fill the seats by spreading the word to family, friends, and readers through that network you built while you wrote the manuscript.

Marketing Yourself: I Write; Therefore, I Promote

Few are the authors who can leave all the marketing to the publisher and sell millions of copies. Economic considerations force publishers to put the bulk of their marketing budgets and efforts behind a few big potential *lead titles* each season. Those titles garner high-profile ads, book-signing tours, pitched features to major media, and keynote speaker gigs at conferences and book festivals. The rest of the season's books (the *list*) get a standard marketing package: submission to a core set of reviewers and awards committees, pitching to *niche* media (small, topic- or genre-focused markets), and local media exposure. This focus isn't a matter of limited interest on the part of the publishers (who would *love* to market all their books as bestsellers and then have sales follow); it's an issue of time and resources.

Even if you have access to a marketing department or a freelance publicist, you need to participate in the process, adding your expertise, insights, and connections. You're more motivated, determined, and knowledgeable about your book than anyone else, which makes you its best promoter.

This section provides tools and resources for promoting yourself and your books. You discover the basic promo must-haves and must-do's, how to create a marketing platform for yourself, and which outlets you can exploit to get the word out about you and your book . . . and keep it out. Use this information to decide which pieces you want to include in a marketing strategy that suits your goals, your abilities, your time, and your budget.

As a YA writer, you have special marketing considerations. Your readership (which you identify in Chapter 2) is somewhere between ages 9 and 18. You must be careful in how you interact with them; you're a grown-up, and your access to unknown kids has limits. You certainly can't be collecting their e-mail addresses or chatting with them on social networking sites. Both the Federal Communications Commission (FCC) and the Federal Trade Commission (FTC) enforce laws protecting kids from adults who use the Internet for inappropriate or downright nefarious purposes. The Children's Online Privacy Protection Act (COPPA), for example, requires websites to obtain parental permission before collecting the personal information of children under age 13. Instead of targeting young readers as direct customers, you market primarily to parents, teachers, librarians, reviewers, and booksellers — collectively referred to as *gatekeepers*. Every YA book must pass through at least one of these folks before landing in a kid's hands. In a nod to your teen audience, though, you can present your website and the materials on it in a teen-friendly manner so that after young readers get your books, they can go to your site, feel at home, and become fans.

Creating and maintaining a platform

Your marketing efforts should start with the one thing that doesn't change no matter how many books you write or how widely your topics range: you. When you communicate your expertise, your credibility, and your personality to an audience that comes to know and trust you, you are creating a *marketing platform,* or a stage from which you can talk to an identified, accessible audience. You are, in essence, branding yourself and establishing a following that you can go to with book news and can count on for book sales.

The most obvious example of a platform is a celebrity with a large fan base already in place before the book deal comes. That fan base can be counted on for a large number of sales, and the marketing can be tailored to their known profile and disseminated to them through pre-established avenues such as the celebrity's fan club.

Celebrities haven't cornered the market on platforms. You can create and maintain your own platform with these tools: a website and blog, social media, articles and newsletters, appearances and teaching gigs, leadership roles in organizations, and participation in author promo groups. Your ultimate goal is to sell books, and platform-building helps you achieve that goal by raising awareness about you and your books. Keep three tenets in mind as you work on your platform:

> ✓ **Lead with your strengths.** Are you a great public speaker? Propose a regular feature about children's books to local news stations with you as the host. Do you have a gift for teaching? Set up workshops for writers' groups and teach writing classes at the local college or writing clinic. Lead with your strengths, establish yourself as an expert in those areas, and then run with the opportunities that evolve.

Making time for marketing

Take it from a busy mom of triplets: Marketing is doable. If you're strategic about your goals, you're practical in your choices, and you remain committed, you can fit in marketing.

I didn't build my platform overnight, and you probably won't, either. That's okay, because publishing isn't an overnight-sensation business. If a baby step is all your life allows right now, then take that baby step with confidence. Marketing in small but manageable chunks is far better than biting off more than you can chew. Here are some tips as you decide what to tackle and when:

✔ **Choose a starting date.** Use the time before your manuscript is finished to build your base online presence through social networking. Your book-specific strategizing should begin 6 months prior to publication. Turn strategy into action at least 3 months prior to publication.

✔ **Focus.** Don't try to do it all. Focus your efforts and your message. Are you trying to be the expert on something related to your genre, story topics, and themes? Then focus on that as you build your online presence and network. If you want to become known as an expert blogger, then focus on providing frequent and engaging content and getting people to follow your blog and link to it. If public speaking is your strength, focus on drumming up appearances, building great speech content for schools and writers' groups, and wowing your audiences so they'll tell others about you . . . right after they buy all your books.

✔ **Allocate marketing time.** Block out marketing time, with set days for set tasks: *Monday: 30 minutes blogging, 1.5 hours writing. Tuesday: 10 minutes on Facebook, 15 minutes in the writers' forum, 1 hour*

writing. And so on. Keep your schedule realistic. Don't jump in and out of tasks throughout the day. You'll just feel scattered, and when Friday comes, you'll have six things only partially done. How about reaching Friday with three things totally checked off your marketing to-do list? Tackle the other three next week.

✔ **Be accountable to Father Time.** Use a timer. Seriously. Use the alarm on your computer or buy an egg timer. And be as tough with yourself as you were when you put your characters through the wringer. A timer may sound rigid, but keep this in mind: Being a writer can be a hobby, but being a published author cannot. It's a job, and jobs require commitment, structure, discipline, and follow-through.

✔ **Know yourself.** If you're a person who likes to read when you're eating, read articles or blogs about craft or the biz at lunch time. If you're a midday slumper, designate that low-energy time as your reading block.

✔ **Take a break.** Do your marketing in separate pushes instead of year-round to give yourself time off. Book promoting can be exhausting and seem never-ending. Efforts pay off, but you need a break periodically to keep your energy up. That may mean dedicating the final days of every month to reviewing the results of that month's marketing and planning the next month's marketing tasks. Or perhaps you can schedule a several-day block of time every couple of months to assess, strategize, and launch the next marketing push.

Above all, be realistic. If you can't fully commit to something, don't do it. Life goes on even if you don't participate in all 17 social-networking venues you've identified.

✓ **Have something to say.** Formulate a message that you can believe in and that has universal appeal or meaning. Maybe your message is a theme, such as telling stories that help readers feel good about themselves. Or maybe it's a mantra, such as "I tackle the issues that tackle teens every day." Or perhaps it's a mission, such as promoting teen literacy. Everything you do as a promoter should in some way tie into your message.

✓ **Act with focus and think long term.** Don't get overwhelmed by all the marketing possibilities out there. Focus on your strengths, your message, and your goals. Just as writing a novel takes time, so does marketing it — and marketing yourself. Be patient and persevere.

You can measure the strength of your platform by the number of blog subscribers and visitors, website hits and newsletter subscribers, social media "friends" and "followers," and book sales that represent your readership. You can also gauge platform strength with the less statistics-friendly but still meaningful support of your communities (the writers' groups or other organizations in which you're an active, well-known member, for example).

In this section, I discuss some of the tools you can use to build your platform.

Creating a professional website

You don't have to speak HTML as a second language to have a website, but you do need a website, and you need to set it up with a specific goal in mind. Do you want your website to stand as a bulletin board or a clearinghouse of all things *you?* Or do you want people to keep coming back to your site, in which case you need to keep things new, and coolly so? Your goal determines what your site should look like and which features it should have.

The basic elements of your website are your books, bio, and contact information (your own or your publisher's or agent's). However, even if you want a low-maintenance billboard-like site, the more information you offer, the better. Provide content that's as captivating as your YA novels, which may mean adding features such as the following:

✓ Book excerpts

✓ Reviews

✓ Book club guides

✓ Interviews and articles about you (in full or as links to other sites)

✓ Frequently asked questions (FAQs)

✓ A news page with updates about your signings and awards

Your website is one of your few chances to interact with — and market directly to — teen readers. Consider that as you choose the look and function of your site. Teens like interactive websites with quizzes, games, book trailers, blogs, and downloadables such as book club guides or sample chapters. An edgy look and feel goes over well with this audience. Young people are web-oriented and particularly quick about going to a website, so reward them for taking the effort to view your site, and use the opportunity to entice them to buy more of your books.

Before you design (or redesign) your website, review the websites of your favorite authors. Note the features the sites offer, the things you like about the sites, and the things you don't. Creative minds come up with creative websites, so you can get great ideas. But as with every aspect of marketing, don't feel you have to do it all. Adopt only the features that serve your site's goals, your overall marketing strategy, and your time and skill level. Strive for a clean, easy-to-navigate website with engaging content. Make your website look professional; it represents you, after all.

You can find plenty of website templates, even free ones, to give your site a polished look. Just sign up with a *web host* (a company that acts as a virtual landowner, letting you park your website on its piece of the Net) and pay a small fee each month for basic service. Hosts have whole sections of website templates to choose from. You can cut-and-paste your information into the template of your choice in a very short time. Or you can upgrade to fancier packages with lots of bells and whistles — or rather, *widgets,* as the programs for the add-on features are called. Creating a basic and professional-looking website is surprisingly easy.

If you don't want to use a stock template, you can hire a web designer to build you a personalized site. The designer creates your site, updates it for you as needed, helps you get a web host, and takes into account *search engine optimization* (SEO) when building the site. SEO refers to ways you can rig your website to pop up more often when people do searches on the Internet.

Starting a blog

A *blog* is an online journal that you can update anytime you want with any information you want and that invites readers to respond via a *comments* section. Most writers include blogs as a component of their websites, embedding them within the actual site or linking the two via buttons that visitors can easily spot and click. Blogs are easy, dynamic, and valuable platform-building tools. They let you get personal with your readers, talking directly to them in a casual, in-the-moment manner that isn't possible on a comparatively static website that allows no interaction. And because readers can post comments, they feel a direct connection to you.

Win followers by holding a contest

Online contests drive traffic to your website or blog, widening your audience and increasing book sales. Who doesn't like a free book? Or a free local speaking engagement, or a free t-shirt, or a character named after them in your next book? Offer people something they want, and they'll take the time to enter. Here are tips for a successful contest:

✔ **Choose a theme.** Have an anchoring reason for holding the contest, such as a holiday, an important date in your story, or your site's anniversary. Celebrate a milestone for your book with a contest, for example, or hold a contest in honor of Banned Books Week (the last week of September) or National Poetry Month (April in the United States and Canada, October in the United Kingdom) or even National Good Neighbor Day (September 28). Use whatever's appropriate to your books, your site, and your readership.

✔ **Choose prizes people want.** Make the contest worth everyone's while. Prizes can be speaking engagements if you want to target local booksellers, teachers, or writing groups. For teens or general readers, choose t-shirts, signed books, or even fuzzy dice if fuzzy dice are in your story. Be creative. Be fun. Just make sure you're giving away something people would want and reflects well on you. And hey, FYI: It's illegal to offer a prize only for people who buy something from you. It must be a "no purchase necessary" contest.

✔ **Post clear rules.** Tell folks exactly what they'll win, what they need to do to enter, the deadline for entering, and any other rules associated with the contest. If you're collecting e-mail addresses, tell people what the addresses will be used for. This being the Internet, you're likely to get some international entries, so include a country restriction in your rules if you don't want to spend the money to send the prize overseas.

✔ **Make it child safe.** There are laws regarding e-mailing with minors and collecting their personal information. Because you're a YA writer, assume young adults will be entering your contests. Keep everyone on the right side of the law (and in compliance with the Children's Online Privacy Protection Act) by including a very visible line such as "If you're under 13, submit a parent's name and e-mail address."

✔ **Make it easy to enter.** The simpler it is to enter, the more entries you'll get. Always ask for an e-mail address to notify the winner. (Remember, keep it child safe!)

✔ **Make the contest easy to manage.** If your contest goes the way you hope, you'll have lots of entries. Keep it manageable from the get-go. For example, if you let people enter by posting a comment at the bottom of your blog, the comments section can get messy with all the entries and questions about the contest and wishes for good contest luck and what all. Instead, have people send entries to your site's contact e-mail account using your website's Contact Me button and form. Or set up an e-mail account just for this contest, providing that e-mail address in the entry instructions. Tell entrants to write a specific phrase in the subject line of their e-mails for easy identification (like "Launch Party Signed Book Giveaway" or "Pick Me!"), and then just drag those e-mails into a folder for storing until the contest deadline.

To keep things low maintenance, you can do a random drawing contest in which you assign each entry a number based on the order it came in and then use a free randomizer website to generate the winning number. If you want to hold a contest where people write something, as in "The Best Opening Line Contest," limit the number of entrants to keep your workload small. Be sure to state who will be judging the contest.

✔ **Promote the contest.** The whole point of a contest is to bring new readers to your website, so get the word out. Post an announcement on your website and blog and then announce the contest (with a link to your announcement post) on your social networking sites. Ask family, friends, and other contacts to forward the news, along with the link to the contest announcement. You're giving something away, so they won't mind spreading the word on their social networking sites. Consider offering additional entries to anyone who spreads the word about the contest, as long as they send you a link to the blog or social networking entry they used to do so.

Don't use some general contest announcement website. You want to hook potential blog readers and book-buyers, not just any Joe who's looking for a freebie and hasn't picked up a book since he was a young reader himself. That may pop up your site's traffic numbers, but it doesn't gain you the long-term readers you're aiming for.

Some writers balk at blogging because they think they must fill their blogs with big treatises about writing. You don't! Use your blog to post reviews of your books, news about you and your books or about topics within your books, tour schedules, and photos from book events (but avoid posting pictures of kids' faces). Kids love it when you give them shout-outs on your blog after school appearances or post extra information or links that you promised during the visit (a trick that brings the kids to your website after the event). You can link to other authors' sites and they'll respond in kind, building a virtual network. You can even hold contests on your blog. A blog entry doesn't have to change the world; it just has to personalize you for your readers.

However you use your blog, view each blog *post* (or entry) as a writing sample. Be anecdotal, educational, and entertaining, but don't be revealing or provocative. You want readers to like you, not debate you or get into your family dramas. Teens will be reading these posts, so keep them G-rated and rant-free.

Best of all, a blog is *free* marketing. Most web hosts offer free blogs along with their website templates, and there are plenty of free blog hosts out there that you can link to your website even though you maintain the blog separately, such as Blogger or WordPress.com. Just type "blog hosts" in your search engine to pick one, or ask friends which blog hosts they use. Blogs are incredibly easy to get up and running.

Connecting with social media

Social media is the umbrella term for those websites that let you interact with other people in real time, forming communities and groups of contacts in full view of everyone else. Facebook, Twitter, and LinkedIn are some of the most prominent, but each serves its own niche group. JacketFlap (www.jacket flap.com), for example, is aimed specifically at children's book publishers and creators. And KidLitosphere Central (www.kidlitosphere.org) brings together children's book bloggers. Goodreads (www.goodreads.com) is an enormous meeting ground of booklovers that offers an Author Program designed to connect authors and their target audience. Every site's individual popularity waxes and wanes, the but the overall trend is here to stay: These are communities where information is spread easily and freely.

Social media is a useful marketing tool because it allows you to spread news about your books to a large group of people in an instant. It's great for connecting with people, allowing you to build a network and expand your platform. But be careful: You can also lose a lot of time in social media (it's addictive!) or risk your professionalism by revealing TMI (too much information). Potential editors, agents, and publishers can read your entries, as can writer colleagues, gatekeepers, and even young readers. Be wise about what you post.

Don't gather young readers into your social media circle. Online predators are a serious security risk for teens, and despite your good intentions, such contact can get you into trouble. Instead, set up fan pages in the online communities that kids can follow. Post book news, not personal commentary.

Writing articles

Writing articles for appropriate magazines or for local papers is a wonderful way to build your platform and get the word out about your novels. Your articles shouldn't be about your book, though. You plug your book in your byline or in a short author bio at the end of the article.

Magazines and newspapers want you to offer their readers information, not a long advertisement. Write an article about a topic you've mastered through writing your book or about something you learned in the writing process that's potentially edifying to others. For example, if your novel is about a boy aspiring to be a competitive eater, write an article about competitive eating or eating disorders in boys. This is a great way to raise your credibility and standing as an "expert," and people feel good about you because you've given them valuable information.

People aren't so keen on your repeatedly contacting them to push yourself and your books. But if you offer them something — information, entertainment, giveaways, your support of their news and endeavors — they're usually happy to hear your news and spread it to others. Word of mouth leads to book sales. Keep this in mind as you market yourself and your books.

Publishing a newsletter

Publishing a newsletter spreads your name, keeps it in front of people, and enhances your image. Your newsletter may contain features about the craft of writing or the topics in your books, or it may offer news about your book events or your website or blog. A newsletter also features articles by guest writers who will return the favor by plugging you and your newsletter on their own websites, blogs, and social media.

Here are a few newsletter tips:

- ✔ **Limit your newsletter to a few pages.** That way, people can read it in one sitting.

- ✔ **Publish your newsletter regularly.** A manageable publishing pace for you may be seasonally or bimonthly. Quality newsletters take time to put together, so be realistic about your time commitments.

- ✔ **Distribute the newsletter electronically.** This is cheaper and more efficient than printing your newsletter and paying postage. People are also more likely to share their e-mail addresses than their home addresses, so distributing electronically can get you more readers.

- ✔ **Create a newsletter template that you just fill in each time.** This also helps you keep your message focused and consistent. Most word processing programs have newsletter templates you can just open up and use. Or you can type "free newsletter template" into a search engine and download a free template. Another option is to lay out your newsletter using desktop publishing software that's probably lurking in your computer's "office software suite."

- ✔ **Save and distribute the final (proofread!) newsletter as a PDF.** PDFs are read-only, and your recipients can easily open the files on their computers. You can attach PDFs to e-mails as well as post them on most social networking sites. An alternative is to use a customizable HTML e-mail newsletter template (type "free html newsletter template" into a search engine to download one) that lets you embed your newsletter content within the body of an e-mail that you then send out to your subscribers.

- ✔ **Post each newsletter on your website for visitors to read.** This is a great way to refresh your website content for repeat visitors.

- ✔ **Create a mailing list.** Collect e-mails at appearances and put a "sign up for my newsletter" feature on your blog and website (there are free widgets for this). Subscribers get automatic inbox delivery, which they like, and you get consistent access to your audience, which you like.

Typos are a writer's worst enemy. They undermine your credibility as a wordsmith. Always proofread your marketing materials. Have someone else read your marketing materials, or set them aside to return to with fresh eyes on another day.

Making appearances

An author appearance is your opportunity to connect face-to-face with your readers. Teens love meeting a real, live author! And guess what — so do grown-ups. There's nothing better for sealing a sale. So get out there and hawk your goods. Meet teens in school appearances, talk to writers' groups and librarians, pitch sessions at writers' conferences, and set up signings at local bookstores and book festivals.

Exploring venues and planning your presentation

YA author appearances fall into four categories:

- ✓ **School visits:** The most effective high school author visits aren't about the books but rather about the students. Remember, teens tend to be a self-absorbed bunch. Focus on how books relate to the students' daily lives and what it means to be a writer and how they can become writers themselves. Bring in props related to your books if appropriate. (Just be careful: These aren't grade-schoolers. The props better be cool.) Give the kids behind-the-scenes looks at the making of the books they love. Incorporate pop culture and promote literacy in general.

WARNING!

Never, ever try to sell books to the kids during school visits. It's not appropriate. But *do* give them a reason to go to your website, an extra step that may be enough for a kid to buy your book. Offer the class a shout-out on your blog, for example, or invite students to read excerpts or to download a sample chapter. Leave them with bookmarks that list your website. You'll be surprised at how many students will e-mail you or comment on your blog about your inspirational visit. School visits are warm fuzzies in disguise.

- ✓ **Writers' groups:** Put together a useful presentation or workshop for other writers based on your book or your expertise or an area of craft interest. Chapters of SCBWI (the Society of Children's Book Writers and Illustrators) and other writers' groups are always looking for inspiring speakers with useful information. You can also offer to be a guest speaker at local universities, colleges, junior colleges, and writers' clinics.

An alternate way to present is through "appearances" in online writers' forums. There, you prepare a post (basically an online article) about a particular topic of interest for the group and then make yourself available to do Q&A (question-and-answer exchanges) for a specified time afterward.

TIP

Here's a sneaky fact: A lot of YA writers are teachers in their day jobs. They share the books and writers they like with their students, which means that if teachers are in your audience at a writers' group appearance, you may just get a classroom visit out of the deal.

- ✓ **Book signings:** If your publisher isn't sending you on a book tour (and most new authors don't get tours), you can do one on the cheap by staying with family and friends or by planning appearances in the cities you're already planning to vacation in. Piggy-back 'em. And be creative. You can hold an event at the zoo if your book is about a teen on safari. Got a YA historical fiction novel featuring a young sailor on a 19th-century sailing ship? Contact the organizers of nearby maritime festivals about hosting a book-signing booth. Look for opportunities specific to you and your topic.

✔ **General events:** Watch for speaking opportunities such as writers' conferences, teacher and librarian conferences, public book festivals, or community events that may be connected to your book's themes or topics.

You can maximize your success as a speaker by being professional and tailoring your appearances to each audience. Know the group and its interests before you pitch your visit, and then ask your contact about the group's latest interests so you can tailor your words to the group's current needs. Return calls and e-mails promptly, follow through on your promises, and get materials to people quickly. End each appearance on a professional note by following up with a thank you. Better yet, post a public thanks on your website or blog — both you and your group get another plug in the process.

Getting a gig

Make things as easy on your potential hosts as possible. Put up an appearance page on your website that lists the following:

✔ The kinds of events you speak at

✔ Some ideas for speaking topics

✔ Testimonials from previous appearances

✔ Your hometown and whether you're willing to travel

✔ Your contact information

You can also include your own honorarium request or a line like "honorarium is negotiable" on your website. An *honorarium* is a payment for appearing. Writers' conferences and groups pay honorariums, and schools do, too, but there's a catch for YA authors: Elementary schools are more likely to spend their public-speaker money on authors than high schools are. (High schools spend their money on anti-drug speakers and the like — go figure.) For current speaker honorariums, peruse other authors' websites, which frequently list this information.

Some writers get around the lack of high school funds by offering free classroom visits to local high school teachers. Free visits allow authors to drum up word of mouth, hone their speaking skills, and maintain a connection with young readers. And hey, you never know what a free appearance can lead to. I've had free appearances lead to radio interviews, TV appearances, and lucrative, all-expense-paid trips to out-of-state private schools.

Want to do out-of-town appearances but are unable to travel or need to keep costs down? Offer to use free Skype or other video-conferencing technologies for a virtual visit. Schools generally can handle low-tech, Internet-based video conferences in individual classrooms. And for today's technologically savvy teens, interacting with a face on a TV screen is totally normal.

Teaching classes

Teaching establishes your expertise and raises your credibility as a writer. Propose classes or guest lectures to local universities, colleges, junior colleges, and writers' clinics, or put together workshops for writers' groups. These gigs are easier to land as you get published books under your belt.

One of my first acts in building my image and reputation as a writing expert was teaching a 9-week night class about writing children's books. It's a good thing I did, because three important things happened: 1) students booked me for speaking appearances with their writers' groups, which led to more appearances, interviews, and guest blog posts; 2) several students hired me for freelance editing, which led to referrals and the foundation of my editorial business when I left my full-time office editorial gig to raise my trio; and 3) I learned something about myself in the process: I *love* to teach. I hadn't known that before. I embraced this discovery, turning teaching into a strength and then into a platform and then, well, into this book. All this happened because I took a single brand-building action to launch my platform and then expanded it as time and circumstances permitted.

Taking leadership roles in organizations

Taking on a leadership role in an organization related to writing, YA fiction, or the topics/themes in your books sets you up as an expert and immerses you in a community, which is great for platform-building and general networking. If you don't see a group that's right for you, start one of your own. If you want a leadership role but can't find one in your organization, propose a new office or initiate a project that needs a project leader. In return for your service, you'll have opportunities to share your book news and meet people who can help you and whom you can help in return.

Having an active role in a group can take up a lot of your time, of course, but it can also open major doors. SCBWI regional advisors do a lot of work for their chapters, but they get to attend the events for reduced prices or sometimes for free and then interact personally with editors and agents when they help put on events. You can't buy that kind of networking . . . but you can work for it. At the very least, be a participating member of an organization. You'll gain as much as you give.

SCBWI (the Society of Children's Books Writers and Illustrators) is the main organization for children's book writers. At any level of participation, you'll find it an amazing resource on craft, the marketplace, and the publishing business. Find more on SCBWI in Chapter 3.

Joining an author promotional group

An excellent way to tackle marketing is to combine resources with other writers in an *author promo group*. Pick a common denominator — your genre, your topic, something that encompasses all your books — and rally around that. Choose "mommy paranormal YA writers," for instance. Push that angle with press, signings, and appearances.

Joining forces can give you more marketing power for less work. Five authors spreading the word about one signing? That gives you greater coverage and hopefully wider turnout than any of you could do on your own. You can hold your own blog tours, giving you an event to hype, and you'll have access to each other's audiences in guest blogs or newsletter articles, growing your own audience in the process. The group's members can step up their participation or dial it back in a group ebb-and-flow, depending on the curveballs life throws. Above all, the emotional support of a core group can be immensely buoying.

Here are some things an author promo group can do:

- ✔ **Group marketing:** Split the costs while multiplying word of mouth. Pool your resources to pay for ads in genre- or topic-specific publications, which are generally out of the budget for individual authors. Create a group website, with everyone contributing content and taking turns with a group blog on the website.

- ✔ **Group newsletters:** Generate a group newsletter, with members taking turns writing the features. Spread the workload among the group.

- ✔ **Guest blogging:** Feature group members on your personal blog, and be featured on theirs, increasing everyone's exposure.

- ✔ **Blog tours:** A *blog tour* allows you to create buzz without ever leaving your writing nook. Like its big sister the book-signing tour, a blog tour starts and ends on specified dates, makes stops at scheduled and pre-promoted venues (in this case, blogs with an audience that matches your target audience), and offers the audience a chance to interact with you while giving your host an opportunity to promote an event. You can put together a blog tour for yourself, but a blog tour by an author promo group creates a weightier big "event" feel. Plus you can make stops at each other's blogs in addition to the outside blog tour hosts.

  You can set up the tour yourself or hire a blog tour company to handle the searching, contacting, and coordinating. Effective blog tours incorporate book reviews, author blog posts, Q&A, book giveaways, and links galore, letting everyone on the tour score some cross-promotion action. Although blog tours are not paid appearances, all the participants benefit from the exposure.

You'll find potential members for your author promo group through your networking in online writing communities, through your writers' group or chapter, by spreading the word among writing friends and colleagues, or even through your agent or publisher, who may know of other writers interested in teaming up.

Gathering your marketing materials

After you target your marketing audience and devise a strategy for reaching them, it's time to create your materials. This section offers a rundown of the basic items every author must have along with things you can tackle beyond that, such as print mailings and expanded electronic marketing (also known as *e-marketing*).

The basics

In terms of promo materials, there are four absolute musts for a YA author:

- **Author photo:** Every author needs a photo to accompany his basic bio. The photo will be used for your appearances, interviews, website, blog, social media, print materials, even your book jacket.

  Your photo represents you to your readers, and it must be professional. Don't use some fuzzy shot of you sitting at a party. You'd be wise to keep this photo personable or serious; silly photos can easily backfire because not everyone shares your sense of humor. And you know, when teens don't think you're funny, they call you a dork.

  Hire a professional photographer or set aside a block of time with a patient friend and a really good camera. Take a million shots, with different backgrounds and different camera settings, until you get a polished one. Due to space and size considerations, keep the photo focused on your head. In fact, consider using tight cropping to fill the frame with your face. And maybe tilt the camera or take it from an unexpected angle. Don't get all proppy; focus on you.

- **Bookmarks, cards, or postcards:** You need one of these items to hand out as your business card. Keep a stack at the ready, no matter where you go. If someone talks to you, mention that you're a writer, hand out a card, and say, "Read excerpts on my website. Here's the address," to give that person a reason to go to your site. The more action people direct toward your book, the more likely they are to buy it.

  You can create bookmarks, traditional business cards, and mail-ready postcards cheaply online without being a techno stud. The online printers have templates and instructions for you, and plenty of free "make your own business cards" sites are out there. Ask writer friends who they use for their cards to find reasonable and quality printers (yet another reason to be networked!), or hire a graphic designer to come up with a design and make a printer recommendation for you. Print tons of these cards so you won't hesitate handing them out like candy.

✔ **Author website:** You don't have to go all bells and whistles, but you do need an author website if you're writing for teens. They expect it. And frankly, adults do, too. They get suspicious if you don't have one. See the earlier section "Creating and maintaining a platform" for my whole spiel about websites and why you need one to build a platform.

✔ **Promo copies of your book:** *Promotional copies* are prepublication editions of your novel that are distributed to reviewers ahead of the publication date, with enough lead time for them to read the book and have the reviews ready when the final bound books hit store shelves. Promo copies are also called *galleys* or *ARCs* (advance reading copies). They're usually printed and bound before the final editing is complete, so most come with warnings about confirming excerpts against the final book before printing them in reviews. Your publisher can provide you with ARCs to send out to your review contacts. But be selective — ARCs are costly to produce and mail, so you want to be sure your targeted reviewers have a solid audience and are worth the expense.

Mailings: Postcards and other printables

The goal of direct mailings is to provide useful and relevant information (including ordering information) in a fun and easy-to-implement format, which in turn makes a personal connection and generates sales. Direct mailings are a great way to reach librarians and teachers. Publishers usually have lists of teachers and educators nationwide. If your publisher doesn't have the right list for you, or if you're self-publishing, you can buy mailing lists from providers of education marketing information and services.

Your mailing materials should focus on your title and on a theme related to the education market, such as April's National Poetry Month. If possible, the materials should suggest classroom activities that incorporate your book and the theme, giving teachers a reason to take action, which is one step closer to buying your book or putting it into students' hands. You can also do a mailing of sample chapters or promotional copies to any key opinion-makers you identify in the marketplace, such as influential librarians, teachers, or authors, or even high-profile local media personalities or national celebrities. Such folks have large platforms and can spread the word about books that connect with them. If you have a specialized topic that would appeal to a large, organized niche audience, send sample chapters or promo copies to the organization leaders. For example, a novel about a group of young aspiring firefighters could get a great plug in a junior firefighters' publication if you send promo materials to the group's president or other influential people.

Downloadables and web features

After you've gathered your basic marketing materials, you can start adding powerful support materials to your website and to your general marketing larder. The goal here is to give people more reasons to think or talk about your book, as well as more reasons to interact with your website. Teens particularly love interactive sites, and teens are forwarding-crazy. If you want kids to get excited enough about something on your site to forward it to their friends, make it 1) cool and 2) worth forwarding. Then let teens do the marketing for you.

Here goes with some general bells and whistles you can offer:

- **Sample chapters and excerpts:** Let your writing speak for itself: Include excerpts or full chapters on your website. Make them viewable on the site or create read-only versions (PDFs or GIFs) that visitors can download and print if they want. End these teasers at cliffhanger moments so readers feel they *must* get the book to find out what happens next.

- **Study guides:** Also called *discussion guides* or *curriculum guides,* these four- to six-page documents are for teachers and other instructors. They're for classroom use, providing background information for the story, researched facts about your topic, and discussion questions and activities that complement curriculum. You may include a creative writing activity, for example, or a mapping activity or a role-playing activity. Some books lend themselves to social studies, history, and even science lessons.

  Provide your study guide to teachers when you're planning school visits. Encourage teachers to work one or more activities into their lesson plans before or after your visit to extend the lesson for the kids.

- **Book club guides:** Less intensive than study guides, book club guides offer discussion questions for teen book clubs. Keep the guides to a page or two so they don't intimidate the kids. Write questions that encourage kids to apply the book's themes to their own lives. The more fun you can make the questions, the better.

- **School appearance packages:** Put together a set of materials that teachers can download prior to your visit and gather those materials on the Appearances page of your website. You may include a flyer with your photo and bio, summaries and excerpts from your books, discussion guides, and so forth — anything to prepare the class for your visit, to get the students to interact with the book and/or its themes, and to help the teacher extend the lesson.

- **Behind-the-scenes articles:** Teens love seeing what went into creating the book in their hands. Did the characters have different names in early drafts? Where did you get your ideas? What's the background of things you mentioned in the story? I have a section called "Behind-the-Books Blog Series" on my blog (it's also accessible through the main menu of my website) that features the history of hot dogs, gummi bears, superheroes, and even my book jackets — all things that appear in or somehow relate to my novels. I talk up this feature with students during visits and encourage them to go to my blog for the quirky details. Behind-the-scenes articles are a fun and easy feature to add to your website or blog, and they don't require maintenance. You write an article and post it, and then you're done.

Author Darcy Pattison talks book trailers

In fall 2010, Naomi Bates, a Texas high school librarian, surveyed 100 librarians about their usage of book trailers in their school libraries. The results are astounding. The first question in the survey was "How effective are book trailers in presenting a book to students?" The poll shows that 66.3% of librarians said, "Very effective," 33.7% said, "Somewhat effective," and only 1% said, "Not effective."

Conclusion: If you're interested in promoting a teen book, you need a book trailer. Bookstores and the trade market may not be very influenced by book trailers, but the school market definitely is. And school is where your audience lives.

The biggest objection to book trailers is that this video advertisement takes away the role of the reader's imagination. That is, the trailer uses certain images or actors to portray a synopsis of the story or an exciting scene, and that image imprints, replacing the reader's imagination. That's a valid objection: You have to walk a fine line between enticing a reader and respecting the reader's imagination. But effective trailers manage to do both.

How? Three options are available for creating a great book trailer:

- **Movie trailer aesthetic:** Book trailers that imitate movie trailers have been one of the Holy Grails of this growing field. These slick, high-dollar productions are usually created by the publisher and a few authors with big budgets. They are indeed lovely to look at, and if done well, the script pulls in readers. These are the most likely kinds of trailers to cross the line into imagining a story for a reader, but they can be very compelling. *Aesthetics:* Slick, professional production on all fronts.

- **Slideshow aesthetics:** On the opposite end of the budget scale is the slideshow book trailer. These are usually author created and feature a combination of static text and static images. These are likely to be a format that many authors choose because they don't require a big layout of funds. The danger here is the risk of boring a reader; after all, silent movies went out in the 1920s. *Aesthetics:* Create the right mood with music, text, and images.

- **YouTube aesthetics:** As with any other video intended primarily for online sites such as YouTube, this kind of book trailer has a more informal aesthetic. YouTube thrives on humor, immediacy, and authenticity. Creativity matters more here than pristine audio or video. Short videos that allow for easy sharing, remixing, and as the basis for a spoof or parody are perfect for this irreverent media. Think flying squirrel, not story synopsis. **Note:** Instead of YouTube, many schools use TeacherTube. com or SchoolTube.com. *Aesthetics:* Creativity.

Everything about book trailers — as with writing a great teen novel — demands creativity. Don't usurp the reader's role of imagining a story, but don't bore him with static images, either. Find creative ways to stay within your budget and still pull in readers.

Darcy Pattison is an award-winning children's book author, writing teacher, and popular speaker on writing techniques. She runs a popular blog on writing and is widely known for her Novel Revision Retreat and her book The Book Trailer Manual. Visit www.darcy pattison.com *and* www.thebook trailermanual.com.

✔ **Audio/video:** Book trailers, interview videos, and audio clips are great additions to any site. These require more advanced technical knowledge, but you can find plenty of sources out there for learning it.

Don't limit yourself to these materials. Be creative. If your book features a journey, consider creating an interactive map for your website. If yours is an epic tale, consider a section on your site that has the community history or short stories about ancillary characters. Just be sure to lay out the site in an easy-to-navigate way. Your primary rule is "user-friendly," with "teen friendly" being a close second.

Garnering book reviews

Book reviews are important marketing tools because positive reviews — especially *starred* reviews, a way some publications call out above-the-crust titles — can mean increased sales. Professional book-buyers such as teachers, librarians, and booksellers depend on reviews to tell them what a book is about and whether it will complement their collection or sell to their customers. Consumers look to reviews for their next purchases.

Children's book review sources have one of three primary audiences:

✔ **Trade:** Aimed at the publishing industry, including publishers, agents, authors, booksellers, wholesalers; *Publishers Weekly* is by far the most significant publishing industry trade publication

✔ **Institutional:** Aimed at the school and library market — meaning teachers, librarians, school and library wholesalers, school district review centers, library review centers, and state departments of education

✔ **Consumer:** Aimed at the general book-buying public; this includes national magazines and newspapers like the *New York Times* or *Seventeen* magazine, as well local publications

Focus your book review efforts on the institutional and trade markets, where professional YA book-buyers look to stock their shelves for their teen readers, and on local and special interest consumer publications. Yes, the big consumer sources like the *Los Angeles Times* have humongous audiences, but their coverage of teen fiction is slim and focused on high-profile titles.

Publishers usually take care of submitting review copies to key review publications. Ask your publisher's marketing department which review sources they'll be submitting your book to. Cross those off your list and start sending out to the others. It's your job to blanket your hometown publications with review copies (local papers like to run news about local writers) because you're in a better position to know those publications.

To get your book reviewed, send your advance reading copies (ARCs) to reviewers several months prior to your publication date. Be sure to include a cover letter that clearly lists the book's category and genre, audience age range, ISBN, price, publisher, and pub date. Reviewers usually want ARCs 3 to 6 months prior to publication; they'll time their printing of the review to your pub month. Some reviews do appear after a book publishes, but you'll lose your window with many publications if you wait to send them final bound books post-publication. Check each review publication's website for its requirements. The publication may send you a copy of its review after it's printed, but not always. Most publishers pay a review clipping service to collect reviews for them as they're printed; in that case, copies of your reviews will eventually wend themselves through the review clipping service, to your editor or marketing staff's offices, and into your mailbox. Or you can periodically do online searches. Many print reviews also appear online, as do exclusively online reviews like those on Teenreads.com. (More on specific reviewers in a moment.)

Children's books is the category for all books for young readers, including board books for toddlers, picture books, chapter books for beginning readers, and young adult literature — with the term *young adult* being a cumulative term for MG and YA.

Established reviewers of MG/YA

Here is a list of the established trade and institutional YA fiction review sources. For now at least, they're all available both in print and online, with some offering their full content online and others requiring subscriptions for full access. Many offer e-newsletter updates, usually for free. After you subscribe to those, the newsletters show up in your inbox automatically. Each publication's website gives a full rundown of its audience description, circulation data, and guidelines for submitting a book for review consideration. Definitely check their rules for what falls within the scope of their reviewing programs before you send an advance reading copy their way.

- ✔ **ALAN Review:** The ALAN Review is published three times a year (fall, winter, and spring) by the Assembly on Literature for Adolescents for the National Council for Teachers of English (NCTE). It offers articles about YA literature and its teaching, author profiles and interviews, publishing trend reports, and book reviews. Visit www.alan-ya.org.

- ✔ **Booklist:** This publication of the American Library Association (ALA) is aimed at librarians, and it's a biggie. *Booklist* reviews thousands of new titles for children and adults every year. It offers a quarterly supplement called *Book Links* that brings further news about children's books to classroom teachers and librarians, with each issue focusing on a theme and suggesting books that fall into those themes. Visit www.booklist online.com.

✔ **The Bulletin:** Technically called *The Bulletin of the Center for Children's Books,* this monthly children's book review journal serves school and public librarians. It reviews new books for children and young adults and offers the prestigious *Bulletin* Blue Ribbon Awards each year. Visit bccb.lis.illinois.edu.

✔ **Horn Book:** *The Horn Book Magazine* features bimonthly commentary, articles, book reviews of selected new titles, and other information related to children's and young adult literature. Its sister publication, *The Horn Book Guide,* appears twice a year and contains only reviews — more than 2,000 in each issue. Visit www.hbook.com.

✔ **Kirkus Reviews:** A biweekly review publication for librarians, *Kirkus* reviews approximately 4,000 to 5,000 print books per year (including adult titles). Visit www.kirkusreviews.com.

✔ **Multicultural Review:** This quarterly journal and book review for educators and librarians focuses on race, ethnicity, spirituality, religion, disability, and language diversity. The journal reviews books and other media with multicultural themes and topics, and it offers articles on critical issues in multicultural literature and education. It's the official publication of EMIERT, the Ethnic and Multicultural Information Exchange Round Table of the American Library Association. Visit www.mcreview.com.

✔ **Publishers Weekly:** This is the primary trade journal for the publishing industry. *PW* provides news and articles on publishing trends and reviews of new books for adults and children. Twice a year (February and July), *PW* publishes a special edition highlighting the spring and fall seasons for children's books. (Some publishers have a third selling season, offering a new list of books every spring, fall, and winter.) *PW* offers free e-newsletters, two of which are right up your alley: the more general *PW Daily* and the children's book–focused *Children's Bookshelf.* Visit www.publishersweekly.com.

✔ **School Library Journal:** *SLJ* is a primary reviewer of books, multimedia, and technology for children and teens, with articles about timely topics of interest for school library media specialists. *SLJ* reviews thousands of new books for children and teens each year. It offers free e-newsletters, including *SLJ Teen,* for librarians, teachers, and consumers with teen-interest books and other media, and *Curriculum Connections,* which ties children's and teen books into curriculum for classroom and library use. Visit www.schoollibraryjournal.com.

✔ **VOYA:** The bimonthly journal *Voice of Youth Advocates* offers reviews, articles, and editorials on YA literature to librarians, educators, and other professionals who work with young adults. At least one annotated booklist for teen readers appears in every *VOYA* issue, covering as many as 200 titles on each list. Visit www.voya.com.

Be sure to target topically appropriate publications with your review copies. *Locus Magazine*, for example, serves sci-fi/fantasy readers — an audience just champing at the bit for the next great fantasy epic. Send them yours.

If you get a review you don't agree with, resist the urge to reply or to rant about it on your blog. No matter how justified you are, your protests will just come across as a case of sour grapes. If there's a legitimate fact error, yes, you can politely point it out, but beyond that, take the high road. Everyone knows a review is subjective, and if it's a vicious one (rare, but it does happen), folks can recognize that, too.

Online bookseller reviews and marketing opportunities

Authors are finding online booksellers to be increasingly powerful marketing outlets where they can have direct impact on book sales. There are a number of small online booksellers, but the two biggest in the U.S. are Amazon.com and Barnes & Noble.com. Virtual bookstores have gained significant stature in the publishing industry over the years, with readers often turning to their listings for their initial information on a title, editorial reviews, and in-the-trenches reader reviews.

Online booksellers understand the connection between authors' self-marketing efforts and book sales, so they provide many great marketing opportunities for authors. Here are some ways to maximize your marketing presence in online bookseller sites and potentially increase your book sales:

- **Create an author page.** Online booksellers usually offer author pages that allow you to share information about yourself and your books with readers. Amazon.com lets you create your author page through its Author Central. Customers access your author page by clicking on your name on your book's *detail page* (product page). You can post your bio and author photo, gather your titles on one page in a visual bibliography, add video, photos, and blog entries, and even track your sales for that site.

- **Write reviews.** The most powerful (and easy) way to convert browsers to buyers is to have positive and useful reviews in your book's comments section. Research shows that shoppers put a lot of stock in customer reviews, so ask your contacts (family, friends, fans, and fellow writers) to write customer reviews for your books. Aim for a minimum of four customer reviews for each book.

- **Review your reviews.** You should know what people are saying about your book in online bookseller sites — and you should know how to manage those reviews to the extent that you can. When you see a review you like, you can raise its profile by clicking "Yes" in answer to the question "Was this review helpful to you?" and asking your contacts to do the same. Unflattering reviews will get buried at the bottom of the list. Shoppers can still read them, of course, but at least those reviews won't be sitting at the top of the heap.

Resist responding to negative comments; not everyone in the world will love your book, and responding to them only makes you look bad.

Online booksellers also post editorial reviews from major review publications on a book's detail page. This is a contracted arrangement between the bookseller and the review publication, and you have no control over which reviews appear there. Asking the bookseller to remove unflattering reviews won't get you far; the booksellers are more dedicated to the integrity of their book review feature than in making a single author happy.

✔ **Tag your book.** At least one online bookseller, Amazon.com, lets you add tags to your book listing. *Tags* are keywords such as *fantasy, magic, trolls,* or *teen fiction* that relate to your book and help readers find that book through keyword searches. For example, if a reader types "teen fiction trolls" into the book search field, books with those tags will show up in the search results. Increase your book's chances of landing on Amazon search results lists by adding tags to your book. Go to your book's detail page and type "tt" to access the "Tag this product" feature. You must have a Real Name or Pen Name in Amazon to save your tags. Anyone can tag any book — and the more people who tag your book, the higher it ranks in search results (there are many factors in ranking; this is just one) — so ask your friends to tag your book, too, using the same tags you used.

✔ **Post a promotional video.** Online booksellers often let you post promotional video on your author page. Here's a good use for a book trailer. (For more on book trailers, read the "Author Darcy Pattison talks book trailers" sidebar.) Whatever kind of video you post, it should represent you well with strong quality and content. You may be tempted to embed a link to your author website in your video, but don't. Major booksellers don't accept videos with external links.

✔ **Post customer images.** You can increase your book's content depth by posting photos related to your book. If you have unusual interior spreads, you can post photos of those. If you have a cool map at the front of your YA fantasy, post a photo of that. These extra images typically appear directly below your cover image on the detail page.

✔ **Check your content.** Sometimes boo-boos make it into bookseller listings. Double check all your information, make sure your book image is there, and see whether the "look inside the book" or "read an excerpt" feature is enabled. If you see a problem with your listing, contact your publisher or the bookseller directly.

Online booksellers continue to add new features that can enhance your presence on their sites and potentially improve your sales. Be on the lookout for the latest and greatest. Don't forget to attend to your listings on international bookseller sites such as Amazon UK (www.amazon.co.uk) or Canada's Indigo Books & Music (www.chapters.indigo.ca) if your book is sold outside the U.S.

And here's a bonus: Most online booksellers have affiliate programs that let you earn a commission every time a user clicks through a link on your website and ends up buying a book in their store. So add bookseller links to your website (perhaps on a "Buy the Books" page) and become an affiliate.

Bloggers and teen fiction forums

Regardless of how much promotion your publisher can put into your specific book, you have it in your hands to launch a *web campaign* of your own. Using the publication of your book as the driving event, you can contact blogs and online forums that specialize in children's books (especially teen fiction) and offer them review copies, sample chapters, cover images, guest blog posts, author interviews, and contests. Your goal is to drive traffic to your website and ultimately to the bookstore. To effectively market your book through blogs and forums, identify and reach out to the following:

- ✔ **Young adult fiction websites for teens:** These websites have solid, established teen audiences. The sites post author interviews and teen-friendly promotional items such as book trailers, sample chapters, and favorite cover images; host blog tours; and provide book news and reviews (often written by teens themselves). Check out `www.teen reads.com` and `www.yareads.com`.

- ✔ **Top children's book bloggers:** These blogs usually list other good blogs in their "resources for writers" or "links" sections. The children's book community is like that, love 'em. You'll quickly see that certain blogs show up in everyone's links sections. Target those.

- ✔ **Blogs, websites, and forums that specialize in your genre or book topic:** If your book is about baseball, look for baseball-lover sites and contact the administrators who run the sites. They may feature your book straight out, do an interview with you, or let you write them a short feature post based on something in your book. Writer and genre LISTSERV-type e-mail lists (online discussion communities that focus on specific topics of interest) are great resources for spreading the word, too. Some of these communities require you to register, and all have rules about self-promoting. Lurk in a forum for a bit to get a feel for the tone, interest, and level of activity.

Researching blogs and forums leads you down all kinds of virtual side roads — some useful, some just distracting, and all potentially overwhelming. To keep your focus, do your blog marketing in three stages:

1. **Identify the blogs you may want to target.**

   Set up a spreadsheet or other document to note the names and addresses (URLs) of the sites you identify, their audiences, and what materials you'll offer each one when you contact them. Here you're free to write down *every one* of the neat-o sites that caught your attention.

2. **Sort the sites.**

   Categorize the sites as YA fiction websites for teens, top children's book bloggers, and genre-specific sites and forums. Target the primary ones for first contact. Blog marketing is very time-consuming, and you'll likely find yourself striking some less-useful sites from your list.

3. **Make contact and follow up.**

   Keep careful notes of whom you speak with, what they want, and when they want it. Communication is very important for turning all this effort into actual blog posts.

Your web campaign uses word of mouth and people's tendency to forward. As with all your marketing efforts, if you can offer readers something beyond a shameless plug — such as advice, information, or sample chapters — they'll have a reason to take notice and tell their friends. But your generosity should have a limit: You'll find a million bloggers willing to give your book a shout-out for a free copy. Determine whether a site has a significant readership before you send a precious advance reading copy (ARC). If the site doesn't, offer the blogger a free electronic chapter to give him a feel for your book and for him to post for his readers. Both blogger and blog followers will feel like they've gotten something for free, so they'll be happy before they even open the chapter file.

Part V
The Part of Tens

The 5th Wave   By Rich Tennant

WORKING DECKSIDE, AUTHOR JANINE
WALKER MISTAKENLY COATS HERSELF
WITH WRITER'S BLOCK INSTEAD OF SUN BLOCK

In this part . . .

The *For Dummies* team's idea of a "happily ever after" ending is to serve up some final and very vital points, tips, and insights in a top-ten list format. Sounds like a satisfying finale to me! Here, then, are three lists of important must-knows for everyone who writes and publishes for young readers. I warn you about the ten most common pitfalls in writing young adult fiction, I answer the ten most common publishing contract questions, and I give you ten ways to turn writers' conferences into positive, productive experiences.

Chapter 16

Ten Common Pitfalls in Writing YA Fiction

*W*riters of young adult fiction face a litmus test not applied to writers in other categories: What you write must hook, convince, and entertain teenagers. And you're in a position to do a lot of influencing. Could you pick a more daunting job? This chapter covers ten common missteps in crafting stories for those impressionable, judgmental, and very important young people.

Dating a Book

Although going out with hotties is certainly a crucial topic of teendom, I don't mean that kind of dating here. I'm talking about the kind of dating that tells readers, "This book is old. This book is out of touch. This book is not for hip, in-the-now you, and there's no way you'll relate to it." At least, that's how teens react when they read about passé music groups and technologies older than they are.

Unless your story takes place in a certain historical era and you're creating a sense of place by sprinkling cultural details throughout, do not mention musicians, movie stars, politicians, or any other such famous folks by name. Be vague instead. Refer to "the president" instead of naming the sitting commander in chief. Refer to the "killer concert" instead of the "awesome Justin Bieber gig." Have the character "crank up the bass" or "zone out to some generic rom-com." If you must name names, make up your celebrities, groups, and movies. Or pick references that never fade away or suddenly go geek, such as the Rolling Stones or the Beatles. With tried-and-true references like that, you can enrich your character's personality and the overall story with cultural references without torpedoing them in the process.

See Chapter 8 for more on creating atmosphere and believability with props and setting details.

Slinging Slang

Slang, or the talk of a particular cultural group at a particular time in history, is fun stuff — but that doesn't mean it belongs in your teen novel. It's very hard for a grown-up to sound anything but lame when slinging teen slang. Lame is never good when you're trying to impress young people. On top of flirting with lameness, there's the dating issue I talk about in the preceding section: Slang is usually limited to its user group, and when teens age out of your target audience, the incoming audience is likely to roll their eyes at the dated lingo.

Of course, you wouldn't be writing teen fiction if you weren't fearless. There are instances where slang can call a teen novel home. M. T. Anderson's National Book Award Finalist novel *Feed* swims in slang. It's a first-person point of view story told by a teenage boy who narrates exactly how he'd talk — slang and all. Things "suck" and characters "go all gaga" over things. This kind of narration is highly stylized, meaning it doesn't follow convention but rather defines itself. In fact, Anderson positions the entire book as a satire, a style of writing that seeks to call attention to the details and devices within. What's most important to note, though, is that Anderson uses freewheeling grammar more than slang, and that's what really gives the narration its youth and per-sonality. More than anything, loose grammar is the key to making slang work in a teen novel without sounding lame or dating your story.

You can certainly try your hand at a stylized narration laced with slang and creative grammar. Such crafting is what Chapter 9 is all about, so flip back there and brush up. If you nail the narration, your readers will sink into the tale, and the style will stop being a "device" and just feel right. If you don't pull readers into the story, though, they'll never get past the device.

If you decide to attempt slang-slinging, make sure you really know how to talk the talk. Do lots of eavesdropping on teens, do lots of conversing with teens, and even consider asking teens to read your manuscript out loud to you, stop-ping when they get to something weird so they can tell you how they'd really say it. Above all, make sure your storytelling craft is up to the task of pulling readers into your world. Render the slang a part of your story for teens, not a hindrance to it.

S-E-X

Can you think of a more controversial topic for a teen novel than sex? Can you think of a topic teens are more interested in?

You, fearless writer of teen fiction, get to tiptoe the fine line of handling teens' top topic without blowing gatekeepers' tops. Oh, it's easy to vilify gate-keepers when you're talking about the need for sexuality, sex-related issues, and sexual activity in teen novels. Parents, librarians, teachers, and booksell-ers are going to bring to bear their preferences when judging a book's appro-priateness for the young readers under their literary care. The thing is, that's something all adults do, and can you really fault people for trying to look out for their kids? Too often people complain that parents *aren't* monitoring kids' cultural intake. The task is subjective, though, and jurisdictions can get controversial.

Including graphic sex in a teen novel will prevent that novel from reaching some teens. It may assure your book lands in other teens' hands, of course. You must decide whether you're willing to forgo some readers for the sake of keeping it real.

Look for ways around the graphic stuff. You can have the sexy stuff happen offstage. You can be vague about it if it's happening onstage. You can avoid the graphic stuff altogether and stick to a PG-rated version of young love. Sex isn't always about the physical act.

Writing Cliché Characters and Situations

Teens have been at the storytelling game long enough to know a stock char-acter when they see one. It's hard to get excited about yet another nerd, another jock, and another bimbo blonde cheerleader. Editors and agents are just as hard on cliché characters and situations. Offer more. Think creatively. Move these characters out of the standard settings, and aim to surprise your-self as much as anyone with how they react in unexpected scenarios.

See Chapter 5 for info on kicking clichés out of your teen fiction.

Preaching

Teens and tweens get enough lecturing in a day; they don't want it in their leisure reading. As much as you want your moral or your message to come across to your readers, resist the urge to state it directly. Show actions and consequences in your story; let readers see lessons learned and maturity evolve. Your readers will get it. They may be young, but they're sharp.

Check out themes in Chapter 2, and read up on the technique of showing instead of telling and the ins-and-outs of the teen mindset in Chapter 9.

Dumbing It Down

Readers who come to teen fiction as grown-ups are often surprised by how sophisticated, daring, and masterful the writing is. Great writers for young readers generally respect their audience's ability to think independently and critically.

Make sure you don't dumb down your content out of fear that young readers won't get something. They will. If you need convincing of that, just read some teen-authored reviews like those on www.teenink.com or in the comments sections of online bookstore listings. And when your fan e-mail starts rolling in, you'll be convinced of it. YA writers are nurturing future adult readers and exposing young people to the ways of the world beyond their immediate experience; serve up things they can really sink their teeth into.

Writing for 18+

YA fiction with protagonists who are post high-school or in their early twenties can be hard sells, and you're severely limiting your submission prospects if you aim for that demographic. These novels fall in the gap between YA's traditional age-18 cutoff and books for adults. A gap is rarely a good place to sell things. No one really knows where to shelve such books or how to market them. Teens like to read about kids their age or just ahead of them, and when you're 18 or 19, you're more likely to jump to the adult fiction section of the bookstore than scour the YA section for the few YAs that still speak to you.

That said, publishers are joining the rest of the entertainment and advertising industries in venturing into the upper teen/early twenties demographic. It's still a tenuous place for books, but that doesn't mean it'll always be so. If you choose to push the upper boundaries of YA, do your darnedest to position your book for a solid, identifiable niche — preferably one with adult crossover appeal.

Putting Adults at the Helm

A hallmark of teen fiction is the empowerment of the teen protagonist, so don't let the adults in your novel come to the rescue. That's a surefire way to get a rejection letter from an agent or editor.

Tweens and teens are at a point in their lives when they desperately want to be able to fix their own problems, which means they want to read about other kids solving *their* problems. That makes readers feel empowered, which makes them feel satisfied upon finishing a novel. Keep the reins of your story in your teen lead's hands.

The Waving Author

No one wants to be reminded that there's an author behind the story they're reading, especially not teens. When this happens, you've done something to jolt readers out of the world you've created. Or worse, you never let readers sink into it in the first place.

In teen fiction, readers can feel the adult author's presence if the author doesn't fully disguise himself with a youthful mindset. The narration in such a book is usually too sophisticated in language or sentiment to let readers forget that this is a grown-up's interpretation of a kid going through kid stuff with a kid way of viewing the world. Get out of your readers' way. Let Chapter 9 be your guide.

Writing to Trends

Teens are a notoriously trendy bunch, and it's hard to think of writing books for them without considering that tendency. Everyone's seen the wizard books and vampire books and teen-clique horror books fill bookstore shelves only to fly off as quickly as they landed. What writer doesn't want a piece of such high-profile bookselling action? The problem is that getting in on a trend is almost impossible if you don't already have a novel in development or completely done when a teen trend hits its stride. Writing a manuscript takes time, submitting the manuscript to agents and editors takes time, and revising, producing, and promoting the book takes time. By then, trend over! Or market glutted.

Now, if you can predict the next teen fiction trend, then you're in like Flynn. Marketers and sales reps are as interested in the hottest topics, genres, and categories as you are, but alas, no one has yet unearthed a crystal ball for teen trends. Your best bet is to be as aware as you can about teen interests and write about universal teen issues with a unique twist that makes your story stand out. Chapter 4 takes you through this as you develop a story that has both high teen and marketplace appeal — and that intrigues you enough that you stick with it through all the ups and downs of the creative process.

Chapter 17

Ten Facts about Book Contracts

Although a published writer and veteran editor ain't no lawyer, she can certainly answer the ten most commonly asked questions about publishing contracts in a way that won't get her hauled into court. Here goes . . .

Does the Publisher Own the Copyright to My Book?

No. You own the copyright to the work itself, from the very moment you create it. The publisher is buying only the rights to publish it. Because copyright law protects your ownership from the moment of creation, you don't need to copyright your work through the United States Copyright Office before sending it out.

In fact, you never really need to register copyright. The purpose of registering is to create legal proof of ownership should you ever become involved in litigation about that work. Some writers find even the possibility of yucky legal stuff reason enough to go through the registration process. Others are fine with including "copyright © [year] by [your name]" on the first page of their manuscripts — although you don't even need to do that. Regardless of your comfort level and how you tag your manuscript, be assured that your publisher will register the copyright in your name for you when the book is published. (Publishers don't like yucky legal stuff, either.)

Make sure your publisher registers the copyright in your name, not theirs. There should be a clause in your book contract that specifies this. If there isn't, ask your publisher to add it. And have a very candid conversation about why this standard item wasn't included in the first place. It's not a common situation, but some vanity publishers and author services companies (see Chapter 14) want rights that should belong to you — which should raise a red flag in your mind. That said, there are instances, such as with a trademarked series, where the publisher will want the copyright in their name. Talk to your publisher about this when you're negotiating your contract.

The nice thing about a copyright is that it lasts a long time. U.S. copyright law sets the term of the copyright for works created after 1978 at the author's lifetime plus 70 years, after which the work goes into the *public domain* and no longer has copyright protection. After the work goes into public domain, it's anybody's to publish as they see fit. (How do you think we get all those dirt-cheap copies of Shakespeare's tragedies? Public domain, baby.) See the United States Copyright Office website (`www.copyright.gov`) for more information about copyrights.

Ever heard of the "poor man's copyright"? That's the practice of sending a copy of your own work to yourself through the U.S. mail to establish an official date of creation. Technically you didn't create it the very day you mailed it, but the point is to have a date officially marked should a copyright issue arise. Problem is, U.S. copyright law doesn't provide for this type of protection, so this practice isn't a substitute for registration. But it is a nifty way to get one of those Elvis Presley memorial postage stamps. Who doesn't love finding the King in their mailbox?

What Does "Buy All Rights" Mean?

Many publishers buy *all rights* to your story. This means you sell all your interest in the work, allowing the publisher to publish your book in any country, in any language, as well as any work that should stem from it *(derivative works)*, such as sequels, books featuring the same characters *(companion books)*, or alternate formats (such as movies or audio books).

You can negotiate a limit on those rights, such as selling first printing rights only, or you can designate a timeline that reverts the rights back to you at a specific time or in a specific situation, such as when book sales drop below a floor threshold in any given accounting period (generally, publishers have two accounting periods per year, which is when you get paid your royalties).

Selling your story's rights to a publisher doesn't mean the publisher would keep all the money from these deals; it just means the publisher's crew would do the legwork and take a cut every time they secure a *license* for your book — that is, sell someone the right to use your work. You still get a portion, too.

Although the idea of selling rights to a possible future movie or theme park may sound like a terrible idea at first, consider that often the publisher is in a better position to exploit those rights, having the connections to production companies, merchandising companies, book clubs, foreign publishers, and so on. In fact, publishers typically have staff dedicated to handling these rights: the Subsidiary Rights Department, or simply Subrights.

What are Subsidiary Rights?

Subsidiary is a fancy world for *secondary,* which itself is a fancy word for all that stuff that isn't necessarily print-related. Here's the breakdown between primary and subsidiary rights:

- Primary book-publishing rights are hardcover, trade paperback (sold in standard bookstores), mass market (smaller, lower-priced paperbacks sold in stores that don't specialize in books, such as grocery stores or Wal-Mart), and direct mail (catalog-based selling to specific mailing lists). These are the areas publishers are best primed to exploit.

- Secondary, or *subsidiary*, rights include periodical rights, first serial rights, book club rights, dramatic rights, motion picture rights, television rights, radio rights, animation rights, merchandising or commercial tie-in rights, electronic rights, and video and audiocassette rights.

You can choose to grant only the rights that the publisher can adequately exploit. If you're contracting with a book publisher, granting the publisher rights to print, publish, and sell printed books makes sense. Book club rights usually go to the hardcover book publisher, too, as do other print-related rights, such as paperback reprint editions, condensations or abridgments in anthologies and textbooks, and first and second serial rights (such as publication in newspapers and magazines). Those are the formats publishers are wired for.

Literary agents like to hang on to nonprint subrights, especially film and merchandising, in order to license them out themselves through their own Subrights staff or through specialized subsidiary rights co-agents. That cuts the publisher out of the deal, meaning more money for you.

The book contract specifies the subrights splits. Although the splits can vary from publisher to publisher, generally the minimum split is 50 percent for you, 50 percent for the publisher, with increases in that percentage (up to 75 percent for you, 25 percent for the publisher) going in your favor.

When negotiating the rights language in your book contract, be as specific and clear with the language as possible. Present copyright law says that you retain any rights you do not expressly grant to the publisher. But vague contract language can cause all kinds of legal hoo-ha. If you have an agent, then he or she is just as vested in protecting your rights as you are, but if you're on your own, consulting a publishing attorney before signing the contract may be in your best interest. A few bucks upfront may save you big bucks down the line.

Make sure your contract stipulates that the rights will be returned to you if the book goes out of print (OP). This is a tricky item (what was that I said about enlisting a publishing attorney?), because the publisher can let a title sit OS (out of stock) for long periods of time before declaring it OP, in effect allowing them the chance to reprint the book anytime they see a prime reason to get it back out there. It also lets them hang on to the rights for *print-on-demand,* a printing method that lets them publish individual books as customers order them instead of printing a batch of books and then holding them in warehouses or shipping them out to stores. Letting a title remain out of stock also lets publishers lock up your rights as they wait for new technologies that offer new-edition opportunities.

Many author organizations advise that electronic and print-on-demand editions should not constitute *in print,* which should instead be defined as available for sale in the United States in English-language hardcover or paperback editions. If your contract doesn't already have an Out-of-Print Clause, you can negotiate one that stipulates your ability to terminate the contract and regain all your rights (called *reverting* your rights) if book sales fall to a specified minimum number per accounting period. That way, publishers can't claim a few print-on-demand sales as reason to lock up your rights, and they can't sit on those while they wait to see who invents what. You don't have to have earned out your advance for such termination and reversion. (See "What Does 'Advance Against Royalties' Mean?" to find out what *earning out your advance* means.)

What's the Deal with Electronic Rights?

These days, terms such as *book form* and *electronic rights* are major hot buttons. As technology is outpacing publishers, many publishers are incorporating expansive language such as "including all known and unknown technologies" into contracts to make sure they don't lose out on electronic editions whenever a new technology is developed. And writers are understandably concerned about getting the shaft.

What should you do about broad electronic-rights language in your contract? If you see in the Grant of Rights clause that your publisher is reserving the exclusive ability to publish or allow others to publish electronic versions of your book, you can ask them to insert a stipulation requiring the publisher to negotiate royalty and subrights splits with you before they enter into any electronic-rights licensing agreements or publish a new electronic edition themselves. Or you can ask for the publisher to specify in the contract exactly which electronics rights they want to license, such as full text editions, Internet downloads, or specific multimedia formats. Then again, you can simply reserve all or specific electronic rights to license yourself or hold for a later date, depending on who invents what.

Even publishers are struggling to understand and define technology's role in publishing. Try not to be intimidated by electronic rights. Everyone's in the same boat, even if some do have seats with better views.

The Authors Guild is a vocal advocate for author rights in the digital age. For the latest on electronic rights issues, go to the Legal Services section (under Services) of the Authors Guild website, www.authorsguild.org.

What Does "Advance Against Royalties" Mean?

After your book is published, you receive a portion of its earnings, or *royalties*. Luckily, you don't have to wait until your book actually starts selling to get some moola. Your publisher pays you an *advance against royalties* before publication. This advance is a sum of money that the publisher agrees to pay you upfront, when you sign the contract. It's neither free money nor a bonus — that sum will be deducted from your royalties until the advance is fully recouped by the publisher, at which point your advance is said to have *earned out*. After that, your share of the royalties comes to you without being dinged by the publisher.

Here's an example: You get a $10,000 advance for a book, with a 10 percent royalty. This means the publisher pays you $10,000 before the book publishes and then keeps your 10 percent share of the earnings until that amount reaches $10,000, at which time your advance has earned out. Now your 10 percent share of the subsequent royalties starts showing up in your mailbox.

That example clarifies the earning-out process, but the example is actually quite simplified. In truth, every penny of contracted income that your book brings in helps you earn out that advance, be those pennies from physical book sales or audio book licensing or movie rights sales. Another factor is *reserves,* which are the funds publishers hold "in reserve" in case your books get returned by bookstores because customers aren't buying them. The accounting can get quite complicated. Your publisher will send you statements several times each year accounting for all these details.

Work-for-hire: Writing for a fee

In a *work-for-hire* arrangement, a publisher pays you a one-time, lump sum fee as a consultant or an employee to create material for them. The publisher owns the copyright and all rights to the material. You get no royalties, and you may or may not be credited for the work. Think "ghostwriter."

Work-for-hire is often the arrangement for a series to which many authors contribute, such as the classic Nancy Drew series. It may not be high-glam, but many authors get their start doing work-for-hire, honing their chops, gaining credibility, and just plain paying the bills. For that reason, work-for-hire is a good gig if you can get it. Writers who can write well and meet deadlines are always wanted by *book packagers,* who create works-for-hire as their bread and butter. For info on book packagers, check out the American Book Producers Association at www.abpaonline.org.

Publishers pay advances when the contract is signed, although your advance may be doled out as you hit manuscript delivery deadlines that are specifically stated in your contract. A common scenario has you being paid a portion of the advance upon signing, a portion upon delivery of half the manuscript, and the final portion upon delivery of the complete manuscript.

Publishers generally calculate the amount of your advance based on their predictions of the number of books they'll sell. That means advances vary hugely, depending on the publisher, the market, and your stature in the marketplace. So if the publisher thinks you have a big enough name and/or the book has a big enough commercial potential, then you'll get a bigger advance because, hey, they think they're gonna sell more copies. Makes sense, doesn't it?

What's the Difference between Royalties on "Net" and "Gross"?

Gross is the book's list price, also known as the *cover price* or *retail price*. *Net* is the amount of money the publisher actually receives on all sales, after expenses such as overhead, marketing, production costs, bad debts, and special deals to its customers have been factored out.

Because net is usually about half the list price, you make more money on gross-based royalties. Luckily, most young adult book publishers base royalties on the list price. Not all do, though, so keep an eye on this detail when you get your contract. Typically, authors get between 10 and 15 percent of gross for each book sold.

Whether you're getting royalties on net or gross, sometimes those royalties can *escalate*. That means your royalty increases as you reach certain sales thresholds. In one common escalator scenario, you'd get a 10 percent royalty on the first 10,000 books sold, 12.5 percent on the next 5,000 books sold, and 15 percent thereafter. Publishers are often more willing to negotiate escalators than larger advances because royalties are paid when books are actually sold; advances, on the other hand, are based on sales projections, and crystal-ball technology hasn't yet been perfected. (Remember, your first earnings pay off your advance; you won't get any checks in the mail until after the publisher recoups that advance.)

Do some math when you're considering your publisher's offer — you may find that you'll be better off in the long run negotiating an escalating royalty rather than digging in your heels for a few thousand dollars more on the advance. High advances are pretty glamorous, and some folks believe that the higher the advance, the more promotional effort the publisher will kick in. That may be so, especially when you're talking astronomical advances. But most writers aren't Big Name Authors with sales projections in the millions, so they don't get million-dollar offers.

Why Do My Royalties Go to My Agent?

Every book contract that involves a literary agency includes an Agency Clause. This clause instructs the publisher to send all your royalties and advances directly to your agent. Don't worry; she's not keeping it! She deducts her commission and disburses the remainder to you. To do that, she deposits the money in a separate client trust account rather than a general account to protect it from any possible creditor action should the agency encounter financial problems.

If your agent doesn't have a separate client trust account, request that your Agency Clause stipulate your right to cancel the clause in the event of the agent's bankruptcy, death, or disability. Your agent should give you an annual accounting when she provides you with your IRS Form 1099 each tax season.

The Agency Clause also empowers your agent to act on your behalf in any matters that arise from that particular agreement. If you and your agent should break up, then after you're done burning all your photos of the two of you together, be sure to notify your publisher in writing that you've had a rep change so the contract may be amended.

For more on the agent-author relationship, see Chapter 13. If you have specific questions about agency agreements, the Association of Author Representatives (AAR) has resources available on its website, www.aaron line.org.

What's a Boilerplate?

A *boilerplate* is simply a standard form contract. Think template. Every publisher has a boilerplate contract, and in their eyes, it's the perfect basic agreement — for them. Wait, wait, I'm not saying publishers draft the boilerplate to be unfair to you. The folks behind the big doors of the publishing house are usually very nice people who want you to succeed; I know because I was one of them. That said, the boilerplate is skewed in the publisher's favor.

You should consider the boilerplate your starting point for contract negotiations. Publishers do. They know and expect that writers and their agents will negotiate the contracts until the agreement has been molded to suit everyone's needs as much as possible. It's part of the process.

Never shy away from requesting changes to the boilerplate or just asking questions to clarify your understanding. No one's going to be miffed at you. This is a legal document, and no one — not you, not the publisher — wants a legal mess later on. Contract negotiation is the time to get everything out on the table and work toward an agreement that you can all sign in good faith and with high hopes for a successful partnership.

Most publishers have *agency boilerplates,* which are contracts that reflect each literary agency's basic musts. That way, agents don't have to negotiate every detail for every contract the agency enters into with that publishing house. This saves everyone time.

The same goes for you: When you sign with a publisher, all your future contracts with that publisher will start with your current contract as your boilerplate. That doesn't mean the negotiation ends there. Your needs and your ability to exploit rights may change, and your current contract should reflect that.

Am I Protected from Libel Suits?

You're treading in the world of warranties and indemnities now, and for that, you'd best consult a publishing attorney if you don't have an agent involved in your book contract negotiations.

Your book contract will almost certainly require you to "indemnify and hold harmless" the publisher against claims — including libel or copyright — or breaches of contract related to the work. Essentially, they're covering their britches against your breaches. Your "warranty" is your promise to the publisher that you've never published this work before, you haven't plagiarized, and you haven't libeled or in any other way defamed someone or violated his or her privacy rights. Indemnifying and holding harmless the publisher means that you agree to foot the bills if the legal logs start rolling.

You can ask a publisher to strike the warranty and indemnity clause from your contract . . . but they probably won't. This is where you ask your publishing attorney or your agent what to do. Based on her knowledge of publishing law and precedents, of the content of your particular work, and of your individual needs, she may recommend that you

- ✔ Ask to be added to the publisher's *media liability insurance,* which protects against copyright and infringement claims and invasion of privacy and defamation. This insurance sometimes provides assistance in paying attorney's fees.

- ✔ Purchase your own professional liability insurance.

- ✔ Request contract language that limits your obligation to "final judgments" (meaning you won't have to cover the costs of lawsuits that eventually get thrown out as frivolous).

- ✔ Ask for language that limits your warranties to "the best of Author's knowledge."

Some national writers' groups, such as the Authors Guild, have agreements with media liability insurance companies, allowing their members to purchase the insurance at specially negotiated rates. If you're a member of a national writers' group, check their membership benefits to see what they can offer you.

What's an Option, and Why Would I Grant It?

An *option* gives the publisher the *right of first refusal,* or the right to read and buy or reject your next work before you show it to anyone else.

Although a publisher may ask for an option, you don't have to grant it. An option isn't really in your favor, except perhaps as a statement of the publisher's investment in you. For a publisher, it's a hedge against sequels or companion novels, if not a blatant grab at your future manuscripts.

If the publisher insists on an option — as they may do when there's a strong likelihood of a sequel or a companion book, or in the case of a series — make the option as specific as possible. Have the language state that they get an option on a book featuring the same characters, the next book in a series, or a book in the same genre as the contracted work. And make sure the clause specifies a time period — such as 90 days — during which the publisher must review the work and give you a thumbs up or a thumbs down.

Chapter 18

Ten Ways to Make the Most of a Conference

. . . .

. . . .

Attending a writers' conference is a great way to brush up on craft, keep abreast of publishing news and trends, network with fellow writers, and interact directly with industry pros. It can also be an intense — even overwhelming — experience. Writers find the wheels in their heads spinning furiously as everything everyone says triggers new ideas that make them want to rush to their keyboards. Trust me, you'll be strategizing, plotting, and brainstorming your way through the entire event, even as you try to focus on a plethora of tips and insights. And because every writer around you is experiencing something similar, the vibe can really juice you up.

Here are ten ways to prepare for a conference so you can stay focused yet relaxed throughout, letting you maximize your time while you're there and then effectively regroup and follow up on connections after you get home. I focus on the larger national and regional conferences, but you can apply these tips to smaller events as well. Your goals, preparation, execution, and follow-up will just be smaller in scope. (See Chapter 3 for the differences among national conferences, regional conferences, and weekend writing retreats.)

Set Reasonable Goals and Make a Plan to Achieve Them

Go into every conference with a list of things you want to achieve at the event, taking into account your current stage and needs. You may be just starting out, you may be heavy into the writing and revising, you may be eye-balling the submission phase, or you may be published and mulling over your next story. Figure out where you are in the process before each conference and develop your goals around that.

When you set your goals, make them tangible. "I want to learn as much as I can about writing for teens" is too vague. Have you been struggling with a particular issue? Are you hearing consistent themes in your critique feedback? Do you run into predictable trouble spots? Write those things down and then turn your list into goals that you can take action on at the conference. You may find it useful to phrase each goal as a question and/or to give yourself number-related goals, such as "What are three techniques for creating more natural dialogue?" Keep the list to a realistically achievable size. Here's what your conference checklist may look like:

- ✔ Learn two new techniques for creating more natural teen dialogue.
- ✔ Learn how to end chapters so they push readers into the next chapter.
- ✔ Identify a possible new member for our online critique group.
- ✔ Learn the key elements of a successful middle grade series.
- ✔ Ask about the state of the paranormal market during the agent panel.
- ✔ Ask Agent X if I can send a post-conference submission.
- ✔ Get suggestions for planning a successful weekend writing retreat.

If landing a book deal is your main goal in attending a conference, the odds of walking out disappointed are high. You've probably heard conference success stories where writers landed a deal, and yes, that does happen, but deals at conferences are the exception, not the rule. And they happen only when writers arrive at the conference with work that's fully polished. Besides, agents and editors don't walk around conferences with blank contracts in their pockets. When they like sample chapters they see at conferences, they ask the author to send the full manuscript to their offices and then the project goes through the full submission process.

When your goals list is done, look through your conference's presentation schedule and identify sessions (presentations) that address those topics. Don't spread yourself thin, trying to learn a little about everything. You can't learn everything about writing and the industry at one event. So focus first on sessions that strengthen your weaknesses before filling up the gaps in your schedule with other stuff that's interesting but still on long-range sensors.

Go to the conference with a friend, if you can, and then split up. You can each attend different sessions and then trade notes later.

Research the Faculty

The heart of a conference is its faculty, those industry experts and experienced writers who present the workshops, do the paid critiques, deliver the keynote speeches, and fill the *panels* (question-and-answer sessions with multiple experts). You should be familiar with all the faculty for the following reasons:

- ✔ **You'll pick your sessions not only for topics but also for the experts presenting them.** If you're writing a middle grade adventure for boys, for example, a session about dialogue with a writer of swashbuckling pirate books would be a better choice than a dialogue session with a contemporary chick lit writer.

- ✔ **You need to know what the experts bring to the table so you can get a feel for what you'll take away from the session.** Why was this expert chosen to talk on that topic in that session? What do you think she can teach you? Do you need that right now?

- ✔ **You need context for what the expert is saying.** After you get into that session, knowing a writer's craft strengths, genre or topic interests, and specific books can deepen your understanding of the session content. Knowing an agent's client list or an editor's biggest books helps you know his literary sensibility and inform you on his recommendations regarding craft and marketplace.

- ✔ **You need to know who's sitting next to you at lunch.** The children's book community is known for being welcoming, and faculty usually mingle. Know whether the person sitting next to you is a faculty member and what she publishes so you don't have to say, "What do you do? Oh! You're an editor at Random House? Wow, what's your name again? Do you publish anything I know? Would my book be something for you?" That's not a meeting to refer to later in a query letter.

The organization hosting the conference may include faculty bios in your registration packet, and you can certainly find bios on the conference website. Read the bios and then visit each person's website to see the breadth of their titles and to read book blurbs, excerpts, their interviews, and some of their blog posts. If you're attending a smaller event, read at least one book for each speaker because that's the best way to get a feel for a writer's sensibility and strengths. Use what you learn about the faculty to pick your sessions, choosing presenters who fit into your particular needs and goals.

Mark your sessions on your conference schedule in advance. A schedule may come with your registration materials, or you can pull one off the host's website. Mark backup sessions, too. Sometimes a session isn't what you thought it would be. When this happens, don't stick around. Politely duck out and slip into your backup choice.

Pay for One-on-One Critiques

If it's within your budget, pay the extra fee to sign up for a one-on-one critique with a faculty member, which is a standard feature at writers' conferences. Expert feedback on your work is worth the extra investment. And if that critique is with an agent or editor, all the better. That face-to-face time is invaluable: you'll be getting feedback straight from the horse's mouth, and you'll be making a personal connection that you can reference when your work is revised, polished, and ready for formal consideration. This is your own little "in," getting you past those no-unsolicited-manuscripts policies.

Ask your conference hosts whether they allow you to request a critique by a particular faculty member. If they do, put in a request or two based on your faculty research.

Go into your critique expecting to come out with homework. The point of a critique is to find out how you can improve your overall writing and that story in particular. That means the critiquer will point out your strengths and weaknesses and offer suggestions for addressing those weaknesses. Don't be nervous or defensive — the feedback is usually offered tactfully and with good intentions. Take notes and ask the critiquer to repeat or clarify as necessary.

Critiquing is subjective, so you may not agree with all the feedback you get. That happens sometimes. Flip to Chapter 11 for tips on how to handle feedback.

Perfect Your Pitch

"What are you working on?" is the second most-common question you get at a conference, topped only by "What's your name?" Scratch that; you'll be wearing a name tag. It's *the* most common question you get. When the question comes, lay your pitch on 'em. The person's follow-up questions or enthusiastic nods can tell you lots.

Conferences are great places to practice your pitch. Testing out your pitch is valuable for making sure you've struck a strong balance between information and tease. Whether you're talking with editors or agents during critiques, chatting with fellow writers during lunch, or participating in a formal *pitch session* (wherein attendees get on-the-spot critiques of their pitches), you'll have countless opportunities for focused feedback.

Your *pitch* is your key sales tool and mission statement for your project, comprised of your one-sentence *hook* followed by two- to three-sentence expansion of that. The hook includes your genre, the age of your main character, her goal and/or main conflict, and possibly your main theme. (Chapter 4 is all about hooks, and Chapter 13 tackles submission pitches.)

You can deliver a pitch no matter what stage you're in with your work-in-progress. If you're still developing your concept, you can reshape based on what you hear at the conference and on the feedback that follows your delivery. If you're done with your manuscript and have signed up for a critique session, ask your critiquer what he thinks of your pitch: Have you hit the right tone? Does it jive with what he read? Does he have any suggestions for refining it? This is your chance to hone.

You may have a chance to pitch to an agent or editor at a conference, although the most likely scenario unfolds like this: After an agent or editor's session, you go up to her to thank her for sharing the information, and then (assuming you've determined that your project would be a match with her needs and wants) you simply say, "I've got a historical fiction (or whatever) that sounds like it would be right for you. May I send it to you after the conference?" You needn't give your pitch in this situation because she's not prepared to state her like or dislike in such a quick encounter. All you're doing is trying to secure permission to circumvent any no-unsolicited-manuscripts policy. Odds are she'll say yes. You can write in your query letter that you met her at the conference and repeat something interesting she said, thus distinguishing yourself among the rest of her queries.

Prepare Your Manuscript

Because you never know what opportunity will present itself, always walk into a conference with a few copies of your sample chapters in case you want to share it with others. If you're going to an event that includes workshops, the workshop organizer will specify the materials you must bring. Prepare everything as if you were submitting it. Here's what to include:

- ✔ **One-sheet:** This takes the place of a query letter, doing the same job of pitching without specifying an addressee. A one-sheet has your title, your hook statement (Paragraph 1 from your query), your pitch (Paragraph 2 from your query), and your bio and contact information (Paragraph 3 from your query), all on the front of one 8½" x 11" sheet of white paper.

✔ **Synopsis:** This is your plot summary, two to three pages long. Consider writing a *brief synopsis,* which is limited to a single page. Brevity of materials is a strength at conferences.

✔ **Sample chapter:** Stick with a single chapter unless your first chapter is very small, in which case include two chapters. You don't want to be schlepping around a stack of paper, nor does anyone else want to walk away with that stack of paper themselves. Never bring your whole manuscript. If someone wants to read more, you can send it later.

Have your materials as developed and polished as you possibly can before the conference. Proofread everything carefully and apply all the formatting I cover in Chapter 13.

Bring your laptop to the conference so you can hole yourself up at night in a fit of frenzied revision enthusiasm.

Create a Conference Notebook

Being organized allows you to focus on writing instead of on finding (see Chapter 3), and that applies to conferences big time. Get yourself a three-ring binder and turn it into a conference notebook. You only need to set up a notebook once, because you use the same one for every conference you attend — perhaps for every writing event at all, including festivals and writers' group meetings.

Even if you prefer to type your session notes directly into your laptop, you need a physical notebook. Much of conference life happens on your feet, not sitting down with a fired-up laptop on your knees. Have a notebook at the ready to jot things in — and just as importantly, to hold things in. You'll be amazed at the slew of notes, handouts, schedules, maps, flyers, business cards, and scribbled-on napkins that'll clog your computer bag and pockets if you don't have a way to organize them on the go.

Here are some suggestions for setting up your notebook:

✔ **Use a three-ring binger.** Spiral notebooks aren't as handy, because you can't add pages or handouts. The conference host will probably give you a folder filled with your registration materials, but that's not your permanent solution. Folders easily become jumbled messes of papers that you have to sort through every time you want something.

✔ **Stock your conference notebook.** Include blank paper for note-taking, plastic sleeves for slipping in handouts, and plastic business card sleeves for the cards you collect as you network.

✔ **Keep a tape dispenser or glue stick in your bag or hotel room for attaching small items to blank pages so they don't get lost.** You don't want to waste time transcribing the scribbles into your notebook.

✔ **Keep a colored pen or highlighter to call out Action Items in the margins of your notes.** You'll scan the margins post-conference and prioritize the highlighted Action Items into a to-do list. Examples: "Read Riordan's new book," "Get keynote notes from Jenny," "Look up Simon & Schuster's author guidelines."

✔ **Put your marked-up session schedule in an easy-access plastic insert or tuck the schedule in the binder's front pocket.** You want to be able to check the session schedule on the go if you have to remind yourself of session room numbers. Big conferences like the Society of Children's Book Writers and Illustrators' annual summer conference (which takes place on several floors of a very large hotel and stretches out over east and west wings and several ballrooms) give you a map; keep that freely accessible, too, with your session locations already marked. Often you don't have much time between sessions.

✔ **Include a printout of your conference goals checklist (see the first section in this chapter).** Review it often during the conference to make sure you get all the answers you wanted.

Bring an index card and pen to all the meals and evening mixers you attend at the conference. You can tape filled index cards onto a blank page in your conference notebook when you get back to your room, saving you the time and trouble of transcribing the scribbles from cocktail napkins.

Bring Bookmarks or Business Cards

Networking should be one of your primary conference goals, so come stocked with a supply of business cards (or bookmarks if you choose that format for your contact information). You'll be making contacts who may help you down the road, if not with your current book. Sometimes you'll make friends and form critique groups or informal manuscript exchanges.

You may need a card for an editor or agent contact, but don't count on it. Business cards are fairly meaningless to editors and agents at conferences. Editors and agents aren't going to follow up with you; you're going to follow up with them — and what they want in that follow-up is a query letter or a manuscript (both of which have your contact information), not a card.

Don't use your regular job-related business cards if you're not in the writing industry; get a business card dedicated to your writing career. Make sure those cards represent you well professionally. That doesn't mean go expensive; you can print customized cards quite cheaply, and plenty of free basic-but-still-lovely card designs are available online.

If you're unpublished, include your name, e-mail address, and website if you have one (omit your home mailing address). If you're previously published or in a writers' organization, include your book titles and organization affiliation on the card, too. (For more on business cards and other marketing tools, jump to Chapter 15.)

Make Notes on the Business Cards You Receive

People easily blend together in the conference-logged brain. As soon as possible after you get a card, pause to note on the back of the card the circumstances of your meeting (mutual friends, a shared enthusiasm for a speaker or genre, and so on). Slip that card into a plastic business-card sleeve in your conference notebook.

Always make an action note on the back of the card, stating what you should do to follow up when you get home — "Read her excerpt online" or "Contact her about guest posting or guest article for newsletter." Reinforce that networking moment with a follow-up contact.

Another option for handling cards is to tape them onto a blank page in your conference notebook, transcribing your back-of-card notes onto the notebook page beside the card. When you get home, you can see at a glance all your action notes and then physically check them off as you work through them. Folks who maintain contacts in electronic phone books find this a useful way to keep cards from people who don't necessarily warrant a phone book entry. For example, you may not be thinking about book trailers at all when someone mentions a great article she read about creating them, but a year later, you're eager to try your hand at one. *I met someone who told me about the best article for book trailers. I wish I could remember the article. Who told me about it? Who . . . who . . . who . . .* Just flip through your notebook and there she is, right next to a note about the book trailer article.

Save Conference Expense Receipts for Tax Records

You can deduct writing-related expenses from your taxes as long as you're pursuing publication and not just writing as a hobby, so keep track of your conference expenses. Save receipts for things that enhance, advance, or promote your writing career. Starting the moment you sign up, print out electronic receipts for all registration and travel, and then carry a receipt envelope around in your purse, pocket, or notebook at the conference.

After the conference, log those expenses into your running Writing Expenses spreadsheet for that year. If you don't have a Writing Expenses spreadsheet, start one. Writing for publication is a business even if it's not your full-time employment. You can bet you'll be taxed on advances and royalties as income when those come in!

Check with your tax preparer for the most current tax rules and restrictions regarding deductions for writers. They can get pretty complicated, so have a tax expert explain the latest rules, prepare the forms for you, or instruct you regarding which forms to use. Also consult the IRS's webpage (www.irs.gov), which has a search function to help you look up the latest articles and FAQs; use "business or hobby" and "hobby loss" as your search terms.

Set Aside a Post-Conference Recovery Phase

Your conference will eventually come to an end — but that doesn't mean you're done with it. You need to take all that information and inspiration and put it to use. You need to recoup, regroup, and then react:

- ✓ **Recoup:** After a conference, you'll be mentally and probably physically wiped. Give yourself permission *not* to think books for a period of time, several days to a week. Reconnect with family and the real world. Exercise. If you're up to it, read the books you bought. Faculty members' books will be on sale at the event; buy them and study how those writers apply what they preach. But don't let your recouping phase go on too long. You don't want to let the inspiration slip away.

- ✓ **Regroup:** This is when you'll be very *very* happy you took my advice about preparing your goals and using a conference notebook, because the first action you take post-conference should be reviewing all the information you collected and making your plans for moving forward:

    • Scan the margins of your conference notebook for Action Items and prioritize them.

    • Read your notes from each session. Interact with those notes, circling and highlighting to cement the points in your mind.

    • Go through your conference checklist and see whether you've answered all your questions and attained your goals. If not, follow up with one of the contacts you made to see whether they got the answer.

    • Make a revision checklist. List the elements of your story that you want to tackle in revision. Plan what you can do in each pass, because you won't be able to do it all at once. (For info on negotiating stages of revision, see Chapter 11.)

- Make a revision plan. Use your post-conference energy to its fullest, reviewing your writing schedule and seeing where you can improve or shift it. You'll likely have heard lots of deliciously sneaky writing-time tips from fellow attendees (it's a hot topic in conference chit-chat!). See whether any of those apply to you.

Some writers find that the "regroup" phase is their "recoup" phase, too. Or they like to regroup before they set things aside to recoup. I'm in the latter group, preferring to organize, highlight, and strategize while it's all still fresh and *then* go outside to play after the action plan is locked in. You'll know after your first conference.

✔ **React:** This is when you take action on what you learned about your story, your writing, yourself, and your industry at the conference. Put your new tools to work:

- Send follow-up notes and/or thank you notes. This should be the first item on your post-conference task list, because this step involves other people and is essential for reinforcing your networking connections. E-mails work just fine, unless you're writing an agent or editor, in which case a physical note is appropriate. Keep the note simple, thanking recipients for their time and sharing their expertise, and note any personal interaction you had with them.

- Move through the rest of the post-conference task list you created.

- Revise any work that received requests from editors or agents. If you're not close to submission-ready, send a note to say thanks and that you're working on your story, and then give yourself a deadline, aiming for less than 3 months if possible. If it takes 6 months or longer, that's fine — everyone knows successful post-conference revision takes time. Just explain the delay when the submission is ready: "I've been revising and feel now that it's ready to submit to you."

- If there was an open invitation to all attendees to submit, do your post-conference revisions before sending your submission. You do have time, and this is your only freebie with that editor or agent. Follow the rules on any handouts or guidelines provided at the conference. Always cite the invitation in the opening paragraph of your query, and note the invitation, too, on the front of the submission envelope: "Requested Material: X Conference."

Index

• I •

• J •

• Z •

e & Macs

For Dummies
0-470-58027-1

ne For Dummies,
Edition
0-470-87870-5

Book For Dummies, 3rd
on
0-470-76918-8

OS X Snow Leopard For
mies
0-470-43543-4

ness

kkeeping For Dummies
0-7645-9848-7

Interviews
Dummies,
Edition
0-470-17748-8

umes For Dummies,
Edition
0-470-08037-5

ting an
e Business
Dummies,
Edition
0-470-60210-2

k Investing
Dummies,
Edition
0-470-40114-9

cessful
e Management
Dummies
0-470-29034-7

Computer Hardware

BlackBerry
For Dummies,
4th Edition
978-0-470-60700-8

Computers For Seniors
For Dummies,
2nd Edition
978-0-470-53483-0

PCs For Dummies,
Windows
7th Edition
978-0-470-46542-4

Laptops For Dummies,
4th Edition
978-0-470-57829-2

Cooking & Entertaining

Cooking Basics
For Dummies,
3rd Edition
978-0-7645-7206-7

Wine For Dummies,
4th Edition
978-0-470-04579-4

Diet & Nutrition

Dieting For Dummies,
2nd Edition
978-0-7645-4149-0

Nutrition For Dummies,
4th Edition
978-0-471-79868-2

Weight Training
For Dummies,
3rd Edition
978-0-471-76845-6

Digital Photography

Digital SLR Cameras &
Photography For Dummies,
3rd Edition
978-0-470-46606-3

Photoshop Elements 8
For Dummies
978-0-470-52967-6

Gardening

Gardening Basics
For Dummies
978-0-470-03749-2

Organic Gardening
For Dummies,
2nd Edition
978-0-470-43067-5

Green/Sustainable

Raising Chickens
For Dummies
978-0-470-46544-8

Green Cleaning
For Dummies
978-0-470-39106-8

Health

Diabetes For Dummies,
3rd Edition
978-0-470-27086-8

Food Allergies
For Dummies
978-0-470-09584-3

Living Gluten-Free
For Dummies,
2nd Edition
978-0-470-58589-4

Hobbies/General

Chess For Dummies,
2nd Edition
978-0-7645-8404-6

Drawing
Cartoons & Comics
For Dummies
978-0-470-42683-8

Knitting For Dummies,
2nd Edition
978-0-470-28747-7

Organizing
For Dummies
978-0-7645-5300-4

Su Doku For Dummies
978-0-470-01892-7

Home Improvement

Home Maintenance
For Dummies,
2nd Edition
978-0-470-43063-7

Home Theater
For Dummies,
3rd Edition
978-0-470-41189-6

Living the
Country Lifestyle
All-in-One
For Dummies
978-0-470-43061-3

Solar Power Your Home
For Dummies,
2nd Edition
978-0-470-59678-4

able wherever books are sold. For more information or to order direct: U.S. customers visit www.dummies.com or call 1-877-762-2974.
customers visit www.wileyeurope.com or call (0) 1243 843291. Canadian customers visit www.wiley.ca or call 1-800-567-4797.

Internet

Blogging For Dummies,
3rd Edition
978-0-470-61996-4

eBay For Dummies,
6th Edition
978-0-470-49741-8

Facebook For Dummies,
3rd Edition
978-0-470-87804-0

Web Marketing
For Dummies,
2nd Edition
978-0-470-37181-7

WordPress
For Dummies,
3rd Edition
978-0-470-59274-8

Language & Foreign Language

French For Dummies
978-0-7645-5193-2

Italian Phrases
For Dummies
978-0-7645-7203-6

Spanish For Dummies,
2nd Edition
978-0-470-87855-2

Spanish
For Dummies,
Audio Set
978-0-470-09585-0

Math & Science

Algebra I
For Dummies,
2nd Edition
978-0-470-55964-2

Biology For Dummies,
2nd Edition
978-0-470-59875-7

Calculus For Dummies
978-0-7645-2498-1

Chemistry For Dummies
978-0-7645-5430-8

Microsoft Office

Excel 2010 For Dummies
978-0-470-48953-6

Office 2010 All-in-One
For Dummies
978-0-470-49748-7

Office 2010 For Dummies,
Book + DVD Bundle
978-0-470-62698-6

Word 2010 For Dummies
978-0-470-48772-3

Music

Guitar For Dummies,
2nd Edition
978-0-7645-9904-0

iPod & iTunes For
Dummies, 8th Edition
978-0-470-87871-2

Piano Exercises
For Dummies
978-0-470-38765-8

Parenting & Education

Parenting For Dummies,
2nd Edition
978-0-7645-5418-6

Type 1 Diabetes
For Dummies
978-0-470-17811-9

Pets

Cats For Dummies,
2nd Edition
978-0-7645-5275-5

Dog Training For Dummies,
3rd Edition
978-0-470-60029-0

Puppies For Dummies,
2nd Edition
978-0-470-03717-1

Religion & Inspiration

The Bible For Dummies
978-0-7645-5296-0

Catholicism For Dummies
978-0-7645-5391-2

Women in the Bible
For Dummies
978-0-7645-8475-6

Self-Help & Relationship

Anger Management
For Dummies
978-0-470-03715-7

Overcoming Anxiety
For Dummies,
2nd Edition
978-0-470-57441-6

Sports

Baseball
For Dummies,
3rd Edition
978-0-7645-7537-2

Basketball
For Dummies,
2nd Edition
978-0-7645-5248-9

Golf For Dummies,
3rd Edition
978-0-471-76871-5

Web Development

Web Design
All-in-One
For Dummies
978-0-470-41796-6

Web Sites
Do-It-Yourself
For Dummies,
2nd Edition
978-0-470-56520-9

Windows 7

Windows 7
For Dummies
978-0-470-49743-2

Windows 7
For Dummies,
Book + DVD Bundle
978-0-470-52398-8

Windows 7 All-in-One
For Dummies
978-0-470-48763-1

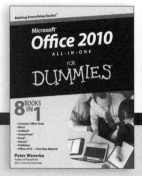

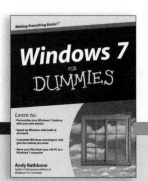

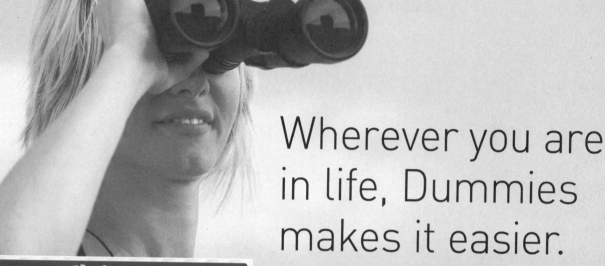

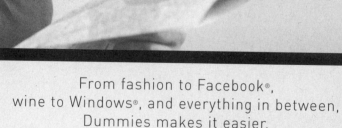

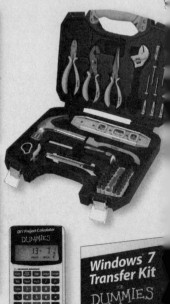